T0354326

William James
on
The Stream of Consciousness

All the Evidence

Frederick R. Bauer
Author of *The Essence of Ethics*,
Logial Fictions,
The Wonderful Myth Called Science, and
William James on Common Sense

iUniverse, Inc.
New York Bloomington

William James on the Stream of Consciousness
All the Evidence

iUniverse books may be ordered through booksellers or by contacting:

iUniverse
1663 Liberty Drive
Bloomington, IN 47403
www.iuniverse.com
1-800-Authors (1-800-288-4677)

ISBN: 978-1-4401-3662-7 (sc)
ISBN: 978-1-4401-3661-0 (e-book)

Printed in the United States of America

iUniverse rev. date: 5/12/2009

CONTENTS

PREFACE

James' writings are an undiscovered gold mine. Randall Albright, editor of *Streams of William James*, the publication of the William James Society, felt that the phrase, "An undiscovered gold mine," captured the status of James's writing at the start of the 2000's. Nothing has happened since to change that fact.

And nothing will change that fact until people use the right key to that gold-mine. This book, read in conjunction with *William James on Common Sense*, will describe that key, namely, a revised description of the stream of consciousness.

All 'higher' learners begin with the common-sense model of the universe. *William James on Common Sense,* * a prologue to this volume, explained common sense, the one-space, one-time structure of our everyday thinking. Unfortunately, it was not until William James (1842-1910) was in his sixties that he began to adequately appreciate the 'magnificence' of everyday thinking, that is, the common-sense worldview. By then, however, his thought *habits* had hardened into a model or framework that, instead of refining common sense, eliminated two of its most fundamental premises, namely, the independent-of-consciousness self and the independent-of-one's-private-experience world. He called that alternative-to-common-sense framework, "radical empiricism." (*That book ended with "What ought w" to create what James called "expectancy, specifically the expectancy that something more should follow.)

But radical empiricism must be recognized for what it is, an alternative that doesn't work. Most Jamesians who have tried to collect and unify his best insights have tried unsuccessfully to make radical empiricism work. In the words of Albert Einstein, what must be done is to *refine common sense* or everyday thinking in a way that retains those two most fundamental truths.

The refinement of everyday-thinking common sense begins with the brain. The common-sense philosophy of every normal five- and six-year-old can be thought of as having answers to two distinct questions. "What exists?" is the first question. "How do we *know* what exists?" is the second.

The basic common-sense answer to the *first* question is, "What exists is my body, the sun, moon, and stars up in the sky, and all the persons, animals, vegetables, minerals, and their places down here on earth." The naïve, uninformed, serenely confident answer to the *second* question is, "We *know* those things exist because we can see and touch them!"

The discoveries collectively referred to as "Modern Science" have utterly demolished the common-sense answer to the second question, the *psychological* one. Already in 1641, the publication of René Descartes' (1596-1650) *Meditations on First Philosophy*, announced to the world the inadequacy of the 'everyday thinking,' common-sense view regarding *knowing*. James, heir not only to Descartes' 1641 *Meditations* but to all of the later psychological discoveries made between 1641 and his own 1878 signing of a contract to write a psychology textbook, agreed. In the fifth of his 1906-07 *Pragmatism* lectures, he made his agreement clear.

> Science and critical philosophy thus burst the bounds of common sense. With science *naif* realism ceases: 'Secondary' qualities become unreal; primary ones alone remain. With critical philosophy, havoc is made of everything. The common-sense categories one and all cease to represent anything in the way of being; they are but sublime tricks of human thought, our ways of escaping bewilderment in the midst of sensation's irremediable flow. (*Writings* II:567)

This 'bursting of the bounds' began with the recognition by Descartes that the brain is a barrier that prevents direct contact between the mind and any outside-the-brain reality. For the same reason, the brain prevents any outside-the-brain reality from directly affecting the mind without it first affecting the brain. The corollary to that premise-conclusion is that humans do not directly know the outside world by means of sensation.

Sense-experience will always serve as clues for deciding how our inner thoughts relate to the external world. We are not, however, eye-witnesses of that external world. We are jurors who must rely on personal, even private evidence to decide which of our thoughts about that unseen-by-us external world are true.

Today's views of the universe are created by imagining. No one who takes time to look into the night sky and to think hard about what they see can fail to realize how innovative was Ptolemy's astronomy. He dreamed that *everything in the world* is located somewhere in a system of bodies spread out in space, with a huge, round, not-flat body called "Earth" at the center. What an imagination he had! No one who takes time to look into the night sky will ever see *a geocentric system*, composed of the stationary earth on which he or she is standing, with a moon, a sun, and planets—or are those stars?—tracing orbits around it, plus an outermost, star-studded, crystal globe enclosing them all?

When Copernicus challenged Ptolemy's astronomy, his theory's calculations were based on a different, even more imaginative picture of a system no one ever saw. In place of the earth at the world's center, Copernicus took the moving sun (watch it move!), pictured it as rock-solid and stationary, and put it at the center of the universe. Instead of the earth being rock-solid stationary (feel it!), he asked us to believe it is circling around the sun, that is, traveling millions of miles in the course of each three-hundred-sixty-five-day period, and also spinning like a top more than a thousand miles per hour at the equator as it does so.

In other words, both Ptolemy's and Copernicus' highly-mathematical theories were constructed on pictures or models invented by the kind of creative imagination that Einstein once said is more important than knowledge.

The only students of the universe who hesitate—even for an instant—to nod in full agreement that those views of the cosmos are the product of imagining, not of looking, are those who have not made a habit of looking into the night sky and comparing what they *see* with what they *think*! If it were possible to see what they think, Moses and the other authors of the Bible would never have written nonsense about a flat earth resting on pillars and covered with a dome!

Efforts to understand the psyche are also built on imagined models. There is far too little recognition of the obvious truth that students of the human psyche rely as heavily as physicists, biologists, and chemists do, on models or image'd pictures as frameworks for their theorizings. A brief historical survey of a few great psychologists will show just how obvious that truth is.

For instance, Socrates was the first thinker we know of who used a two-part model to build a case for his theory about the moral purpose of humans' lives. Each human, he claimed, is an immaterial being only temporarily 'living inside' a material organism. (See Plato's *Phaedo*.) Who doesn't see that it is impossible to look at someone and see two things, a soul and a body?

Plato developed that model in two different ways. He took the fact that our bodies or material organisms have distinct sense organs, namely, eyes, ears, nose, tongue, and skin, and decided that, in similar fashion, the soul or psyche has distinct organs. In Book IV of his *Republic*, Plato uses everyday human experiences as evidence that the soul has three organs or, as they came to be called, "faculties" or "capacities." We experience desires; they come from the soul's desiring faculty. We can think and reason; we do that by using our reasoning power. We can consult reason in order to decide which desires should and which should not be acted upon; our ability to accede to or to resist our desires he called the psyche's "spirited part."

In the *Theatetus*, Plato gives his strongest argument to prove that human thinking or theorizing is radically 'more' than mere sense experience. This Platonic *distinction between sensation and thinking* profoundly influenced subsequent Western psychology. Does anyone imagine that Plato looked at a soul and said "Look, see those three parts of the soul: a desiring part, a spirited part, and of course both of them below that top part, reason"?!

What about more recent psychologists? Where did Kant get his huge array of items whose names (translated into English) are "autonomy," "axiom," "category," "concept," "deduction," "ideal," "manifold," "noumena," "paralogism," "phenomena," "reason," "practical reason," "pure reason," "schematism," "understanding," and so on? Does anyone seriously believe that Freud looked and saw what no one else had seen before him, namely, an id, ego, and superego?!

The next time you have some leisure on your hands, try to imagine how anyone whose psyche is essentially like yours ever acquired ideas of such items as those that Plato, Kant, and Freud wrote about.

Back to the beginning. The preceding segments of this preface bring us back to its beginning:

James' writings: an undiscovered gold mine. Randall Albright, editor of *Streams of William James*, the original but now discontinued publication of the William James Society, felt that the phrase, "An undiscovered gold mine," captured the way things stood at the start of the 2000's. Nothing has happened since to change that fact.

And nothing will change that fact until people use the right key to that goldmine. This book, read in conjunction with *William James on Common Sense*, will describe it.

And what is that key? The quintalist model or framework.

As the chapters of this book will explain, James knew of the elements needed for a five-part framework that has ample room for all of his brilliant insights into the human psyche. But he died, still trying to squeeze everything into a too-small, two-part model whose elements he referred to with such phrases as 'percept and concept,' 'perception and conception,' or 'the perceptual view and the conceptual view.'

The aim of *William James on the Stream of Consciousness*. This book will expand James's two-part model to a five-part one, from a variety of dualism to what—in imitation of "quintessential," "quintet," and "quintuplet"—will be called "quintalism." The aim will be to show that James has left for all of us careful readers an abundance of evidence to recognize three types of things in our private streams of conscious experience: sense-data, memory-images, and complete thoughts.

CHAPTER I

Full-Bodied Sense-Data Are Things

Every one, however instructed, still thinks of a 'thing' in the common-sense way, as a permanent unit-subject that 'supports' its attributes interchangeably. No one stably or sincerely uses the more critical notion, of a group of sense-qualities united by a law. (W.James, *Pragmatism*, lect.V)

Two Preambles

First, the title. If you happen to be a 'modern philosophy' student, you probably will think there is such a thing as 'the' sense-datum theory. In that case, you might skip this chapter, either because, like one eminent 'philosopher of science,' you don't think 'the' sense-datum theory is credible or because, like a student from Brown University, you were taught that 'the' sense-datum theory was refuted once and for all during the twentieth-century.

Nonsense. There is no 'the' sense-datum theory.

James's pluralism points to the truth. In the whole of human history or the plural histories of plural humans, every minor theory, regardless of what 'it' was about, was part of a unique worldview or philosophy held by some unique, individual thinker.

Applied. Bertrand Russell had a sense-datum theory. G. E. Moore had one. C. D. Broad another one, H. H. Price yet another, A. J. Ayer (a student of Price) one of his own, and so on. And they all differed in various ways, because—to repeat—each one's theory about what sensing is and what its objects are was tailored to fit the mindset-context of his or her overall world-view or philosophy.

The same was true about James. He used the phrase, "sense-data." But he did so to refer to the theory of those predecessors who maintained that human knowledge begins with 'atoms of sensation.' The most important of those ancestors were Locke, Berkeley, Hume, and the Mills. If anything about James is certain, it is that he absolutely rejected every version of an 'atoms of sensation' theory. That is why he coined the phrase, "stream of thought," which he later broadened to

1

"stream of consciousness." Nevertheless, he often 'used' the theory as a helpful fiction, a pragmatic model, in his description of any stream of consciousness similar to his own.

The position here is like that of James. The phrase, "sense-data," derived from the Latin to mean "the givens of sensation," is ambiguous. Rather than avoid it, however, it is necessary to do only two things. One is to keep James's objection in mind by occasionally recalling that, for instance, visual sensing is like filming a movie. The other is to qualify "sense-data" with the phrase "full-bodied." When we see, we see a total visual field of many colored-shapes or shaped-colors, never just a single patch of red or a simple impression of red or an apple-shaped idea of red. When we hear, we often hear, not just a single stroke of a single sound, but an entire quadraphonic medley of sound(s).

By pondering—really pondering!—the true facts of sense experience, we can then understand why James's chapters on comparison, discrimination, and association are so essential for everyone whose ambition it is to become a Jamesian psychologist, that is, a *good* student of humans' psyches.

Second, switching mindsets. In his all-important fifth *Pragmatism* lecture, James told his audience that "Science and critical philosophy thus burst the bounds of common sense." He did not pause to argue for the truth of that claim. He simply referred his listeners to the views of nineteenth-century physicists and to the tradition-shattering theories of the earlier Locke and Berkeley.

Those in James's audience who were unfamiliar with the arguments believed to have 'burst the bounds' of common sense could hardly have understood much of James's sixth and seventh *Pragmatism* lectures. Worse, no one in the twenty-first century who is unfamiliar with the arguments made by Galileo, Descartes, Locke, Berkeley, and Hume against the naïve-realism component of everyone's common-sense philosophy, will understand either James's first masterpiece, *The Principles of Psychology,* or his later radical-empiricist belief-system. This opening chapter, therefore, will present a relatively brief synopsis of the arguments *against* common sense's naïve realist component and *for* a full-bodied version of a 'sense-datum view' of sense experience.

Before presenting that synopsis, however, it will help if a few paragraphs are devoted to explaining the huge psychological hurdle faced by anyone still blithely unaware that their everyday sense experience is, in the phrase of Jonathan Harrison, "a consistent hallucination."

The hurdle can be described very directly. To explain a full-bodied sense-datum theory, it is necessary to use two convictions of common sense. i) The first is the assumption that persons, animals, vegetables, and minerals really exist *and that they are completely independent of us.* For instance, our parents were here before we were born; they did not wait till we opened our eyes and saw them in order to begin existing. ii) The other conviction is that the reason we can be certain those things really exist is because *we can see and touch them.* This second conviction is partially false. The things we see and feel do exist; and, at least so long as we see and feel them, we can be absolutely certain about their existence. But the things we see and feel are not what we grow up believing they are.

For instance, you can be certain that what you're seeing as you continue to read really exists so long as you are seeing it. And, if you think about it, you'll realize that you do not see only one thing; you see everything that is in your total visual field right now. However, *the things you see are not words, not a book, not even your hands holding it.* The things you see are the patterned colors that make up a movie-like, total visual field of colors in your mind.

Here is the hurdle: this is hard to believe! To understand James, however, you'll have to at least understand the preceding paragraph. It can be done. The very fact that, at first, everyone finds the things stated in that paragraph hard to believe is evidence that they have at least vaguely understood it!

To become wholly clear in your thinking about what you see and, *even more obviously, what scientists see,* you will have to use a skill you've possessed from your youth, one you most likely haven't paid much attention to. It will be called "mindset switching."

Everyone with common sense does it quite easily. For instance, children play games in which they pretend they are cops or robbers, moms or dads, cowboys or indians, etc. To play such games, they pretend. They use their imagination. But as soon as the game is over, they switch from 'let's pretend' to 'reality.' Then, too, if you've ever enjoyed a movie or television show, you've done so only because, without noticing it, you were using your imagination to think about people, animals, events, etc., that you *weren't* seeing, all the while you were not thinking about the colors you *were* seeing! That is, while you were seeing nothing but colors 'projected' onto a movie screen or created on a television screen and hearing nothing but sounds from a speaker, your mind was spurred into creating people, places, and events existing only in your imagination. If someone suddenly asked, "Is that really so-and-so or is it literally just colors on the movie- or TV-screen?", you'd immediately switch from one train of thought to another. Finally, if you've ever pointed to a photograph and said "Look, there's so-and-so in the back row; did you know he died last year?", you were using your imagination to think about a person you weren't seeing, as you'd admit if someone asked, "Do you think that's a living person you're pointing to?"

In this chapter, you will have to learn how to read—for instance— "It seems that this is a book in you hands, but 'this' is actually part of a visual field of colors in your mind" and, as you 'read' it, to use it to practice switching back-and-forth between your common-sense mindset and a radically different one.

The final *insight* comes from a further mindset-switching. Your ability to form an idea of thinking with the straightforward, common-sense mindset and to form an idea of thinking with the pretending-mindset requires a broader point of view that embraces both ideas simultaneously so as to compare and contrast them. The ultimate worldview will be one that can be used to think about, contrast, and rank all mindsets. It can be thought of as *the pinnacle of insight.*

1. James: Contradictions or Mindset-Switchings?

Not Paradox, but Clear-Cut Contradictions. We can agree with Gordon Allport that in many cases, what look like contradictions in James's writings are better viewed as pragmatically productive paradoxes. Often, the inconsistency is merely verbal, the use of one 'word' to signify two quite opposed concepts.

But what about his answers to questions about brains, consciousness, colors, and the relations between them? If there are such things as contradictions, there is more than sufficient evidence that James's diverse answers to questions regarding *those* topics cannot be labeled as anything but "blatant contradictions."

Three Questions: a Test-Case for Interpreting James. The test-case consists of three seemingly simple questions.

1) Did James believe in brains?
2) Did he believe in consciousness?
3) Did he believe each causally acts upon the other?

Of course the third question is moot unless the answers to the first two questions are both "Yes," in the same way that "Have you stopped beating your wife?" is a moot question when the 'you' addressed is not married or is married but never started beating his wife. So, to repeat, did James believe in brains? Did he believe in consciousness? Did he believe each causally acts upon the other?

Those three questions do not deal with minor areas in James's thinking. They go to the very core of his worldview. His answers constitute three vital stitches in the entire fabric of James's belief-system. They stand at the center of his 'world.'

James's First Documented Answers. We can begin with the third question, "Did he believe that the brain and consciousness exert causal influence on one another?" If the answer is "Yes," then it will highlight the obvious importance of the other two questions.

(1) Did James believe that the brain and consciousness interact? Descartes became famous for his theory that mind and brain are separate entities and that each can act on the other. The brain is a funnel between the non-physical mind and the physical things outside of the brain. All traffic between the outside world and the mind must be routed through the brain. The brain is the only thing in the entire universe with which the mind has direct contact, and the brain is the only item in the entire universe which has any direct effect on the mind. This was Descartes' model. James used Descartes' model for *The Principles of Psychology* and its later abridgements.

Begin with the brain vis-à-vis the body. James viewed the brain as both a message center to which are sent all the signals received by the eyes, ears, nose, tongue, and skin from the external physical environment. The brain is also a command center from which orders are sent out to legs, arms, torso, vocal cords, eyes, and any other part of the body. The brain's capabilities are 'shaped' by both the incoming signals and the outgoing commands. James viewed such 'shaping' as habit-acquisitions, both knowledge-habits and behavior-habits. That he used this model as the basis for his *Principles of Psychology* is unmistakable.

If habits are due to the plasticity of materials to outward agents, we can immediately see to what outward influences, if to any, the brain-matter is plastic. Not to mechanical pressures, not to thermal changes, not to any of the forces to which all the other organs of our body are exposed; for nature has carefully shut up our brain and spinal cord in bony boxes, where no influences of this sort can get at them. She has floated them in fluid so that only the severest shocks can give them a concussion, and blanketed and wrapped them about in an altogether exceptional way. The only impressions that can be made upon them are through the blood, on the one hand, and through the sensory nerve-roots, on the other; and it is to the infinitely attenuated currents that pour in through these latter channels that the hemispherical cortex shows itself to be so peculiarly susceptible. The currents, once in, must find a way out. In getting out they leave their traces in the paths which they take. The only thing they *can* do, in short, is to deepen old paths or to make new ones; and the whole plasticity of the brain sums itself up in two words when we call it an organ in which currents pouring in from the sense-organs make with extreme facility paths which do not easily disappear. For, of course, a simple habit, like every other nervous event—the habit of snuffling, for example, or of putting one's hands into one's pockets, or of biting one's nails—is, mechanically, nothing but a reflex discharge . . . For the entire nervous system is nothing but a system of paths between a sensory *terminus a quo* and a muscular, glandular, or other *terminus ad quem.* (PP I:107-08)

What about the mind? How does the brain relate to it? "Do the brain and the mind exert mutual causal influence on each other?" The question obviously has two halves, "Does the brain influence consciousness?" and "Does consciousness have any effect on the brain?"

As for the first half, the thesis that the brain influences consciousness is the postulate upon which James based *The Principles.*

And a very small amount of reflection on facts shows that one part of the body, namely, the brain, is the part whose experiences are directly concerned. If the nervous communication be cut off between the brain and other parts, the experiences of those other parts are non-existent for the mind. The eye is blind, the ear deaf, the hand insensible and motionless. And conversely, if the brain be injured, consciousness is abolished or altered, even although every other organ in the body be ready to play its normal part. A blow on the head, a sudden subtraction of blood, the pressure of an apoplectic hemorrhage, may have the first effect; whilst a very few ounces of alcohol or grains of opium or hasheesh, or a whiff of chloroform or nitrous oxide gas, are sure to have the second. The delirium of fever, the altered self of insanity, are all due to foreign matters circulating through the brain, or to pathological changes in that organ's substance. The fact that the brain is the one immediate bodily condition of the mental operations is indeed so universally admitted nowadays that I need spend no more time in illustrating it, but will simply postulate it and pass on. The whole remainder of the book will be more or less of a proof that the postulate is true. (PP I:4)

Events in the brain "have the first effect." How else can this be interpreted than by acknowledging that neural events are the causes of—or the conditions for—the abolition or alteration of "consciousness." It would be tedious to go through his book and list every mention on every page which supports the affirmative answer to our question. One such passage will suffice. In it, James explains what happens when muscles are contracted. The muscles activate the brain, and the brain activations are accompanied by sensations we become aware of.

Let A, B, C, D, E, F, G represent an habitual chain of muscular contractions, and let a, b, c, d, e, f, stand for the respective sensations which these contractions excite in us when they are successively performed. Through them, and through them alone, we are made aware whether the contraction has or has not occurred. (PP I:116)

The second half of our first question is "Does consciousness have a reciprocal influence on the brain processes which control the body?" Because he wrote with one eye on his 'professional' peers, James approached the issue very carefully. He knew that Huxley and others espoused a view that is usually referred to now as "epiphenomenalism." According to that theory, human beings are conscious robots or automata. Mental or conscious states are useless byproducts of brain activities and can do nothing to further or to impede events in the world of matter where the laws of thermodynamics allow for no interference from such 'outside forces' as consciousness or willing.

In an 1879 essay that asked, "Are We Automata?", James answered with a firm "No!" Much of the essay was used later in Chapter V of *The Principles*.

My conclusion is that to urge the automaton-theory upon us, as it is now urged, on purely *a priori* and *quasi-metaphysical* grounds, is an *unwarrantable impertinence in the present state of psychology.* [. . .]

But there are much more positive reasons than this why we ought to continue to talk in psychology as if consciousness had causal efficacy. The *particulars of the distribution of consciousness,* so far as we know them, *point to its being efficacious.* Let us trace some of them. (PP I:139)

The reasoning James used in Chapter V, entitled "The Automaton-Theory," was also repeated in Chapter XI entitled "Attention." There, he renamed it the "effect-theory." Once more, he protested against the view that consciousness is ineffective and powerless to change anything.

When, a few pages back, I symbolized the 'ideational preparation' element in attention by a brain-cell played upon from within, I added 'by other brain-cells, or by some spiritual force,' without deciding which. The question 'which?' is one of those central psychologic mysteries which part the schools. When we reflect that the turnings of our attention form the nucleus of our inner self; when we see (as in the chapter on the Will we shall see) that volition is nothing but attention; when we believe that our autonomy in the midst of nature depends on our not being pure effect, but a cause, . . . we must admit that the question whether attention involve such a principle of spiritual activity or not is metaphysical as well as psychological, and is well worthy of all the pains we can bestow on its solution. It is in fact the pivotal question of metaphysics, the very hinge on which our picture of the world shall swing from materialism, fatalism, monism, towards spiritualism, freedom, pluralism,—or else the other way.

It goes back to the automaton-theory. If feeling is an inert accompaniment, then of course the brain-cell can be played upon only by other brain-cells, and the attention which we give at any time to any subject, whether in the form of sensory adaptation or of 'preperception,' is the fatally predetermined *effect* of exclusively material laws. If, on the other hand, the feeling which coexists with the brain-cells' reacts dynamically on that activity, furthering or checking it, then the attention is in part, at least, a *cause.* . . .

I have stated the effect-theory as persuasively as I can. It is a clear, strong, well-equipped conception, and like all such, is fitted to carry conviction, where there is no contrary proof. The feeling of effort certainly may be an inert accompaniment and not the active element which it seems. No measurements are as yet performed (it is safe to say none ever will be performed) which can show that it contributes energy to the result. We may then regard attention as a superfluity, or a 'Luxus,' and dogmatize against its causal function with no feeling in our hearts but one of pride that we are applying Occam's razor to an entity that has multiplied itself 'beyond necessity.'

But Occam's razor, though a very good rule of method, is certainly no law of nature. The laws of stimulation and of association may well be indispensable actors in all attention's performances, and may even be a good enough 'stock company' to carry on many performances without aid; and yet they *may* at times simply form the background for a 'star-performer,' who is no more their 'inert accompaniment' or the 'incidental product' than Hamlet is Horatio's or Ophelia's. Such a star-performer would be the voluntary effort to attend, if it were an original psychic force. Nature *may*, I say, indulge in these complications; and the conception that she has done so in this case is, I think, just as clear (if not as 'parsimonious' logically) as the conception that she has not. To justify this assertion, let us ask just what the effort to attend would effect if it were an original force.

It would deepen and prolong the stay in consciousness of innumerable ideas which else would fade more quickly away. The delay thus gained might not be more than a second in duration—but that second might be critical; for in the constant rising and falling of considerations in the mind, where two associated systems of them are nearly in equilibrium it is often a matter of but a second more or less of attention at the outset, whether one system shall gain force to occupy the field and develop itself, and exclude the other, or be excluded itself by the other. When developed, it may make us act; and that act may seal our doom. (PP I:447-48, 452-53)

Always in the back of James's mind is the idea of rival systems. What he says next should remind everyone of what happens at well-presented debates. There, 'in the constant rising and falling of considerations in the mind, where two associated systems of them are nearly in equilibrium, it is often a matter of only a moment of extra attention to some detail that leads to one system gaining enough force 'to occupy the field.' That moment can come at any time, perhaps right after the debate when, remaining to converse with one group rather than another, one's mind, still 'in equilibrium,' can be exposed to thoughts which will tilt it in one direction rather than the other.

The tilt need not be permanent, provided that the 'mind' in question does not prematurely close. The remarkable thing about our belief system is that it is subject to revision each morning when we wake up once more and find ourselves able to decide which friends we will 'hang' with, which books we will read, which courses we sign up for, which TV programs we watch, which gurus we listen to, etc. James ends this mini-section with an allusion to 'scientists' whose minds are not open, and with an invitation to readers not yet 'set' in their views.

Under these circumstances, one can leave the question open whilst waiting for light, or one can do what most speculative minds do, that is, look to one's general philosophy to incline the beam. The believers in mechanism do so without hesitation, and they ought not to refuse a similar privilege to the believers in a spiritual force.

I count myself among the latter, but as my reasons are ethical they are hardly suited for introduction into a psychological work. The last word of psychology here is ignorance, for the 'forces' engaged are certainly too delicate and numerous to be followed in detail. Meanwhile, in view of the strange arrogance with which the wildest materialistic speculations persist in calling themselves 'science,' it is well to recall just what the reasoning is, by which the effect-theory of attention is confirmed. It is an argument from analogy, drawn from rivers, reflex actions and other material phenomena where no consciousness *appears* to exist at all, and extended to cases where consciousness seems the phenomena's essential feature. *The consciousness doesn't count*, these reasoners say; it doesn't exist for science, it is *nil*; you mustn't think about it at all. The intensely reckless character of all this needs no comment. It is making the mechanical theory true *per fas aut nefas*. For the sake of that theory we make inductions from phenomena to others that are startlingly *un*like them; and we assume that a complication which Nature has introduced (the presence of feeling and of effort, namely) is not worthy of scientific recognition at all. Such conduct may conceivably be *wise*, though I doubt it; but scientific, as contrasted with metaphysical, it cannot seriously be called. (PP I:454)

This is an extremely careful passage. A great deal of the time, though, James simply and without fanfare asserts that, yes, the mind does influence the brain.

In habitual action, on the contrary, the only impulse which the centres of idea or perception need send down is the initial impulse, the command to *start*. This is represented in the diagram by V; it may be a thought of the first movement or of the last result, or a mere perception of some of the habitual conditions of the chain, the presence, e.g., of the keyboard near the hand. (PP I:116)

To sum up, then, James often answered "Yes!" to our first question, "Do the brain and consciousness exercise mutual causal influence on one another?"

(2) Did James believe that brains exist? If we go by appearances, then the preceding quotes from *The Principles* are consistent with a resounding "Yes!" But, because he insisted that his 'psychology' would need revision when the time came to put it into the broader context of 'metaphysics,' and because he even went so far as to say that further reflection leads to idealism, we know that James did not always give us his 'ultimate truth' answers in his psychology text. What about his other works? Did he always believe in brains? The answer appears to be a firm "Yes!"

For instance, two years after completing *The Principles*, James was criticized for making his psychology a 'natural science' by so often attributing the initiative to the brain and so often suggesting that the mind's role is better discussed by metaphysics or critical philosophy. In response, he wrote "A Plea for Psychology as a Natural Science," published in the March 1892 issue of *Philosophical Review*. His plea was based, first, on the progress being made by brain-investigators. More than that, however, it was based on his hope that investigations into the brain might someday lead to the cure of depression and other mental disorders.

The kind of psychology which could cure a case of melancholy, or charm a chronic insane delusion away, ought certainly to be preferred to the most seraphic insight into the nature of the soul. (CER:327)

In *Talks to Teachers*, 1890's lectures based on his psychology and published in 1899, he repeated his concern for the importance of the brain:

. . . mental action is conditioned by brain action, and runs parallel therewith. But the brain, so far as we understand it, is given us for practical behavior. Every current that runs into it from skin or eye or ear runs out again into muscles, glands, or viscera, and helps to adapt the animal to the environment from which the current came. It therefore generalizes and simplifies our view to treat the brain life and the mental life as having one fundamental kind of purpose. (TT:34-35; *Writings* I:728)

Incidentally, the title James gave to the chapter from which that passage is copied was "The Child as a Behaving Organism." Picturing the child as an organism makes it easy to understand his focus on the child's brain. Later, in Chapter IX, on "The Association of Ideas," he wrote "I myself am disposed to think that the phenomena of association depend on our cerebral constitution" (*Writings I:*760), and in Chapter XI on "Attention," he drew another verbal picture of his thesis:

The attentive process, therefore, at its maximum may be physiologically symbolized by a brain-cell played on in two ways, from without and from within. Incoming currents from the periphery arouse it, and collateral currents from the centres of memory and imagination reinforce these. (TT:82; *Writings* I:775)

Two years earlier, James had delivered the Ingersoll Lecture on "Human Immortality." In it, he speculated that the brain might have a function other than producing thought. But still, he assumes that the brain exists.

My thesis now is this: that, when we think of the law that thought is a function of the brain, we are not required to think of productive function only; *we are entitled also to consider permissive or transmissive function*. And this the ordinary psycho-physiologist leaves out of his account. (Human Immortality:15; *Writings* I:1110)

Perhaps, he adds, "the genuine matters of reality, the life of souls as it is in its fullness, will break through our several brains into this world in all sorts of restricted forms" (*Human Immortality*:17; *Writings I:*1111). Ten years later and two years before his death, in Lecture IV of *A Pluralistic Universe*, James remarked in passing that "All the consciousness we directly know seems tied to brains" (Writings II:702). Somewhat further on, he added that "The immediate condition [for changes in attention] is probably cerebral in every instance" (same, p.753). In his last (uncompleted) work, *Some Problems of Philosophy*, the final problem he took up in the final chapter concerned the relation of mind to brain.

Perception has given us a positive idea of causal agency but it remains to be ascertained whether what first appears as such, is really such; whether aught else is really such; or finally, whether nothing really such exists. Since with this we are led immediately into the mind-brain relation, and since that is such a complicated topic, we had better interrupt our study of causation provisionally at the present point, meaning to complete it when the problem of the mind's relation to the body comes up for review. (*Writings* II:1093)

Given these statements from various periods of his life, is there anyone who can doubt that James believed brains exist? He explicitly says that scientific psychology is about the brain vis-à-vis consciousness, he insists that studying the brain is better than swooning over the soul, and he assures us that he leans toward the view that association-phenomena and attention relate to the brain. We have his word on the fact, his written word, his written published word. Unless he had a reason to lie, we have to ask what more evidence anyone would need in order to be sure, that is, to feel 100% confident, that James believed in brains?

(3) Did James believe consciousness exists? There is abundant evidence that he did, and even if we just browse in his lesser *Psychology: Briefer Course*, we discover how vividly he could capture facts of experience so mundane and obvious that some materialist 'philosophers' trivialize them by calling them "trivial"! If we happen to think that Descartes was more on the right track than any of his modern critics, it warms our heart to see how robust was James's insistence on the 'primacy' of mind and consciousness vis-à-vis the brain and physiology. *Psychology: Briefer Course* offers everything an eager Cartesian could wish for:

> The Fundamental Fact.—The first and foremost concrete fact which every one will affirm to belong to his inner experience is the fact that consciousness of some sort goes on. 'States of mind' succeed each other in him. If we could say in English 'it thinks,' as we say 'it rains' or 'it blows,' we should be stating the fact most simply and with the minimum of assumption. As we cannot, we must simply say that thought goes on. (PBC:19; *Writings* I:152-53)

How tame that announcement of "the fundamental fact" and how dull if compared with Descartes' dramatic build-up for his famous "I think, therefore I am." Still, James's follow-up pages describing consciousness firmly plants the conviction in us that James had no doubt whatever about the existence of consciousness, plain and simple. Our confidence grows when we return to *The Principles* and locate the abridgment's original. It has been cited already, but here it is once again.

> *Introspective Observation is what we have to rely on first and foremost and always.* The word introspection need hardly be defined—it means, of course, the looking into our own minds and reporting what we there discover. *Every one agrees that we there discover states of consciousness.* So far as I know, the existence of such states has never been doubted by any critic, however sceptical in other respects he may have been. That we have *cogitations* of some sort is the *inconcussum* [unshaken fact] in a world most of whose other facts have at some time tottered in the breath of philosophic doubt. All people unhesitatingly believe that they feel themselves thinking, and that they distinguish the mental state as an inward activity or passion, from all the objects with which it may cognitively deal. *I regard this belief as the most fundamental of all*

the postulates of Psychology, and shall discard all curious inquiries about its certainty as too metaphysical for the scope of this book. (PP I:185)

Our confidence takes a momentary dip when we notice the word "postulate." Why would James use "postulate" at the end rather than the word "fact" which he used two years later when he abridged this paragraph? Still, he did use "fundamental fact" rather than "postulate" last. Perhaps by the time he wrote *Briefer Course*, he realized that, if "conscious states exist" is the only remaining fact that has not yet been weakened by any skeptic's attacks, it makes little sense to use the weaker term, "postulate." Our confidence is fully restored when we read what James declared even later in his 1896 "Will to Believe."

I am . . . myself a complete empiricist so far as my theory of human knowledge goes. I live, to be sure, by the practical faith that we must go on experiencing and thinking over our experience, for only thus can our opinions grow more true; but to hold any one of them—I absolutely do not care which—as if it never could be reinterpretable or corrigible, I believe to be a tremendously mistaken attitude, and I think that the whole history of philosophy will bear me out. There is but one indefectibly certain truth, and that is the truth that pyrrhonistic scepticism itself leaves standing,—the truth that the present phenomenon of consciousness exists. That, however, is the bare starting point of knowledge, the mere admission of a stuff to be philosophized about. The various philosophies are but so many attempts at expressing what this stuff really is. (WB:14-15; *Writings* I:466-67).

In his 1901-02 lecture series, *The Varieties of Religious Experience*, James was still more emphatic about the reality of the mental states or experience which hard-nosed, objective 'scientists' prefer to ignore:

In spite of the appeal which this impersonality of the scientific attitude makes to a certain magnanimity of temper, I believe it to be shallow, and I can now state my reason in comparatively few words. That reason is that, so long as we deal with the cosmic and the general, we deal only with the symbols of reality, but *as soon as we deal with private and personal phenomena as such, we deal with realities in the completest sense of the term.* (*Writings* II:446)

Finally, all of the last five chapters which he managed to complete of his intended magnum opus, *Some Problems of Philosophy*, are devoted to one central issue, namely, novelty. From moment to moment in this world of ours, there is always something new coming into being. What is it? New phenomenal being. Concrete perceptual experience. Fields of consciousness. Pure experience. Because these chapters were written so late (1909-10) and because they are wrapped up with his reference at the end to 'the mind-body relation' quoted earlier, it makes sense to trust them as evidence of James's truest convictions.

> So far as physical nature goes few of us experience any temptation to postulate real novelty. The notion of eternal elements and their mixture serves us in so many ways, that we adopt unhesitatingly the theory that primordial being is inalterable in its attributes as well as in its quantity, and that the laws by which we describe its habits are uniform in the strictest mathematical sense. These are the absolute conceptual foundations, we think, spread beneath the surface of perceptual variety. It is when we come to human lives, that our point of view changes. It is hard to imagine that 'really' our own subjective experiences are only molecular arrangements, even though the molecules be conceived as beings of a psychic kind. A material fact may indeed be different from what we feel it to be, but what sense is there in saying that a feeling, which has no other nature than to be felt, is not as it *is* felt? Psychologically considered, our experiences resist conceptual reduction, and our fields of consciousness, taken simply as such, remain just what they appear, even though facts of a molecular order should prove to be the signals of the appearance. Biography is the concrete form in which all that is is immediately given; the perceptual flux is the authentic stuff of each of our biographies, and yields a perfect effervescence of novelty all the time. (*Writings* II:1058-59)

Given so many unequivocal assertions about the absolute confidence James felt in assenting to the statement, "Consciousness exists," and given his repeated assurance that no other fact was as fundamental (because conscious experience is the "stuff to be philosophized about"), can anyone doubt that James believed consciousness is as real as brains? And yet . . .

If those direct quotations mean what they seem to mean, it is no wonder readers experience shock, disbelief, then extreme puzzlement when they discover that James called the brain "a fiction," declared that consciousness does not exist, and denied that it has yet been proven that the brain and consciousness causally affect each other.

James' Second Documented Answers. Our three questions—Did James believe in brains?, Did he believe in consciousness?, and Did he believe the brain and consciousness causally affect each other?— taken together constitute the 'experimentum crucis' test for anyone attempting to unify James best beliefs. The first set of documented answers are easily understood if approached with the common-sense mindset. Every reader who reads further can also understand what G. Allport predicted in "The Productive Paradoxes of William James":

> At first, led along by lucidity and inspiration, he finds himself assenting eagerly to a great many discrete observations, as arresting in their brilliance as anything he ever encountered. But soon he comes upon propositions that contradict one another and do violence to his sense of syllogism. The further he reads, the more the contradictions pile up, and his discomfort becomes acute. In reading the *Principles* he probably feels as Bertrand Russell felt in reading *Pragmatism*—as if he were taking a bath in water which heated up so imperceptibly that he didn't know when to scream. (*Psych. Rev.*, 50:97)

(1) Did James believe that the brain and consciousness interact? We can begin by returning to the suggestion which he proposed in his 1897 Ingersoll Lecture on "Human Immortality." To the possibility that the brain and mind interact, James immediately proposed an alternative:

> My thesis now is this: that, when we think of the law that thought is a function of the brain, we are not required to think of productive function only; *we are entitled also to consider permissive or transmissive function.* And this the ordinary psychophysiologist leaves out of his account.
>
> Suppose, for example, that the whole universe of material things—the furniture of earth and choir of heaven—should turn out to be a mere surface-veil of phenomena, hiding and keeping back the world of genuine realities. . . .
>
> Admit now that *our brains* are such thin and half-transparent places in the veil. What will happen? Why, as the white radiance comes through the dome, or as the air now comes through my glottis determined and limited by its force and quality of its vibrations by the peculiarities of those vocal chords which form its gate of egress and shape it into my personal voice, the life of souls as it is in its fullness, will break through our several brains into this world in all sorts of restricted forms, and with all the imperfections and queerness that characterize our finite individualities here below.
>
> According to the state in which the brain finds itself, the barrier of its obstructiveness may also be supposed to rise or fall. It sinks so low, when the brain is in full activity, that a comparative flood of spiritual energy pours over. At other times, only such occasional waves of thought as heavy sleep permits get by. And when finally a brain stops acting altogether, or decays, that special stream of consciousness which it subserved will vanish entirely from this natural world. But the sphere of being that supplied the consciousness would still be intact; and in that more real world

with which, even whilst here, it was continuous, the consciousness might, in ways unknown to us, continue still. (HI: 15-17; *Writings* I:1110-11)

His phrase, "the furniture of earth and choir of heaven," comes from the idealist, G. Berkeley's *Principles*, sec. 6. Yet, even if James did believe in material brains, he here takes the view that they do not cause consciousness, but only open and close the pipeline running from an ocean of consciousness to the mind. Around the same period in his life, James was giving his *Talks to Teachers*. In a letter written off the record to his friend, G. H. Howison, he noted that the teachers who came to his talks lacked the ability to think large and flexibly enough. If a teacher hears a single good idea, "he lies down on it with his whole weight like a cow on a doorstep so that you can neither get out or in with him. He never forgets it or can reconcile anything else you say with it, and carries it to the grave like a scar" (R. B. Perry II:131). But those same, plodding, common-sense teachers became keenly aware of James's constant explanations of mental operations in terms of the material, biological, unspiritual brain. And they did not hesitate to express their concerns. So, a little before he ended his final lecture which was on the will, he tried to calm their fears:

I have been accused of holding up before you, in the course of these talks, a mechanical and even a materialistic view of the mind. I have called it an organism and a machine; I have spoken of its reaction on the environment as the essential thing about it; and I have referred this, either openly or implicitly, to the construction of the nervous system. I have, in consequence, received notes from some of you, begging me to be more explicit on this point; and to let you know frankly whether I am a complete materialist, or not.

Now in these lectures I wish to be strictly practical and useful, and to keep free from all speculative complications. Nevertheless, I do not wish to leave any ambiguity about my own position; and I will therefore say, in order to avoid all misunderstanding, that in no sense do I count myself a materialist. I cannot see how such a thing as our consciousness can possibly be *produced* by a nervous machinery, though I can perfectly well see how, if 'ideas' do accompany the workings of the machinery, the *order* of the ideas might very well follow exactly the *order* of the machine's operations. (TT:128; *Writings* I:819)

That said, James launched into a brief explanation to say why he regarded free-will as a sufficiently strong reason for him not to become either a fatalist or a materialist. In fact, however, he was a relentless critic of the idea that the brain controls our thoughts, feelings, and decisions.

Did he believe the mind causes things to happen in the brain? He insisted till the very end that he had never claimed that we have empirical evidence that our willing, our effort, or our feeling of mental energy literally cause changes in the physical brain. See "The Experience of Activity." (*Writings* II:797, ff)

Still, all of the preceding excerpts from James's writing make it sound as if James never wavered in his belief that brains exist. He might be questioning what they do, but brains can be neither sources of influence nor recipients of it unless they exist. And so, we ask . . .

(2) Did James believe in brains? The answer is "No," unless "reality" and "fiction" mean the same thing!

> *The 'entire brain-process' is not a physical fact at all.* It is the appearance to an onlooking mind of a multitude of physical facts. 'Entire brain' is nothing but our name for the way in which a million of molecules arranged in certain positions may affect our sense. On the principles of the corpuscular or mechanical philosophy, the only realities are the separate molecules, or at most the cells. Their aggregation into a 'brain' is a fiction of popular speech. Such a fiction cannot serve as the objectively real counterpart to any psychic state whatever. Only a genuinely physical fact can so serve. But the molecular fact is the only genuine physical fact—whereupon we seem, if we are to have an elementary psycho-physic law at all, thrust right back upon something like the mind-stuff theory, for the molecular fact, being an element of the 'brain,' would seem naturally to correspond, not to the total thoughts, but to elements in the thought. (PP I:178)

That astonishing claim—that the aggregation of discrete cells or molecules into one entity, a brain, "is a fiction of popular speech"— was originally tucked into a page near the end of Chapter VI of *The Principles*. When James abridged the 1400 pages of *The Principles* into the *Briefer Course*, he yanked the passage from its originally obscure setting, plunked it down almost dead-center in the Epilogue he wrote to conclude the *Briefer Course* and, if anything, made his position even more unmistakably clear:

> Our own formula has escaped the metempiric assumption of psychic atoms by taking the entire thought (even of a complex object) as the minimum with which it deals on the mental side, and the entire brain as the minimum on the physical side.

But the 'entire brain' is not a physical fact at all! It is nothing but our name for the way in which a billion of molecules arranged in certain positions may affect our sense. On the principles of the corpuscular or mechanical philosophy, the only realities are the separate molecules, or at most the cells. Their aggregation into a 'brain' is a fiction of popular speech. Such a figment cannot serve as the objectively real counterpart to any psychic state whatever. Only a genuinely physical fact can so serve, and the molecular fact is the only genuine physical fact. Whereupon we seem, if we are to have an elementary psycho-physic law at all, thrust right back upon something like the mental-atom-theory, for the molecular fact, being an element of the 'brain,' would seem naturally to correspond, not to total thoughts, but to elements of thoughts. Thus the real in psychics seems to 'correspond' to the unreal in physics, and *vice versa*; and our perplexity is extreme. (PBC:331; *Writings* I:429-30)

In his third *Pragmatism* lecture, he presented an alternative "No" answer to the question, "Do brains exist?" He told his audience that "Matter is known as our sensations of colour, figure, hardness and the like. . . . These sensations then are its sole meaning."

Here is how Berkeley explained his view of such things as apples. And brains. The following is a passage from Berkeley's work, *Of the Principles of Human Knowledge.*

Thus, for example, a certain color, taste, smell, figure, and consistence, having been observed to go together, are accounted one distinct thing, signified by the name 'apple.' Other collections of ideas constitute a stone, a tree, a book, and the like sensible things; . . . That neither our thoughts, nor passions, nor ideas formed by the imagination, exist without the mind, is what everybody will allow. And it seems no less evident that the various sensations or ideas imprinted on the sense, however blended or combined together (that is, whatever objects they compose), cannot exist otherwise than in a mind perceiving them. (*Op. cit.,* par's 2-3)

If James agreed with Berkeley that "apple" is only shorthand for "a certain colour, taste, smell, figure, and consistence" and if such qualities as color, etc., are merely ideas or sense-data in the mind, then "brain" is also only shorthand for "so much by way of sensation." Anyone who can listen to the six o'clock weather forecaster say that "the sun will rise tomorrow at 5:38 am," without thinking she or he has reverted to Ptolemy's view that the sun and not the earth does the moving should be able to interpret James's apparent concessions to 'common but inaccurate modes of speech' which, though useful for daily life, do not express the literal truth.

Those alternative views of what James meant by "brain" must

be interpreted within the context of his overall view(s) of material things in general. Knowing that he was already leaning toward radical empiricism by 1890, it is not difficult to believe that what he wrote in *The Principles*, "[The brain] is the appearance to an onlooking mind of a multitude of physical facts," expressed his Berkeleyan, phenomenalist, anti-dualist view that "matter" *means* phenomena in the mind. The added idea that "brain" might also be shorthand for the motions of "a million [later, billion] of molecules arranged in certain positions" which produce the 'phenomena' or 'appearances' in our minds, allows for the possibility that, even if brains do not exist, millions or billions of swarming molecules do.

Nevertheless, even if James became a phenomenalist idealist, that is, even if he held that material bodies as such do not exist, he surely did not deny the existence of consciousness, did he?

(3) Did James believe in consciousness? A final shock meets us when we open to the first of his *Essays in Radical Empiricism* and discover that James used, as its title, the question, "Does 'Consciousness' Exist?" The entire essay is his answer, but it is summed up on the second page. (If we did not know better, we might think that Watson, when he wrote *Behaviorism*, merely plagiarized James.)

> It [consciousness] is the name of a nonentity, and has no right to a place among first principles. Those who still cling to it are clinging to a mere echo, the faint rumor left behind by the disappearing 'soul' upon the air of philosophy. During the past year, I have read a number of articles whose authors seemed just on the point of abandoning the notion of consciousness, and substituting for it that of an absolute experience not due to two factors. But they were not quite radical enough, not quite daring enough in their negations. For twenty years past I have mistrusted 'consciousness' as an entity; for seven or eight years past I have suggested its non-existence to my students, and tried to give them its pragmatic equivalent in realities of experience. It seems to me that the hour is ripe for it to be openly and universally discarded. (*Writings* II:11411-42)

Reading this brings to mind an admission James slipped into the earlier Epilogue to *Psychology: Briefer Course*. It came only a few pages after he stunned us with his claim that "brain" names a fiction of popular speech. It, too, was a disclaimer about consciousness.

States of consciousness themselves are not verifiable facts.—But 'worse remains behind.' Neither common-sense, nor psychology so far as it has yet been written, has ever doubted that the states of consciousness which that science studies are immediate data of experience. 'Things' have been doubted, but thoughts and feelings have never been doubted. The outer world, but never the inner world, has been denied. Everyone assumes that we have direct introspective acquaintance with our thinking activity as such, with our consciousness as something inward and contrasted with the outer objects which it knows. Yet I must confess that for my part I cannot feel sure of this conclusion. Whenever I try to become sensible of my thinking activity as such, what I catch is some bodily fact, an impression coming from my brow, or head, or throat, or nose. It seems as if consciousness as an inner activity were rather a *postulate* than a sensibly given fact, the postulate, namely, of a *knower* as correlative to all this known; and as if '*scious*ness' might be a better word by which to describe it. But 'sciousness postulated as an hypothesis' is practically a very different thing from 'states of consciousness apprehended with infallible certainty by an inner sense.' For one thing, it throws the question of *who the knower really is* wide open again, and makes the answer which we gave to it at the end of Chapter XII a mere provisional statement from a popular and prejudiced point of view. (PBC:334; *Writings* I:432)

"Does 'Consciousness' Exist?" was first published in 1904. Recall that *The Principles* was published in 1890, the *Briefer Course* in 1892, and "The Will to Believe" in 1896. This means that all three of those works were put before an unsuspecting public during the twenty years when, as he confessed in "Does 'Consciousness' Exist?", he had been having qualms about the answer!

What comes as an even greater shock to anyone who reads James's texts with the speech-habits of common-sense readers is James's seeming adoption of materialism. The last section of "Does 'Consciousness' Exist?" begins with an imagined objection from common-sense readers: "We, for our part, *know* that we are conscious. We *feel* our thought, flowing as a life within us, in absolute contrast with the objects which it so unremittingly escorts. We cannot be faithless to this immediate intuition." To which James replied:

My reply to this is my last word, and I greatly grieve that to many it will sound materialistic. I can not help that, however, for I, too, have my intuitions and I must obey them. Let the case be what it may in others, I am as confident as I am of anything that, in myself, the stream of thinking (which I recognize emphatically as a phenomenon) is only a careless name for what, when scrutinized, reveals itself to consist chiefly of the stream of my breathing. The 'I think' which Kant said must be able to accompany all my objects, is the 'I breathe' which actually does accompany them. There are other internal facts besides breathing (intracephalic muscular adjustments, etc., of which I have said a word in my larger Psychology), and these increase the assets of 'consciousness,' so far as the latter is subject to immediate perception; but breath, which was ever the original of 'spirit,' breath moving outwards, between the glottis and the nostrils, is, I am persuaded, the essence out of which philosophers have constructed the entity known to them as consciousness. *That entity is fictitious, whilst thoughts in the concrete are fully real. But thoughts in the concrete are made of the same stuff as things are.* (*Writings* II:1157-58)

Are we shocked? We shouldn't be. This only repeats in 1904 what we find buried in *The Principles'* section on the 'spiritual me' (PP I:296-305). Here are some samples:

But when I forsake such general descriptions and grapple with particulars, coming to the closest possible quarters with the facts, it is difficult for me to detect in the activity any purely spiritual element at all. Whenever my introspective glance succeeds in turning round quickly enough to catch one of these manifestations of spontaneity in the act, all it can ever feel distinctly is some bodily process, for the most part taking place within the head. . . . In consenting and negating, and in making a mental effort, the movements seem more complex, and I find them harder to describe. The opening and closing of the glottis plays a great part in these operations, and, less distinctly, the movements of the soft palate, etc., shutting off the posterior nares from the mouth. My glottis is like a sensitive valve, intercepting my breath instantaneously at every mental hesitation or felt aversion to the objects of my thought, and as quickly opening, to let the air pass through my throat and nose, the moment the repugnance is overcome. . . . In a sense, then, it may be truly said that, in one person at least, *the 'Self of selves,' when carefully examined, is found to consist mainly of the collection of these peculiar motions in the head or between the head and throat. . . .* If the dim portions which I cannot yet define should prove to be like unto these distinct portions in me, and I like other men, *it would follow that our entire feeling of spiritual activity, or what commonly passes by that name, is really a feeling of bodily activities whose exact nature is by most men overlooked.* (PP I:300-01)

Niels Bohr is said to have said that whoever is not shocked by quantum theory does not understand it. It is equally true that whoever is not shocked by the contradictory views expressed by James over the last twenty years of his life has not understood the significance of those contradictions. These are not footnotes to his system. *They are the main text.* Unless these contradictions can be explained away as merely an appearance of contradiction, we who wish to salvage his magnificent insights must choose. We must choose which of his opposed lines of thought are true. Then we must either reject out of hand the other things he wrote or else find a way to revise them and make them consistent with his best thoughts.

2. James Tried to Unify Two Incompatible 'Visions.'

Looking for the Center of James' Vision(s). This unification of James's best thoughts begins the way he did, namely, with confidence that an all-embracing worldview can be found. He saw radical empiricism, not as a limited theory about part of reality. He hoped it would provide a universal framework for the whole of reality. Still, the very fact that "empiricism" was part of the name he chose for that framework indicates that "How do we know?" is a major aspect of that framework.

On all or nearly all of the major issues concerning knowledge that have been debated during the long history of western thinkers, James knew all the wrong solutions. But he also had in his hands all the right ones, if not in this place in this essay, then in that one in that book. In the instances where he adopted a view in one place which contradicts what he advocated in another, we must choose the pieces of the puzzle which fit with the best of the rest.

This will often require that we give more value to what he *does* than to what he *says*. For instance, in spite of his frequent attacks on intellectualism and his lack of respect for 'formal' logic, he was an intellectualist, logical to his fingertips. Were this not so, he would not have worried so incessantly about his own logical inconsistencies, he would not have paid so much attention to Kant's, Hegel's, Bradley's, and Royce's intellectualist theorizings, nor would he have been so delighted to have found in Bergson a well-reasoned, intellectual justification for rejecting what often seemed to be experience-ignoring, purely verbal deductions urged by 'intellectualists.'

If James was the genius that so many have concluded he was, there must have been reasons for his contradictions. Let us assume that there is a way to explain the logic behind them, by trying to do for James what he urged us to do for other thinkers. Here, from his *Pluralistic Universe* lecture on Bergson, is his description of how to approach those others.

Place yourself similarly at the centre of a man's philosophic vision and you understand at once all the different things it makes him write or say. But keep outside, use your post-mortem method, try to build the philosophy up out of the single phrases, taking first one and then another and seeking to make them fit 'logically,' and of course you fail. You crawl over the thing like a myopic ant over a building, tumbling into every microscopic crack or fissure, finding nothing but the inconsistencies, and never suspecting that a centre exists. I hope that some of the philosophers in this audience may occasionally have had something different from this intellectualist type of criticism applied to their own works! (*Writings* II:750-51)

What, then, is the center of James's philosophical vision, at least insofar as the brain, consciousness, and the interrelations between them are concerned?

The answer is that he had two visions. Neither vision wholly satisfied him, a fact that he confessed in his fifth *Pragmatism* lecture. Nevertheless, the two incompatible visions had a common center or core.

James Had Two Dominating Visions. He praised the everyday mindset which he called "*common sense.*" But he also rejected it as a final version of the truth, preferring his *radical-empiricist* version. He made heroic efforts to circumvent certain of the bedrock convictions of his common-sense 'vision,' but he was never able to iron-out the inconsistencies that resulted. He could not show how common sense could be incorporated logically into his radical-empiricist vision.

We, however, can put ourselves 'at the center' of his two visions. When we do, we discover that they have the same core.

We begin by asking, "How did the world seem to James?" But we must ask it twice. First, how did the world seem to him *most of the time*? Most of the time, the world seemed to him the way it seems to everyone else who is 'in' the common-sense mode of thought. At such times, he 'used' his common-sense worldview without any second thoughts about whether or not it was true. Should he try to become a professional painter-artist and make a living that way? He may have had deep feelings about the value of building his entire future around that professional activity. (Thank God, he didn't.) We can wager that his decision to give up that plan was not based on doubts about the outer world, doubts to which he referred in the *Briefer Course*'s epilogue. That is, he did not give up the idea of becoming a painter-artist because he worried that he'd be devoting his life to an illusion. And what should he and Alice call their first-born? Can we even imagine him bothered by the fact that he still hadn't made up his mind whether knowers . . . he surely took it for granted his first-born would become one of those! . . . whether knowers really are only evolution-produced organisms, or—as he maintained in his natural-science psychology and his radical empiricism—are really nothing but present thoughts which at each moment appropriate everything from previous moments' thoughts? We can safely bet that his thoughts about naming his first born were 'typical' of all new parents living in a relatively free society where no strict rules about naming have to be followed. And so on.

That is, the world 'felt normal' to James most of the day. We can be confident it felt that way to Berkeley as well. Hume told us it felt that way to him once he walked out of his study and 'did what came naturally.' James's fifth *Pragmatism* lecture about the primacy of common sense doesn't make sense unless the world felt that way to him most of the time.

But we can also be certain of a second point. The world didn't always seem plainly 'common-sensical' to James. The rest of his fifth *Pragmatism* lecture wouldn't make sense unless he was genuinely dissatisfied with common sense. There were those long hours when he was trying to reshape his 'vision' to accommodate 'science' and 'critical philosophy' as well as everyday common sense. It was during those hours of intense thinking that he worked out the various theses to which he gave such names as pluralism, pragmatism, and especially radical empiricism. And it is when we try to do what he did, namely, to assemble all those most deeply-felt theses into a single, coherent 'vision,' that we find it hard at first to 'get inside his mind' and to look at the world 'through his eyes.' It is difficult at first even to be certain *what he meant* when he said he was going to approach psychology as a natural science, which *meant* he would . . . That is the problem. He said what it *meant* in ways that were contradictory. First, he wrote as if his psychology could avoid 'metaphysical speculations.' Later, he confessed that 'metaphysics' leaked in 'at every joint.' (Chapter VI of the 1890 *Principles* begins with "The reader who found himself swamped with too much metaphysics in the last chapter will have a still worse time of it in this one.") And, in an 1885 letter to his brother in law, he confessed to some of the difficulties which he never could resolve to his full satisfaction:

I've just been lecturing on idealism . . . and found myself unable to come to a conclusion. The truth is, all these preliminaries lead one along very well to *immaterialism*. But when it comes to a *positive* construction of idealism, such questions as how many spirits there are, how the divine spirit sends us our representations if we are separate from him, and how if we are only bits of him we can have separate consciousness at all, and a host of others, start up and baffle *me*, at least, completely. (Cited in *Perry* I:578)

The more resolutely we seek an answer to "What was James's central vision?", the more certain it becomes that he was torn between common sense and radical empiricism.

Experience is the Overlapping Core of Both Visions. In James's thought, common sense and radical empiricism agree on one thing. Things are experienced. Add that is we who do the experiencing, and the formula becomes, "We experience things." *Our thesis* is that one of the meanings of "We experience things" is central both to everyone's common sense and to James's later, radical-empiricist or phenomena(list) idealism.

But to defend that thesis, a huge ambiguity must be recognized and kept permanently in view when we read anything that James ever wrote. Anything!

Start, Not with 'Definitions,' but with Everyday Thinking. Everyone who picked up *The Principles of Psychology* was someone able to read. No matter how radically any reader had subsequently modified it, every reader still possessed the common-sense philosophy they had acquired by the age of five or six. James took that fact for granted when, at the outset of his central ninth chapter, "The Stream of Thought," he skipped any effort to define "thought" or "consciousness" or "experience." Instead, he listed five 'characters' of experience, warned that he would 'plunge *in medias res*' [jump right into the middle of things] rather than define his terms, and then immediately began to describe the first character.

When I say *every thought is part of a personal consciousness*, 'personal consciousness' is one of the terms in question. Its meaning we know so long as no one asks us to define it, but to give an accurate account of it is the most difficult of philosophic tasks. (PP I:225)

The purpose of this book is to show that James succeeded in that 'most difficult of philosophic tasks,' namely, in giving an accurate account of ongoing thought, And there is no other way to do that, than by imitating James and assuming that you will be able to understand what you read. (Recall the Rorty Rule: "Everybody understands everybody else's meanings quite well indeed." See R. Rorty, *Philosophy and the Mirror of Nature*, p.88.)

Take the term "experience." Like the terms "sensation" and "sight," the word "experience" has two easily recognizable senses. Each of those three terms can refer either to i) a conscious *act* or ii) to the *object* of a conscious act.

Consider some everyday expressions. "We experience many things, ranging from lovely sunrises to deep depression," seems to make sense. But, if someone adds, "And depression is not a 'fun' experience", the combination leads to the conclusion that we can experience experience. That statement is best analysed by taking the verb form to refer to 'being conscious' of something, whereas the noun form refers to the 'thing' we can be conscious of.

Now take the analysis a step farther. We can experience many 'somethings.' We can experience sunrises and depression, but the two nouns refer to very different objects. Add to those examples the idea that we can experience colors, sounds, odors, tastes, tickles, pains, and all sorts of emotions. Such thoughts, pursued in further detail, help any reader to understand a premise basic to John Locke's lengthy psychology, *An Essay Concerning Human Understanding*. He claimed quite simply that "All knowledge comes from experience," and then wrote hundreds of pages to explain in endless detail what that 'generalization' meant.

We do not need to add hundreds more pages to Locke's. For the purpose of systematizing and unifying James's best thoughts, it is sufficient to distinguish two senses of "experience." And of "sight" as well as "sensation." Such terms can be used either to refer to *a kind of activity*, being aware or conscious of (something), or else to refer to *an object*, that is, something we can be aware or conscious of.

3. History: The 'Road' From Common Sense to Radical Empiricism.

Start with "What Do I See?" Why with sight? To counter a mammoth myth that clouds the thinking of most educated citizens. What myth? The myth that there is a special kind of knowledge called "science" acquired by the use of a special truth-producing method *based on direct observation.*

It falls apart once *readers* take seriously the fact that early all of the 'direct observation' (the most crucial component of that supposedly superior method) is seeing, and that 'normal' *reading* relies on the identical sense, *visual seeing,* that astronomers, physicists, chemists, biologists, and other so-called 'scientists' rely on. Pick up any psychology text and study it to see whether researchers have found that the senses of 'scientists' work differently from normal readers' senses! Or differently from the senses of eye-witnesses at criminal trials who must answer the question, "What did you see?" Simply asking such questions shows how absurd the myth is.

Consider. Everyone's eyes, optic nerves, brains, and minds work exactly the same way. It doesn't matter, therefore, whether the seeing is like the seeing you are doing as you read right now or whether it is seeing stars 'through' telescopes, seeing microbes 'through' microscopes, seeing numbers on various meters, seeing squiggles on paper, or seeing lines on a nuclear-accelerator-produced photograph.

Keep this fact in mind as you continue reading.

And seeing.

James' Answer(s) to "What Do I See?" James wrote *The Principles* with the tacit assumption that readers could see brains and books. He treated that fact as if it is perfectly obvious and uncontroversial. Consider the footnote he attached to the book's opening chapter:

*Nothing is easier than to familiarize one's self with the mammalian brain. Get a sheep's head, a small saw, chisel, scalpel and forceps (all three can best be had from a surgical-instrument maker), and unravel its parts either by the aid of a human dissecting book, such as Holden's 'Manual of Anatomy,' or by the specific directions ad hoc given in such books as Foster and Langley's 'Practical Physiology' (Macmillan) or Morrell's 'Comparative Anatomy and Dissection of Mammalia' (Longmans).

The second chapter of *The Principles* went on to present an 1880's description of the various parts and functions of human brains. In fact, the entire two-volume masterpiece is explicitly constructed on a two-part, brain-and-mind model, and on the postulate that there are correlations between what goes on in one's unobserved-by-one's-self, skull-imprisoned brain and what one directly experiences in the privacy of one's own stream of consciousness. However . . .

However!!! James knew that, since Descartes' revolutionary revision of common sense, the most important thinkers took it for granted that no one can see material bodies, such as brains and books. Moreover, not only did he know what those most important thinkers, viz., Descartes, Locke, Berkeley, Hume, Kant, and others, took for granted. He agreed with them!

That is, the things we experience are not brains or books! No matter whether we acquiesce in our common-sense mindset or switch to James's radical-empiricist mindset, the most precise answer to the question, "What do I see?" is "sense qualities." Or "sense-data," "sensa," "qualia," "impressions," etc. (Terminology, even in English, varies widely.) But there is a huge contradiction between our other common-sense convictions and James's radical empiricism. The question that must be faced is, "Why doesn't everyone recognize that immediately?"

The answer is "Ambiguity." The contradiction gets smothered, because the same words are used to express radically different beliefs which are parts of radically different belief-systems. James switched from one mindset or worldview to the other whenever he tried to answer the question, "What do I see?" When his oscillating mindsets were common sense and radical empiricism, his first answer would be the same: "I see the colors of things." The ambiguity emerges when you try to find out his answer to "What do you mean by 'thing'?"

Nowhere in his published works did James ever give as clear an answer to that question as the one he gave in the fifth of his *Pragmatism* lectures. The answer is "I mean two utterly different things."

Every one, however instructed, still thinks of a 'thing' in the common-sense way, as a permanent unit-subject that 'supports' its attributes interchangeably. No one stably or sincerely uses the more critical notion, of a group of sense-qualities united by a law. (*Writings* II:565)

"A permanent unit-subject that 'supports' its attributes interchangeably" is *the common-sense meaning* behind "I see the colors of things." "A group of sense-qualities [or sense-data] united by a law" is *the radical-empiricist meaning* behind "I see the colors of things."

The Common-Sense Notion of "a Permanent Unit-Subject . . ." Every reader capable of understanding James is someone who spent the first five or six years of a personal learning career by acquiring what James called "the magisterial notions" of the common-sense philosophy, which notions he briefly described in his all-important fifth lecture. At the top of his list of magisterial notions is "thing." What, then, do we think of as things while in our common-sense mindset?

Among other things, things are what we see. Find someone who is looking into the night sky when it is cloudless and sunlight is reflecting from our large nearby satellite. Ask them "What do you see?" If they did not answer "the moon," it should surprise us. It would be surprising if they even added the attribute "white" to "the moon." It would, of course, be surprising if, asked "What color is the moon?", they answered anything but "White."

This sequence of answers is all that is necessary to explain what James meant by a *"permanent unit-subject that 'supports' its attributes interchangeably."* The moon is an example of one. We ordinarily think of it as i) permanent; it has existed for years (even on nights when clouds hide it). We think of it as ii) one single reality or unit, not zillions of separate molecules or atoms. We think of it as iii) something distinct from and supportive of the color, shape, and size attributed to it, even though the color, shape, and size of the moon would perish if the moon was ever to perish. Even little children listening to *Alice in Wonderland* know that, if the cat disappears, its grin will disappear with it.

Good libraries will have reams of writing discussing these ideas. This short work, in other words, is not the place to explain how complex is the thinking even of young children who give the expected answers to such questions as "Have you ever seen grass?" or "What color is it?" Or to "Did you ever see a cow?" and "What kind of sound does it make?" To explain how children learn to answer such questions—or how they can understand the lyrics of "Old McDonald Had a Farm"—it would be necessary to understand the topics dealt with in James's chapters on comparison, discrimination, and association.

But James believed that 'science' and 'critical philosophy' have demolished the common-sense philosophy, including the common-sense "How do we know?" component, which is part of common sense's psychology component.

History is Essential for Learning "the More Critical Notion [of a 'Thing']." What is necessary now is to learn what James meant by "the more critical notion [of a 'thing']," that is, the notion "of a group of sense-qualities united by a law." To do so is impossible for anyone who has not mastered some of the basics of Aristotle's thought, then the basics of Descartes' thought, and so on, right up to and including Kant's thought.

The history is essential for understanding the distinction between two ideas or concepts. They have many labels, even among those who use English terms only. i) One idea is signified by "substance," "underlying reality," "subject," even "thing." ii) For the other, "accident," "attribute," "quality," "property," "characteristic," "feature," and so on, have been used.

The chaos in terminology makes it necessary to become clear on the ideas that any particular term- or word-user is thinking about or referring to. Names are less important than the ideas we 'take' them to signify.

Be warned. Never assume that those who use the same names are thinking of the same thing. For the same reason, never assume that those who use different names must be thinking of different things.

As for James, his common-sense idea of "I see a thing" uses the idea of a substance. His other idea of "I see a thing" uses the idea of qualities.

Aristotle and Being Precise About Different 'Objects.' Aristotle is the master when we are looking for the earliest thinker who captured in an *explicit* model the tangled, *tacit* principles that make up the theoretical, conceptual framework for our everyday thinking. St. Thomas Aquinas is the master who took Aristotle's writings and streamlined the great systematizer's psychological framework.

Begin again. As long as they have grown up among people accustomed to giving different *names* to different things, five-year old children can discuss the colors of the sky, clouds, vegetation, animals, skin, and rainbows, as easily as they discuss eyes, ears, nose, mouth, tongue, hands, and feet. By the age of five, normal children have learned that we see with our eyes, hear with our ears, smell with our noses, taste with our mouths and tongues, feel fur with our hands and grass with our feet. They know that, unlike red, green, blue, and orange colors which can be seen, loud voices and whispers are sounds to be heard, that smoke and perfume can be smelled, that sweet and bitter are tastes, that hot and cold are opposites, and so on. Rare would be the five-year old who could write an essay on such things, but equally rare would be the five-year old in a first-world country who would be unable to carry on Platonic-type dialogues about them. These unimaginably complex commonplaces are all that learners need later on to understand Berkeley whose thought is so critically important for grasping the core of James's two 'visions.'

Aristotle was the first writer to 'put order into' the complex and initially confusing ways in which we talk about our sensings and the objects of our sensings. He did so by inventing or, in Einstein's vocabulary, *creating* a three-part model or classification scheme to handle the whole range of possible answers to the question, "What do we sense?" The results, made 'canonical' by the scholastics during the long period known as 'the Middle Ages,' are summarized in Aristotle's work, *On the Soul.*

In dealing with each of the senses we shall have first to speak of the objects which are perceptible by each. The term 'object of sense' covers three kinds of objects, two kinds of which are, in our language, directly perceptible, while the remaining one is only incidentally perceptible. Of the first two kinds one (a) consists of what is perceptible by a single sense, the other (b) of what is perceptible by any and all of the senses. I call by the name of special object of this or that sense that which cannot be perceived by any other sense than that one and in respect of which no error is possible; in this sense colour is the special object of sight, sound of hearing, flavour of taste. . . .

'Common sensibles' are movement, rest, number, figure, magnitude; these are not peculiar to any one sense, but are common to all. There are at any rate certain kinds of movement which are perceptible both by touch and by sight.

We speak of an incidental object of sense where e.g. the white object which we see is the son of Diares; here, because 'being the son of Diares' is incidental to the directly visible white patch, we speak of the son of Diares as being (incidentally) perceived or seen by us. Because this is only incidentally an object of sense, it in no way as such affects the senses. Of the two former kinds, both of which are in their own nature perceptible by sense, the first kind—that of special objects of the several senses—constitute *the* objects of sense in the strictest sense of the term. . . . (Aristotle, *On the Soul*, trans. J. A. Smith, Bk II, Ch. 6; 418a 6-23)

Aristotle's three-part model for mentally class-ifying or group-ing objects must be kept in mind throughout this chapter's examination of the post-Descartes answers to the deceptively simple question, "What do I see?" (Or hear, smell, taste, feel?) Rather than give a blanket answer, such as "Persons, animals, vegetables, and minerals," Aristotle's model invites us to first ask, "Which of the senses are you asking about?"

If the question is "What do I see?", Aristotle would insist that my first answer must be "Colors" (the special object of sight). The reasoning behind his insistence is pure common sense. No one can see anything's shape, size, or location (common objects) if the thing is as colorless, i.e., as transparent as the air we breathe or the sounds traveling through it. As for the incidental object, it is obvious that a wax or plastic replica of an apple can have the same color, shape, etc.

For similar reasons, Aristotle would insist that, if I am asked "What do you hear?", my answer must be "Sounds." Colors and sounds are the 'proper' or 'special' objects of sight and hearing, respectively. No one can see sounds or hear colors. "Etc." for the other senses.

Aristotle's analyses are the first step in the reasoning that leads from analysis' starting point, viz., common sense, to Descartes' great discoveries. Mathematically precise answers are called for here as much as they are for any inquiries in physics, chemistry, biology, etc. I must not say simply "I see the book I am reading." I must say "I see the color of the surface of the pages facing me (the other pages or even the other side of these pages might have a different color) surrounding the color of the ink spread out on them." Even that is an imprecise or rather incomplete answer if I can simultaneously see other things as well, such as my hands (the color of the skin, etc.), the table in front of me (its colors), etc.

Only if the tight link between sight and color, hearing and sound, etc., is kept in mind, can we learn to be precise when the most crucial question related to the so-called 'scientific method' is raised. What question is that? "What is observed?" The idea that we can see, hear, and (at times) feel the locations and movements of some things is strictly-speaking false. We sense colors and sounds. We only *infer* the locations and movements of the things (incidental objects) we naïvely believe we are sensing.

Descartes and Later Thinkers Inherited Aristotle's Distinctions. Though Descartes often used "mode" in place of "quality," he and his successors continued to use Aristotle's distinction between substance-things and their qualities.

However, he used the distinction in order to remove 'incidental objects' from Aristotle's list of objects that can be sensed. *They cannot be sensed at all.* They can be known only by intellect or reason.

The distinction between what we sense and what we only infer by reason was basic to Descartes' revolutionary psychology. In the second of his *Meditations*, he used an excellent example to show what he meant. A cool piece of wax fresh from the hive is opaque, hard, capable of emitting a sound if tapped, fragrant, etc. Heated in a pan, all of its sensed qualities change: it is no longer opaque but translucent, its hardness turns into liquidity, its fragrance evaporates, and it makes only a splashing sound. Still, he observes, we are as convinced that the wax itself remains genuine wax, as we are that the rock-hard ice we walk across in winter is the same liquid H_2O we swam in during the summer.

Such 'physics' began with our naïve-realist philosophy. In everyday life, we assume that the infant who becomes a five-year old and later on a fifty-year old is one, same, perduring person, even though such qualities as her or his size, weight, shape-details, even hair-color (or hair-period!) have changed. This Aristotle-type *explicitation* of *implicit* common sense is what James had in mind in his fifth *Pragmatism* lecture's reference to "subjects" vs "attributes" and to the "unit-subject that supports its attributes interchangeably" concept. The various sense objects are attributes, their subject—according to Aristotle's explicitation of common sense—is not grasped by sense, but only inferred by reason.

These inferences become instantaneous. Newborns may see colors, hear sounds, feel pain, but they have no idea that they are seeing people, hearing words, or feeling pins. By the age of five or six, however, thoughts or inferences come so instantly and, for all practical purposes, so simultaneously, that we need reasoning to pry them apart and then to construct a complex theory to fit experience. For instance, we infer subjects or substances that remain the same, but we also infer subjects that are different. The unseen wax, cold or warm, remains a single subject. But two different subjects may have the same color and the same shape. For instance, the visible yellow of a banana-fruit and the visible yellow of a banana-shaped piece of plastic are the same, but the invisible fruit and plastic substances are not the same.

In every case, the equivocal "same" must be handled with care. It can mean "one," or it can mean "similar." The wax is the same, meaning there is only *one* subject 'beneath' dissimilar attributes or appearances. In the banana-vs-plastic example, each subject possesses only its own color, but the two (not one) colors can be *similar* or *alike*. The word "same," therefore, is like a hidden, unnoticed iceberg, and more than one voyage of discovery has ended in a shipwreck of wholesale confusion.

A Fatal Equivocation: Qualities? Or Ideas '*of*' Qualities? By the time James began writing about sensing and its objects, it was customary to use the phrase "secondary qualities" as shorthand for colors, sounds, odors, etc., which had previously been called "the proper objects of the senses." Also by that time, a fatal and too-little-noticed ambiguity had crept into the way people used "secondary qualities."

John Locke's *Essay Concerning Human Understanding* is an ideal text for studying the fatal ambiguity. Like Descartes, Locke distinguished ideas in our minds from things (substances and their qualities) outside our minds. For the purpose of his psychology, Locke replaced Aristotle's vocabulary with a new set of terms. In place of "incidental objects," Locke used "substances outside the mind." He replaced Aristotle's "common objects" with "primary qualities," and replaced Aristotle's "proper objects" with "secondary qualities." The three categories of items outside the mind have powers to produce—through the brain—three types of ideas in the mind, namely, i) ideas of substances, ii) ideas of shape, size, rest and motion, and iii) ideas of colors, sounds, odors, etc.

But, like Descartes, Locke denied that we ever experience any qualities of any bodies outside the mind. We have access only to ideas OF them, and the ideas are *effects produced by the brain in the mind.* There may be qualities in bodies, but we can know about them only through the ideas OF them which are in our mind. And...

And... Right there is the source of the fatal equivocation. Locke said that our ideas OF primary qualities are similar to the outside (primary!) qualities but that our ideas OF 'secondary' qualities do not resemble anything in outside things. After Locke, however, "secondary qualities" came to be used to refer i) to (non-existent) attributes of physical substances outside our mind and ii) to colorless, silent, odorless, etc., ideas OF (those non-existent) colors, sounds, odors, etc.

Think about Locke's model. He believed that we have ideas of substances and that substances exist. We can have an idea of an apple-substance that 'supports' the shape and size, the color and taste. We can have an idea of shape and size, and the apple really possesses shape and size. We can have an idea of color and taste, but there is no color or taste as such, only the 'power' to produce colorless ideas of color and tasteless ideas of tastes. (Ideas, of course, do not have colors or tastes, do not make sounds, are not warm or cool, etc.)

After Locke, it became common to say that primary qualities are real and exist in things, and that secondary qualities are not real. We have ideas OF all three, ideas of bodies, ideas OF their shapes and sizes, and ideas OF colors and tastes. But the fact that we have ideas OF colors, tastes, etc., does not prove that colors, tastes, etc., should be listed in the long answer to "What exists?" We also have ideas OF leprechauns, even though we know that leprechauns are not listed under "Things that exist."

Color, Sound, Odor, Taste, etc., Were Eventually Banished from the World. Locke built on ideas he received from his study of Descartes, Newton, and other great seventeenth-century philosophers of nature. During the 1600's, when new discoveries about physical bodies were being made at an accelerating rate, attention became focused more and more exclusively on the 'objects' which Aristotle had called "common sensibles," namely, movement, rest, number, figure, and magnitude, and which Locke renamed "primary qualities." Only those features of bodies seemed important for such researchers as Galileo, Newton, and others seeking mathematically precise laws governing physical bodies.

The other—secondary—qualities slowly faded from view. James, as we will see, was always acutely aware of this catastrophe of modern history. He drew attention to it on numerous occasions. One of those occasions came during his fifth *Pragmatism* lecture:

> Science and critical philosophy thus burst the bounds of common sense. With science, *naïf* realism ceases: 'Secondary qualities' become unreal; primary ones alone remain. (*Writings* II:567)

There were excellent reasons why Galileo and others revived the ancient atomists' theory that evicted secondary qualities from external nature. According to the atomists and those who revived their view, grass has no color, apples no taste, roses no fragrance, etc. Libraries have abundant information on the reasons which can only be alluded to here. For instance, it had long been noted that colors, sounds, odors, tastes, warmth, coolness, etc., are perceived differently at different times.

Still, there is an infinite distance from the idea that colors, sounds, and so on appear to change to the idea that those qualities do not exist. The first step had simply uprooted colors, sounds, etc., from nature and relocated them as effects or ideas inside us. Is there anyone who has not heard of the legendary tree which can fall soundlessly in the humanless forest? Here is how Galileo proposed the relocation in 1632.

> [. . .] I think, therefore, that these tastes, odors, colors, etc., so far as their objective existence is concerned, are nothing but mere names for something which resides exclusively in our sensitive body, so that if the perceiving creatures were removed, all of these qualities would be annihilated and abolished from existence. But just because we have given special names to these qualities, different from the names we have given to the primary and real properties, we are tempted into believing that the former really and truly exist as well as the latter. (Galileo, *The Assayer*, 1632, in *The Scientific Background to Modern Philosophy*, ed. M. Matthews, pp.56-57)

But it was John Locke's careful analyses that finally 'annihilated and abolished' tastes, odors, colors, etc., entirely. Here is a sample of the way his mind moved from common sense to that annihilation and abolition:

The now secondary qualities of bodies would disappear, if we could discover the primary ones of their minute parts.—Had we senses acute enough to discern the minute particles of bodies, and the real constitution on which their sensible qualities depend, I doubt not but they would produce quite different ideas in us, and that which is now the yellow color of gold would then disappear, and instead of it we should see an admirable texture of parts of a certain size and figure. This microscopes plainly discover to us; for, what to our naked eyes produces a certain color is, by thus augmenting the acuteness of our senses, discovered to be quite a different thing; and the thus altering, as it were, the proportion of a bulk of the minute parts of a colored object to our usual sight, produces different ideas from what it did before. Thus sand or pounded glass, which is opaque and white to the naked eye, is pellucid in a microscope; and a hair seen this way loses its former color, and is in a great measure pellucid, with a mixture of some bright sparkling colors, such as appear from the refraction of diamonds and other pellucid bodies. Blood to the naked eye appears all red; but by a good microscope, wherein its lesser parts appear, shows only some few globules of red, swimming in a pellucid liquor; and how these red globules would appear, if glasses could be found that yet could magnify them one thousand or ten thousand times more, is uncertain. (Locke, *An Essay Concerning Human Understanding*, Bk. II, ch. XXIII "Of Our Complex Ideas of Substances," par. 11)

Privative Definitions or Theories. Locke claimed that his *Essay* was intended only to clear away old ideas in order to make room for the true theories proposed by Isaac Newton. But, by sweeping ideas of color *as such*, odor *as such*, etc., from 'scientific' philosophy, he finished with a theory of "secondary qualities" that can serve as a classic example of what James called "privative definitions."

Ever since Socrates we have been taught that reality consists of essences, not of appearances, and that the essences of things are known whenever we know their definition. So first we identify the thing with a concept and then we identify the concept with a definition, and only then, inasmuch as the thing *is* whatever the definition expresses, are we sure of apprehending the real essence of it or the full truth about it.

So far no harm has been done. The misuse of concepts begins with the habit of employing them privatively as well as positively, using them not merely to assign properties to things, but to deny the very properties with which the things sensibly present themselves. (*Writings* II:728)

". . . to deny the very properties with which the things sensibly present themselves." Locke first states that all of our knowledge begins with experience. He then sub-divides experience into sensation and reflection. His description of sensation subtly shifts between things that cause and ideas that are caused effects. Is sensation an active awareness or experience of some thing or the production of an invisible, intangible idea? Watch.

> *Secondary qualities.*—*Secondly*, such qualities, which in truth are nothing in the objects themselves, but powers to produce various sensations in us by their primary qualities, i.e, by the bulk, figure, texture, and motion of their insensible parts, as colors, sounds, tastes, etc., these I call *secondary* qualities. . . .
> How secondary [qualities produce ideas in us].—After the same manner that the ideas of the original qualities are produced in us, we may conceive that the ideas of secondary qualities are also produced, viz., by the operation of insensible particles on our senses. (Locke, *Essay*, Bk. II, ch. VIII, par. 10 and 13)

Just as the ideas of primary qualities do not have shape, size, etc., the ideas of secondary qualities have no color, sound, etc. The former really exist out in bodies. The latter, it turns out, exist nowhere in all of God's creation.

When the distinctions between colors, powers in things to produce ideas, and colorless ideas OF colors are fudged, the highway to 'privative definitions' of color, sound, odor, etc., is smoothly paved. Even Newton was less than clear in his treatment of color as such. Edwin Burtt, author of a deservedly honored history of these matters which he called *The Metaphysical Foundations of Modern Science*, offers this description of Newton's views about color.

> Newton conceived his experiments on refraction and reflection to have definitely overthrown the theory that colours are qualities of objects. . . . Apparently Newton's first alternative to the rejected theory of colours as qualities of objects, is that they are qualities of light, having its rays for their subject. We discover at the end of the quotation, however, that this must have been a slip of language. Newton there absolves himself from any intention of mingling conjectures with certainties. This remark implies that the preceding assumption is no conjecture, namely, that colours have no existence even in light, but are phantasms produced in our minds by the modes or actions of light; the only conjectural matter being the process by which this takes place. In the *Opticks* this position is asserted at somewhat greater length. "If at any time I speak of light and rays as coloured or endued with colours, I would be understood to speak not philosophically and properly, but grossly, and according to such conceptions as vulgar people in seeing all these experiments would be apt to frame. For the rays to speak properly are not coloured. In them there is nothing else than a certain power and disposition to stir up a sensation of this or that colour. For as

sound in a bell or musical string or other sounding body, is nothing but a trembling motion, and in the air nothing but that motion propagated from the object, and in the sensorium 'tis a sense of that motion under the form of sound; so colours in the object are nothing but a disposition to reflect this or that sort of rays more copiously than the rest; in the rays they are nothing but their dispositions to propagate this or that motion into the sensorium, and in the sensorium they are sensations of those motions under the forms of colours." (E. Burtt, *Op. cit*, pp.235-36)

Burtt's paragraph is doing two things, and *they must be distinguished.* First, it reports a point that cannot possibly be overemphasized: Newton denied that light is color *as such*, or has a color *as such*. That is, Newton refused to identify color and light, that is, to treat "color" as a naïve way to refer to what is really light. He was right to do so. No one has ever experienced light *as such*. Test it. Can you see the light bouncing from this page into your eyes? Test it again. Most of the night sky around the moon is flooded with invisible sunlight. Can you see it? (The long 'shadow' created when the earth cuts off the sun's light accounts for the moon's darkening or eclipse when it passes from the sunlit area of the night sky into the 'shadow.')

But, Burtt's paragraph contains a fudge factor that becomes evident upon a close reading of Newton's words. Is Burtt right to say that, according to Newton, colors "are phantasms produced in our minds by the modes or actions of light"? Did Newton believe at all in colors, *as such*? He talks about ideas of motions "under the forms of colours." But this introduces us to a popular verbal dodge. Materialists are fond of the expression, "the brain interprets certain nerve impulses *as* colors." But this is clearly an evasion. "As colors" really means "*as if* they are colors, though they aren't!" Since the brain does not sense nerve impulses, it can hardly interpret them. (Has anyone ever interpreted a letter they were not allowed to see?) And even if a brain could do any interpreting, it would at best be *mis*-interpreting here, that is, *misinterpreting* the nerve-impulses *as if* they are colored, even though they aren't.

A Contemporary View. The views of many contemporary thinkers is well captured by C. Hardin in his 1986 *Color for Philosophers: Unweaving the Rainbow.* According to him, there is no problematical, real color *as such* anywhere in this colorless world, not in the 'blue' sky, not in 'red' roses, and certainly not in pitch-dark brains.

[. . .] Problems that are intractable either at the extradermal physical level or at the phenomenal level promise to yield to analysis in neurological terms. Of course, at the present rudimentary state of our knowledge of the visual system, most of this is promise, program, and principle. But enough has already been done to suggest that it is not mere hot air. Furthermore, there is plenty of evidence that all the alternative ways of proceeding are dead ends.

With this wave of the magic wand, we may resolve the problem of the ontological status of color in the following way: Since physical objects are not colored, and we have no good reason to believe that there are nonphysical bearers of color phenomena, and colored objects would have to be physical or nonphysical, we have no good reason to believe that there are colored objects. Colored objects are illusions, but not unfounded illusions. We are normally in chromatic perceptual states, and these are neural states. Because perceptions of color differences and perceptions of boundaries are closely intertwined neural processes, we see colors and shapes together. Roughly speaking, as color goes, so goes visual shape. Consequently, there are no visual shapes in the ultimate sense, just as there are no colors. But visual shapes have their structural analogues in the physical world, namely, shapes *simpliciter*, and colors do not. (C. Hardin, *Color for Philosophers*, pp.111-12)

Hardin's verdict, that there is no room in the physical world, i.e., *among bodies,* for colors or visual, seen shapes, is the bottom line with which we must all agree. But it is nothing more than the old wine of Locke's earlier verdict bottled in more recent vocabulary. Nothing literally new has been added to the three

Berkeley's Sensational (Re-)Discovery of Color, etc., *As Such*. In his 1904 "Does 'Consciousness' Exist?", James chided those who believed in consciousness—he added "as an entity"—for not being "quite radical enough, not quite daring enough" (*Writings* II:1141). At the beginning of a new millennium, we can look back and feel confident that behaviorists and other naturalist-materialists showed the world what happens when radical thinkers *are* daring enough to declare that consciousness 'as an entity' does not exist but *not* equally cautious in deciding what does exist.

The time has come to be truly radical and to deny, as James did twice, that brains as such exist and to assert, as he did on both occasions, that thoughts exist, including fictions (thoughts or concepts for things that do not exist). Brains may not exist, but our concept of 'the brain' is a useful notion constructed by our 'onlooking' mind (us).

But our daring must go far beyond the brain. Not only are our concepts of 'brains' theoretical fictions, but every last item in our theories of the physical world is a concept created by our powerful imaginations. That fact brings back the question, "What does exist?" Which of our concepts represent realities rather than fictitious entities? St. Thomas and those other medieval thinkers called "scholastics" believed that we can prove the existence of God with five different lines of reason. All of them, however, begin with the illusions of naïve realism, the illusions that Descartes had exposed and which Locke carried further. For, before we can use the cosmos to prove God, we must first prove the cosmos.

Does the cosmos even exist? Before we can answer that question, we must go back to James's radical-empiricist concept of "thing." When we think of the cosmos, we think of stars, planets, continents, oceans, forests, and other kinds of things which, as the analysis of common sense shows, are 'unit-subjects which support their attributes interchangeably.'

But there are no such 'unit-subjects' according to James's radical empiricism. What we call "a thing," an apple for instance, is actually only "a group of sense-qualities united by a law." *The 'law' is the law of association.* We pick up an apple. We feel its smoothness. We look at it. We see its color. We bite into it. We enjoy its taste. We experience the shape, the color, and the taste either at the same time or in quick succession. When, later on, someone mentions the word "apple," we recall all three sense-qualities (or rather memory-images of them) which, because they were sense-experienced together, are now associated in our memory. Chapter XXIII of Locke's *Essay* is a delightful essay on the process whereby we create all of our complex, idea-groups of 'things' from simple ideas of shape, color, taste, etc.

What must count as one of the most sensational theory-revolutions in recorded history came when a youthful George Berkeley devoured the ideas of such thinkers as Descartes, Newton, and Locke, and realized how absurd was their elimination of color as such, taste as such, odor as such, and so on. The best and easiest way to describe what Berkeley did is this. He accepted the tradition begun by Aristotle of distinguishing proper objects of sensation from common objects of sensation, and both from substances or incidental objects of sensation.

Then he thought hard and realized that we do not experience colorless ideas OF color, tasteless ideas OF taste, silent ideas OF sound. No! We experience colors, tastes, sounds, and other qualities. *As such,* i.e., as distinct from everything else.

Unfortunately, Berkeley followed Locke and called them "ideas," but only in order to insist that they exist in the mind, not outside in an external world where they can exist without us. A better and far less misleading way to express what Berkeley was trying to convey is to say that colors, tastes, sounds, etc., are the 'things' we experience, *and they are entirely immaterial.* Or . . .

Or, using a Jamesian vocabulary, we can say that the most obvious components of anyone's stream of consciousness or field of experience are 'sensuous givens,' viz., fields of patterned colors, wrap-around sounds, and other qualities mis-labeled "secondary." Since there is no way to prove bodies exist, the allegedly 'primary qualities' of bodies may not exist. The secondary qualities should be honored as being truly 'primary.' They constitute our only evidence for inferring that physical things even exist.

It is too late, of course, to change the labels. Most of the books since Locke would have to be rewritten, even the works of James. In our own minds, though, we must recognize with Berkeley that secondary qualities are the ones whose importance is primary.

Berkeley was right because Aristotle was right. Aristotle was right because our everyday common sense is right. *Colors do exist,* and we can be certain they do because we experience them. We do not see rainbows outside our mind which are colorless subatomic particles. *Sounds do exist,* and we can be certain they do because we experience them. We do not hear falling trees in forests outside our minds which are soundless particles that do not even touch each other. *Odors do exist,* and we can be certain they do because we experience them. We do not smell violets or roses outside our minds which are swarming, odorless particles. *Tastes do exist,* and we can be certain they do because we experience them. We do not taste apples or bananas outside our minds which are tasteless, infinitesimal bodies.

Of course, the colors, sounds, odors, tastes, tickles, and pains exist *only while we are experiencing them.* They do not float off while we are asleep. They do not get stored in brain-atoms while we are not experiencing them. "What creates them while we experience them?" is a separate question to be taken up later. (They are proof that creation *ex nihilo*, i.e., from nothing, goes on constantly.) The first task is to notice how obvious it is that they exist. If they didn't, "What creates them?" would be moot.

This is where a mindquake is called for, in order to understand Berkeley. Were he here to give a speech, it would go as follows. "You keep blah-blah'ing about things we don't sense and ignoring things we do. Color, sound, odor, etc., are real. They are what we experience. If they are in the mind and not where we first believed they were, so be it. They are effects and we know them, even if we are unsure of their cause which materialists say is the brain and I say is God. We are both guessing about a cause neither of us senses. When people use the word 'wine,' they think of color, taste, sound, etc., which, as Locke said, are ideas (effects) in their mind. 'Wine' to ordinary people *means* this group of secondary qualities or ideas in the mind. Hence, even if there are such things as never-sensed and never-to-be-sensed liquid particles outside the mind, it will never make any difference to anyone except philosophers who have time to ruminate over useless questions."

In short, if there were external bodies, it is impossible we should ever come to know it; and if there were not, we might have the very same reasons to think there were that we have now. Suppose (what no one can deny possible) an intelligence without the help of external bodies, to be affected with the same train of sensations or ideas that you are, imprinted in the same order and with like vividness in his mind. I ask whether that intelligence hath not all the reason to believe the existence of corporeal substances, represented by his ideas, and exciting them in his mind, that you can possibly have for believing the same thing? Of this there can be no question; which one consideration were enough to make any reasonable person suspect the strength of whatever arguments he may think himself to have for the existence of bodies without the mind. (Berkeley, *Principles*, sec.20)

Berkeley went on to rebut Locke's claim that the microscope gives us an ever better view of the true, colorless nature of physical things such as blood. We simply experience a series of different, visual, 'secondary' qualities (effects) produced by a not-experienced something (cause) whose 'primary' qualities are unknown! Berkeley, in effect, returned to Aristotle's claim that the 'special' sense objects are quite obviously distinct.

Strictly speaking, Hylas, we do not see the same object that we feel; neither is the same object perceived by the microscope, which was by the naked eye. But in case every variation was thought sufficient to constitute a new kind or individual, the endless number or confusion of names would render language impracticable. Therefore to avoid this as well as other inconveniences which are obvious upon a little thought, men combine together several ideas, apprehended by diverse senses, or by the same sense at different times, or in different circumstances, but observed however to have some connexion in nature, either with respect to co-existence or succession; all which they refer to one name, and consider as one thing. Hence it follows that when I examine by my other senses a thing I have seen, it is not in order to understand better the same object which I had perceived by sight, the object of one sense not being perceived by the other senses. And when I look through a microscope, it is not that I may perceive more clearly what I already perceived with my bare eyes, the object perceived by the glass being quite different from the former. But in both cases my aim is only to know what ideas are connected together; and the more a man knows of the connection of ideas, the more he is said to know of the nature of things. (Berkeley, *Three Dialogues Between Hylas and Philonous*, 3rd dialogue)

Berkeley's successor and one of Kant's most important predecessors, David Hume, complained. "If that is true, then no one can ever have certainty about anything real, e.g., a table outside her or his mind." Here is Hume's reasoning.

It seems evident, that men are carried, by a natural instinct or prepossession, to repose faith in their senses; and that, without any reasoning, or even almost before the use of reason, we always suppose an external universe, which depends not on our perception, but would exist, though we and every sensible creature were absent or annihilated. Even the animal creation are governed by a like opinion, and preserve this belief in external objects, in all their thoughts, designs, and actions.

It seems also evident, that, when men follow this blind and powerful instinct of nature, they always suppose the very images, presented by the sense, to be the external objects, and never entertain any suspicion that the one are nothing but representations of the other. This very table, which we see white, and which we feel hard, is believed to exist, independent of our perception, and to be something external to our mind, which perceives it. Our presence bestows not being on it; our absence does not annihilate it. It preserves its existence uniform and entire, independent of the situation of intelligent beings, who perceive or contemplate it.

But this universal and primary opinion of all men is soon destroyed by the slightest philosophy, which teaches us, that nothing can ever be present to the mind but an image or perception, and that the senses are only the inlets, through which these images are conveyed, without being able to produce any immediate intercourse between the mind and the object. The table, which we see, seems to diminish, as we remove farther from it; but the real table, which exists independent of us, suffers no alteration: it was, therefore, nothing but its image, which was present to the mind. These are the obvious dictates of reason; and no man, who reflects, ever doubted, that the existences, which we consider, when we say, this house and that tree, are nothing but perceptions in the mind, and fleeting copies or representations of other existences, which remain uniform and independent.

So far, then, are we necessitated by reasoning to contradict or depart from the primary instincts of nature, and to embrace a new system with regard to the evidence of our senses. But here philosophy finds herself extremely embarrassed, when she would justify this new system, and obviate the cavils and objections of the sceptics. (Hume, *Enquiry Concerning Human Understanding*, Sec.XII, Pt.I)

We can't have absolute certainty about physical things. But we certainly can have all the certainty we need for ordinary purposes about those primary existents, the 'secondary qualities' we are experiencing, whether they are in the physical world as Aristotle and the schoolmen (like all of us during our naïve-realist days) believed or not in the physical world as Berkeley held.

Finally, William James and 'the More Critical View of Things.' To learn where James stood after he had assimilated the preceding lessons of history, the best thing any reader could do would be to read the third of James's *Pragmatism* lectures, the one entitled "Some Metaphysical Problems Pragmatically Considered." He began that lecture by using chalk and wood to give a brief synopsis of the common-sense distinction between substance and attribute, i.e., between 'incidental' objects and their qualities. Then he paraphrased Berkeley's claim:

Now it was very early seen that all we *know* of the chalk is the whiteness, friability, etc., all we *know* of the wood is the combustibility and fibrous structure. A group of attributes is what each substance here is known-as, they form its sole cash-value for our actual experience. The substance is in every case revealed through *them*; if we were cut off from *them* we should never suspect its existence; and if God should keep sending them to us in an unchanged order, miraculously annihilating at a certain moment the substance that supported them, we never could detect the moment, for our experiences themselves would be unaltered. (*Pragmatism*, lect. III.)

But, after being so clear, James introduced an ambiguity different from the earlier one, an ambiguity that Berkeley first invented. Before reading it, re-read the preceding passage. It should be obvious that, if you understood it at all, you knew what was meant by 'God continuing to send us the attributes or sense-qualities but annihilating the substance that supports them.' A few paragraphs later, James in effect says that there is no distinction between ideas of mind-occupying 'sensations' and ideas of (external) material substances:

> Material substance was criticized by Berkeley with such telling effect that his name has reverberated through all subsequent philosophy. Berkeley's treatment of the notion of matter is so well known as to need hardly more than a mention. [Would that we true!] So far from denying the external world which we know, Berkeley corroborated it. It was the scholastic notion of a material substance unapproachable by us, behind the external world, deeper and more real than it, and needed to support it, which Berkeley maintained to be the most effective of all reducers of the external world to unreality. Abolish that substance, he said, believe that God, whom you can understand and approach, sends you the sensible world directly, and you confirm the latter and back it up by his divine authority. . . . Berkeley doesn't deny matter, then, he simply tells us what it consists of. It is a true name for just so much in the way of sensations. (*Pragmatism*, lect. III; comment added.)

"Berkeley doesn't deny matter." At this point, the ambiguities of language take over. If by "matter" is meant "apples, brains, and books as we conceive them while in our common-sense mindset," and if by the latter 'definition' we mean "permanent unit-subjects which support their attributes interchangeably," then it is outrageous for James to say that "Berkeley doesn't deny matter"!

The Common Core of James' Two Visions. The common core of common sense and radical empiricism should now be clear. According to common sense, if you are seeing anything as you read on and on, some of what you see is the *white color* of the paper and the *black color* of the ink. According to radical empiricism, if you are seeing anything as you read on and on, some of what you see is *white color* and *black color*. Call what-you-see "experience," and it becomes easy to 'see' why—so long as "experience" refers to seen colors, heard sounds, etc.—experience is the same core in both of James's visions.

What James felt certain about was seen colors, heard sounds, etc. This is clear from a vast number of passages sprinkled throughout his works:

> The nearer the object cognized comes to being a simple quality like 'hot,' 'cold,' 'red,' 'noise,' 'pain,' apprehended irrelatively to other things, the more the state of

mind approaches pure sensation. (PP II:1) THE PARAMOUNT REALITY OF SENSATIONS. (PP II:299) *Sensible objects are thus either our realities or the tests of our realities. Conceived objects must show sensible effects or else be disbelieved. . . . Sensible vividness or pungency is then the vital factor in reality when once the conflict between objects, and the connecting of them together in the mind, has begun. . . .* Witness the obduracy with which the popular world of colors, sounds, and smells holds its own against that of molecules and vibrations. Let the physicist himself but nod, like Homer, and the world of sense becomes his absolute reality again. (PP II:301-02) All these elements are subjective duplicates of outer objects. They *are* not the outer objects. The secondary qualities among them are not supposed by any educated person even to resemble the objects. Their *nature* depends more on the reacting brain than on the stimuli which set it off. (PP II:631) I do not see why a critical Science of Religions of this sort might not eventually command as general a public adhesion as is commanded by physical science. Even the personally non-religious might accept its conclusions on trust, much as blind persons now accept the facts of optics—it might appear as foolish to refuse them. Yet as the science of optics has to be fed in the first instance, and continually verified later, by facts experienced . . . (*Varieties of Religious Experience*; *Writings* II:409) If you ask what any one bit of pure experience is made of, the answer is always the same: "It is made of *that*, of just what appears, of space, of intensity, of flatness, brownness, heaviness, or what not." Shadworth Hodgson's analysis here leaves nothing to be desired. Experience is only a collective name for all these sensible natures . . . ("Does Consciousness Exist?" *Writings* II:1153) [. . .] the secondary qualities, to which our world owes all its living interest . . . (*Pragmatism*; *Writings* II:567-69) Berkeley doesn't deny matter, then; he simply tells us what it consists of. It is a true name for just so much in the way of sensations. (Same; *Writings* II:525) The first part of reality from this point of view is the flux of our sensations. (Same, *Writings* II:593) 'The insuperability of sensation' would be a short expression of my thesis. (*Some Problems of Philosophy*; *Writings* II:1022) All conceptual content is borrowed: to know what the concept 'color' means you must have *seen* red or blue, or green. (Same; *Writings* II:1023) A material fact may indeed be different from what we feel it to be, but what sense is there in saying that a feeling, which has no other nature than to be felt, is not as it *is* felt? (Same; *Writings* II:1059)

The Hard But Necessary Solution to James' Contradictions. It is a solution he both recognized and rejected. It has three parts.

First, amend Descartes and Locke by accepting Aristotle's, Berkeley's, and Hume's claims that *a precise way to describe* that the things we sense and are most certain about is to say that they are colors, sounds, odors, etc.

The second part is logically easy, but difficult psychologically. Great thinkers from Aristotle to Kant accepted a two-part model to discuss knowledge: some things are out in the physical world, e.g., stars, forest trees, and towns, but other things are inside souls or minds, e.g., memories, feelings, and ideas. When Berkeley appeared on the scene, colors, sounds, odors, etc., i.e., secondary qualities, had been declared nonexistent or unreal, even though we have (false) colorless, soundless, odorless, ideas OF them, much as we have (false) ideas OF leprechauns.

Berkeley's great realization was that what we experience are not colorless ideas OF colors, sounds, etc. What we experience ARE colors, sounds, and the rest. Calling them "ideas" only means that they are in minds. They are immaterial, non-physical, and exist only so long as we are experiencing them. However much they seem to be the physical things we've always thought they were, what-we-see, what-we-hear, what-we-smell, etc., are not stars, forest trees, towns, etc. And the act by which we perceive them is best called "awareness," though James preferred "feeling."

The final step follows logically from those two conclusions-now-premises. The only things any human being has direct access to are components of his or her private stream of consciousness. Everything else, beginning with his or her own brain and body, but including other persons and their private streams of consciousness, as well as the farthest away stars, can only be learned about *by understanding thoughts about them* and testing those thoughts against the rest of his or her stream of consciousness.

The full-bodied sense-data, i.e., the colors, sounds, and so on, that each person experiences, are not public. They are private. They are the most obvious, intrusive, inescapable ingredients of each person's personal, individual, private, immaterial stream of consciousness. And, as James noted in 1890, in *The Principles'* chapter on the stream of consciousness, the 'breaches' between individuals' streams are 'the most absolute breaches in nature.' (PP I:226)

A final note about the 'hard part.' Just two years before his *Pragmatism* expression of agreement with Berkeley, an agreement which he tried to defend as good common sense, James was composing his essays on radical empiricism. In the second one, "A World of Pure Experience," he profoundly *dis*agreed with Berkeley!

With transition and prospect thus enthroned in pure experience, it is impossible to subscribe to the idealism of the English school. Radical empiricism has, in fact, more affinities with natural realism than with the views of Berkeley or of Mill, and this can easily be shown.

For the Berkeleyan school, ideas (the verbal equivalent of what I term experiences) are discontinuous. The content of each is wholly immanent, and there are no transitions with which they are consubstantial and through which their beings may unite. Your Memorial Hall and mine, even when both are percepts, are wholly out of connection with each other. Our lives are a congeries of solipsisms, out of which in strict logic only a God could compose a universe even of discourse. No dynamic currents run between my objects and your objects. Never can our minds meet in the *same*.

The incredulity of such a philosophy is flagrant. It is 'cold, strained, and unnatural' in a supreme degree; and it may be doubted whether even Berkeley himself, who took it so religiously, really believed, when walking through the streets of London, that his spirit and the spirits of his fellow wayfarers had absolutely different towns in view. (W. James, *Writings* II:1176)

The explanation can be found in James's radical-empiricist claim that matter and mind are simply two different ways of conceptualizing the same stuff, namely, pure experience. Nowhere in the entire corpus of James's writings is there a more blunt outburst of James's passionate desire to persuade his readers that it was he, not materialists, whose views were in line with the common-sense conviction that when we wake in the morning, we open our eyes on the identical, single, one, public world that everyone else opens their eyes on.

But it just ain't so. If only God can connect what otherwise would be a congeries of solipsisms, then only God can do it. Many times over the years, James publicly referred to the possibility that God actually does it! Even more times, perhaps, he referred to that possibility in private notes he made which have only recently been published in *Manuscript Lectures* and *Manuscript Essays and Notes*. His most controversial theory of all, presented in his lecture, "The Will to Believe," was a theory defending belief in trans-empirical realities.

Yet, for many reasons, beginning with his radical-empiricist decision to not-appeal to anything that was "trans-empirical," James held back from accepting what his everyday-thinking logic told him might be the truth. A year before he died, in the introduction he wrote for *The Meaning of Truth*, a collection of essays, he wrote:

Radical empiricism consists first of a postulate . . . The postulate is that the only things that shall be debatable among philosophers shall be things definable in terms drawn from experience. [Things of an unexperienceable nature may exist *ad libitum*, but they form no part of the material for philosophic debate.] (W. James, *Writings* II:826)

The price he paid for that postulate, for that holding-back, was a high one: an unsuccessful forty-year struggle with solipsism. That, however, is a subject for the next chapter.

4. James, like Aristotle and Berkeley, Was Right About Color, etc.

Preliminaries, a to e. The preceding bit of history should help to make clear what Berkeley and James meant by "sense qualities" and "experience."

a. **But Were They** *Right?* Were Descartes and Locke *right* to conclude that we have no direct sense-experience of independently existing physical bodies? Were Hume and Kant *right* in believing that experience shows that everyday thinking, naïve-realist common sense is (partly) wrong?

Was James right in agreeing with them? That is the big, $64,000 question here.

The answer must be an unequivocal "Yes!" *The Wonderful Myth Called Science*, published in April, 2008, is a stripped down version of the 'case' for that answer, that is, for this chapter's part of what is being called "Jamesian quintalism." That 'case' incorporated what this chapter is calling a "full-bodied sense-datum theory."

But self-imposed limits on space and time made it impossible to include there the further details needed to make each step of the case for sense-data more compelling. In this fourth section of Chapter I, a fuller argument for a 'full-bodied sense-datum' thesis will be presented. *But it will do something else, too.* It will show that, at one time or another, in one writing or another, James agreed with each part of the argument *against* common sense's naïve-realist component, *and in favor of* a robust Berkeleyan version of James's stream-of-consciousness theory.

The first step in arguing that James was right must begin by recalling several of the things James said in his fifth *Pragmatism* lecture concerning our common-sense, fundamental ways of thinking.

Our fundamental ways of thinking about things . . . form one great stage of equilibrium in the human mind's development, the stage of *common sense*. Others stages have grafted themselves upon this stage, but have never succeeded in displacing it. . . . Even today science and philosophy are still laboriously trying to part fancies from realities in our experience; . . . . Science and critical philosophy thus burst the bounds of common sense. . . . There are thus at least three well-characterized levels, stages or types of thought about the world we live in, and the notions of one stage have one kind of merit, those of another stage another kind. . . . Common sense is *better* for one sphere of life, science for another, philosophic criticism for a third; but whether either be truer absolutely, Heaven only knows. (*Writings* II:560, 563, 567, 568, 569)

"Science and critical philosophy thus burst the bounds of common sense." As the preceding section on the recent history of psychological exploration has shown, Berkeley's answer to "What do I sense?" was the final outcome of that 'bursting' of the 'bounds.' That final outcome was the core in both of James's two visions.

From James's works, then, the threads of argument that begin with common sense, that reject some of common sense, and that finally yield an unequivocal, full-bodied sense-datum answer, will be presented. There is no longer any reason to doubt which unifying theory is 'truer absolutely,' no longer any need to continue waiting for more 'facts,' no longer any need for prolonged wriggling.* (*A reference to the April 14, 1898 note James wrote for himself: "Does n't it seem like the wrigglings of a worm on the hook, this attempt to escape the dualism of common sense?")

b. Newton's One-Space Model. The first step in answering the question, "What do I sense?", is to return to common sense and its 'magisterial concept' of a one-space universe. The decision to concur with James's confidence that the one-space and one-time concepts are part of our common-sense philosophy must be unequivocal. (For details, see *William James on Common Sense*.)

Common-sensically, a red apple sitting on top of William Tell's head is where it is and we who use our eyes to see it with are where we are. If we can measure distances accurately enough to know that the sun is slightly less than ninety-three million miles from earth and that a photon traverses 299, 792, 458 meters of that distance every second, then it is exquisitely common-sensical to believe that the distance between the apple and our eyes could 'in principle,' as they say, be measured with utter precision. Common sense also tells us that, if we walk around William Tell the way the campers mentioned in *Pragmatism*'s second lecture walked around the tree-climbing squirrel, we can do so without changing in any way the location or color of the apple we are looking at.

Numerous theories have been proposed to get around the common-sense idea of a one-space universe in which bodies are where they are this very instant, particularly since Einstein's relativization of space and time became widely adopted by physicists. A. N. Whitehead, for instance, protested against the common-sense idea, calling it the "simple location" aspect of "The Fallacy of Misplaced Concreteness." He also told us why. Like James in his "Pure Experience" outburst, Whitehead found the theories of Berkeley and Hume "quite unbelievable." (*Science and the Modern World*, p.51,ff.) That is why the discussion of relativity ideas of space and time in *The Wonderful Myth Called Science* is so vital to this unification of James's best thoughts.

Because all of our later-in-life theorizing builds from our five-year-old's common-sense philosophy, that is where the following argument begins. And there can be no doubt that what James called "the one-space" concept is part of our first, common-sense worldview. The psychological discoveries by Descartes, Locke, and others were all constructed on that platform. So, too, is today's neuroscience.

c. Spread out in Space: Bodies, Including Recently-Discovered Things. The original world-view that every normal human learner acquires includes belief in persons, places, and three types of things, namely, animals, vegetables, and minerals. At the beginning of this new millennium, our textbooks offer lengthy descriptions of additional items that newborn infants, ancient ancestors, and illiterate aborigines are ignorant of. These include: (i) over a hundred different classes of largely-empty-space atoms which behave in extraordinarily complex ways; (ii) photons or waves with varying frequencies and lengths of separation, either or both of which travel from one point in space to another with a velocity of 186,000 mps; (iii) sound waves which travel through air at roughly 1100 fps; (iv) microscopic particles that detach from such things as roses, cheeses, perfumes, etc., and find their way into our nostrils; (v) particles of food which, dissolved in saliva, activate the taste-buds on our tongues; (vi) trillions of cells making up various sense-organs, among them the retinas in our eyes, the tiny bones and auditory receptors in our ears, as well as neurons connecting our sense organs with our brain and neurons connecting our brain with our muscles; as well as numerous additional existents.

The discovery of these additional existents would have been impossible, were it not for the fact that our original, common-sense belief-system made it possible to notice details in our experience which, once sufficient attention was paid to them, led curious ancestors to ask questions and make their new discoveries. The history of these discoveries is available in dozens of books that can be found in any well-stocked library. What follows in this chapter will show how to fit those discoveries into an extended line of reasoning which led James, as it has led many others, from their naïve realism to the momentous discoveries of Descartes, Locke, Berkeley, and Hume. At each step, certain assumptions will be described, and evidence will be offered to show that James was both aware of, and in agreement with them.

d. Four One-Space, Simple-Location Answers to "What Do I See?" The question must be personalized. Each of us must see everything for ourselves. No one else can do our seeing for us. To read about what others think we see, we must see, first-hand, the 'words' they write. They, of course, are in the same situation. They must rely on their own first-hand sensing as much as we rely on our own.

We start with our naïve realism and ask "What is there to see?" Having acquainted ourselves with the discoveries of Galileo, etc., we can group everything in the universe into four different categories, beginning with those which are distant from us and ending with those which are closest to us. The first class is made up of things that are not in direct contact with our body and its sense organs, and the second consists of things which are in direct contact. The third class consists of our brains and whatever is in them, while the fourth class includes any 'more's' or 'extras' that do not fit into those three categories. This mental grouping furnishes us with four different answers to the question, "What do I see?", as well as to the more general question, "What do I sense?" They cannot all be true, but they can all be understood.

(1) The naïve-realist answer. This is what everyone lives by most of the time and what most people never dream of doubting. Don't we all 'know' from a very young age what we can see, hear, feel, etc.? We see books, the print on the pages, the walls of the room in which we are seated, and so on. The best collective, naïve-realist answer to "What do we sense?" is "Things which are distant from us." The stars we see at night are the most distant. The sun, planets, and moon are closer. Clouds seen from earth, oceans and forests and cities seen from aloft, the birds that fly in the sky, the trees they build nests in, etc., are closer yet. When things get too close to us, they appear blurred. To be seen clearly, they must be at least a little distant from our eyes.

(2) The sense-organ answer. A better name might be "the intra-organic object theory," but "sense-organ theory" is easier to remember. Our sense organs are our eyes, ears, nose, tongue, and skin. This theory holds that what we are aware of are not distant things, but the stimuli inside our sense organs. We sense light-patterns ('retinal images') in our eyes, sound vibrations in our ears, pheromones in our nostrils, food particles on our tongue, and various excitations of the nerves embedded in our skin. That is why "the intra-organic object theory" is a clearer name. So long as we do not take "sense organ theory" to mean we sense our eyes, ears, etc., but what is inside them, the name is not only convenient but also quite safe.

(3) The brain-function answer. According to this theory, we do not sense things distant from us nor the stimuli inside our sense organs. What we call seeing, hearing, smelling, and so on, are activities within our brain itself. Though terminology varies greatly—finding the appropriate vocabulary has become a major preoccupation—most materialist thinkers at the end of the twentieth century accepted some version of this theory. They believe what U. T. Place was defending when he said that green after-images do not exist. According to them, "consciousness" is the name for brain functions or brain processes.

(4) The full-bodied sense-datum answer. Sensing is our awareness of colors, sounds, tastes, and other objects which literally are not part of the physical world of bodies at all. There are different versions of this theory. The easiest way to approach it is with James's concept of 'more.' Sense-data are more than, over and beyond, all the physical things making up the physical part of reality. Materialists reject this

theory generally, though some are willing to take a tiny step beyond materialism by admitting sense-data as useless byproducts of the brain's functions. In that case, sense-data as objects of sensing form part of a theory known as epiphenomenalism. Most versions of the latter theory hold that, besides sense-data, there are memory-images, feelings, etc., among the brain's byproducts.

e. Required: Some Consistency in Vocabulary. A certain degree of consistency in our vocabulary is required in order to arrive at a clear and distinct—and true—answer to the question, "What do I see?" James himself made this point in his sixth *Pragmatism* lecture, "Pragmatism's Conception of Truth."

> All human thinking gets discursified; we exchange ideas; we lend and borrow verifications, get them from one another by means of social intercourse. All truth thus gets verbally built out, stored up, and made available for every one. Hence, we must *talk* consistently just as we must *think* consistently: for both in talk and thought we deal with kinds. Names are arbitrary, but once understood they must be kept to. We mustn't now call Abel 'Cain' or Cain 'Abel.' (*Writings* II:579)

The idea is that one's worldview must consist of beliefs which all fit together. The 'sense' of truth vs error, which includes our 'sense' of logical consistency, must take us by the hand and guide us in our quest for wisdom. Nothing else will help us sift the nuggets of true insight from the gravel of error and distraction as we read on.

Thus ends these preliminaries.

The 'Process of Elimination' Approach. The 'process of elimination' operates best when the alternatives can be stated with a reasonable amount of clarity and when they can then be lined up in a way that problems with one theory seem soluble by the next. Because the four answers in this case are so clear when we start with the common-sense mindset, the elimination process can work perfectly.

For instance, facts against naïve realism seem soluble by the sense-organ theory, facts which tell against the sense-organ theory seem soluble by the brain-process theory, and so on.

Elimination Step #1: We Do Not Sense Anything Distant. Travel is the key to this first step in understanding why James wrote, "Science and critical philosophy thus burst the bounds of common sense."

The concept of travel is the concept of things moving from one location to another. Nothing can be more simple. The idea of changing location is everyday common sense.

Begin with the sense of touch. We cannot feel bodies which do not reach our skin. The baseball must reach our hands if we are to feel it. Our hand must reach up and pick the apple before we can feel it. Etc. Because of sense-related expectancies to which James drew attention, we may anticipate a still-to-come sensation. But we feel nothing when the ball is only half-way to us, nothing when it is three-quarters of the distance to us, nothing when it is a foot away. There must be contact if the tactile nerves embedded in our skin are to be activated.

The same is true for taste. Only when we put the apple up to our mouth, bite into it, and allow the part of the apple inside our mouth to make contact with our taste buds, do we experience its taste.

Smell and hearing are a bit harder than touch and taste. In these cases, it appears that the things we sense do not have to travel to us. Our senses can 'reach out' and detect them directly. It is only when we stop to think about certain experiences that we recognize the need for a more complex theory. For instance, we wake on Sunday morning and from our bedroom upstairs we can smell the coffee brewing in the kitchen downstairs. We rise, put on our bathrobe, go to the kitchen, but discover that those who were there ahead of us drank all the coffee. We come into a room where limburger cheese sat out all night, but—though we smell the cheese—none of it can be found. Someone, we learn later on, came, ate it, and left just before we arrived. The cigarette's smoke is clearly visible across the table, but we do not smell it until it wafts across to our nostrils. And so on. Nowadays, we take it for granted that there is 'more' to be included in the picture than just the distant bodies and our nose. We must include the tiny particles which travel from the distant object to our nostrils. We must admit that, strictly speaking, it is not distant objects but their traveling 'evaporants' which our nose detects.

As for what we hear, our physics course will have taught us all we need to know about vibrations or waves of vibrations called "sound waves" which travel approximately 1100 feet per second through the ocean of air which blankets the earth's surface and carries those vibrations from their distant sources or causes to our receptive ears. But we do not need the physics text if, like long-ago ancestors who had no textbooks, we begin to pay close attention during thunderstorms. As soon as we do, we notice that there can be time-lapses between the time we see the lightning and hear the thunder. The only way those time-lapses have ever been explained is by recognizing that sounds take time to travel from where the lightning occurs to our ears.

Most of us do not find those ideas difficult to accept. But everything changes when we apply the same reasoning to sight. Then, our whole normal sense of what is happening rebels. Surely we can see our own hands and the books we hold in them while we read. Certainly we can see one another. We can even see such distant things as the stars far off in the sky. No wonder the psychologist James began the last chapter of his unfinished *Some Problems of Philosophy* with the observation, "Most persons remain quite incredulous when they are told that the rational principle of causality has exploded our native believe in naïf activity as something real . . .", and that one of his illustrations is the fact that "we think a certain star's light is the cause of our now seeing it, but ether-waves are the causes, and the star may have been extinguished long ago."

In 2008, however, certain discoveries, if accepted, prove beyond dispute that our life-long conviction that we see distant things is false. James knew that the argument is easiest to grasp when we start with the example of the stars. This is because, in the case of stars, truly cosmic distances and travel-times are involved. So swift is light that when Aristotle wondered whether or not light travels instantaneously, he concluded that it did. The expanse we call "the sky," extending from horizon to horizon, is so vast that, if the light of dawn did not travel instantaneously, we would see dawn's early light slowly crossing the vast distance from horizon to horizon the same way we see clouds and birds doing it. Not until 1676 did a Swedish astronomer, Olaus Roemer, find the first empirical evidence that light does not travel instantaneously. By studying Jupiter's moons' eclipses, he calculated the time it takes light to travel the extra distance when we move from being closest to Jupiter to being farthest away during our twelve-month journey around the sun. So confident are physicists about the finite velocity of light that the foundation stone for Einstein's general relativity theory is that nothing can move faster than light as it streaks from distant stars and planets to us. Roemer's discovery was the 'final nail in the coffin' of naïve realism.

By the time that James began his 'higher learning,' the libraries were already filled with texts which told about light, its velocity, how it is reflected and refracted, how complex are the formulas for predicting how various materials will affect the light rays or waves that travel through them, how the eyes work, etc. He was familiar with the controversies between those who hypothesized with Newton that light is particles and those who sided with Huygens and speculated that it is waves carried by the invisible ether. As one who almost took up painting as a career, he had a keen interest in everything relating to vision and colors. His *Principles'* chapter on "The Perception of Space" can still be read with great profit by anyone interested in the vast range of related facts discussed there.

The first conclusion we arrive at after this sketch of the 'case' against naïve realism is an elimination, a negative. *We cannot sense anything distant from our sense organs.* A fuller description of the evidence against naïve realism is massive. And available.

But, if naïve realism does not give us the right answer to "What do I see?", which theory does? The first of the remaining three easy-to-understand theories seems at first to be the obvious choice. It apparently is supported by the evidence just invoked against naïve realism.

The Case FOR the Sense-Organ Theory of Sensed Objects. Real things are located inside our sense organs. Many recent thinkers who count themselves as adherents of common sense are sufficiently persuaded by the evidence against naïve realism to reject it, but they do so reluctantly. While admitting that the things we sense *directly* are not what we initially mis-take them for, viz., distant physical objects, they hold that the sensed objects are real and, though inside our sense organs, are sufficiently like distant objects that the closer objects enable us to know the more distant ones through them.

Two recent supporters of St. Thomas's thought have adopted the 'sense-organ' theory. The first is R. P. Phillips.

The confusion between interpretations and intuitions is the main source of the objections to the Thomist doctrine, and it is these objections themselves which are the strength of the opposing view of the Illationists. Thus it is argued that the intuitionist view would oblige us to attribute contradictory predicates to the same realities; for since the colour, size, and shape of objects vary according to their distance from us, the angle from which they are looked at, and the media through which they are viewed, it will follow that we shall have to say that they are simultaneously of different sizes, shapes, and colours: e.g., a penny will be at once half and a quarter of an inch in diameter, both light and dark brown, circular and oval simultaneously. It is, however, plain that according to our theory we do not sense the penny on the table but the projection of light reflected by it to the eye, and this intraorganic object is in fact of different dimensions, shapes and colours according to the point of view from which the penny is looked at. (*Modern Thomistic Philosophy*, 1935; Vol.II, p.70)

J. Owens, in *An Elementary Christian Metaphysics*, took the same position.

What is immediately seen is just the object that touches the retina, what is immediately felt is the inner surface of the skin in contact with the nerve ends, what is immediately heard is only the sound within the ear, and so on. These are all objects really distinct from the knowing subject. They are not subjective modifications of him as the knower. They are modifications of bodies immediately in contact with and reacted upon by the sensory organs. They are in the bodies that constitute the sustaining media of colors, sounds, odors, tastes, temperature, hardness and softness, and so on. Through habits of touch in conjunction with sight the perception of distance is gradually acquired, and through similar habits the immediately perceived data are interpreted, on the basis of groupings and changes, in terms of different natures like stones, plants, animals and men. In these ways, there is a complicated mediation in human knowledge of external things. (*Op. cit.*, 1963; pp.219-20)

What is inside our eyes, ears, etc., are real things. If light is real and if, by opening and closing our eyelids, we can let light in and shut it out, then it is clear that what is inside our eyes is real light. The same thing is true of vibrating air-molecules, odorous and tasty particles, and kinetic energy. If those real things are what we sense, then we plainly do not sense distant objects.

We all resort to verbal circumlocutions in order to skate over the cracks or inconsistencies in a naïve-realist epistemology. Today's 'scientific' psychology texts invariably employ a circumlocution that James himself used, namely, a distinction between sensing and perceiving. "Sensing" can be used for physiological changes in the nervous system, for a conscious process, or for both. "Perception" can be used to refer to awareness or to interpreting, and both can be conceptualized either as physiological or psychological. We can speak as if we 'sense' stimuli in our sense organs and 'perceive' distant things. We can especially savor the way one 2003 text skates over several cracks—chasms?—at once:

> Light rays from the top of an object are focused at the bottom of the image on the retinal surface, whereas rays from the right side of the object end up on the left side of the retinal image. The brain rearranges this upside-down and reverse image so that people see the object as it really is.

Seeing: is it sensing, perceiving, both at once, or whatever you wish to call it when cornered in a debate. Some say we have direct contact with patterned light which reaches our retinas, with air-molecule vibrations which reach our inner ears, with particles which reach our nostrils, and so on, and—the 'and' in this case is psychologically reassuring— that *through* them we indirectly sense the distant objects. This gives us theories of 'indirect (sense) realism.' Joseph Gredt, another twentieth-century scholastic, wrote that, although the immediate object of sight is "the extended, colored object received in the eye and existing in the ether which immediately touches the retina," there is a mediate object as well.

> . . .] in the same simple act of sensation by which the [retinal] image is known, that which is represented by the image is known as well. In seeing the image, the eye sees that which is represented by the image, inasmuch as it is contained in the image. Whence it sees both: the image and that which is represented by the image, but not as distinct, since a simple sensation is not able to institute a comparison between them. (J. Gredt, *Elementa Philosophiae Aristotelico-Thomisticae*, 6th ed., 1932; Vol. I, p.385)

The impulse to avoid a blunt admission that we do not see, hear, feel, smell, or taste any distant physical realities is a powerful one. Since such an admission may be the first step on the path to Berkeley's claim that nothing physical exists, anyone who has spent all of her or his early years simply acquiescing in naïve realism—that means all of us— can sympathize wholeheartedly with Gredt's attempt to blur the lines between what is inside and what is outside. We can also understand the direct-vs-indirect view of an 1983 work on sensing.

> Unlike Berkeley, whose power to believe in the incredible is one of the wonders of the philosophical world, I am, like Locke, a merely commonsensical Newtonian who presumes that there are mind-independent objects which we succeed in a [sic]

perceiving by sense. These objects, therefore, I hold that we indirectly perceive; also, that within perception the sensuous qualities belonging to us of which we are directly aware represent for us objective properties of physical objects before our sense organs. (M. Perkins, *Sensing the World*, p.1)

It is tempting to adopt such compromises without feeling as if the truth is being evaded. Once we are confronted with the possibility that a blunt denial that we ever see stars, trees, animals, or other people, will lead to what seems too absurd to be believable, namely, Berkeley's claim that no physical things exist at all, it feels as if sanity itself demands that we find an alternative. Any alternative!

Or is it any dodge? Probably most experts today think anything is preferable to risking the problems that result once it seems we have no proof that physical bodies exist.

Elimination Step #2: Against the Sense-Organ Theory. That James was super-conscious of the problems involved in seeing or any kind of sense-awareness is made clear in *The Principles*. At first, nothing seems more uncomplicated. We open our eyes while looking upward at night, and we see stars. We open our eyes while at sea, and we see the ocean and sky meeting on a distant horizon. We open our eyes while holding a book in our hands, and there before us are rows and rows of black ink marks on the white pages. What could be more simple?

James knew, however, as Descartes, Newton, and others before him did, that there was nothing simple at all about seeing. At least there is nothing simple about the various physical and physiological processes going on at every instant:

If a common person is asked how he is enabled to see things as they are, he will simply reply, by opening his eyes and looking. This innocent answer has, however, long since been impossible for science. There are various paradoxes and irregularities about *what* we appear to perceive under seemingly identical optical conditions, which immediately raise questions. To say nothing now of the time-honored conundrums of why we see upright with an inverted retinal picture, and why we do not see double; and to leave aside the whole field of color-contrasts and ambiguities, as not directly relevant to the space-problem—it is certain that the same retinal image makes us see quite differently-sized and differently-shaped objects at different times, and it is equally certain that the same ocular movement varies in its perceptive import. It ought to be possible, were the act of perception completely and *simply* intelligible, to assign for every distinct judgment of size, shape, and position a distinct optical modification of some kind as its occasion. And the connection between the two ought to be so constant that, given the same modification, we should always have the same judgment. But if we study the facts closely *we soon find no such constant connection between either judgment and retinal modification, or judgment and muscular modification, to exist.* (PP II:211-12)

That James would reject any claim that we directly sense our retinal images is clear from that passage. It introduces the most obvious of the sense-organ theory's fatal weaknesses. If it were true that we see the objects in direct contact with our retinas, we should *always* see two pictures, one for each eye. But we don't. *Everything* we see should be upside down. But it isn't. No one should be color blind, since the objects in direct contact with the retinas of the color blind are the same as those in contact with everyone else's eyes. But some people are. And we shouldn't see anything correlating with our eye's blind spot. But we do.

The blind spot. Nothing perhaps is more astonishing than it. (Every decent psychology text will explain it.) We do *not* see what is there on our retina. But that's not nearly so shocking as the fact that *we do see what is not there!* Even in the experiments in which a large black dot covers the blind spot in the retinal image which matches the black dot on the piece of colored paper held in front of the eye, what we see is an unbroken expanse of *whatever* color surrounds the black spot. In *Color for Philosophers*, C. L. Hardin describes this filling in:

It [the blind spot] covers an area with a 6 degree visual diameter, enough to hold the images of ten full moons placed end to end, and yet there is no hole in the corresponding region of the visual field. This is because the eye-brain *fills in* with whatever is seen in the adjoining regions. If that is blue, it *fills in* blue; if it is plaid, we are aware of no discontinuity in the expanse of plaid. (*Op. cit.*, p.22)

The plain fact is that no sensing whatever takes place in the sense organs. The evidence against the sense-organ or intra-organic object theory is as conclusive as the evidence against naïve realism. According to the current, 'scientific' worldview, the one James called the "corpuscular science" system, the sense organs merely convert or (in recent jargon) 'transduce' stimuli that are *heterogeneous*—ranging from light to sound waves to odorous particles, etc.—into nerve impulses that are *homogeneous*, and these homogenous impulses must reach the brain before any seeing, hearing, etc., occurs. If the optic nerve, the auditory nerve, or any of the other afferent nerve bundles leading from the sense organs to various parts of the brain are severed, no sensing takes place.

James indicated his approval of this principle near the very opening of *The Principles*, in a passage cited earlier:

> And a very small amount of reflection on facts shows that one part of the body, namely, the brain, is the part whose experiences are directly concerned. If the nervous communication be cut off between the brain and other parts, the experiences of those other parts are non-existent for the mind. The eye is blind, the ear deaf, the hand insensible and motionless. And conversely, if the brain be injured, consciousness is abolished or altered, even although every other organ in the body be ready to play its normal part. . . . The fact that the brain is the one immediate bodily condition of the mental operations is indeed so universally admitted nowadays that I need spend no more time in illustrating it, but will simply postulate it and pass on. The whole remainder of the book will be more or less of a proof that the postulate is true. (PP I:4)

Differences in the type of sensing—seeing, hearing, smelling, tasting, etc.—depend only on which part of the brain the nerve impulses reach. A tiny electrode can produce different sensations by being applied to different afferent nerves. This helps to explain why colorless electrodes, applied to the brain areas which receive impulses from the optic nerves, produce points of 'light' called "phosphenes." (*Scientific American*, March 1994, p.108), why soundless cochlear implants produce sounds, why unfelt stimulation of areas deep within the brain produces pain and pleasure, etc. As long ago as April 19, 1971, *Time* magazine used its cover story to introduce the public to these ideas. It included José Delgado's dramatic experiment of stopping a bull's charge with a jolt to its brain delivered via a radio signal.

The Case FOR the Brain-Process Theory. If what we see are not images in our eyes, what we hear are not air-molecule vibrations in our ears, etc., then the next location to investigate is our skull-imprisoned brain. The author of a 2004 'scientific' psychology text captures the thinking behind this theory in delightfully vivid fashion:

> We talk as though objects possess color. We say, "A tomato is red." Perhaps you

have pondered the old question, "If a tree falls in the forest and no one hears it, does it make a sound?" We can ask the same of color: If no one sees the tomato, is it red?

The answer is no. First, the tomato is everything but red, because it rejects (reflects) the long wavelengths of red. Second, the tomato's color is our mental construction. As Isaac Newton (1704) noted, "The [light] rays are not coloured." Color, like all aspects of vision, resides not in the object but in the theater of our brains.

The brain-process theory would not exist if Descartes' successors had not accepted his 1600's recognition that 'modern science' discoveries made it necessary to resurrect the ancient view of Hippocrates that the brain is the only bodily organ linked directly with any conscious experience. It was Descartes who first used 'phantom limb experiences' to expose the error of believing that what *seem* to be parts of our body, beginning with our feet and progressing to our jaw, eyes, and scalp, are parts of a physical, biological organism. In fact, they are parts of an entire 'phantom body.' Despite the potentially misleading phrase, "in as far as it is in the brain," what Descartes means is quite clear.

PRINCIPLE CXCVI

That the soul does not perceive anything excepting in as far as it is in the brain.

It is however easily proved that the soul feels those things that affect the body not in so far as it is in each member of the body, but only in so far as it is in the brain, where the nerves by their movements convey to it the diverse actions of the external objects which touch the parts of the body [in which they are inserted]. For, in the first place, there are many maladies which, though they affect the brain alone, yet either disorder or altogether take away from us the use of our senses; . . . Secondly, from the fact that though the brain be healthy [as well as the members in which the organs of the external senses are to be found], if the paths by which the nerves pass from the external parts to the brain be obstructed, that sensation is lost in these external parts of the body. And finally we sometimes feel pain as though it were in certain of our members, and yet its cause is not in these members where it is felt, but in others through which the nerves pass that extend to the brain from the parts where the pain is felt. And this I could prove by innumerable experiments; here, however, one will suffice. When a girl suffering from a serious affection of the hand was visited by the surgeon, her eyes were usually bandaged... (Descartes, *The Principles of Philosophy*, Pt. IV; trans. E. Haldane, G.Ross, p.293)

The post-Descartes brain-process theory was already well-known a century ago. A famous description of it was offered by Karl Pearson in 1892:

> We are accustomed to talk of the "external world," of the "reality" outside us. We speak of individual objects having an existence independent of our own. The store of past sense-impressions, our thoughts and memories, although most probably they have beside their psychical element a close correspondence with some physical change or impress in the brain, are yet spoken of as inside ourselves. On the other hand, although if a sensory nerve be divided anywhere short of the brain we lose the corresponding class of sense-impressions, we yet speak of many sense-impressions, such as form and texture, as existing outside ourselves. How close then can we actually get to this supposed world outside ourselves? Just as near as but no nearer than the brain terminals of the sensory nerves. We are like the clerk in the central telephone exchange who cannot get nearer to his customers than his end of the telephone wires. We are indeed worse off than the clerk, for to carry out the analogy properly we must suppose him never to have been outside the telephone exchange, never to have seen a customer or any one like a customer—in short, never, except through a telephone wire, to have come in contact with the outside universe. (K. Pearson, *The Grammar of Science*, pp.60-61)

Eleven years earlier, in 1879, that is, a year after James signed the contract to write his text on psychology, he described—and mocked—this theory that identifies i) what occurs in the pitch dark, dead silent brain with ii) what the brain-owner experiences . . . and that (like the passage cited above) further identifies what is in the brain with the outside-the-brain object!

> When Lewes asserts in one place that the nerve-process and the feeling which accompanies it are not two things but only two "aspects" of one and the same thing, whilst in other passages he seems to imply that the cognitive feeling and the outward thing cognized (which is always other than the nerve-process accompanying the cognitive act) are again one thing in two aspects (giving us thereby as the ultimate truth One Thing in Three Aspects, very much as Trinitarian Christians affirm it to be One God in Three Persons),—the vagueness of his mode only testifies to the imperiousness of his need for unity. (W. James, "The Sentiment of Rationality," in CER:91-92)

Nevertheless, the brain-process theory has become the darling of those who are dazzled by recent discoveries that mirror, on a minute scale, the dazzling discoveries of the heavens by modern astronomers. The brain-process theory is the dominant theory among neuroscientists who think of consciousness only in terms of physiology. That is why it is important to examine it both carefully and thoroughly.

One of the very best brief books on visual sensation is Richard L. Gregory's *Eye and Brain*. (The title is significant. A recent psychology text states, "a more correct expression would be that 'our eyes are in the back of our brains'.") The fourth edition of *Eye and Brain* (1990) ends this way:

> Consciousness is indeed difficult to think about. But for the physicist, matter and force and time, and any other unique attributes of the world, are just as difficult. Science is good at discovering and describing relations; but it is powerless with unique cases. The question 'what is matter?' is as difficult to answer as the question 'what is consciousness?' To suggest that matter is substance is mere tautology. Physics describes matter in terms of structures. It does not ask the ultimate question: 'what are the atomic structures of matter made of?' Similarly, it seems meaningless to ask: 'what is the substance of mind?' When we know enough to describe brain processes capable of giving perception in machines, the problem of consciousness may be solved—or shelved, as the substance of matter is ignored in physics. Then we need not be ashamed of our ignorance of ourselves. (*Op. cit.*, pp.247-48)

The same author enlisted the help of dozens of experts to produce *The Oxford Companion to the Mind* (1987). There is a link between the two works. They both present the 1990's 'official' scientific view that conscious experience is either identical with or completely parasitic upon brain processes. In fact, *The Oxford Companion to the Mind* could easily be renamed *The Oxford Companion to the Brain*. A 'tutorial' of nearly twenty-one pages is included as the entry under "Nervous System," and explains the bold statement made on the opening page of the Preface, namely, "For, in a physical sense, the structure and function of the nervous system are what we are" (*Op. cit.*, p.v). The current mood is perhaps best summed up in the title of a lecture series given at Notre Dame in 1991: "Our Brains, Ourselves." Richard Restak, author of several books on the brain, translates the maxim "Know thyself" into "Know thy brain" (see *Brainscapes*, p.3). We are our brains, then, and our brains are us. The rest of the body serves as both a support system and a taxi for our brain. The ancients thought, as Descartes often did, that our bodies are ships piloted by souls. Today's materialists have replaced ship-steering souls with taxi-driving brains.

Advocates of the brain-process theory routinely anthropormophize about 'information' in presenting their case. Light is no longer just light but information. Nerve impulses traveling through the optic nerves are no longer just nerve impulses but information. The subsequent reactions in the brain are no longer neurons being activated, secreting, and absorbing neurotransmitters, but neurons doing information-processing. Related synonyms are also used, e.g., messages, instructions, commands, codes, etc. Here, for instance, is a passage from the tutorial written for *The Oxford Companion to the Mind*:

How the nervous system sends messages. The behaviour of the central nervous system consists of passing messages from one lot of neurones to another. The message itself is sent in the form of a Morse code consisting only of dots. As the dots are always grouped together, they are usually referred to as a volley of nerve impulses, or just as a volley. The nerve fibre conducts impulses in one direction only. Afferent nerves outside the central nervous system conduct impulses towards the spinal cord and brain, and efferent nerves conduct them away from the central nervous system to the muscles and glands. Within the central nervous system, each nerve fibre is a one-way street.

One can talk of taking messages, for the nerve impulse is an instruction to the cell that receives it to do something. The message or impulse is an electric current, somewhat like the current sent along a telegraph or telephone wire. (*Op. cit.*, p.516)

With the help of modern technologies whose functions are designated with letters of the alphabet—EEG, CAT, MRI, PET, etc.—researchers have come to feel more and more confident that the brain is finally surrendering its long-held mysteries. In his 1971 book *Beyond Freedom and Dignity*, B. F. Skinner insisted that behaviorists do not believe the organism is a black box with nothing going on inside. He admitted that "A great deal goes on inside the skin, and physiology will eventually tell us more about it" (*op. cit.*, p.186). By the time he died in 1990, 'physiology' had told us so much about the brain that Skinner's critics concluded there is no longer any doubt that "brain" and "mind" refer to a single existent and its doings. The result is a theoretical model or picture of the brain whose features are being mapped out with ever greater precision. The latest edition of *Eye and Brain* notes that . . .

The notion that there are many channels for brightness, colour, shape, movement, and so on, has now become a central notion with strong physiological evidence for how the visual system is organized. Yet it remains a mystery how the contributions from these physiologically separate channels with their own brain locations (so that movement and colour and so on are represented in different regions of the cortex) come together to form consistent perceptions. Ann Triesmann has, however, shown that movement and colour can separate or become mixed up: in short exposures, colours may be seen in wrong places. (*Op. cit.*, p.11)

The only difference between Descartes who died in 1650 and those who adhere to the theory that what we sense are actually activities of our pitch-dark, skull-imprisoned brain is that today's adherents have access to a greater volume of details. The quantity of details is also the sole difference between James and us.

But what do the details prove? Discovering that there are black as well as white swans does not constitute new evidence regarding the difference between swans and humans. Discovering a thousand new details about the correlation between what is hypothesized to occur in one's brain and what one has direct, conscious evidence for does not constitute a smidgeon of different evidence vis-à-vis the question, "What am I experiencing as I read about such historical facts which I have never witnessed and therefore must take on faith?" Added details may add to our confidence that our conclusions are indeed true, but today's details are of the same generic type as those which great psychologists, from Descartes to James, were thoroughly familiar with.

Elimination Step #3: Why the Brain-Process Theory Fails. Over a century ago, James already pointed out *three fatal errors* in the brain-process theory or, as it is known today, the mind-brain-identity theory. (Note. As in all of these cases, there are multiple versions of this theory.)

The first of them is that the plurality-of-destinations conflicts with *our unity-of-consciousness experience*. Careful brain researchers themselves recognize this problem. Gregory referred to it in the passage cited above: "it remains a mystery how the contributions . . . come together to form consistent perceptions." One reflection James offered to help notice this unity of consciousness is found in Chapter VI of *The Principles*.

Take a sentence of a dozen words, and take twelve men and tell each one word. Then stand the men in a row or jam them in a bunch, and let each think of his word as intently as he will; nowhere will there be a consciousness of the whole sentence. We talk of the 'spirit of the age,' and the 'sentiment of the people,' and in various ways we hypostatize 'public opinion.' But we know this to be symbolic speech, and never dream that the spirit, opinion, sentiment, etc., constitute a consciousness other than, and additional to, that of the several individuals whom the words 'age,' 'people,' or 'public' denote. The private minds do not agglomerate into a higher compound mind. (PP I:160)

"Nowhere will there be a consciousness of the whole sentence." It is assumed by brain researchers that *heterogeneous* stimuli of all kinds (light waves, sound vibrations, odorous particles, tasty morsels, kinetic energy, etc.), after their conversion into *homogeneous* impulses, are sent to disconnected parts of the brain. How do they ever 'come together' to form seemingly seamless streams of conscious experience?

This objection has been tackled by various theorists. For instance, Richard Restak reports a suggestion by Dr. R. Llinas' in Chapter IV of *Brainscapes*:

One of the unsolved mysteries of the human brain raised by the newer technology is described by Rodolfo Llinas, Professor of Neuroscience at New York University: "How are the separate bits of activity in different parts of the brain made into a single event?" . . . A common sense explanation would hold that at some as yet undetermined area of the brain all of the various components of experience are synthesized into a unity. But so far neuroscientists haven't discovered such a Master Control Center, leading many of them to conclude that the brain must employ other means to synthesize the separate components of our mental life into a unity.

One influential theory holds that the binding is not a spatial but a temporal one. According to Dr. Llinas, a 40-cycle-per-second wave sweeps the brain from front to back every 12.5-thousandth of a second. He believes this wave serves to link information from those parts of the cortex handling vision, hearing, and other sensations, with the *thalamus*, the lower brain structure that is a way station for sensory impulses on their way to the cerebral cortex. (*Op. cit.*, pp.90-91)

The only word for why Llinas or anyone else would take seriously the idea that a 'lower' part of the brain can 'read waves' is *desperation*. It is an attempt to come up with something—anything!—to explain how the single "I" can simultaneously read (see), recall, and reason, even compare a theory about unfelt 'waves' with the ongoing complexities of felt experience, and to do so without opening the door to claims that there is more than matter in this universe of ours. Anyone not suffering from MPD (multiple-personality-disorder) understands what James meant by a 'consciousness of the whole sentence' or—better—a unified understanding of the total sentence's *meaning*. In fact, this unity is the linchpin in his historic achievement, namely, the first solid description of ongoing human thought.

That second difficulty with the brain-mind-identity theory connects directly with another 'unity' fact. *The concept of a unified, single-thing brain is a fiction.* No such unified entity exists. In more recent terminology, "the brain" is the name for a theoretical construct. James pointed this out more than a century ago.

The 'entire brain-process' is not a physical fact at all. It is the appearance to an onlooking mind of a multitude of physical facts. 'Entire brain' is nothing but our name for the way in which a million of molecules arranged in certain positions may affect our sense. On the principles of the corpuscular or mechanical philosophy, the only realities are the separate molecules, or at most the cells. Their aggregation into a 'brain' is a fiction of popular speech. Such a fiction cannot serve as the objectively real counterpart to any psychic state whatever. Only a genuinely physical fact can so serve. But the molecular fact is the only genuine physical fact—whereupon we seem, if we are to have an elementary psycho-physic law at all, thrust right back upon something like the mind-stuff theory, for the molecular fact, being an element of the 'brain,' would seem naturally to correspond, not to the total thoughts, but to elements in the thought. (PP I:178)

James's claim is pure common sense. There is no evidence that, even if neurons (which have never been seen) existed . . . there is not a scintilla of evidence that they are any more conscious than the twitching of the severed leg of one of Golgi's frogs. Imagining that 'jamming unconscious neurons together' will create a conscious brain is like believing that piling eleven unconscious football players on top of one another will create one conscious football team! (For a linguistic, materialist critique of current neuroscience, see M.R. Bennett and P.M.S. Hacker, *Philosophical Foundations of Neuroscience*, 2003.)

It is essential to be clear about two things here, namely, about what does and about what does not exist. If "brain" is the name for a fiction, for a concept of what does not exist, then there is no brain. Brains do not exist. But if the brain does not exist, what does? James's answer was unequivocal: "On the principles of the corpuscular or mechanical philosophy, the only realities are the separate molecules, or at most the cells." This, of course, is consistent with what he wrote in the later, final chapter of *The Principles*: "The essence of things for science is not to be what they seem, but to be atoms and molecules moving to and from each other" (PP II: 633-34).

James's idea that there are no such realities as unified-thing brains has been proven a thousand times during the twentieth century. The electron microscope, designed with both microscopic particles and wave properties in mind, has amply verified James declaration that "brain" is shorthand for many distinct things, either brain cells or even smaller entities which do not aggregate or make up anything larger. Whoever believes they do must face Ryle's accusation that they believe in such ghosts as invisible structures, forms, patterns, harmonies, etc. No one has told the story which confirms James's century-old claim better than R. Restak in his 1979 *The Brain: the Last Frontier*.

[. . .] For over a hundred years, two schools of thought vied with each other on this question. The first believed the brain was composed of a continuous net of cells, each nerve cell directly connected to its neighbor. According to this view, the brain consisted of layer on layer of interconnected cells with impulses traveling through the brain like water through an intricate network of pipes.

The other view was proposed by a Spanish artist-turned-physician, Ramon y Cajal, who developed special chemical stains that showed the nerve cells to be composed of a central cell body, a long process known as an axon, and finally innumerable smaller processes, the dendrites. Cajal shared the Nobel Prize in 1906 for his concept (published in his own medical journal in Madrid) that nerve impulses are conducted along the axon of one neuron to the dendrite of a second neuron. If the stimulus passes to yet another neuron, the process is repeated. The impulse leaves via the axon of one neuron, and makes contact with the dendrite of another.

For years the debate raged as to whether the brain is composed of individual neurons completely separated from each other, or whether the true state of affairs is closer to an elaborate spider web. Some measure of the difficulty scientists had at the time in deciding between these two views can be deduced from the Nobel Prize Committee's choice, in 1906, for a person to share the prize in medicine with Cajal. Camillo Golgi, the foremost proponent of the net theory of brain function, along with his lifetime rival, Cajal, jointly shared the honor, since the scientific world was unable to decide between their competing theories.

Looking back now on the debate which, as I will discuss later, still has not been entirely settled, one can't help but suspect that occasionally Cajal must have felt that he was laboring on the short end of the odds. If the neurons are separate and not a part of a vast nerve net, then how does nerve-cell communication take place.

At one point Cajal's view seemed to suffer a fatal blow. A world-famous brain scientist announced that he had developed a stain showing tiny fibers connecting one nerve cell to another. Cajal, reacting in an inspired flash of brilliance, immediately substituted a milder solution of the same stain and demonstrated that the tiny fibers belonged to individual neurons rather than forming the interconnections between neurons. To prove his point, Cajal sketched his anatomical slides on the tablecloth of a nearby Madrid café where the earliest psychobiologists met daily to debate the microscopic architecture of the human brain.

Today, we know that Cajal was correct. With increasingly sophisticated stains that would have appealed to Cajal the artist, brain scientists over the ensuing fifty years have demonstrated that neurons in reality are separate cells that communicate with each other but are never in direct physical contact. This rules out the view that nerve impulses pass through the brain like water through a system of pipes. (*Op. cit.*, pp.164-65)

The neurons are *dis*connected at the synapses, since synapses are actually gaps. (Etymologically, the use of "synapse" is an egregious oxymoron: gaps that connect!) That conclusion is repeated in dozens of books currently sitting on library shelves. It should be added, "apparently sitting on library shelves." If there are no brains, there are also no books, no shelves, and no libraries either. Not even electron microscopes.

James wrote that "On the principles of the corpuscular or mechanical philosophy, the only realities are the separate molecules." Today, we replace "molecules" with "sub-atoms." Restak's story about the nature of 'the brain' referred to a tablecloth, and "tablecloth" reminds us of tables, and that, in turn, reminds us of A. Eddington, the world-famous scientist who, in the oft-cited introduction to *The Nature of Modern Science*, described the utter discrepancy between our naïve-realist view of tables and the modern-science view.

I have settled down to the task of writing these lectures and have drawn up my chairs to my two tables. Two tables! Yes; there are duplicates of every object about me—two tables, two chairs, two pens.

This is not a very profound beginning to a course which ought to reach transcendent levels of scientific philosophy. But we cannot touch bedrock immediately; we must scratch a bit at the surface of things first. And whenever I begin to scratch the first thing I strike is—my two tables.

One of them has been familiar to me from earliest years. It is a commonplace object of that environment which I call the world. How shall I describe it? It has extension; it is comparatively permanent; it is coloured; above all it is *substantial*. By substantial I do not merely mean that it does not collapse when I lean upon it; I mean that it is constituted of "substance" and by that word I am trying to convey to you some conception of its intrinsic nature. It is a *thing*; not like space, which is a mere negation; nor like time, which is—Heaven knows what! But that will not help you to my meaning because it is the distinctive characteristic of a "thing" to have this substantiality, and I do not think substantiality can be described better than by saying that it is the kind of nature exemplified by an ordinary table. And so we go round in circles. After all if you are a plain commonsense man, not too much worried with scientific scruples, you will be confident that you understand the nature of an ordinary table. I have even heard of plain men who had the idea that they could better understand the mystery of their own nature if scientists would discover a way of explaining it in terms of the easily comprehensible nature of a table.

Table No.2 is my scientific table. It is a more recent acquaintance and I do not feel so familiar with it. It does not belong to the world previously mentioned—that world which spontaneously appears around me when I open my eyes, though how much of it is objective and how much subjective I do not here consider. It is part of a world which in more devious ways has forced itself on my attention. My scientific table is mostly emptiness. Sparsely scattered in that emptiness are numerous electric charges rushing about with great speed; but their combined bulk amounts to less than a billionth of the bulk of the table itself. (A. Eddington, *The Nature of the Physical World*, pp.xi-xii)

James, of course, never heard of Eddington. He died before the tumultuous series of new theories and experimental confirmations shattered the mechanist worldview, popular among nineteenth-century physicists. This, of course, is not the place for even trying to summarize the history of this century's physics. Nor is it necessary, when so many able authors have told the stories so well, none better than Banesh Hoffman in his superb classic, *The Strange Story of the Quantum*. However, nuclear-science discoveries have confirmed, a thousand times over, the truth of James's declaration that brains do not exist, that our concept of 'it' is at best a useful fiction. What is needed now is an honest recognition that there is no justification for protecting everyday common-sense—or 'religious'—beliefs by walling them off from conclusions lumped together as "science."

Below is a handful of quotations from a variety of books, all of which reinforce the conclusion Russell, Einstein, and Eddington arrived at. The texts will be presented without comment. Each reader must decide whether she or he will will-to-believe them or not. Every well-stocked library will offer plenty of 'rebuttals' for those who will to not-believe.

Texts Without Comment For Readers Free to Believe or to Not-Believe.

. . . when I hear to-day protests against the Bolshevism of modern science, I am inclined to think that Rutherford, not Einstein, is the real villain of the piece. When we compare the universe as we had ordinarily preconceived it, the most arresting change is not the rearrangement of space and time by Einstein, but the dissolution of all that we regard as most solid into tiny specks floating in the void. That gives an abrupt jar to those who think that things are more or less what they seem. The revelation by modern physics of the void within the atom is more disturbing than the revelation by astronomy of the immense void of interstellar space.

The atom is as porous as the solar system. (A. Eddington, *The Nature of the Physical World*, p.1)

The space in the atom outside the nucleus is enormous compared with the size of the nucleus, or with the much smaller size of an electron. In the atom of hydrogen the single electron is near the outer rim of the atom. If its nucleus were enlarged to the size of a baseball, its electron would be a speck about eight city blocks away. Actually, of course, this atomic distance is small. The diameter of a hydrogen atom is nearly 1/200,000,000 of an inch; in other words, 200,000,000 hydrogen atoms could be placed one next the other in an inch. Relative to the nucleus or to the electron, however, the atomic space is prodigious. (Selig Hecht, *Explaining the Atom*, p.64)

From that day in 1911, when Rutherford described the inside of the atom, our whole idea of matter has been changed. The atom, formerly likened to a solid billiard ball, has become a transparent sphere of emptiness, thinly populated with electrons. The substance of the atom has shrunk to a core of unbelievable smallness; enlarged a thousand million times, an atom would be about the size of a football, but its nucleus would still be hardly visible—a mere speck of dust at the center. (Otto R. Frisch, *Atomic Physics Today*, p.13)

The new atomic model was definitely planetary. The surprising thing of the planetary model was how small the nucleus appeared. If the golf ball-sized atom was once again inflated, this time to the size of a modern sports arena or football stadium, the nucleus of the atom would be the size of a grain of rice. (Fred A. Wolf, *Taking the Quantum Leap*, p.75)

Now how do we know this is true if we can't see it? What proof have we that matter is made up of these quintillions of infinitesimal particles? Robert Millikan, one of the world's most noted physicists, said, "We can count the exact number of molecules in any given volume with more certainty than we can count the population of a city or a state."...

An atom is the smallest part of an element that can exist either alone or in combination with other particles. There are more atoms of hydrogen in a pail of water than there are drops of water in all the oceans of the world combined. So small is the diameter of an atom that half a million atoms piled, one on top of another, would not even equal the thickness of this page! The volume of the average atom is about 1.56×10^{-25} of a cubic inch, which means that there are approximately fifteen-thousand-six-hundred-billion-million-million atoms to a cubic inch. Of course, such a number is totally incomprehensible, yet in spite of its inconceivable minuteness, the atom is mostly empty space! Its entire mass is packed into its nucleus which, believe it or not, is one trillionth the size of the atom itself. This is very fortunate. If the atom were all nucleus without any space in it, a glass of water would weigh as much as a two-ton truck and you would weigh as much as half a dozen locomotives...

Because they are so incredibly close to the nucleus these electrons make approximately 10,000,000,000,000,000 revolutions around it every second... (Jerome S. Meyer, *The ABC of Physics*, pp.22, 34-35)

A bar of gold, though it looks solid, is composed almost entirely of empty space: The nucleus of each of its atoms is so small that if one atom were enlarged a million billion times, until its outer electron shell was as big as greater Los Angeles, its nucleus would still be only about the size of a compact car parked downtown. . . . Nor, to return to the old classical metaphor, does a cue ball strike a billiard ball. Rather . . . on the subatomic scale, the billiard balls are as spacious as galaxies, and were it not for their like electrical charges they could, like galaxies, pass right through each other unscathed. (Timothy Ferris, *Coming of Age in the Milky Way*, pp.288-89)

In every single drop of sea water, there are fifty billion atoms of gold. One would have to distill two thousand tons of such water to get one single gram of gold...

If we magnify the atom to the size of a football, the nucleus would be but a speck in its center and the electron, still invisible, would be revolving around its surface. Similarly, if we picture the atom as large as New York's Empire State Building, the electron, the size of a marble, would be spinning around the building seven million times every millionth of a second. There is relatively more empty space in the atom than between the planets in the solar system. (Bernard Jaffe, *Crucibles: The Story of Chemistry*, p.83)

James, once a student in a chemistry class taught by Charles Eliot who, as Harvard's president, later hired him, would have welcomed Rutherford's discovery. He often used the water molecule to illustrate his conviction that many of our concepts are mental shorthand for making simultaneous reference to things which retain their plural individualities or separatenesses. In his *Principles of Psychology*, he used that example to argue against those who proposed what he called 'the mind-stuff' theory of consciousness.

In other words, no possible number of entities (call them as you like, whether forces, material particles, or mental elements) can sum *themselves* together. Each remains, in the sum, what it always was; and the sum itself exists only *for a bystander* who happens to overlook the units and to apprehend the sum as such; or else it exists in the shape of some other *effect* on an entity external to the sum itself. Let it not be objected that H_2 and O combine of themselves into 'water,' and thenceforward exhibit new properties. They do not. The 'water' is just the old atoms in the new position, H-O-H; the 'new properties' are just their combined *effects*, when in this position, upon external media, such as our sense-organs and the various reagents on which water may exert its properties and be known. . . .

[. . .] The mind-stuff theory, in short, is unintelligible. Atoms of feeling cannot compose higher feelings, any more than atoms of matter can compose physical things! The 'things,' for a clear-headed atomistic evolutionist, are not. Nothing is but the everlasting atoms. When grouped in a certain way, *we* name them this 'thing' or that' but the thing we name has no existence out of our mind. (PP I:159, 160)

Nearly twenty years later, in the fifth of his 1908 lectures, *A Pluralistic Universe*, James repeated the view he had defended in the 1890 *Principles*:

[. . .] When a chemist tells us that two atoms of hydrogen and one of oxygen combine themselves of their own accord into the new compound substance 'water,' he knows (if he believes in the mechanical view of nature) that this is only an elliptical statement for a more complex fact. That fact is that when H_2 and O, instead of keeping far apart, get into closer quarters, say into the position H-O-H, they affect surrounding bodies differently: they now wet our skin, dissolve sugar, put out fire, etc., which they did n't in their former position. 'Water' is but our name for what acts thus peculiarly. . . .

A third difficulty is this: The bird-metaphor is physical, but we see on reflection that in the *physical* world there is no real compounding. 'Wholes' are not realities there, parts only are realities. 'Bird' is only our *name* for the physical act of a certain grouping of organs, just as 'Charles's Wain' is our name for a certain grouping of stars. The 'whole,' be it bird or constellation, is nothing but our vision, nothing but an effect on our sensorium when a lot of things act on it together. It is not realized by any organ or any star, or experienced apart from the consciousness of an onlooker. In the physical world taken by itself there *is* thus no 'all,' there are only the 'eaches'—at least that is the 'scientific' view. (*Writings* II:713-14, 717)

James's idea is clear. Had he known what discoveries would be made during the twentieth century, he might have been even bolder in his insistence that, if one believes in discontinuous, individual particles, the conclusion must be that sums of things do not exist, period!, and that all of our concepts of macroscopic bodies are 'fictions of popular speech.' We can imagine whole things having 'potential' parts which will become actual if the whole is cut, just as we can imagine that each whole is 'potentially' part of a larger, not-yet-actual whole. But 'part' and 'whole' are invented concepts the same way that 'cause' and 'effect' or 'large' and 'small' are. It is up to us to decide when we should use these 'eternal' or 'unchanging' concepts by applying or projecting them 'onto' realities. This is the same issue he discussed in his seventh *Pragmatism* lecture:

> What shall we call a *thing* anyhow? It seems quite arbitrary, for we carve out everything, just as we carve out constellations, to suit our human purposes. For me, this whole 'audience' is one thing, which grows now restless, now attentive. I have no use at present for its individual units, so I don't consider them. So of an 'army,' of a 'nation.' But in your own eyes, ladies and gentlemen, to call you 'audience' is an accidental way of taking you. The permanently real things for you are your individual persons. To an anatomist, again, those persons are but organisms, and the real things are the organs. Not the organs, so much as their constituent cells, say the histologists; not the cells, but their molecules, say in turn the chemists. (*Writings* II:597-98)

What ought to be the third and final nail in the coffin of the brain-process or brain-mind-identity theory is one that each and every student of the psyche must discover first-hand for her- or himself. It will only come by determined pondering of James's clear-headed *difference between the stream of consciousness that we experience and never-experienced physical bodies* that may exist out beyond the perimeter of that stream. Even in *Some Problems of Philosophy*, his final effort to write a radical-empiricist textbook, he highlighted that distinction. (Ignore only his pre-quantum-theory, deterministic reference to "the laws . . . are uniform in the strictest mathematical sense.") Whether or not James was always consistent, it is clear that he did often view the world as he describes it there. This passage from Chapter IX serves as an introduction to his strongest reason for rejecting the brain-process answer to "What do I see?"

> So far as physical nature goes few of us experience any temptation to postulate real novelty. The notion of eternal elements and their mixture serves us in so many ways, that we adopt unhesitatingly the theory that primordial being is inalterable in its attributes as well as in its quantity, and that the laws by which we describe its habits are uniform in the strictest mathematical sense. These are the absolute conceptual foundations, we think, spread beneath the surface of perceptual variety. It is when

we come to human lives, that our point of view changes. It is hard to imagine that 'really' our own subjective experiences are only molecular arrangements, even though the molecules be conceived as beings of a psychic kind. A material fact may indeed be different from what we feel it to be, but what sense is there in saying that a feeling, which has no other nature than to be felt, is not as it *is* felt? Psychologically considered, our experiences resist conceptual reduction, and our fields of consciousness, taken simply as such, remain just what they appear, even though facts of a molecular order should prove to be the signals of the appearance. Biography is the concrete form in which all that is is immediately given; the perceptual flux is the authentic stuff of each of our biographies, and yields a perfect effervescence of novelty all the time. (*Writings* II:1058-59)

"The perceptual flux is the authentic stuff of each of our biographies, and yields a perfect effervescence of novelty all the time." Think about that. Each time you open your eyes to begin another day that you will write about in your private diary (does anyone still keep diaries?), you expect that, however similar the *new* day's experiences—e.g., eating an apple—will be to any *old* day, it can only be *similar*, not identical. How many times can you eat one apple?!

Now think about what James referred to. If neurons exist, and if the neurons you think-together under the label "my brain" are the *identical* neurons you had yesterday and last year and the year before, then your life-experience is not varied and interesting as it appears to be but only the boring jiggling and rejiggling of the same old bowlful of cerebral jelly! No need to wait another billion billion years to see whether or not Nietzsche's theory of the eternal return of 'the same old things' is true. Try to recall whether even one eighteen-hour span of your experience has been a repeat of even one previous day's waking experience. (It once took a pair of experimental psychologists 435 pages of a book to describe what one boy did during one single day!)

Again, "the perceptual flux is the authentic stuff of each of our biographies, and yields a perfect effervescence of novelty all the time." This 1909 passage rejoins all of those citations gathered near the end of this chapter's third section. (The final citation is from the passage just cited.)

This is what overwhelmingly contradicts the brain-process theory which is one long string of inferences about never-seen, colorless brains and disconnected neurons. According to Berkeley and James, and we should add Russell and Einstein, no one has ever seen a brain, most of all their own! According to Berkeley and James, we experience panoramas of color, symphonies of sound, pungent varieties of odor, seven-course banquets of taste, life-like phantoms of bodies which walk, work, breathe, beget, tire, and tingle.

Yes, we think, we rationalize, we mentally assess logical trains of thought, we relish intellectual pursuits. Yes, we dream, we image, we create models, we subject them to endless tinkering and testing. But we also experience 'sensed worlds,' ranging from what *seem like* sandy beaches beneath the warm sun, hard pews in the quiet of darkened chapels, bustling city streets crowded with traffic and shoppers, thick-carpeted living rooms with fireplaces crackling, studies whose walls are lined with books similar to the doubly-non-book you are reading.

But the 'seem like' is the crucial qualification, kept in the back of our mind and readily available whenever a mindset-switch is necessary.

Some Views of the 'Authorities.' Do you believe that psychologists agree in their analyses of sensing, especially seeing, the centerpiece in the wonderful myth called "the scientific method." Whoever thinks so needs help. In 1979, James Gibson, known especially for his work on sense perception (or should it be sensation and perception?), gave this as his answer:

> The conclusions that can be reached from a century of research on perception are insignificant. The knowledge gained from a century of research on sensation is incoherent. We have no adequate theory of perception, and what we have found in the search for sensations is a mixed batch of illusions, physiological curiosities, and bodily feelings. The implications are discouraging. (J. Gibson, "Conclusions from a Century of Research on Sense Perception," in S. Koch and D. E. Leary, ed., *A Century of Psychology as Science*, pp.229-230

James's fame is currently in eclipse. Albert Einstein's is just the opposite. In 1999, he was named "Person of the Century" by *Time* magazine. It is fortunate that this most famous 'scientist' of the twentieth century can serve as the patron of those who are bold enough to seriously reexamine the validity of their naïve-realist convictions.

Abraham Pais believes it was around 1950 when Einstein, with whom he was taking a walk, stopped and "asked me if I really believed that the moon exists only if I look at it." Surely a startling question! But it is less startling once we know what Einstein wrote when asked in

1944 to make a contribution to Paul Schilpp's volume on *The Philosophy of Bertrand Russell.*

[The] more aristocratic illusion concerning the unlimited penetrative power of thought has as its counterpart the more plebeian illusion of naïve realism, according to which things "are" as they are perceived by us through our senses. This illusion dominates the daily life of men and of animals; it is also the point of departure in all of the sciences, especially of the natural sciences.

These two illusions cannot be overcome independently. The overcoming of naïve realism has been relatively simple. In his introduction to his volume, *An Inquiry Into Meaning and Truth*, Russell has characterized this process in a marvelously concise fashion:

> "We all start from "naive realism," i.e., the doctrine that things are what they seem. We think grass is green, that stones are hard, and that snow is cold. But physics assures us that the greenness of grass, the hardness of stones, and the coldness of snow are not the greenness, hardness, and coldness that we know in our experience, but something very different. The observer, when he seems to himself to be observing a stone, is really, if physics is to be believed, observing the effects of the stone upon himself. Thus science seems to be at war with itself; when it most means to be objective, it finds itself plunged into subjectivity against its will. Naive realism leads to physics, and physics, if true, shows that naive realism is false. Therefore naive realism, if true, is false; therefore it is false." (B. Russell, *An Inquiry Into Meaning and Truth*, Introduction)

Apart from their masterful formulation these lines say something which had never previously occurred to me. For, superficially considered, the mode of thought in Berkeley and Hume seems to stand in contrast to the mode of thought in the natural sciences. However, Russell's just cited remark uncovers a connection: if Berkeley relies upon the fact that we do not directly grasp the "things" of the external world through our senses, but that only events causally connected with the presence of "things" reach our sense organs, then this is a consideration which gets its persuasive character from our confidence in the physical mode of thought. For, if one doubts the physical mode of thought in even its most general features, there is no necessity to interpolate between the object and the act of vision anything which separates the object from the subject and makes the "existence of the object" problematical.

It was, however, the very same physical mode of thought and its practical successes which have shaken the confidence in the possibility of understanding things and their relations by means of purely speculative thought. Gradually the conviction gained recognition that all knowledge about things is exclusively a working-over of the raw material furnished by the senses. In this general (and intentionally somewhat vaguely stated) form this sentence is probably today commonly accepted. (A. Einstein, *Ideas and Opinions*, pp.30-32)

"Gradually the conviction gained recognition that all knowledge about things is exclusively a working-over of the raw material furnished by the senses." It is hard to imagine any statement with which James would have more heartily agreed. The color we call 'green,' the resistance we name 'hardness,' and the touch we describe as 'cold' are not qualities inherent in bodies outside us, but are *effects* produced in us by *causal* agents whose existence and features can only be inferred or guessed at. In the context of seeing, sight, or visual sensing, the effects are shaped colors.

This is Descartes' revolutionary conclusion. For everyone who truly grasps it, it leads immediately to the question, "Then how can we be certain of anything in the outside or external world? For instance, the moon?"

In fact, Einstein's question was a reversion to naïve realism. He ought to have asked, "Since what we see is *never* the moon, but only effects produced in our stream of consciousness, how do we even know the moon exists at all?"

For brain-process materialists, the question is even more pointed. *"How could a brain, if any exist, know what goes on outside of itself?"* To feel the force of that question, compare 'seeing a star' to 'reading a letter from Paris.' In the physical world, if it exists at all, things are simply what and where they are. Before any humans walked the earth, the sun and moon were sending light toward the earth at 186,000 miles per second, much the same way that falling trees were sending sound waves through the forest at 1100 feet per second. We and our sense organs have now been added to the picture. Our eyes intercept some of the arriving light. Via our afferent nerves, our skull-encased brains receive 'messages' about what is taking place outside our skull. But . . .

But, suppose a person in Paris sends a letter to a person in New York without ever leaving Paris. The letter reader in New York must first receive the letter, open it, *and look at it.* Only then will it be possible for the letter reader to *interpret* it in order to learn about the person in Paris and whatever that person wanted her or him to learn. Similarly, the brain must receive the coded nerve-impulses, become aware of them, and *interpret* or translate them into useful information about what is taking place in the outside environment.

However, a letter in New York is not a person in Paris, nor are nerve impulses anything but nerve impulses. How do we ever learn about never-seen stars, sun, moon, and other things, long before we learn about never-seen light-waves, air-molecule vibrations, kinetic energy, rods, cones, cochleas, taste buds, afferent neurons, nerve impulses, thalami, cortexes, and so on? The brain-process theory rests on anthropomorphizing faith that a brain, with no access of any kind to things outside of itself, can create a vast and complex common-sense worldview 'about' them, and then make the *inferential* discoveries summarized in these few pages about processes it is utterly unaware of, in order to finally realize that it—the brain—has no access of any kind to what exists outside of itself, even to consider the possibility that it doesn't exist?

As Russell noted and Einstein agreed, it is naïve realism which we begin with. Naïve realism is what we build our sciences of physics and physiology on. And it is our 'knowledge' of those wondrous things supposedly taking place in the physical world that shows naïve realism to be false. The more that researchers believe they have discovered about brains, the more obvious it should be that no one has any direct *experience* whatever of brains, not others' brains, not even their own!

Richard Restak, an advocate of the 'sensing is a brain process' hypothesis, acknowledged that brains—or we!—can deal only with representations.

> First, a fundamental principle: The brain exists in order to provide an internal representation of "reality." Quotation marks are employed here in deference to the fact that no creature, including ourselves, can ever know any other "reality" than the representations made by his brain. These representations, in turn, depend upon the brain's organization, which differs from one creature to another and, in our own species, from one person to another. (R. Restak, *Brainscapes*, pp.3-4)

Harvard professor, Steven Pinker, concurred: "Plato said that we are trapped inside a cave and know the world only through the shadows it casts on the wall. The skull is our cave, and mental representation is all that we can know about the world." (*How the Mind Works*, 1997, p.84.)

"Representations." That is precisely what Descartes and Locke held! *Every objection against their systems strikes directly at the systems of brain-mind-identity theorists.* And what is most obvious is that no theory gives a more inadequate answer to the most basic question which every would-be scientist must answer: "What do scientists or scientific observers observe, that is, see?!" Since *most* of what scientists or scientific observers believe they know about brains is acquired—it seems!—*by reading words* rather than *interpreting nerve impulses,* we can narrow the question down to this: "What do readers see when they engage in the many coordinated activities referred to as 'reading'?"

Descartes proposed an answer to the objection against representationalism. James often referred to the answer that Berkeley proposed. This is not the moment to examine their answers. It is the moment to point out that all representationalists face the same 'solipsist' challenge that James had to face.

P. S. To test your grasp of this Jamesian argument, analyse the logic (or lack of it) in the following answer of a prominent neuroscientist to the question, "What do you believe that you cannot prove?"

> For me, this is an easy question. I believe that animals have feelings and other states of consciousness, but neither I nor anyone else has been able to prove it. We can't even prove that other people are conscious, much less other animals. In the case of other people, though, we at least can have a little confidence since all people have brains with the same basic configurations.

Note. Confidence in the brain-process theory of sensing is not drawn primarily from studying sensing. Far more convincing for most people are the effects of brain damage on experience, but especially the explosion of psycho-pharmacology for treating undesirable states of consciousness. In no instance, however, is there more than correlation, which is not causation. But the more basic and important fact is that correlation assumes distinction, and distinction is the opposite of identity.

Step #4. Is There Anything Left?! There are two answers.

The first is the strict materialists' answer. No, there is nothing left that has not already been accounted for. Why? Because 'nature is all there is' (premise one), and 'there is no color, sound, odor, etc., as such, in nature' (premise two). It should be added that, because they adopt the first premise as their mantra, many of today's materialists prefer to be called "naturalists."

The other answer is that of James. Yes, the sense-objects we began with are what is left. That is, *what is left after the three eliminations is what every ex-five-year-old, normal college student begins the quest for 'higher' education with*, namely, the experienced objects mentioned above: panoramas or total visual fields* of color, symphonies of sound, pungent varieties of odor, seven-course banquets of taste, life-like phantoms of bodies which walk, work, breathe, beget, tire, and tingle. In a nutshell, what is left is everything that materialist or naturalist thinkers leave out. (*Henceforward, "total visual field of colors" will be replaced by a convenient acronym, TVF.)

For James, what is left are the proper sense objects (Aristotle) or secondary qualities (Berkeley). They should never have been eliminated. They cannot be eliminated. They are the 'stuff' of our experience. It is to them that, for most people, life 'owes all its living interest.'

> If common sense were true, why should science have had to brand the secondary qualities, to which our world owes all its living interest, as false, and to invent an invisible world of points and curves and mathematical equations instead? (*Writings* II:567)

Those lines, from the fifth of his *Pragmatism* lectures, are the reason why he ended by confessing that he could not make up his mind about which is the truest worldview, that of common sense, science or critical philosophy.

Be clear about what he meant by life's "living interest." Who would prefer what materialists believe in? Roses as colorless as light, music as silent as John Cage's 4'33" (look it up), food as tasteless as tofu, perfume as odorless as air, and a body as unfeelable as the most distant star. That's the literal meaning of Galileo's—and Newton's!—claim that nature is wholly devoid of sensed qualities, including tickles and painful burns.

The Challenges. The challenge is to imitate the greatest psychologists of the past, beginning with Plato and Aristotle, progressing at least through Hume and Kant, and ending, of course, with the greatest of them all, William James. The imitation must take the form of thinking hard enough to discover that there is 'MORE'—a term James often used—that is, MORE than what materialists or naturalists dream of. There is *more* than atoms and molecules, cells, organs, and organisms.

The greatest challenge of all, however, is recognizing that the more's which materialists or naturalists ignore are the very things they and naïve realists *believe* are the twinkling of stars, the sounds of falling trees, the fragrance of roses, taste of banana splits, or the felt hands or wiggling toes. Those more's are not what they *seem*, i.e., what naïve realists *believe*—falsely!—they are. *They are secondary qualities* which, in our naïve-realist mindset, we *mis*-take for independent, external, material, physical things.

Not till we are bold enough to face the hard truth about the more's we *mis*-take for 'material' things can we feel confident we have truly imitated the greatest psychologists. (Why do so many 'scientists' believe that the ultimate 'grand unifying theory' will be discovered by physicists rather than psychologists?)

5. Our Virtual-Reality, Movie 'World.'

Peirce's Dream. James claimed that his pragmatism was little more than a publicity campaign for a theory that his friend, C. S. Peirce, had put forth in "How to Make Our Ideas Clear," published in 1878, but ignored by the world for twenty years. Pragmatism, James maintained, was mostly a theory about meaning, especially the meaning of "truth."

What is especially curious is that, in that 1878 article, Peirce envisioned a day in the future when everyone devoted to the 'scientific method' of discovering truth would find themselves agreeing on everything. When that day arrives, we will be in possession of the full truth about reality. Especially relevant to James's pragmatism is the way Peirce linked truth and reality:

[. . .] all the followers of science are fully persuaded that the processes of investigation, if only pushed far enough, will give one certain solution to each question to which they can be applied. . . Different minds may set out with the most antagonistic views, but the progress of investigation carries them by a force outside of themselves to one and the same conclusion. This activity of thought by which we are carried, not where we wish, but to a foreordained goal, is like the operation of destiny. No modification of the point of view taken, no selection of other facts for study, no natural bent of mind even, can enable a man to escape the predestinate opinion. This great law is embodied in the conception of truth and reality. The opinion which is fated to be ultimately agreed to by all who investigate is what we mean by the truth, and the object represented in that opinion is the real. That is the way I would explain reality. (C. S. Peirce, "How to Make Our Ideas Clear," sec. iv)

Today's Academic-World Chaos. How wrong Peirce was! *The Wonderful Myth Called Science* drew attention to the most obvious feature of today's 'academic world.' There is more disagreement today about *everything* than at any previous time in recorded history. *There is chaos everywhere.*

But the chaos goes almost unnoticed. And it does so for one blindingly clear reason. Call it "the Myth of Distinct Disciplines." Investigators or researchers are imagined to be toiling in distinct, autonomous areas humorously called "fields." But visit the fields, survey the opinions about the foundational issues in each field, and the chaos comes into focus or, if you prefer, the forest dissolves into the trees. Physicists are so divided that Einstein declined to comment on some of the essays contributed to *Albert Einstein: Philosopher-Scientist.* Mathematicians disagree about the basic question, "Do numbers as such exist?" Psychologists form rival, hostile societies. Even if most historians agree that there was a Holocaust, they can't agree on whether or not Lee Harvey Oswald acted alone. Literature teachers deconstruct each others' theories of interpretation. Sociologists sometimes study the 'social realities' [sic] known as 'other disciplines,' but does anyone think that sociology itself is built on anything but a socially constructed myth? And so on.

Individual Critical Choosing. The goal Peirce envisioned, a future day when disagreement or contradiction would be eliminated, should remain the goal of everyone in pursuit of a grand unifying theory.

But the goal can only be achieved by individuals. And individuals can achieve it only by becoming *critical choosers,* that is, thinkers who can pick out the true opinions of the disagreeing physicists, the right opinions of the disagreeing mathematicians, the best opinions of the disagreeing psychologists, and so on.

That means that Jamesian quintalists must be critical choosers. The purpose of this and the earlier *William James on Common Sense* is to demonstrate how, when individual readers pick out James's *best* and *truest* thoughts from the rest, they will see how they do in fact fit together into a grand unifying theory.

But the picking out must be firm and decisive. And bold.

How to Deal With James' As-As Indecisiveness. Recall James's crucial distinction between things conceived as 'permanent unit-subjects that support attributes interchangeably' and things conceived as 'groups of sense-qualities united by the law of association.'

That distinction, found in the fifth *Pragmatism* lecture and analysed at great length earlier in this chapter, was a result of Immanuel Kant's influence on James. Call it the "as-as" distinction.

It is a distinction all of us can understand. "As a husband and father, Rockefeller might have been a caring person, but as a businessman he was utterly ruthless," "As a young girl, she was quite beautiful, but as an old woman she had lost her attractiveness," "As one component of salt, chlorine is harmless, but alone, as a liquid or gas, it is a deadly poison," are examples. In the common-sense worldview, those statements make perfect sense, since in each case *only one unit subject* which supports attributes interchangeably is involved.

Repeat. In those cases, there is only one unit-subject of which the attributions are being made.

However, in James's case, *there is no unit-subject that is both a permanent unit-subject and a group of sense-qualities!* This truth goes to the heart of the contradictions that run through James's writings. What we each must do is to get in the habit of distinguishing legitimate as-as distinctions from illegitimate ones.

Only with that habit of drawing the line between legitimate and illegitimate as's in the right place, can readers unlock the treasures in James's works.

How the Illegitimate As-As's, Especially Kant's, Are Created. All of us use the expression "as" routinely. What's more, all of us are at least common-sense philosophers and, as philosophers, all of us can understand as-as distinctions. But watch how, used carelessly—or to lure us into accepting a carefully planned but illegitimate use—the as-

as distinction can go from ambiguity to out-and-out contradiction . .
.

. . . By age five, we naïvely believe "The sun comes up each morning and goes down each evening." In time, we learn to say with Berkeley, "The sun appears to rise even though it is really just the earth turning so that we are once again able to see the sun." Shortened, that becomes "The sun *appears* to rise." In time, we don't object if someone tells us "*As it appears* to us, the sun rises, but *as it really is in itself,* it isn't moving." Maybe we don't. But we should.

It's wrong! A thousand times WRONG! The sun outside our mind never appears to us at all, and what does appear to us is not the sun but phenomena, sense-data, impressions, ideas in our mind . . . whatever, depending on whose vocabulary we prefer.

The dual as-as 'sun' example perfectly illustrates the illegitimate type of as-as use that Kant constructed his three hugely influential *Critique*'s on. In imitation of Berkeley, Kant lured his readers (most likely himself as well) into believing that, instead of there being two things, the sun 'out there' and the sense-data 'in here,' there is a single 'it' that both is in itself but also appears to us. It is 'as if' there is only one thing, the sun, which is both 'the-sun-as-it-appears' *and* 'the-sun-as-it-is-in-itself.' Kant then extended his equivocation to all of 'nature" and assured readers that his new 'designation' was the one that is "proper"! The following passage offers a perfect Kantian counterpart to James's crucial 'as a unit-subject' vs 'as a group of sense qualities' distinction.

> But it has just been shown that the laws of nature can never be known *apriori* in objects so far as they are considered, not in reference to possible experience, but as things in themselves. And our inquiry here extends, not to things in themselves (the properties of which we pass by), but to things as objects of possible experience, and the complex of these is what we here properly designate as nature. (*Prolegomena to Any Future Metaphysics*, Sec.17)

"*Objects* . . . as things in themselves"? "Things as *objects* of possible experience"? "*Objects* . . . properly designated as nature"?! Gone are Berkeley's 'ideas in the mind.' In its (their) place we have 'things as we experience them.' Gone are Berkeley's 'never-sensed substances' which do not exist. In their place we have things in themselves whose properties 'we pass by.' In place of the stars, the moon, and other parts of Mother Nature which pre-existed humans, we have the complex of things as objects of possible experience which "we properly [!] designate as nature." Kant lulls us into a lazy attitude toward what we see and touch: "We can be sure of how the things we see and feel appear, even though we must admit that what they are really like 'in themselves'. . . , well, no one knows that for sure."

Note that Kant begins that passage with a reference to the laws of nature. If you doubt that he was not referring to stars, the moon, and others parts of nature as five- or ten-year olds think of them, that is, as permanent unit-subject 'things' that were in existence long before any five- or ten-year-old was born, watch what Kant has to say about the laws which 'govern' those things that appear to us. In the original edition of his *Critique of Pure Reason*, when his actual meaning was less disguised by verbal veils than it later became, he tells us about those laws of nature. Where Berkeley had acknowledged God as the law-giver for the 'ideas' he designated as "nature," Kant assures us that 'the pure understanding' gives the laws to 'nature.'

> However exaggerated and absurd it may sound, to say that the understanding is itself the source of the laws of nature, and so of its formal unity, such an assertion is none the less correct, and is in keeping with the object to which it refers, namely, experience. Certainly, empirical laws, as such, can never derive their origin from pure understanding. That is as little possible as to understand completely the inexhaustible multiplicity of appearances merely by reference to the pure form of sensible intuition. But all empirical laws are only special determinations of the pure laws of understanding, under which, and according to the norm of which, they first become possible. Through them appearances take on an orderly character, just as these same appearances, despite the differences of their empirical form, must none the less always be in harmony with the pure form of sensibility. (Kant, *The Critique of Pure Reason*, 1st ed., trans. N. K. Smith, A127-28)

Newton's empirical laws of inertia, gravitation, action-and-reaction are 'only special determinations' of the laws of nature whose source is not God but the faculty of understanding!! What Kant said *is* absurd, *but only if* we take him to be referring to laws that 'govern' subatomic particles or atoms or whatever purely physical things, if any exist independently of us and our thoughts. But, and it is a crucial but . . .

Kant's important question. But Kant was trying to find a 'natural science' explanation for an important fact that neither Hume, nor Berkeley, nor Descartes gave enough attention to. Why is it that other people seem to think like us about stars, the moon, the earth's oceans, forests, etc.? In fact . . .

In fact, why do other people seem to see the same colors that we do? Every college freshman, introduced to the sense-datum arguments, at first assumes that everyone sees the same colors. Only when it is explained that normal sighted people may be using the same names but seeing opposite colors (e.g., every unripe apple and patch of grass one calls "green" may *appear* red to someone who has learned to call objects with a color similar to that of unripe apples and patches of grass "green"), do they begin to see the first problem. What Kant wanted to know was i) why everyone believes there are apples and roses, *and* stars, the moon, etc., and ii) why everyone correctly instructed accepts that they are subject to Newton's laws.

Why is it, in other words, that *we all develop the same worldview*, the one James and we are calling "common sense"? Before Descartes, everyone assumed that the answer was "Because we are all sensing the same world!" Descartes, if he ever thought of the question, would have argued that it is because we all have minds which God designed to learn the truth about the one and only world. Berkeley would have said it is because God gives everyone similar ideas. Hume left the answer vague, namely, "It's just that we all develop similar habits or customary ways of thinking." Kant, however, asked the question the others paid no attention to. And, he wanted an answer that would show why Aristotle's logic, Euclid's geometry, and Newton's physics are impregnably true.

Like Kant, James was dissatisfied with pre-Kantian answers. But, during the years between 1878 when he signed his contract and 1890 when he finished his great text on the human psyche, he wrestled with two problems. On the one hand, he wanted to make his psychology empirical, that is, *to base it on experience*. On the other hand, he was aware that, as Descartes had argued, all streams of conscious experience are tied to brains and all brains are isolated from each other by their skull-prisons. i) How could he even prove there were other streams of consciousness than his own? ii) How could he prove that most were similar to his own?

True, his own common-sense belief-system included the conviction that other persons exist and that their experience was like his own. But he had also accepted the verdict of 'science,' namely, that common sense is wrong. Thus, in order to write a 'scientific' text that did not depend on 'metaphysical' premises such as Kant's, he tried to find a different answer. In the fifth *Pragmatism* lecture, he gave it:

> Our ancestors may at certain moments have struck into ways of thinking which they might conceivably not have found. But once they did so, and after the fact, the inheritance continues. . . My thesis now is this, that our fundamental ways of thinking about things are discoveries of exceedingly remote ancestors, which have been able to preserve themselves throughout the experience of all subsequent time. (*Writings* II:560)

Nevertheless, James did not disagree with perhaps the most important feature of Kant's psychology. Both Kant and he did accept Berkeley's claim that we directly experience colors, sounds, odors, tastes, warmth, coolness, tickles, pains, and other 'phenomena.' All three accepted the fact that the naïve-realist claim that we sense permanent, unit-subject things that exist in themselves, i.e., independently of any perceiver, is false and has been refuted by modern discoveries. That is why Kant went on to ask whether it is possible, theoretically, to prove the existence of any things-in-themselves, and to give the answer, "No."

But . . .

The Inner Stream of Consciousness' Inner-vs-Outer Feature. What is the most important feature of Kant's psychology? It is simply this: the "Elimination" case against common sense ends with private phenomena 'inside the perceiver's mind.' But there are also other things—images and thoughts—inside the mind. The different things inside the mind 'appear' differently. The colors, sounds, odors, tastes, etc., which are actually inside us, *appear* to be outside of us. They are inside us, but we do not 'introspect' or look backwards into our mind in order to study them. It seems that we look out to see them and that we reach out to feel them. *That is because they appear to be outside.* That is what makes them so different from things that, by contrast, appear to be inside and not outside: namely, headaches, memory-images, emotions, thoughts, and other components of one and the very same private, *inside!* stream of consciousness.

In a word, some parts of our common-sensically inner, private stream of consciousness appear to be outside and some appear to be inside. James argued however that, at first, everything that appears, i.e., everything that we experience directly, is "one undiscriminated whole object." That was James's ingenious way of beginning his case for a purely 'empirical' version of Kant's 'vision.' He hoped to explain how the inner stream gets sub-divided into two parts, one 'outer' and one 'inner,' without appealing to anything that is not empirically experienced. (Redundancy for the sake of emphasis.) The distinction of the inner stream of consciousness, utterly distinct and cut off from whatever realities 'in themselves,' lie out beyond the perimeter of the private stream, into an 'outer-seeming' and an 'inner-seeming' part, is not, for James, what Kant claimed. It is not dependent on pre-experience 'structures of the mind,' discovered first by Kant*, and only by inference. (*Leibniz offered a vague anticipation of Kant's 'discovery.')

Here, then, is James's description of how the utterly private, inner stream of consciousness appears at first:

[. . .] the undeniable fact being that *any number of impressions, from any number of sensory sources, falling simultaneously on a mind* WHICH HAS NOT YET EXPERIENCED THEM SEPARATELY, *will fuse into a single undivided object for that mind.* The law is that all things fuse that can fuse, and nothing separates except what must. What makes impressions separate we have to study in this chapter. Although they separate easier if they come in through distinct nerves, yet distinct nerves are not an unconditional ground of their discrimination, as we shall presently see. The baby, assailed by eyes, ears, nose, skin, and entrails at once, feels it all as one great blooming, buzzing confusion; and to the very end of life, our location of all things in one space is due to the fact that the original extents or bignesses of all the sensations which came to our notice at once, coalesced together into one and the same space. There is no other reason than this why "the hand I touch and see coincides spatially with the hand I immediately feel." (PP I:488)

"The baby, assailed by eyes, ears, nose, skin, and entrails at once, feels it all as one great blooming, buzzing confusion." That is James's description of the stream of consciousness as it appears to the newborn infant, before there has been any subdividing.

For James, the outer-vs-inner separation comes only gradually and can be explained without any Kantian built-in structure of the mind. ("Whose mind?" became the big question for Kant's immediate successors.) Here is how James described the matter in a 1905 essay entitled "The Place of Affectional Facts in a World of Pure Experience," the fifth of the essays he wrote to present his radical empiricism. Here is his answer to the question, "Are emotions inner or outer?" As might be expected, he describes both the common-sense and the radical-empiricist mindsets *as if they are on the same side* of the debate with intellectualists.

With the affectional experiences which we are considering, the relatively 'pure' condition lasts. In practical life no urgent need has yet arisen for deciding whether to treat them as rigorously mental or as rigorously physical facts. So they remain equivocal, and, as the world goes, their equivocality is one of their great conveniences.

The shifting place of 'secondary qualities' in the history of philosophy is another excellent proof of the fact that 'inner' and 'outer' are not coefficients with which experiences come to us aboriginally stamped, but are rather results of a later classification performed by us for particular needs. The common-sense state of thought is a perfectly definite halting-place, the place where we ourselves can proceed to act unhesitatingly. On this stage of thought things act on each other as well as on us by means of their secondary qualities. Sound, as such, goes through the air and can be intercepted. The heat of the fire passes over, as such, into the water which it sets a-boiling. It is the very light of the arc-lamp which displaces the darkness of the midnight street, etc. By engendering and translocating just these qualities, actively efficacious as they seem to be, we ourselves succeed in altering nature so as to suit us; and until the more purely intellectual, as distinguished from practical, needs had arisen, no one ever thought of calling these qualities subjective. When, however, Galileo, Descartes, and others found it best for philosophic purposes to class sound, heat and light along with pain and pleasure as purely mental phenomena, they could do so with impunity.

Even the primary qualities are undergoing the same fate. Hardness and softness are effects on us of atomic interactions, and the atoms themselves are neither hard nor soft, nor solid nor liquid. Size and shape are deemed subjective by the Kantian; time itself is subjective according to many philosophers, and even the activity and causal efficacy which lingered in physics, long after secondary qualities were banished are now treated as illusory projections outwards of phenomena of our own consciousness. There are no activities or effects in nature, for the most intellectual contemporary school of physical speculation. Nature exhibits only changes, which habitually coincide with one another so that their habits are describable in simple 'laws.'

There is no original spirituality or materiality of being, intuitively discerned, then; but only a translocation of experiences from one world to another; a grouping of them with one set or another of associates for definitely practical or intellectual ends.

I will say nothing here of the persistent ambiguity of relations. They are undeniable parts of pure experience; yet, while common sense and what I call radical empiricism stand for their being objective, both rationalism and the usual empiricism claim that they are exclusively the 'work of the mind'—the finite mind or the absolute mind, as the case may be. (*Writings* II:1210-11)

There is only one solution. *Begin* with the absolutely clear, unambiguous common-sense distinction between 'out there' vs 'in here.' What is—or seems to be—out there, the 'external' world of stars, the moon, etc. (if there are such things), is on its own, independent of us. What is in here, our feelings, memories, thoughts, etc., is dependent on us and would 'go poof' the moment we 'went poof.' This conviction is well in place by every normal learner who reaches the age of five or six. *Begin with it. Hang on to it!*

Every five-year old knows the difference between the tummy ache that is inside and the parents who are outside. The five-year old who is lost in a shopping mall and tearfully wanders around crying for Mom is in no doubt that Mom exists somewhere else but can be found! In a letter to F. C. S. Schiller two years before his death, James was emphatic on the fact that this is common sense's conviction:

[. . .] You write that you shrink a little from my use of independent realities, etc. etc. No need of shrinking! They are an indestructible common sense assumption, and the discussion is kept on terms more intelligible to the common man if you assume them. Moreover, in relation to the *individual man* the object *is* an independent reality with which his thought can 'agree' only by its pragmatic workings. (*The Correspondence of William James*, Vol.XI, p.552)

He was right with the first sentence'd thought. He'd already switched into his radical-empiricist mindset with the second. It is the thing as a permanent unit-subject *versus* the thing as a group of sense qualities all over again.

Such inadvertent (?), certainly unreferred-to! mindset-switching must be recognized, so that the line between legitimate, same-mindset switching and illegitimate, systematically ambiguous switching can be drawn decisively. The key is recognizing the common-sense conviction and *holding it in place* when, later on, further subdividing what is inner experience into what is inner but only appears to be outer (it comes as a shock to discover that the out-there-appearing sense-data are actually in 'here!) and what also appears or feels to be inner.

Clearing up the confusion created by subdividing the 'inner' part of the original 'outer-vs-inner' common-sense distinction into what should then be seen as an 'inner-outer' vs 'inner-inner' distinction, is the key to understanding James. It is the key to correcting him and removing the blatant self-contradictions that result from his ambiguities. P.S. Clearing away those ambiguities is especially important for clarifying the state of mind he was in when he made his misleading "This may sound materialistic to you" statements in 1980's *Principles* and in 1905's "Does 'Consciousness' Exist [as an entity]?"

James Had the Solution for the As-vs-As Problem. Though he failed to make any adequate use of it, the way to eliminate Berkeley's and Kant's equivocations did flit across James's mind long enough for him to make a note of it. To keep our own thoughts clear while we are reading James, or any other author for that matter, we must use the same caution which he advised himself to use in an 1884 note which *Manuscript Essays and Notes* entitles simply "Idealism [III] 1884." In a word, we must not transfer qualifying phrases from acts to objects. When James denied that consciousness exists, he added "as an *entity*." We can add "as an object." The entity, if it existed, would be the object of the *function* or act aptly named "awareness."

Berkeley & Ferrier . . . wish to prove that the world *per se* can't *exist*. They do it by showing that we can't think it to exist *per se*. Not being able to think it so, of course we have no right to say it is so. The propositions by which they seek to show we can't think it so are true propositions enough in one sense, but not in the sense in which Berkeley & Ferrier use them. The true sense is that *we can't think* the world *per se* except so far as we *do* think it. The sense they smuggle in is that we can't think it except *under the form of* an object of thought, or except as an *idea*. The neatest phrase, perhaps, for expressing the ambiguity is: "The world can't be tho't of except *as* thought of." The *as* here may refer to the act of thinking or to the object of the thinking. It may mean *when* thought of; and be true, but insignificant. Or it may mean, *under the appearance of being thought of;* when it is significant, but false. (Perry I:578; see MEN:198-99, which adds "Confusion of psychologists' point of view with subjects'. We can't think of it without thinking of it, but when thinking of it, we think of it *as per se*. ")

"The *as* here may refer to the act of thinking or to the object of the thinking." When Berkeley wrote that "a thing's *esse* is its *percipi*," i.e., for a thing to exist is the same as for the thing to be perceived, he switched from thinking about the object which was perceived—something which is impossible if the thing does not exist—to thinking about the perceiver's act of perceiving the object. There are, we assume, things that exist only while we are thinking about them. For instance, we assume that thoughts (object) exist only while they are being understood (act) by someone, and that headaches (object) exist only while they are being felt (act). But everyone understands quite well the thought that other things exist even when no humans think about or feel them, e.g., the stars, the moon, and other things which every common-sense person 'knows' were in existence long before any humans were around to think about them, even though later human thoughts OF those pre-existing things exist only while humans are in the act of understanding them.

Draw a Map, Then Count and Classify. As explained in *William James on Common Sense*, each new learner gradually builds an inner model or map of the world. The items gradually added to that model can be classified in countless ways.

The way needed here is to divide them according to whether they are on the out- or the in-side of the line we originally draw through that one-space inner map representing each item's location vis-à-vis all the others. Of the things that are in our mind, some are sense-data, some are memory-images, and some are thoughts. From Galileo and Descartes on, it was taken for granted that bodies exist, but that the ideas of 'secondary quality' sense-data are not like any bodies in the external world. But they did believe that some thoughts or ideas inside our minds can truly represent outside bodies. Berkeley argued that there are no bodies for thoughts (ideas) to match. Kant said we can't be theoretically certain our thoughts match anything outside our experience. James decided that radical empiricists should agree not to discuss anything outside our experience. And so on.

The view here is that, of our thoughts, some are hypotheses about never-sensed bodies and some are guesses about never-sensed selves. To the extent that our hypotheses-guesses are true, we can know about the not-experienced things 'through' our thoughts. This view is easy to understand. We may be able to indirectly know things we do not sense, much the way we indirectly know what went on in Paris when we read a letter after it reaches New York.

The real question is, "How can I ever be certain that my thoughts about what I never experience are true?" As we will see in the next chapter, that became James's great worry when, in 1878, he began thinking how he could write a psychology text about other minds he could never experience.

The 'Bottom Line' for this Section: The 'Movie' that is MY 'Physical Reality.'

It is a matter for regret that James did not live long enough to experience more abundantly the marvels of modern technology. Had he attended wide-screen movies often enough, routinely watched television in 'living color,' enjoyed quadraphonic sound reproduction, witnessed synthesizer keyboards making music that sounds as if it is coming from a large ensemble of orchestral instruments, it is quite likely that he would have made use of such technologies to convey the hypothesis that we experience a rich sensory 'world' of color, sound, smells, flavors, muscle flexings, pains, and tingles.

It is quite likely, first, because he more than once emphasized his conviction that similar 'sense-data' (his term; see PP II:184 & 620) can be produced by dissimilar physical and physiological causes. In *The Principles*, he noted that 'Nature' herself demonstrates a notable flexibility in the production of various effects.

> Nature has many methods of producing the same effect. She may make a 'born' draughtsman or singer by tipping in a certain direction at an opportune moment the molecules of some human ovum; or she may bring forth a child ungifted and make him spend laborious but successful years at school. She may make our ears ring by the sound of a bell, or by a dose of quinine; make us see yellow by spreading a field of buttercups before our eyes, or by mixing a little santonine powder with our food; fill us with terror of certain surroundings by making them really dangerous, or by a blow which produces a pathological alteration of our brain. (PP II:625)

It is also quite likely, because in his last work, *Some Problems of Philosophy*, James did use the idea of motion-photography technology (Edison's kinetoscope) to present a Hume-like analysis of our experience of 'causal connection.' In doing so, he anticipated by years the implications of later, well-known experiments by A. Michotte.

> The logical conclusion would seem to be that even if the kind of thing that causation is, were revealed to us in our own activity, we should be mistaken on the very threshold if we supposed that the fact of it is there. In other words we seem in this line of experience to start with an illusion of place. It is as if a baby were born at a kinetoscope show and his first experiences were of the illusions of movement that reigned in the place. The nature of movement would indeed be revealed to him, but the real facts of movement he would have to seek outside. (*Writings* II:1092-93)

An infant taken by mom to watch "Children's Hour" will see and hear what the infant would have seen and heard if taken by mom to the movie set. The movie projector and the sound system are designed to produce light-waves in movie-goer' eyes and air-molecule vibrations in the movie-goer's ears. The patterns of those light-waves and air-vibrations will be *similar* to those produced in the eyes and ears of the movie-goer if she or he had been where the camera and microphone were located on the original film-set. But what a difference between the infant and the ex-infant movie-goer! The infant who made no sense of the colors and sounds, emerges from the theater as an adult, drenched with memory and emotion.

Similarly, non-theater visual fields and sounds which initially 'make no sense' to the infant because they are received into a mind devoid of a worldview, eventually begin to 'make sense' when received into a mind more and more equipped with a common-sense worldview. Once the child has an enormous inner model 'of' things supposedly existing in the outer world and has acquired enough memory-videos of previous sense-sequences, new but similar phenomena will activate that 'prepared mind' to make instant sense of them.

James's radical empiricism is built on these considerations. We experience what we experience, not what causes what we experience. Apart from the shock of our new insight, it does not matter whether our visual sense-data are caused by real people, houses, etc., by movie-projectors, by virtual-reality technology, by a brain hooked up to Hal the computer, by a malevolent demon, or by a deity enjoying a game-of-wits.

James's third *Pragmatism* lecture shows how profound was his conviction that we each must face the question, "How can I know any unseen realities behind the curtain of 'ideas' (Locke and Berkeley), 'impressions' (Hume), 'phenomena' (Kant), or 'flux' (James)?" That lecture is an updated version of Descartes' *First Meditation*.

A more recent presentation of 'the' question is Jonathan Harrison's clever parody of the linguistic turn in "A Philosopher's Nightmare: or, The Ghost Not Laid," which can be found in *The Proceedings of the Aristotelian Society*, vol.67*. In effect, Harrison asks "How do I know that my 'sensed world' is not a consistent hallucination?" James, who wrote "An hallucination is a strictly sensational form of consciousness, as good and true a sensation as if there were a real [physical] object there" (PP II:115), would surely have enjoyed Harrison's subtly funny, deadly serious spoof. (*Incidentally, it is infinitely more educational than a certain later "brain in a vat" presentation.)

Meditating on this 'bottom line' demands a strong stomach or at least a bold spirit. If we are unwilling to face the spectre of 'solipsism,' we can avoid the 'bottom line' question, "If all I experience is what is in my mind, how can I be certain there are real things outside my mind and, even if there are, how can I be certain that I can ever know the truth about them?" We can resist. Others have. But evading facts does not produce wisdom.

The existentialist stress on the ultimate aloneness of the individual is a useful reminder for us. . . . [It] alone makes more problematic and more fascinating the mystery of communication between alonenesses via, e.g., intuition and empathy, love and altruism, identification with others. . . . We take these for granted. It would be better if we regarded them as miracles to be explained. (A. Maslow, "Existential Psychology: What's In It for Us?", in *Existential Psychology*, ed. R. May, p.57)

[Man's] awareness of himself as a separate entity, the awareness of his own short life span, of the fact that without his will he is born and against his will he dies, that he will die before those whom he loves, or they before him, the awareness of his aloneness and separateness, of his helplessness before the forces of nature and of society, all this make his separate, disunited existence an unbearable prison. . . . The deepest need of man, then, is the need to overcome his separateness, to leave the prison of his aloneness. (E. Fromm, *The Art of Loving*, ch.2)

Philosophy, we might say, begins with the recognition of aloneness in the existential sense. Obviously there is no demand that the individual make the experiment of suspension or even bother about the significance of conceptual experimentation. The alternative is not ignorance but unwisdom. In fact, the force of mundanity is such that radical reflection on it is, if not a rarity, a rather scarce commodity. (M. Natanson, *The Journeying Self: A Study in Philosophy and Social Role*, p.15)

Movies can dramatize our 'existential aloneness.' The wrenching scene in *Children's Hour*, when Audrey Hepburn's fiance, James Garner, is badgered by her into voicing a suspicion about her relation with Shirley MacLaine, teaches the lesson central to James's *Principles*, namely, James's insistence that the breach between different people's minds is one of 'the most absolute in nature.' What makes that scene so unusual is its depiction of people's inability to open their thoughts to inspection by others even when they desperately want to. Equally instructive are scenes in which deliberate deceptions are shown, scenes such as that in which Jane Fonda glances at her watch during the movie *Klute*. But no movie is better than *Rashomon* as an introduction to 'the breach.'

> [. . .] The only states of consciousness that we naturally deal with are found in personal consciousnesses, minds, selves, concrete particular I's and you's.
> Each of these minds keeps its own thoughts to itself. There is no giving or bartering between them. No thought even comes into direct *sight* of a thought in another personal consciousness than its own. Absolute insulation, irreducible pluralism, is the law. It seems as if the elementary psychic fact were not *thought* or *this thought* or *that thought*, but *my thought*, every thought being *owned*. Neither contemporaneity, nor proximity in space, nor similarity of quality and content are able to fuse thoughts together which are sundered by this barrier of belonging to different personal minds. The breaches between such thoughts are the most absolute breaches in nature. (PP I:226)

'Watching TV' also makes it easy to think correctly about one's TVF. It takes time to become accustomed to noticing that our visual sense-datum from edge to edge (top to bottom, right to left) is a 'field' of patterned colors very similar to what appears on a movie or television screen. If real TV screens existed, *their color and shape would remain unchanged*, though the items 'in the picture' are constantly changing in size, shape, and position relative to each other. Normally, we pay no attention to the changes, because they instantly trigger our imagination into mentally creating a 'story' about persons, things, events, etc., which do not change size, shape, or size, but come closer, go away, turn, etc. By thinking hard about the difference between the changes in i) what we see and ii) our thoughts about the things 'represented' by what we see, we can acquire a mental template that can be transferred to studying the difference between our changing total visual fields or TVFs (see PP I:185) and the unseen bodies we take to be represented by them. In Chapter XX of *The Principles*, James described the inner psychology of the process:

> But suppose, to take a more complicated case, that the object is a stick, seen first in its whole length, and then rotated round one of its ends; let this fixed end be the one near the eye. In this movement the stick's image will grow progressively shorter; its farther end will appear less and less separated laterally from its fixed near end; soon it will be screened by the latter, and then reappear on the opposite side, and finally on that side resume its original length. Suppose this movement to become a familiar experience; the mind will presumably react upon it after its usual fashion (which is that of unifying all the data which it is in any way possible to unify), and consider it the movement of a constant object rather than the transformation of a fluctuating one. (PP II:215)

Whoever would understand James must learn to think about the objects of visual awareness the way James did, in the way that creators of 'special effects' for movies do, in the way that designers of computer graphics must, etc.

Concluding Application of the Above. To read James with ease rather than mind-exhausting bafflement, it is essential to acquire a ready habit for switching from one mindset to another, from one model to its opposite, etc.

You're reading, right? To read, you look, right? What are you looking at or seeing while you read? These are not really words, right? The initial introduction to this fact is available in *William James on Common Sense*, the pre-quel to this book on the stream of consciousness. Your stream of consciousness. Your *private* stream of consciousness.

Here, as elsewhere, these 'word-clues' which evoke your present train of thought must be 'seen' as part of a project concerning the need to revise your naïve-realist thinking. In the same way that Magritte's painting of a pipe is not a pipe but a painting, the 'words' used here are not words but—like subtitles or credits in a movie—just parts of your changing TVF.

But what would we do, if we did not have the logical-fiction ideas of word-names that we pretend are 'symbols' for concepts, the logical-fiction ideas of sentences that we pretend are 'symbols' for thought-meanings, etc.? What would we do, if we did not have an entire arsenal of 'language' fictions to help us notice the radically different components of our initially unnoticed stream of consciousness?

6. Pragmatism, Paradigms or Useful Fictions.

James's Pragmatic 'Definition' of "True Belief." What do we mean if we say "The woodsman only pretended to carry out the wicked queen's command to kill Snow White" or if we say "Snow White is now living in the forest with the seven dwarfs"? Clearly the thoughts signified by such 'word-cues' are not true in the vocabulary of common sense. Strictly speaking, such claims are literally false. We know that no woodsman existed, that the queen was a fiction, and that Snow White existed only in our imagination. But, unless we want to insist "That's false!" whenever a meteorologist says "The sun rose this morning at 5:59 am," we must become accustomed to thinking in a truly convoluted way that, even though 'scientifically' false, the meteorologist's common-sense statement is 'true.'

Actually, to say that "Snow White is still alive" means that there will be some future movie scenes with 'her' in them. By using Berkeley's analysis of 'sun-rising' statements, it becomes easy to understand James's idea of truth. His pragmatist view that statements about physical bodies are 'true' does *not* mean that such statements (or the thoughts 'signified' by them) *correspond* to unsensed physical bodies outside our mind-experience, but only that the statements (or thoughts) predict the occurrence of specific sense-data in the future. If there are no unsensed physical bodies, as James the radical empiricist believed, that is, if only our stream-of-secondary-qualities life-movies exist, that is, if there is only one category of things to consider and not two, then it makes no sense to define "truth" as "correspondence."

That is, once we understand that James regarded 99% of all the things 'represented' by our concepts as as-if* fictions, useful for making future-predictions vis-à-vis 'the flux of perception,' and also understand that he was naturally reluctant to say that 99% of what most people believe is literally false, it becomes easier to understand why he fought so hard for his approach to 'truth' in *Pragmatism*. We must get used to two different meanings of "true": the everyday, common-sense 'correspondence' view and the 'false but useful for predicting future sensations' view. (*What we experience is *as-if* the sun moves, the sky is blue, etc.)

James's 'Humanism' And Kuhn's '(Group) Revolutions.' Thomas Kuhn's *Structure of Scientific Revolutions* launched a philosophical revolution in the thought-habits of 'philosophers of science.' It popularized the notion that research in 'the sciences' requires great imagination. Phrases such as "theoretical fictions," "working models," "current paradigms," and so on have become common. What is still not sufficiently appreciated is that consensus on equations does not indicate consensus on what those equations refer to. James recognition that much of what is put forward as 'science' is, at best, false-but-useful formulas that enable 'researchers' and the rest of us to make accurate predictions of future observations should be much better known 'by the public.' Works such as John Horgan's collection of interviews with 'leading authorities,' entitled *The End of Science: Facing the Limits of Knowledge in the Twilight of the Scientific Age*, are useful, as 'behind the scenes' revelations of facts that James tried to publicize with his 'pragmatic' approach to "truth." (See also the recent Age of Entanglement, by Louisa Gilder.)

As *The Wonderful Myth Called Science* explains, Einstein himself advocated views similar to those of James. First of all, he was emphatic about the fact that the concepts used in 'the sciences' are not acquired by simply observing nature. They are inventions of creative human imagination.

> I am convinced that even much more is to be asserted: the concepts which arise in our thought and in our linguistic expressions are all—when viewed logically—the free creations of thought which cannot inductively be gained from sense experiences. . . . Thus, for example, the series of integers is obviously an invention of the human mind, a self-created tool which simplifies the ordering of certain sensory experiences. (A. Einstein, *Ideas and Opinions*, p.33)

Furthermore, testing the value of these imagination-created ideas must be done from within the stream of consciousness. Consider a passage from *The Evolution of Physics*, co-authored by Einstein and Leopold Infeld. It is an easy-to-understand description of the 'created models' model of scientific theorizing.

Physical concepts are free creations of the human mind, and are not, however it may seem, uniquely determined by the external world. In our endeavor to understand reality we are somewhat like a man trying to understand the mechanism of a closed watch. He sees the face and the moving hands, even hears its ticking, but he has no way of opening the case. If he is ingenious he may form some picture of a mechanism which could be responsible for all the things he observes, but he may never be quite sure his picture is the only one which could explain his observations. He will never be able to compare his picture with the real mechanism and he cannot even imagine the possibility or the meaning of such a comparison. But he certainly believes that, as his knowledge increases, his picture of reality will become simpler and simpler and will explain a wider and wider range of his sensuous impressions. He may also believe in the existence of the ideal limit of knowledge and that it is approached by the human mind. He may call this ideal limit the objective truth. (Einstein-Infeld, *Op. cit.*, 1938, p.31)

When James agreed that F. C. S. Schiller's term, "humanism," might be more appropriate than "pragmatism," he did so because "humanism" conveys the idea that our views of reality are not naked copies of the world. *All of our concepts and judgments bear traces of their human creation.* At the very least, this demands an effort to sort out ideas that are so metaphorical that they cannot mirror reality from ideas that we feel 'must fit reality.'

The following 'texts without comment' will suggest how immense is the task of analysis that this model-creating and testing-against-later-sensation model of 'science' demands. In every area, the first and most important question remains "What really exists?"

Texts Without Comment From the 'Soft' Sciences.

PERSONALITY. Personality is not purple! Nor is it red, yellow, blue, or pink, square, sweet, loud, or hard. It is not an it. Personality is an idea that caught on some time in the history of our language. No one ever saw it, smelled it, tasted it, heard it, or touched it. If someone tries to sell you some at $1.98 per pound, he ought to be locked up. If you buy some, you ought to be! It is not an it—it is an idea that caught on. It caught on because the idea of personality has helped men make sense out of their own behavior and the behavior of people around them. In some respects the concept of personality is like the concept of force in physics or valence in chemistry. In the technical terminology of the philosophy of science these ideas, by definition unobservable, are called *hypothetical constructs*. These constructs—like force, valence, gravity, personality—help us make sense out of our world. They help us understand the myriads of events constantly occurring about us. These constructs enable us to bring some order and simplicity to the fantastic complexity the environment constantly presents to our millions upon millions of sense receptors. (M. Doherty & K. Shemberg, *Asking Questions About Behavior: An Introduction to What Psychologists Do*, p.7)

WHAT IS A THEORY? Just as everyone knows what a personality consists of, so everyone knows what a theory is! The most common conception is that a theory exists in opposition to a fact. A theory is an unsubstantiated hypothesis or a speculation concerning reality which is not yet definitely known to be so. When the theory is confirmed it becomes a fact. There is a grain of correspondence between this view and the usage we will advocate here for it is agreed that theories are not known to be true. There is also an element of disagreement as the commonsense view asserts that a theory will become true or factual when the appropriate data have been collected if these data are confirmatory. In our view, theories are never true or false although their implications or derivations may be either. (C. Hall & G. Lindzey, *Theories of Personality*, Ch. One)

A current view of the relation of individual to society, shared by most social psychologists of both psychological and sociological backgrounds, can be summarized as follows. Both individuals and societies are *constructs*, not realities, in a metaphysical sense (just as atoms, molecules, and gravity are only constructs), but both are *real* in the sense that they have observable effects. Furthermore, individuals and societies are *interdependent*. Individual behavior is partly a function of biological and physiological factors, partly a function of social experience. Society is *generated* by interactions and relationships between individuals, but has stability and continuity over time independent of any particular individuals. Society is the *pattern* of its parts, though that pattern is far more complex than a simple summation of properties of the individuals who populate a given society at a given time. We will refer to this issue again when we deal with groups in Part Three. (J. E. McGrath, *Social Psychology: A Brief Introduction*, 1965, p.16)

I have said "culture channels biological processes." It is more accurate to say "the biological functioning of individuals is modified if they have been trained in certain ways and not in others." Culture is not a disembodied force. It is created and transmitted by people. However, culture, like well-known concepts of the physical sciences, is a convenient abstraction. One never sees gravity. One sees bodies falling in regular ways. One never sees an electromagnetic field. Yet certain happenings that can be seen may be given a neat abstract formulation by assuming that the electromagnetic field exists. Similarly, one never sees culture as such. What is seen are regularities in the behavior or artifacts of a group that has adhered to a common tradition. The regularities in style and technique of ancient Inca tapestries or stone axes from Melanesian islands are due to the existence of mental blueprints for the group. (C. Kluckhohn, *Mirror for Man*, 1944, p.28)

Reality. We wanted to know what exists and how we know about it. If Quine is right, what's really real? That question is meaningless, he says, even though our language makes us think it's not. "When a discovery is made and a (scientific) law is changed, we don't say that the truth has changed—that it used to be true and now it's not. We say we thought it was true and it wasn't" . . .

"If somehow, as people might imagine, the veil was lifted from reality and we could see what the world was really like and how does it match up—that, to me, is meaningless," he said. "'Real' and 'object' and 'thing,' these terms don't mean anything except as part of this network of concepts and the only source of objectivity of all that is the checkpoints." (Associated Press, "Philosopher delves into mysteries of science," an article about Harvard's W. V. Quine, in *Sunday Telegram*, 9-10-95, p.B13)

If we use "reality" to refer to things that exist, period!, and "fiction" to refer to (real) thoughts about things that do not exist, then we must ask the question, "Who knows what she or he is talking about?" Unless we decide correctly which of the 'things' we talk about is which, we cannot claim to know what kind of thing we are talking about. This, in Russell's opinion, is the situation with pure mathematics.

Pure mathematics consists entirely of assertions to the effect that, if such and such a proposition is true of *any*thing, then such and such another proposition is true of that thing. It is essential not to discuss whether the first proposition is really true, and not to mention what the anything is, of which it is supposed to be true. Both these points would belong to applied mathematics. . . *If* our hypothesis is about anything, and not about some one or more particular things, then our deductions constitute mathematics. Thus mathematics may be defined as the subject in which we never know what we are talking about, nor whether what we are saying is true. (B. Russell, "Mathematics and the Metaphysician," sec.1)

Russell's idea can be extended almost indefinitely.

The view that we do not know what we are talking about when we speak of intelligence is unfortunate not only because it is not true by any comparative standards—actually we know more about intelligence than we do about any other mental function—but because it has nurtured a confusing pessimism and a profitless kind of account taking which almost completely misses the issue at hand. The issue is not, as is commonly supposed, the lack of agreement by psychologists on a standard definition of intelligence. If this were so, the problem might conceivably be resolved by an international convention, as has been done by physicists in defining various units of measurement. Unfortunately, the problem with which psychologists are concerned in defining intelligence is quite different from that which the physicist deals with when he defines amperes, farads and watts, or the biologist when he classifies living things as plants and animals. The difficulty is similar to what the physicist encounters when asked to state what he means by time or energy, or the biologist what he means by life. The fact is that energy and life are not tangible entities but limiting constructs. You cannot touch them or see them under a microscope even though you are able to describe them. We know them by their effects or properties. The same is true of general intelligence. It is not a material fact but an abstract construct. What we can reasonably expect of any attempt at a definition is only a sufficiently clear and broad connotation as to what it comprehends. Mind you, not what it is but what it involves and eventually, what it distinguishes. (D. Wechsler, *The Measurement and Appraisal of Adult Intelligence*, 4th ed., 1958, p.4)

First, then, What is the historical fact? Let us take a simple fact, as simple as the historian often deals with, viz.: "In the year 49 B. C. Caesar crossed the Rubicon." A familiar fact this is, known to all, and obviously of some importance since it is mentioned in every history of the great Caesar. But is this fact as simple as it sounds? Has it the clear, persistent outline which we commonly attribute to simple historical facts? When we say that Caesar crossed the Rubicon we do not of course mean that Caesar crossed it alone, but with his army. The Rubicon is a small river, and I don't know how long it took Caesar's army to cross it; but the crossing must surely have been accompanied by many acts and many words and many thoughts of many men. That is to say, a thousand and one lesser "facts" went to make up the one simple fact that Caesar crossed the Rubicon; and if we had someone, say James Joyce, to know and relate all these facts, it would no doubt require a book of 794 pages to present this one fact that Caesar crossed the Rubicon. Thus the simple fact turns out to be not a simple fact at all. It is the statement that is simple—a simple generalization of a thousand and one facts. (C. L. Becker, "What Are Historical Facts?" sec.1)

Does anyone know what they are talking about? The question is important, because whoever does not know whether they are talking about real things or only about fictions they have created in their imagination doesn't. It is not enough to say what does not exist or to point out that this or that is a fiction. Is anyone willing to say she or he is certain that this or that does exist? Really exists? Was James so wrong in saying that everyone, from geologists to psychologists, must eventually go farther and 'do metaphysics'? In his special sense of metaphysics, of course.

Metaphysics means only an unusually obstinate attempt to think clearly and consistently. The special sciences all deal with data that are full of obscurity and contradiction; but from the point of view of their limited purposes these defects may be overlooked. Hence the disparaging use of the name metaphysics which is so common. To a man with a limited purpose any discussion that is over-subtle for that purpose is branded as 'metaphysical.' A geologist's purposes fall short of understanding Time itself. A mechanist need not know how action and reaction are possible at all. A psychologist has enough to do without asking how both he and the mind which he studies are able to take cognizance of the same outer world. But it is obvious that problems irrelevant from one standpoint may be essential from another. And as soon as one's purpose is the attainment of the maximum of possible insight into the world as a whole, the metaphysical puzzles become the most urgent ones of all. (PBC:457; *Writings* I:427)

Analyse Till Existents Are Reached. There are only three absolutely bottom-line questions. What exists? What do the existing things do? Why? (The third makes itself superfluous, inasmuch as answers to it will fit into the class of answers given to the first two.)

Only things exist. The blunder of the 'ordinary language school' of linguistic analysis was ignoring the fact that one's talk must fit one's thought, not vice-versa. When something nice shows up on our desk on March 17 with a note "From a local leprechaun," our belief that leprechauns do not exist compels us to search for an answer to the question, "Then how did it get on my desk?" Youngsters who believe the tag "From Santa" on a gift found under the Christmas tree will want to know the true source after they discover there is no Santa Claus. Why, then, are we satisfied when authors preface their textbooks with announcements that their theories are constructed around 'useful constructs,' and then fail to answer the question, "Useful for knowing *what real things*?"

When we come to realize that we are making use of 'useful fictions' or 'theoretical constructs,' we must make the 'metaphysical' effort to analyse those fictions or constructs till we reach the bedrock of something real. Pragmatic fictions are perfectly acceptable so long as they are unmasked as fictions and so long as the question "What (real things) are you using your fictions to talk about?" is faced.

For instance, Thomas Szasz has waged a long campaign to argue that "mental illness" names a myth. If the DSM-IV proves anything, it proves that he is right. "Mental illnesses" does not refer to self-existent entities. "DSM-IV" does not, either. When our eyes come to "mental illness" or "DSM-IV," our eyes come to a clue to a word-user's thought, and the thought will require dozens upon dozens of added clues or cues to 'define' what we call "the word" or "the phrase."

For most people, "DSM-IV" will mean nothing. "What is the DSM-IV?", they'll ask. We answer, "It is the fifth edition of *The Diagnostic and Statistical Manual.*" (The fourth was numbered "III-R.") Now do they know what we were thinking? If their mind was blank when they heard or saw "DSM-IV," the only new thing they will know is that 'it' stands for a manual-type book. Only if they inquire further—learn more—will they learn that some people have studied other people's abnormal experiences and/or behaviors and have tried to 'put order' into what they've learned by drawing up lists of shorthand 'names' for the mental groupings they have invented.

The most instructive argument for Szasz's view can be found in history books. Best of all is the long list of different lists created over the course of centuries that can be found in an appendix to Karl Menninger's *The Vital Balance.* When people are told "You have schizophrenia," they should not think "Thank God, now I know what I have!" What they 'know' is what some people call the group of 'symptoms' they (or others) have complained about. James's principle, "No one sees farther into a generalization than his knowledge of details extends," is the key to this and other category- or concept-creations.

This is not to say that there is pure 'nothing' behind the myth of mental illness. It is important to understand how indispensable logical, pragmatic fictions are. But we need to know what real, non-fictitious things they refer to. There are real people. Real people hear 'voices' when no one is nearby. Other real people feel prolonged, extreme anxiety that seems to have no ordinary explanation. Others are tormented by bizarre thoughts. As James argued, it is important to understand the causes of, and find remedies for, the troubling experiences that disrupt real people's lives.

We must learn about reifications (discussed in the pre-quel) and how to apply Ockham's Razor to them. Unless we are alert to the ease with which we convert verbs, adjectives, and adverbs into nouns, and then mis-take those nouns as names for things-that-exist, we will never realize how many non-existent things we talk about during a single day. We convert "You ran well today" into "You ran a good race today." Well, there may be race-tracks and racers, but once the racers are home in bed at night, there are no races left lying around somewhere. Until we get in the habit of looking for the nugget-of-fact 'behind' reifications, we will not know how to reason correctly. For instance, it would be silly to say "You didn't run a good race today," because we have concluded that races do not exist, hence can't be run. Just so, there are donuts, holes do not exist, but it would be wrong to simply say "Donuts have no holes," unless it is clear that the person to whom we are speaking knows that such an expression does not mean donuts look like jelly rolls. "Donuts are baked rings of dough but there is not anything in their middles" might be clearer so long as we are not taken to mean 'middles' exist. Workers at donut shops do not have to sweep up all the uneaten holes or middles along with the crumbs at the end of the day.

Full-length analyses may be so long that we lose patience trying to learn them. For instance, darkness does not exist, but "Darkness fell over the land" will not be misleading if we understand that what really happened is comparable to turning out lights. When we turn out lights, we do not incur added charges on our electric bill to pay for darkness to replace the light. There is still a room, just no light coming from the gases or filaments, hence no light reaching our eyes, hence no afferent impulses reaching our brain, hence no sense-data being created, hence no awareness of them. But our eyes are still open, and where a moment ago we (thought we) saw a lighted-up room, the room has just become dark or black, hence we 'project' and say we see darkness. (Caution points in both directions. Just because consciousness 'as an entity' does not exist, that does not mean we aren't conscious!) The lesson is that *we must be bold and make our talk fit our thought,* not vice-versa.

Because collective bodies of knowledge do not exist, Kuhn's notion of scientific revolutions is valuable only for gross generalizations. However, given our finite mental powers, we cannot know each human being's complex body of knowledge. We must generalize, in order to think simultaneously of similarities in the thinking of numerous individuals. The most helpful generalizations are the ones that capture a period's grand unifying theory. Since Descartes, the most important categories of unifying theories are materialism, idealism, and dualism. The most significant revolution in 'American philosophy' since James was born in 1842 was the revolt against idealism and the triumph of materialism. But even during that nineteenth-century, monist-idealist period, the dominant paradigm did not fit its greatest thinker.

The Final Word re "What Do I See?" The final word, the bottom line, the irrefutable conclusion—call it what you will—is this. We see things as they are. They are just not the things we grow up believing they are.

Appendix A. Color

A Question. Everyone should ponder deeply the question, "Which am I more certain of, the color of the sky on a clear day or the color of my own brain?"

Everyone, or at least every average college freshman, can understand that question. You can, can't you?

Directly related to that question is this: which of those two things have you ever seen? It should take 'pre-scientific' persons only a few seconds to grasp the implication of i) the fact that they have never seen the color of their own brain when contrasted with ii) the fact that they have seen the color of the sky on many clear days. Since they have never seen the color of their brain—because they have never seen their brain, period!—the implication is that they must search for some other reason why they think the color of their brain is gray.

What is most important about the preceding train of thought is how average college freshmen do not react to the original question. The average college freshmen never react by asking "What do you mean by 'color'?" They also do not ask "What do you mean by 'see'?", "What do you mean by 'the sky'?", or "What do you mean by 'brain'?"

That is because the average college freshman—and most of those all-purpose 'people on the street'—are blithely unaware of the far-reaching questions that the revolutionary Descartes and the heirs of his revolution raised. But they are not ignorant. Every last one of them has an incredibly complex philosophy, with an unimaginably complex framework constructed around those 'magisterial notions' which James made explicit during his fifth *Pragmatism* 'ode to common sense.'

A Danger. Unless we come to appreciate common sense the way

James did only during the last decade of his life, it is unlikely that we will appreciate what he was referring to when he wrote about secondary qualities, beginning with color. I speak from first-hand experience when I say that it is easy to amend common sense by simply redefining "color" to mean "light (frequencies or wavelengths)," "light-absorbing and light-reflecting properties," or "brain processes," then redefining "see" so that it refers to events in the retinas or the brain, and so on.

The result of such redefining is a lapse into what James called "privative definitions," a topic discussed earlier in this chapter.

Why is it necessary to 'make a big deal' of this danger? The answer is easy. Unless the danger is seen and avoided, it is difficult if not impossible to grasp fully what Berkeley realized and what James fought for. Above all, it becomes difficult to take seriously what Descartes came to understand:

> If there are finally any persons who are not sufficiently persuaded of the existence of God and of their soul by the reasons which I have brought forward, I wish that they should know that all other things of which they perhaps think themselves more assured (such as possessing a body, and that there are stars and an earth and so on) are less certain. (*Discourse on Method*, Pt. IV; H-R I:104)

More on this in a moment. But first . . .

Everyday Switches in the Meaning of "Color." Insistence on the variety of meanings that any given 'word' can bear is one of the pillars of this reconstruction of the scaffolding needed to support James's best insights. That insistence extends to far more than the vague names experts use for their esoteric philosophies. It reaches down to the most basic of all the terms we use in our familiar, everyday lives. "Color" is one of those most basic terms. But "color" is a general term. That is, it is mental shorthand used to think-together many distinct ideas for distinct items.

Congenitally blind people can use it as shorthand for "the quality X which non-blind people experience in connection with things that have a particular felt shape, felt size, tasted flavor, heard 'plop' sound (when dropped onto a floor), etc.," or as shorthand for "the quality X which non-blind people experience in connection with an unripe apple, i.e., with things that have a particular felt shape, felt size, tart flavor, crisp 'crunching' sound (when teeth sink into it), etc.," as well as for "the quality X non-blind people are assumed by us to 'see,' even though in our own inner model 'color' is like an empty place-marker that stands for 'something, we know not what'."

That is, blind people's concept of 'color' is similar to what Locke said our concepts of 'substance' are like. Begin with our one-space inner model of the outer world. Name the items in that inner model. Then, insert an X for an item that can only be de-fined in relation to the other items in that model. That is why the blind can learn to use specific color terms: "orange" for things with a certain taste, "blue" for sunny, warm-day skies, and so on. They mimic the word-use of those able to see.

But *how non-uniform is sighted, non-blind people's use of the specific names* for color! Children know that "white" is the name for the color of the paper before any colored crayons are applied, hence "white" is the name for the absence of (other) colors. They also know that black can be created either with a black crayon or by applying all the crayons except the black, hence "black" is the name for the combination of all the colors (except black). Physicists, though, say that white is the combination of all the colors before the prism breaks them up, whereas black is the absence of color. Those who go to movies do not regard black-and-white films as being 'in color,' though black, white, and the grays in between are the only colors some color-blind people ever experience.

Even more fascinating is the fact that there are wide variations in the ways different 'cultures' count colors. D. Brown, in *Human Universals*, notes that some peoples employ just two words for the colors they see, whereas others use eleven (p.13). Would anyone say those peoples' eyes, optic nerves, and brains operate differently, or that their children—if adopted and raised in another culture—would be unable to experience 'all the colors'? Before answering, consider the story Harvard anthropologist Clyde Kluckhohn told, relating to the lack of universal correlations between names, concepts, and experienced colors:

[. . .] Each culture dissects nature according to its own system of categories. The Navaho Indians apply the same word to the color of a robin's egg and to that of grass. A psychologist once assumed that this meant a difference in the sense organs, that Navahos didn't have the physiological equipment to distinguish "green" from "blue." However, when he showed them objects of the two colors and asked them if they were exactly the same colors, they looked at him with astonishment. His dream of discovering a new type of color blindness was shattered. (C. Kluckhohn, *Mirror for Man*, p.30)

We are fortunate to be living after the century during which the 'linguistic turn' took place. The library additions, contributed by those who devoted years to examining language from every imaginable angle, are of enormous value in showing that everyone who appeals to 'language' as evidence for any belief at all is appealing to a fiction.

Back now to the color of one's own brain.

Appendix B. James and "the Brain."

"The Brain" was Important for James. Or was it the brain, not "the brain." What *is* the difference? Is it important?

It is difficult to think of anything that is more important for understanding James than the difference between the brain and "the brain." The difference is '1st Grade' common sense. It is the difference between i) a physical thing inside one's dark-prison skull and ii) an English word for the idea of that physical thing.

The difference can be generalized as follows. i) There are things that exist in complete independence of me. I call them "Realities." ii) There are the ideas or thoughts I have acquired about those things, and these ideas or thoughts depend on me. I label them ideas and thoughts collectively as "thought." iii) There are my English *names* for those things. I group the names under the heading, "language."

James used the word "brain" thousands of times. He thought that whatever it was he was referring to was so important that he made the following claim: "The nature and hidden causes of ideas will never be unraveled til the *nexus* between the brain and consciousness is cleared up." (PP II:6) It was precisely that *nexus* that, for James, was the target of 'psychology as a natural science':

Not that to-day we have a "science" of the correlation of mental states with brain states; but that the ascertainment of the laws of such correlation forms the programme of a science well limited and defined. (W. James, "A Plea for Psychology as a Natural Science," in CER:324)

Section 1 of this chapter explained James's contradictory views about the brain, consciousness, and the relation between them. A major reason for his contradictory views is that he used the term "brain" to mean four different things at different times. *Meaning #1*: the common-sense idea of a perduring unit-subject, namely, the biological organ resting between our ears. *Meaning #2*: a pragmatic fiction referring collectively to separate unit-subject neurons or atomic particles. *Meaning #3*: the 'critical philosophy' idea of a group of sense-qualities in a single, continuous stream of consciousness, united by the law of association. *Meaning #4*: the ambiguous, radical-empiricist idea of a group of sense-qualities that can be 'taken' i) in the context of all the sense-qualities which we say make up the duration of an individual's stream of pure conscious experience or ii) in the context of all the sense-qualities that we can say make up many (physical) 'things.' (For the last meaning, see "The Tigers in India" in *The Meaning of Truth*, in *Writings* II:852ff, extracted from "The Knowing of Things Together," in CER:371ff and in *Writings* I:1057ff. For more detail on all four, see "What Did James Mean by 'the Brain'?", in *Streams of William James*, Vol. 6, pp.1-6)

The full story of James's years-long indecisiveness about what was the 'truer' meaning of "the brain" can only be had from a detailed study of W. James, *Manuscript Lectures* and W. James, *Manuscript Essays and Notes*, collections of James's unpublished manuscripts now published by Harvard University Press. The best, one-sentence description of his most fundamental indecisiveness is found in a note he wrote on Friday, April 15, for his 1897-98 course, "Philosophical Problems of Psychology."

Does n't it seem like the wrigglings of a worm on the hook, this attempt to escape the dualism of common sense? And is not the contrast I have been forcibly led to between the brain terminatively or entitatively considered and the brain "in the field" (= the brain *representatively* considered) indistinguishable from the common sense contrast between the objective brain and the brain-thought of? It looks so. Let me, then, try some one of the other problems for better luck! (Perry II:369-70; ML 247-48)

The difference is simple. The objective brain would be like a real Santa running a year-round toy factory at the North Pole. The brain-only-thought-of is like the more usual Santa-thought-of.

James never ceased his wrigglings. While he was writing the third last paragraph of his never-finished *Some Problems of Philosophy*, he was still wriggling about the brain (whatever it is):

Perception has given us a positive idea of causal agency but it remains to be ascertained whether what first appears as such, is really such; whether aught else is really such; or finally, whether nothing really such exists. Since with this we are led immediately into the mind-brain relation, and since that is such a complicated topic, we had better interrupt our study of causation provisionally at the present point, meaning to complete it when the problem of the mind's relation to the body come up for review. (*Writings* II:1093)

CHAPTER II

Images, Too, Are Things!

(Like Sense-Data and Thoughts)

"Everyone knows the difference between imagining a thing and believing in its existence, between supposing a proposition and acquiescing in its truth." (W. James, *Principles of Psychology* II:283)

1. Faiths and 'Worlds'

A Christian's Faith. Centuries ago, Christian leaders decided that it would be helpful to the faithful if each of the basic truths of their tradition were stated briefly and strung together. Each Christian could then memorize the list of basic truths and, on occasion, recite them in the proper sequence. One such list is the following. It is called "the Apostles' Creed."

> I believe in God the Father Almighty, Creator of heaven and earth. And in Jesus Christ, His only Son, our Lord, who was conceived by the Holy Spirit, born of the virgin Mary, suffered under Pontius Pilate, was crucified, died, and was buried. He descended into hell, the third day He arose again from the dead. He ascended into heaven, sits at the right hand of God the Father Almighty. From thence he shall come to judge the living and the dead. I believe in the Holy Spirit, the Holy Catholic Church, the communion of saints, the forgiveness of sins, the resurrection of the body, and life everlasting. Amen.

From the beginning, questions have been raised about those claims, but the majority of the faithful seem content to take what they hear in church 'on faith.' What believer, for instance, would claim to have 'scientific proof' that Jesus Christ was not only an historical person executed before he was fifty years old, but also a divine being existing from all eternity? Or to have 'scientific proof' that this human-divine being once descended into hell*, is this very moment sitting at the Father's right hand, where he will remain till judgment day at the end of the world? Or to have 'scientific proof' that their own body will

119

someday be resurrected and restored to them? And so on? (*In this context, "hell" does not refer to a place of eternal punishment, but to Limbo, a place where good people had to wait till Jesus Christ redeemed the human race, thereby opening the gates of heavenly paradise for them. Christian theologians have recently concluded that Limbo does not exist.)

The Faith of Naïve-Realist Materialists. Naïve-realist materialists are those who do not realize what the preceding chapter explained, namely, that naïve realism leads to physics and neurophysiology, which, if true, show that naïve realism is not merely naïve, but partly false.

The articles of their faith can be listed as follows.

I believe in my own brain which I cannot see or touch and which probably has never been seen or touched by anyone else. I believe that I have seen and felt some parts of my body, e.g., my legs, torso, arms, the tip of my tongue (when I stick it out), and (vaguely) the sides of my nose. I believe I have seen distant stars and the moon in the night sky, the sun and clouds in the day sky, as well as dogs, cats, and the outsides of other people's bodies down here on the ground. Besides my own brain which I have never seen or touched, I believe in many other things I have never seen or touched: dogs', cats', and other humans' feelings, conscious desires, and thoughts. I believe Galileo, Newton, Darwin, and Freud really existed. Finally, I believe in imagination, which Einstein reputedly said is essential for anyone who aspires to be a scientist. Amen.

But "Faith" Means Many Things. There are many ideas that the word "faith" is said to mean. In front of me, for instance, is a recent anthology entitled *Faith and Reason*. In its 350 pages, plus a 10-page introduction, there are 28 essays whose authors tell what they take "faith" to mean. They don't agree.

When thinkers use the word "faith," they clearly mean different things. At times, "faith" is 'the' faith, that is, the *body of truths* to which 'religious' believers give their assent. Because people belong to different religions, "the faith" will in fact be used to refer to very different bodies of alleged truths. At other times, the word may be used for the deliberate *act* by which believers assent to this or that body of alleged truths. At still other times, it is used casually to mean something vaguely conceived of as the opposite of whatever "reason" vaguely refers to, for instance, *a different 'method' of learning truth*, different from the 'scientific' one.

A Stipulative Definition of Faith for this Text. The claim *in this text* will use "faith" in roughly the second sense. It will refer to an act on the part of an individual person who is in the habit of believing that such-and-such is 'a fact,' but *without having any conclusive evidence* for the 'fact' which may, in fact, not be a fact at all.

When a person, for instance, a juror, has deliberately weighed the evidence for and against a 'guilty' verdict, that is, a thought, and when that juror assents to it even though acknowledging that the evidence is not 100% conclusive (that is, the person is only 'morally certain' of the prisoner's guilt), that juror will be said to assent to the thought with *faith*. More briefly, *faith is assenting to a thought when the assenting person's evidence for it is less than conclusive*. It is thus perfectly possible that one person takes 'on faith' what someone else has conclusive evidence for. St. Thomas, for instance, thought that an expert can be certain that God exists, even though most people take God's existence only on faith.

The preceding chapter has referred to the evidence for this text's claim that, if anyone assents to the 'naïve-realist materialists'' list of thoughts, they are actually taking the truth of those thoughts on faith, whether they realize it or not.

Psychology is Based on Faith. Why begin this chapter with faith? Because James, by meticulous reasoning from the evidence presented in the preceding chapter, reached the conclusion that all hoped-for scientific psychology is based on personal, individual, subjective acts of *faith*. He told an 1884 audience, "'Reality' has become our warrant for calling a feeling [or thought] cognitive; but what becomes our warrant for calling anything reality? The only reply is—the faith of the present critic or inquirer." (*Writings* II:835) If true, every claim about any stream of consciousness except one's own is accepted on *faith*.

What James had in mind is complex. He meant that the only genuinely 'cognitive' mental states—that is, the ones we are *justified* in calling "cognitive"—are mental states that actually put us in touch with reality. But people disagree about reality. Each one assumes that what they, but not everyone else, are in touch with is reality and not fiction, which raises the question: "What determines whose mental states are genuinely 'cognitive' and whose are not?" After wrestling with that question for some time, James threw up his hands and concluded that each person is, willy-nilly, *relying on their own faith* when they decide that this or that belief of theirs is truly 'cognitive' of reality!

That version of James's conclusion is found in a relatively early 1884 lecture, "The Function of Cognition." But an even earlier version was part of a never-used draft for a chapter of *The Principles*. (That draft will be discussed later.) Somewhat reworded, the draft eventually became a major part of the 1890 text's Chapter XXI, entitled "The Perception of Reality. "

"Belief," in fact, is the title of the first section of that all-important Chapter XXI. It includes a brilliant treatment of what James refers to as "The Many Worlds," which worlds or 'worlds' are created by different people's different faiths. *Different faiths, different 'worlds.'* For Christians, the reality of God, heaven, immortal souls, etc., are or *feel* entirely real. For naïve realists, stars, the moon, the sun, their own two hands and brain are or *feel* obviously real. But . . .

Which of those two opening credo's is the true one? Whose 'world' truly correlates with reality and whose is a product of imagination? How is anyone in quest of certainty to decide? In other words, how is anyone to decide what is real and what is only a figment of imagination?

At least in several places, James's answer was, "faith." That is the reason for beginning this important chapter with those sample 'creeds.'

2. Reason #1 re "Why Everyone Needs an Imagination."

There Are Three Reasons Why . . . *everyone* in quest of certain truth needs a good imagination. It is needed i) to improve our outside-vs-inside model, ii) to create an accurate model of physical realities, and iii) to create the right model for the stream of consciousness. In other words, everyone in pursuit of wisdom needs an imagination because i) it is the only way to accurately understand in-the-mind vs outside-the-mind, ii) it is the only way to discover what the physical world is like, if, that is, a physical world exists, iii) it is the only way to discover what the immaterial stream of consciousness is like.

But Wait. What Does "Imagination" Mean? Before discussing the three reasons why imagination is vitally important, it helps to know what the term means.

Here is James's answer to the question, "What does imagination mean?" His answer constitutes one of the most important premises for all of his writing. It comes in the very first paragraph of Chapter XXI:

> Everyone knows the difference between imagining a thing and believing in its existence, between supposing a proposition and acquiescing in its truth. In the case of acquiescence or belief, the object is not only apprehended by the mind, but is held to have reality. Belief is thus the mental state or function of cognizing reality. (PP II:283)

"Everybody knows . . ." We begin then with the assumption that, however we wish to explain it, we already have the idea of imagining or imagination. Just to confirm that assumption, pause and consider some of the things you might hear in day-to-day discourse. "Can you imagine spending your life in solitary confinement?" "Picture this: *she* proposed to *him!*" "Just think what it would be like to win a million dollars in the lottery." "As soon as you say 'mind,' neuropsychologists invariably conjure up their idea of a brain." "He spends half his time daydreaming about surfing."

Pause for a few moments to see how many *similar* 'things you might hear' you can think of. Do take a few moments to do it, because that type of 'pausing' is the only way to test whether or not the chapters of this book tell the truth or not.

"Everyone Knows the Difference . . ." Pause next to ask a few questions. While you were reading that series of 'things you might hear,' were you able to understand them? Or did you keep worrying, "Am I able to understand such things?" Would you have to 'go back' and reread those sentences in order to be *certain* you understood them? To understand James, you will have to get in the habit of asking, "Do I really understand this?"

There's something else you'll have to do. Look back at those sentences and ask another question: Did you *notice* the difference in the verbs? Here they are again: picture, imagine, conjure up, think, and daydream.

Now see whether you can understand the following sentences. "Can you picture spending your life in solitary confinement?" "Imagine! *She* proposed to *him!*" "Try to conjure in your mind what it would be like to win a million dollars in the lottery." "As soon as you say 'mind,' neuropsychologists invariably think of the brain." "He spends half the day dreaming about surfing."

Now, *without looking back*, pause again and ask whether the second series of 'things' was the same as the first. (The great advantage of books over lectures is that the different things we read are fixed. We can see both and compare them. Without tape recorders, we have to rely on our memory of different things we've heard.) If, without looking back, you paused and tried to remember whether those two series of 'things you might hear' were similar, were you able to decide whether or not they were?

Why is the question about 'sameness' vitally important? The answer will help you understand the difference between a positive attitude of trying to 'get inside someone's mind' to catch on to their 'vision' and a negative attitude of trying to find where they were wrong. Recall the passage from *Pluralistic Universe* cited in Chapter I:

> Place yourself similarly at the centre of a man's philosophic vision and you understand at once all the different things it makes him write or say. But keep outside, use your post-mortem method, try to build the philosophy up out of the single phrases, taking first one and then another and seeking to make them fit 'logically,' and of course you fail. (*Writings* II:750-51)

Here is the answer regarding the sameness. If you look back, you will see that the verbs have all been switched.

You now have *a crucial decision* to make. Did the switch in verbs make any really important difference in the thoughts conjured by "those crabbed little black marks" (PP I:132) we call "sentences"? The contention here is that we often use a variety of 'words,' 'names,' 'terms,' or what have you, to mean the same thing, i.e., to convey the same thought. Often, though. Not always!

We often use different words for the same idea, just for the sake of variety. Plato understood the difference. (*Theatetus* 184C) At times, he switched terms in order to make certain the imaginations of his readers would not get so fixated on words that they would fail to grasp the lofty thoughts he was trying to 'convey.'

Still, it is imperative that, when it is crucial, we use names, words, terms, etc., with a consistency that will help convey the consistency in our ideas. In the seventh *Pragmatism* lecture, James noted: "Names are arbitrary, but once understood they must be kept to. We mustn't now call Abel 'Cain' or Cain 'Abel'." (*Writings* II:579)

Inconsistency or Variety? How can we distinguish *inconsistency* from simple *variety*? Each of us must decide for ourself. We form our own faith vis-à-vis others' mindset and/or mindsets, vis-à-vis which mindset they are using, etc. By now, it should be clear that such is the only way to read James, sort out his true insights from the false turns, and see how the true insights fit together.

In the context of this and the next chapter, it will be essential i) to give your imagination free rein, while at the same time ii) being able at any moment to bring it under the control of your most basic convictions about what-exists, i.e., reality.

Connect that Difference to Truth vs Falsity. James claimed that everyone knows the difference between imagining and believing. Is that true? Did primitive people know the difference? Do children?

The only way to decide whether James is right is to think hard about our implicit or tacit 'sense' of truth versus falsity. Children old enough to understand "You should always tell the truth," the opposite of "You must never lie," must have a 'sense' of the difference. Very young children learn what 'stories' are. They learn that "Once upon a time" often introduces a train of thought about people who never existed and events that never happened. Johny, who believes in Santa Claus, immediately rejects Susie's taunt, "There's no Santa Claus!", even though he's never learned about 'contradictory propositions' in a logic course. In fact, logic courses simply 'put into so many words' what five- and six-year-olds already understand implicitly or tacitly. Even the 'technical' terms, "tacit" and "implicit," are generalizations that capture explicitly certain tacit features of everyday thinking or common sense.

Does anyone believe that ancient, aborigine people did not know what lying, deception, mistakes, and/or false appearances were? Why, then, would they include such factors in their legends and myths?

We can generalize, then. We can think of imagining as 'pretending that something is true which the pretenders *believe* is false.'

Never Confuse Language, Thought, and Reality. If you find that, with a bit of effort, you can understand the preceding paragraphs, it is because you have at least a tacit sense of the difference between words (language), thoughts (beliefs), and reality (whatever exists, period!, i.e., regardless of what anyone believes and regardless of whether anyone believes anything at all).

First, *language* is not the same as thought. It is estimated that between 3,000 and 10,000 languages are spoken in 2009. If people whose language is English can understand what French speakers say (or write), then it is logical to assume that people who speak different languages can think similar thoughts. An even more obvious proof that language is distinct from thoughts is the fact that some people speak two or more languages fluently. Does anyone believe that someone who is Catholic while they speak English becomes an atheist as soon as they switch, say, to Russian?!

Second, *thought*. If—contrary to the desperate attempts by twentieth-century thinkers to replace theories about invisible and intangible thoughts with theories about language—people who speak different languages can express similar thoughts with different words, then it is crucial to get into the habit of never confusing what people think with the way they try to 'put it into words.'

Finally, *reality*. Everyone who can understand contradictory thoughts at the same time, e.g., the thoughts expressed by "These are words you are seeing" and "These are not words you are seeing," can also understand that the things you see are real, i.e., exist, but cannot really *be* words and really *not be* words at the same time, at least not as long as the word "word" refers to the same, seen existents. That is, the *thoughts* are contradictory, but *what is seen* is whatever it is, period! It exists, at least as long as it is being seen. In the seventh *Pragmatism* lecture, James said of sense-data "*They* are neither true nor false; they simply *are*. It is only what we say about them, only the names we give them, our theories of their source and nature and remote relations, that

126

may be true or not." (*Writings* II:593) What is is, regardless of how we think about it, regardless of whether we think about it. (Infants see things long before they have any thoughts about them.)

"Reality," then, is best defined for our purposes as "whatever exists, period!, regardless of *what* any human thinks about it and regardless of *whether* any human thinks anything at all."

Once we have learned to 'get behind' the words, names, terms, etc., in order to capture the word-user's thought, we can practice doing it. To show that you already can do it was the motive for the two lists of 'things you might hear.'

Watch now, to see how important it is to *never confuse words and thoughts.*

Descartes: An Invitation to Pretend! That is, to imagine. Descartes was criticized by some contemporaries for beginning his great masterpiece, *Meditations on First Philosophy*, by attempting to doubt everything he believed. How, they asked, could "I think, therefore I exist" be the very first thing he could be certain of? He could never have been certain that "I am thinking" is true, if he wasn't certain first of all that he knew what "thinking" meant. And, other critics added, if he couldn't first of all prove what "I" referred to?

The solution, once it is fully realized, is simple. No one can begin to question the truth of any thought who does not already have that complex foundation for all 'higher' or 'later' learning, namely, the broad common-sense philosophy described in *William James on Common Sense*. Despite the lateness of his full appreciation of the fact that all later theories are 'grafted' onto common sense, James relied on common sense. That is what he was doing when he opened Chapter XXI with his bold assertion, "Everyone knows the difference between imagining a thing and believing in its existence . . ." (PP II:283)

If this were a book about Descartes, it would be easy to show that, like James, he was relying on common sense. He tacitly appealed to it in his argument to show that "I am thinking, so I must also be existing" is a judgment that cannot possibly be false. Does any sane person believe they could think even if they didn't exist?! Here is Principle X of his *Principles of Philosophy.*

That conceptions which are perfectly simple and clear of themselves are obscured by the definitions of the Schools, and that they are not to be numbered as amongst those capable of being acquired by study [but are inborn in us]. (R. Descartes, *Philosophical Works of Descartes*, trans. H-R, I:222)

Descartes outlined his argument in Part IV of his *Discourse on Method*. Here are a few lines from it.

I do not know that I ought to tell you of the first meditations there made by me, for they are so metaphysical and so unusual that they may perhaps not be acceptable to everyone. And yet at the same time in order that one may judge whether the foundations which I have laid are sufficiently secure, I find myself constrained in some measure to refer to them. . . Because in this case I wished to give myself entirely to the search after Truth, I thought that it was necessary for me to . . . reject as absolutely false everything as to which I could imagine the least ground of doubt, in order to see if afterwards there remained anything in my belief that was entirely certain. Thus, because our senses sometimes deceive us, I wished to suppose that nothing is just as they cause us to imagine it to be. . .

And then, examining attentively that which I was, I saw that I could conceive that I had no body, and that there was no world nor place where I might be; but yet that I could not for all that conceive that I was not. (H-R, I:101)

That is an English translation of Descartes' original French. Examine the sentence, "Thus, because our senses sometimes deceive us, I wished to suppose that nothing is just as they cause us to imagine." Another translator wrote: ". . . I decided to assume that nothing in the world was such as they presented it to me." A third translator wrote: ". . . I decided to suppose that nothing was such as they led us to imagine." A fourth wrote: ". . . I wanted to suppose that nothing was exactly as they led us to imagine." *Do all four sets of 'words' represent the same thought?*

As for ". . . I saw that I could conceive that I had no body," Descartes' thought is translated by ". . . and seeing that I could pretend I had no body," and by two exactly alike formulas: ". . . I saw that while I could pretend that I had no body." You be the judge of *whether or not those 'words' all represent the same judgment.* (Can thought, judgment, opinion, and belief be used to mean the same thing?)

Be clear about it: Descartes' *Meditation One* is an invitation to naïve readers to pretend that what they *believe* or *are convinced* is false is actually true! As long as normal learners continue to acquire an unimaginably complex common-sense philosophy during their first five or six years of life, cultured despisers of Descartes will be wasting their time trying to prove that his whole approach was false. False?

Does the preceding help to grasp the difference between Descartes' thoughts and his words? And anyone else's?

Mindset-Philosophies as Words' Context. To decide which of a word's possible meanings is the one being used, we must attend to the context. All students *are* taught this rule. Unfortunately, they are *not* taught that the context is not words, but the word-user's *philosophy or mindset.*

What creates the most difficulty regarding context is that, in the case of Descartes, Kant, James, and Einstein, all four had at least two philosophy-mindsets, and they systematically switched from one to the other and back again. To understand them, to 'get inside their minds,' it is necessary to learn more than one belief-system for each of the four.

And, to learn the different mindsets, nothing is more necessary than imagination. If James was right about 'different faiths, different worlds,' then it will require imagination to learn about other people's—Descartes', etc.—faiths and worlds.

Only after learning others' contradictory faiths can we then decide for ourselves which is true. Or which is *partly* true and *partly* false.

"True" vis-à-vis Rival Systems of Beliefs. That is, vis-à-vis rival philosophies. The common-sense notion of truth is easily stated: "A thought is true if it matches or corresponds to reality, i.e., to what exists, period!"

But there are no *isolated* thoughts. Every thought is part of an overall system of thoughts. As noted, however, systems of beliefs can be radically different. E.g., James's common-sense philosophy is radically different, in part, from his radical-empiricist worldview. That is the reason why "The brain is a thing" is 100% ambiguous when James writes it, because it can mean utterly different things, depending on which mindset is serving as the context for his thought at any given moment.

That fact makes the term "true" ambiguous, so long as we focus only on words and ask, for example, "Is 'The brain is a thing?' true?"

It can only be true if it is 'taken' as part of a belief-system whose fundamental premises are true. Vis-à-vis the last chapter, it is false if it is understood common-sensically, i.e., if "brain" refers to a permanent unit-subject *and* if no physical bodies larger than subatomic particles (James's "corpuscles" or "molecules") exist.

That ambiguity must be confronted *every time* James uses the word "truth." In his fifth *Pragmatism* lecture, he explains the difference between common sense, science*, and critical philosophy. (*Careful reading will show that he uses "science" for two different theories.) After explaining that common sense has been blown out of the water by science and critical philosophy, he ends the lecture by asking his audience to 'pretend' or 'imagine' that the common-sense notion of "truth" is not the only one.

> Ought not the existence of various types of thinking which we have reviewed, each so splendid for certain purposes, yet all conflicting still, . . . suggest this pragmatistic view, which I hope that the next lectures may soon make entirely convincing. May there not after all be a possible ambiguity in truth? (Writings II:571)

The situation today is truly chaotic. After Descartes, numerous new belief-systems or worldviews or philosophies were constructed. As a result, every 'word,' even in one language, e.g., English, has been infected with ambiguity. "Language," "thought," and "reality" are among the chief casualties. The word "true" is another. As a consequence, the system-builders have had to propose their own *tests* or *criteria* for their own special meaning of "truth." The breadth of James's knowledge of rival philosophies is nowhere better revealed than in his list of tests in his most famous essay, "The Will to Believe."

> No concrete test of what is really true has ever been agreed upon. Some make the criterion external to the moment of perception, putting it either in revelation, the *consensus gentium*, the instincts of the heart, or the systematized experience of the race. Others make the perceptive moment its own test,—Descartes, for instance, with his clear and distinct ideas guaranteed by the veracity of God; Reid with his 'common-sense;' and Kant with his forms of synthetic judgement *a priori*. The inconceivability of the opposite; the capacity to be verified by sense; the possession of complete organic unity or self-relation, realized when a thing is its own other,—are standards which, in turn, have been used. The much lauded objective evidence is never triumphantly there; it is a mere aspiration or *Grenzbegriff*, marking the infinitely remote ideal of our thinking life. (WB:15-6; *Writings* I:467)

Anytime we ignore the believer's total belief-system which is the particular belief's context, we ignore a major component of any 'test' for that belief's truth. Thoughts or propositions must be evaluated in the context of a system, not in isolation. That is why James was so right to focus on rival systems. They are integral to James's view of human freedom. Mature thinkers freely choose which thoughts they will select to be part of their own unique system. That system will 'constitute' reality for them. We create our 'worlds,' meaning we choose our 'truths.' Freely.

Return Now to Reason #1. Reason #1 for why everyone in pursuit of wisdom needs a good imagination is 'to improve their outside-vs-inside model of the entire cosmos.' Stripped of ambiguity, it is clear that Descartes, Kant, and James all concluded that the only evidence any of us have regarding what is *outside* of or out beyond our own private stream of consciousness or field of experience must be found *inside* that private stream or field. You have thoughts about things outside your private stream of consciousness, but what seem to be the things themselves are themselves a major part of your inner, private stream of consciousness!

You needed all the imagination you could muster to i) understand that conclusion of Chapter I, and you'll need even more imagination to ii) get in the habit of testing and eventually believing it. Imagination was required to grasp the conclusion of Chapter I because it is the only way to correctly distinguish in-the-mind from outside-the-mind, namely, by taking seriously the question at the core of that chapter, namely, "Is what I see and touch a *private*, virtual-reality 'world' and not a *public* world of physical, permanent subject-unit things, such as stars, the moon, sun, my two hands, and so on?"

We open our eyes (it seems), and reality is right there in front of us (it seems). True, our *thoughts* about what is 'right there' are inside us. *They* depend on us. We have some control over *them*. But we have no such control over what is—seems to be—outside of us, on the other side of our eyes. But James, ninety percent of the time, agreed with Berkeley. What seems to be outside, on the other side of our eyes, is really as much inside us as our *thoughts* are! So, too, are the sense-data we mis-interpret as our eyes.

It is at this juncture that naïve realists need imagination the most. To 'get into the mind' of Berkeley and James demands that we try hard to believe—even if we think of it as nothing but *practice* in imagining or pretending—that what we see (e.g., a book with rows of words on each page) and what we feel (e.g., a book that weighs less than a boulder but more than a feather) are actually 'only' sense-data in us, i.e., that the seen 'book' is part of a private TVF or 'movie,' the felt 'book' is a 'phantom body.' *In a word, everything that seems to be 'outside' is really inside!*

To do this pretending rightly, it helps to look (it will seem) at, say, one's hand and to think "What's really out where it seems *that* is, are zillions of unseen, infinitely tiny protons, neutrons, and electrons; but *that* is really part of my private 'inner world'." W. Köhler began his *Gestalt Psychology* with that kind of pretending vis-à-vis the entire environment. He began with a vivid common-sense description, but then abruptly changes base to the Berkeley-James's view. Notice how he refers to the objects of each sense, to feelings, to imagery, etc. Notice also that Köhler begins with the same thought that Einstein began his comment on Russell with: "This illusion [naïve realism] dominates the daily life of men and of animals; it is also the point of departure in all of the sciences, especially of the natural sciences."

There seems to be a single starting point for psychology, exactly as for all the other sciences: the world as we find it, naïvely and uncritically. The naïveté may be lost as we proceed. Problems may be found which were at first completely hidden from our eyes. For their solution it may be necessary to devise concepts which seem to have little contact with direct primary experience. Nevertheless, the whole development must begin with a naïve picture of the world. This origin is necessary because there is no other basis from which a science can arise. In my case, which may be taken as representative of many others, that naïve picture consists, at this moment, of a blue lake with dark forests around it, a big, gray rock, hard and cool, which I have chosen as a seat, a paper on which I write, a faint noise of the wind which hardly moves the trees, and a strong odor characteristic of boats and fishing. But there is more in this world: somehow I now behold, though it does not become fused with the blue lake of the present, another lake of a milder blue, at which I found myself, some years ago, looking from its shore in Illinois. I am perfectly accustomed to beholding thousands of views of this kind which arise when I am alone. And there is still more in this world: for instance, my hand and my fingers as they lightly move across the paper.

Now, when I stop writing and look around again, there also is a feeling of health and vigor. But in the next moment, I feel something like a dark pressure somewhere in my interior which tends to develop into a feeling of being hunted—I have promised to have this manuscript ready within a few months.

Most people live permanently in a world such as this, which is for them *the* world, and hardly ever find serious problems in its fundamental properties. Crowded streets may take the place of the lake, a cushion in a sedan that of my rock, some serious words of a business transaction may be remembered instead of Lake Michigan, and the dark pressure may have to do with tax-paying instead of book-writing. All these are minor differences so long as one takes the world at its face-value, as we all do except in hours in which science disturbs our natural attitude. There are problems, of course, even for the most uncritical citizens of this first-hand world. But for the most part, they do not refer to its nature as such; rather, they are of a practical or emotional sort, and merely mean that, this world being taken for granted, we do not know how to behave in the part of it which we face in our present situation.

Centuries ago, various sciences, most of all physics and biology, began to destroy this simple confidence with which human beings tend to take this world as *the reality*. Though hundreds of millions still remain undisturbed, the scientist now finds it full of almost contradictory properties. Fortunately, he has been able to discover behind it another world, properties of which, quite different from those of the world of naïve people, do not seem to be contradictory at all. (W. Köhler, *Gestalt Psychology*, pp.7-8)

In a footnote, Köhler brings 'the body' inside as well. He warns that the not-sensed physical or biological body must be carefully and consistently distinguished from the experienced 'body.'

We have seen that the same warning applies to the relation between my organism as a physical system and my body as a perceptual fact. My [perceived] body is the outcome of certain processes in my physical organism, processes which start in the eyes, muscles, skin and so forth, exactly as the chair before me is the final product of other processes in the same physical organism. If the chair is seen "before me," the "me" of this phrase means my body as an experience, of course, not my organism as an object of the physical world. Even psychologists do not always seem to be entirely clear about this point. (*Same*, p.17, n.1)

To understand James, then, Köhler's description of "the world as we find it, naïvely and uncritically" must be memorized. But more than abstract memorizing is needed. Each individual must identify in their own here-and-now stream of consciousness or ever-changing field of experience, just which things the 'words' or 'names' should be attached to. The 'things' we experience must be distinguished from any other merely-inferred parts of whatever world lies out of sight, out beyond the sensed 'world.'

To appreciate the strength of Köhler's vivid in-here vs out-there description, see whether you can spot the *difference* between it and one of James's descriptions of our here-now 'worlds.' It comes from "A World of Pure Experience."

> The nucleus of every man's experience, the sense of his own body, is, it is true, an absolutely continuous perception; and equally continuous is his perception (though it may be very inattentive) of a material environment of that body, changing by gradual transition when the body moves. But the rest of the physical world is at all times absent from each of us, a conceptual object merely, into the perceptual realities of which our life inserts itself at points discrete and relatively rare. Round the nucleus, partly continuous and partly discrete, of what we call the physical world of actual perception, innumerable hosts of thinkers, pursuing their own several lines of physically true cogitation trace paths that intersect one another only at discontinuous perceptual points, and the rest of the time are quite incongruent. (*Writings* II:1170-71)

Did you notice? If not, look closely at "The *rest* of the physical world"? That shows the typical Jamesian switch. In fact, the *entire* physical world (if any exists), *all of it*, is absent from our stream of consciousness or field of experience. The things we first *mis*-take for a lake, a forest, a rock, paper, wind, and so on, are not physical at all. Since they are not 'permanent unit-subjects,' they—the things seen, heard, smelled, tasted, felt—are not literally a world or an 'it.' They are distinct sensed qualities which 'make up' what Jonathan Harrison called, in the best sense of the words, "a consistent hallucination."

Now recall James's description of the newborn individual's total object, that is, the whole of what the newborn experiences. "The baby, assailed by eyes, ears, nose, skin, and entrails at once, feels it all as one great blooming, buzzing confusion." (PP I:488) That describes the individual's entire *inner* stream of consciousness, entire *inner* field of experience. It is that *inner*, 'original world-stuff' which the new learner, that is, each one of us, who acquires an *inner*, common-sense theory, divides into two halves. Two halves—be clear about it!—of one, private, 'original world-stuff'!

Looking back, then, over this review, we see that the mind is at every stage a theatre of simultaneous possibilities. Consciousness consists in the comparison of these with each other, the selection of some, and the suppression of the rest by the reinforcing and inhibiting agency of attention. . .

But in my mind and your mind the rejected portions and the selected portions of the original world-stuff are to a great extent the same. The human race as a whole largely agrees as to what it shall notice and name, and what not. . . There is, however, one entirely extraordinary case in which no two men ever are known to choose alike. One great splitting of the whole universe into two halves is made by each of us; and for each of us almost all of the interest attaches to one of the halves; but we all draw the line of division between them in a different place. When I say that we all call the two halves by the same names, and that those names are '*me*' and '*not-me*' respectively, it will at once be seen what I mean. (PP I:289)

That original splitting by the young infant of its one 'original world-stuff'—which is inside!—*is done inside*, in the privacy of the infant-learner's stream of consciousness. It takes place as the child's beliefs develop. But it is done by *unnoticed*, unself-conscious thought- and belief-formation. The young learner has no explicit awareness of what it is doing or, rather, of what is being done.

Learning later what Kant and James learned can only be done retrospectively, by virtue of the hard, relentless thinking needed to learn that what came to be mis-taken as things outside the stream are really part of it. Chapter I traced the steps of the hard, relentless thinking needed to carry out this second, explicit splitting of the original stream of consciousness whose private—all inside—nature goes unsuspected for years, even till death for most people.

If you've understood the preceding chapter, which discussed the outer-vs-inner and then the inner-outer vs inner-inner at length, and this new chapter which has reinforced the first, it is only because you, too, have what is needed: a powerful imagination.

3. Reason #2 for "Why Everyone Needs an Imagination."

Reason #2 is a Corollary to Reason #1. How can anyone in quest of truth learn the truth about what is *really* outside of or out beyond the full-bodied sense-data that only provide possible clues to what is outside? We might make the point clearer by asking, "Why do *physicists* need an imagination?"

One way to describe the 'Cartesian' revolution goes this way. To learn the full truth of one's cosmic situation, it is necessary to 'bring the physical environment into ourself,' that is, into the same 'place' where our thoughts and feelings are. It is necessary to pretend that what seems 'so out there!' is really not out there at all! It is necessary to picture a cosmos, then to zero in to that individual Earth-inhabitant we call "I, myself," then to seal that individual off, as it were, from everything else. At the same time, it is necessary to provide that individual with a sensuous, seemingly real 'world,' plus memories of prior sensuous experience, plus a belief-system complex enough for that individual to discover his or her cosmic aloneness.

An alternative way to achieve the same psychological effect is to expand one's mind, to make it 'spacious,' so that it includes, not only one's feelings and thoughts, but also the most *apparently* but-not-really-distant things one can see, hear, feel, etc.

Both ways demand that we be courageous enough to assent to something scary, namely, that *we are really alone,* alone with our own personal, private stream of conscious experience. And, not only alone, but wholly unable to 'climb out of our mind' to see or touch whatever else exists out there, in the rest of the universe. And yet . . .

And yet, the most remarkable thing of all is that, in 2009, we seem to have more 'scientifically-proven,' therefore 'certainly true' knowledge about the physical universe than any of our ancestors had. We have the vastly improved theories about the heavens above and this earth below, even of the 'worlds' discovered with the help of telescopes and microscopes.

Recall the last segment of the earlier citation from Köhler:

Centuries ago, various sciences, most of all physics and biology, began to destroy this simple confidence with which human beings tend to take this world as *the reality*. Though hundreds of millions still remain undisturbed, the scientist now finds it full of almost contradictory properties. Fortunately, he has been able to discover behind it another world, properties of which, quite different from those of the world of naïve people, do not seem to be contradictory at all. (W. Köhler, *Gestalt Psychology*, pp.7-8)

"Fortunately, he [the scientist] has been able to discover behind it [the experienced 'world] another world, properties of which, quite different from those of the world of naïve people, do not seem to be contradictory at all." There, in a single sentence, is the reason why everyone needs a good imagination.

The Wonderful Myth Called Science went to great lengths to show the stark contradiction between our everyday-thinking, naïve-realist view of physical things and the widely accepted 'scientific' view of physical things or what Einstein called "the illusion" that we base the decisions of our daily lives on.

For instance, we look at one of our hands. As adults, we are as familiar with it as with anything in the universe. It has a color. It is warm. It can be held steady, motionless. If we hold it up to the light, we can't see through it. It is solid.

But a 1986 *National Geographic* publication, *The Incredible Machine*, informs us that our hand has no color. "There is no red to the rose, no yellow to the bumblebee, no green to the bean. It's all in your head." (P.316) Since our hand is not in our head, it has no color. Later, we read the May 1995 issue of *National Geographic* and marvel at the "Worlds Within the Atom" story. It tells us that "physicists are searching for the ultimate building blocks from which all things—the stars, the earth, you, I, and the atom—are made." (P.634) Atoms, however, are nearly 100% empty space. So much for the solidness of our hand. Many of the atom's building blocks are electrons. J. S. Meyer, in *The ABC of Physics*, astounds us with the claim that "these electrons make approximately 10, 000, 000, 000, 000, 000 revolutions" around the atom's nucleus every second. (P.35) What happened to our motionless hand? We open to the first page of Max Born's *The Restless Universe* and get our answer: "It is odd to think that there is a word for something which, strictly speaking, does not exist, namely, 'rest'." That, of course, is consistent with Galileo's announcement that nothing physical is warm or hot. We say our hand is "warm," the physicist translates that as "the infinitesimal bodies have a certain amount of kinetic energy, i.e., motion." (*The Wonderful Myth Called Science*, pp.38-39)

The question is, "How can we discover such things as photons, electrons, protons, atoms, molecules, neurons, synapses, or any other invisible and intangible physical things?" The answer is "By imagining and testing for their possibility."

Theoretical Schizophrenia Hides a Miracle. By "theoretical schizophrenia" or split-mindedness is meant the attitude of almost 100% of the people who think of themselves as 'science minded.' They read books about the surprising things that astronomers have discovered: e.g., that the earth is not flat as it appears, that the sun is vastly larger than the moon that looks to be about the same size, that the earth and not the sun does the moving from sunrise to sunset, that some of the distant 'stars' are really planets much closer than any star, and so on. But it never occurs to them to read books about the minds without which there would be no astronomy.

Nor do they read books that will explain how they themselves got most of their own knowledge about the astronomers' discoveries. Nearly all of their knowledge about astronomers and what astronomers have discovered comes to them through reading. But they rarely if ever read books about reading. The result is that most of the world's billions of human inhabitants are quite ignorant of how their own mind works while they are reading.

In fact, it seems safe to say that millions of people today know more about the heavens and the earth (if they exist) than they know about their own minds. They shrug off the fact that their 'scientific' views clash almost 100% with what they take for granted during most of their waking hours. Most people are content to say that those are just different ways of 'looking at' things, oblivious to the fact that it is not different ways of looking at all. It is contradictory ways of thinking. And believing.

Of course, there are different ways of thinking about the same thing. James offered many illustrations, including the following.

> A substance like oil has as many different essences as it has uses to different individuals. One man conceives it as a combustible, another as a lubricator, another as a food; the chemist thinks of it as a hydrocarbon; the furniture-maker as a darkener of wood; the speculator as a commodity whose market-price to-day is this and to-morrow that. The soap-boiler, the physicist, the clothes-scourer severally ascribe to it other essences in relation to their needs. (PP II:335, note)

But the materialist thinks oil really exists, idealists deny that oil exists, though they will admit that certain clusters of immaterial ideas exist. Most dualists think both things exist. That is, the clash between the naïve-realist view of hands and, for instance, Rutherford's and Eddington's views is between contradictory worldviews.

The last point is crucial. Even 'philosophers' ignore the fact that there is a huge difference between i) two people talking about different parts of one elephant and ii) two people talking, one about elephants and the other about thoughts. Some compare the difference to the shifting 'perceptions' of the Necker Cube, ignoring the fact that no one has ever seen anything physical (such as lines on paper) and that the 'perceptions' are not thoughts but rather alternating, somewhat different TVFs.

That's the miracle that is hidden from most 'science-minded' people: the power of the human mind and the fact that humans can guess so accurately about physical things that no one has ever seen and about the intricate 'laws' those unsensed things 'obey.' That is, if physical things exist.

Philosophers of Nature Have Always Relied on Imagination. James was keenly aware of the miracle. He had a passionate interest in 'the sciences.' It began when he was in his teens. It only intensified as his learning increased:

> Who does not feel the charm of thinking that the moon and the apple are, as far as their relation to the earth goes, identical; of knowing respiration and combustion to be one; of understanding that the balloon rises by the same law whereby the stone sinks; of feeling that the warmth in one's palm when on rubs one's sleeve is identical with the motion which the friction checks; of recognizing the difference between beast and fish to be only a higher degree of that between human father and son; of believing our strength when we climb the mountain or fell the tree to be no other than the strength of the sun's rays which made the corn grow out of which we got our morning meal? (WB:65-66; *Writings* I:506)

In "The Will to Believe," he praised "the magnificent edifice of the physical sciences":

> [. . .] what thousands of disinterested moral lives of men lie buried in its mere foundations; what patience and postponement, what choking down of preference, what submission to the icy laws of outer fact are wrought into its very stones and mortar; how absolutely impersonal it stands in its vast augustness . . . (WB:7; *Writings* I:461)

But never did he forget that that 'magnificent edifice' was not created by looking at 'outer fact.' Many times, when he discussed Berkeley's view of 'matter'—what should be called Berkeley's denial of matter—James showed his awareness of the difference between sense-appearances and possible material substances lying 'beneath' or 'behind' them. For instance, in the third *Pragmatism* lecture, he used as an example a well-known Roman Catholic doctrine about transubstantiation.

Before transcribing what James wrote, it is worthwhile to quote what Peirce, from whom James said he learned his pragmatism, had to say about the doctrine. According to Peirce, the Catholic doctrine is "senseless jargon."

> To see what this principle leads to, consider in the light of it such a doctrine as that of transubstantiation. The Protestant churches generally hold that the elements of the sacrament are flesh and blood only in a tropical sense; they nourish our souls as meat and the juice of it would our bodies. But the Catholics maintain that they are literally just that, meat and blood; although they possess all the sensible qualities of wafer-cakes and diluted wine. But we can have no conception of wine except what may enter into a belief, either—
> 1. That this, that, or the other, is wine; or,
> 2. That wine possesses certain properties.
> Such beliefs are nothing but self-notifications that we should, upon occasion, act in regard to such things as we believe to be wine according to the qualities which we believe wine to possess. The occasion of such action would be some sensible perception, the motive of it to produce some sensible result. Thus our action has exclusive reference to what affects the senses, our habit has the same bearing as our action, our belief the same as our habit, our conception the same as our belief; and we can consequently mean nothing by wine but what has certain effects, direct or indirect, upon our senses; and to talk of something as having all the sensible characters of wine, yet being in reality blood, is senseless jargon. Now, it is not my object to pursue the theological question; and having used it as a logical example I drop it, without caring to anticipate the theologian's reply. I only desire to point out how impossible it is that we should have an idea in our minds which relates to anything but conceived sensible effects of things. Our idea of anything *is* our idea of its sensible effects; and if we fancy that we have any other we deceive ourselves, and mistake a mere sensation accompanying the thought for a part of the thought itself. It is absurd to say that thought has any meaning unrelated to its only function. It is foolish for Catholics and Protestants to fancy themselves in disagreement about the elements of the sacrament, if they agree in regard to all their sensible effects, here or hereafter. (C. S. Peirce, "How to Make Our Ideas Clear," sec.II)

James, for reasons we can only guess about—one thing is certain, it could not have been by inadvertence!—selected that illustration of Peirce and explained how it might be re-interpreted by a different pragmatist, himself. James recognized that there is more at stake than just the sensible effects Peirce believed in.

After telescoping the history of Western thought concerning the reality-vs-appearance or substance-vs-accident debate into a few paragraphs, James used the Catholic doctrine as an example of a "pragmatic application of the substance-idea."

Scholasticism has taken the notion of substance from common sense and made it very technical and articulate. Few things would seem to have fewer pragmatic consequences for us than substances, cut off as we are from every contact with them. Yet in one case scholasticism has proved the importance of the substance-idea by treating it pragmatically. I refer to certain disputes about the mystery of the Eucharist. Substance here would appear to have momentous pragmatic value. Since the accidents of the wafer don't change in the Lord's supper, and yet it has become the very body of Christ, it must be that the change is in the substance solely. The bread-substance must have been withdrawn, and the divine substance substituted miraculously without altering the immediate sensible properties. But tho these don't alter, a tremendous difference has been made, no less a one than this, that we who take the sacrament, now feed upon the very substance of divinity. The substance-notion breaks into life, then, with tremendous effect, if once you allow that substances can separate from their accidents, and exchange these latter.

This is the only pragmatic application of the substance-idea with which I am acquainted; and it is obvious that it will only be treated seriously by those who already believe in the 'real presence' on independent grounds. (Writings II:524)

That is only one sample of James's awareness of the difference between sense-appearances and whatever realities may be lying 'beneath' or 'behind' them. But, whereas Catholics would say, with St. Thomas, that they knew about the change from wine to blood or bread to flesh by *faith* in divine revelation (see the Gospel of St. John), James's pragmatism was the work of imagination-created hypotheses and empirical testing.

There are many examples of James's recognition that the 'surface veil of phenomena' may be hiding genuine realities which can only be guessed at or imagined. Here is a striking example from his 1897 Ingersoll lecture:

Suppose, for example, that the whole universe of material things—the furniture of earth and choir of heaven—should turn out to be a mere surface-veil of phenomena, hiding and keeping back the world of genuine realities. Such a supposition is foreign neither to common sense nor to philosophy. Common sense believes in realities behind the veil even too superstitiously; and idealistic philosophy declares the whole world of natural experience, as we get it, to be but a time-mask, shattering or refracting the one infinite Thought which is the sole reality into those millions of finite streams of consciousness known to us as our private selves. ("Human Immortality," p.15; *Writings* I:1110)

James's reference to a curtain or veil of appearances hiding reality(ies) was no mere passing thought, then. In fact, his radical-empiricist effort to avoid worrying about transcendent (never-experienced) realities grew precisely out of his dislike for the common-sense idea of never-sensed realities behind the curtain or veil of sensible appearances. Still, as is clear from his 1880 "The Sentiment of Rationality," he saw that one must be decisive regarding the difference:

> There can be no greater incongruity than for a disciple of Spencer to proclaim with one breath that the substance of things is unknowable, and with the next that the thought of it should inspire us with awe, reverence, and a willingness to add our co-operative push in the direction towards which its manifestations seem to be drifting. The unknowable may be unfathomed, but if it make such distinct demands upon our activity we surely are not ignorant of its essential quality. (WB:86; *Writings* I:521)

Further study of James's humanism—a name he used for pragmatism in his seventh 1906-07 *Pragmatism* lecture (see the last chapter)—will show how open he would have been to Einstein's later version of Kant'ian epistemology:

> The following, however, appears to me to be correct in Kant's statement of the problem: in thinking we use, with a certain "right," concepts to which there is no access from the materials of sensory experience, if the situation is viewed from the logical point of view.
>
> As a matter of fact, I am convinced that even much more is to be asserted: the concepts which arise in our thought and in our linguistic expressions are all—when viewed logically—the free creations of thought which cannot be inductively be gained from sense experience. . . .
>
> Thus, for example, the series of integers is obviously an invention of the human mind, a self-created tool which simplifies the ordering of certain sensory experiences. (A. Einstein, *Ideas and Opinions*, p.33)

Until we see that *there is a better solution* (the next chapter), we can use Kant's *we-create-our-'world'* thesis as an interim view. Our minds or imaginations are creative. To avoid the error of comparing ourselves to deities capable of creating reality as it is in itself, we qualify the create-to-discover thesis. *We create concepts to discover what we do not create.*

We can then use that model as a stepping-stone to James's better insights.

We *must* use that model for incorporating into our own philosophy the bulk of James's pragmatism and his second or pragmatist definition of "truth" as "a literally false theory that is useful, perhaps even indispensable, for discovering what is literally true."

We especially need it when our goal is i) to fully grasp the switch *from* a simple outside vs inside *to* an adequate outside vs inside-outside vs inside-inside, ii) to discover the real truth about physical things, such as hands (our own and others'), brains (our own and others'), or total bodies (our own and others'), and above all iii) to discover the real truth about non-physical sense-data, images, and thoughts (our own and others'). The 'above all' brings us to the third reason why imagination is so necessary.

4. Reason #3 for "Why Everyone Needs an Imagination."

We Need Models for Learning the Nature of What's Inside! How can anyone in quest of truth learn the truth about everything that is *really* inside the stream of consciousness, that is, for non-physical reality(ies)? We might make the point clearer by asking, "Why do *psychologists* need an imagination?"

That is, why do all of us who believe that we and others like us have unseen thoughts, memories, desires, and so on, need imaginations? We can break the answer down into two sections. i) We need imaginations to know what others experience. And, what is more surprising, ii) we need imaginations to know the true nature of our own experience.

Section One: Others' Consciousness. Descartes was right. What we experience is private to us. Berkeley, and later James, were right. The sense-data we common-sensically *mis*-take as being others' bodies are also private to us. Those discoveries raise a further question: "Since we cannot even see or hear others, how can we know for sure what their experience is like?"

It seems, common-sensically, that we learn what others are thinking or feeling by watching their bodies and/or hearing what they say. In his pro-Berkeley mood, James admitted that 'physical bodies' are 'groups of private sense-qualities united by the law of association.' But in his 1905, anti-Berkeley flare-up, his attack of 'common sense' (see Chapter

I's exclamation about Berkeley and the city of London), he claimed the following:

> To me the decisive reason in favor of our minds meeting in some common objects at least is that, unless I make that supposition, I have no motive for assuming that your mind exists at all. Why do I postulate your mind? Because I see your body acting in a certain way. Its gestures, facial movements, words and conduct generally, are 'expressive,' so I deem it actuated as my own is, by an inner life like mine. This argument from analogy is my *reason*, whether an instinctive belief runs before it or not. ("A World of Pure Experience," *Writings* II:1176)

Yet, even there, he immediately admitted that it's not so simple:

> But what is 'your body' here but a percept in my field? It is only as animating *that* object, *my* object, that I have any occasion to think of you at all. If the body that you actuate be not the very body that I see there, but some duplicate body of your own with which that has nothing to do, we belong to different universes, you and I, and for me to speak of you is folly. Myriads of such universes even now may coexist, irrelevant to one another; my concern is solely with the universe with which my own life is connected. ("A World of Pure Experience," *Writings* II:1176)

That admission creates several *challenges for all psychologists*, including our selves who wish to understand consciousness or, as it is often worded, the mind. We can only guess about the bodies that seem to be our only evidence for others' experience. How, then, can we ever be certain that others' experience is like our own? How, in fact, can we learn the true nature of our own experience?

Pace Behaviorists, No One Has Access to Another's Body. According to Descartes and even according to James's radical empiricism, your 'body' is only a percept. It is only intermittently a percept in *your* field (i.e., only while you are awake) and only intermittently a percept in *my* field (i.e., when you and I are in each other's presence). And, because your 'body' is a percept only at sporadic moments, it is impossible for it to be 'a permanent unit-subject.' How, then, can your percept of your 'body' and my percept of your 'body' ever be one and the same 'thing' as James fervently wished it could be?

It is quite impossible to 'get inside James's mind' unless we confront this question, "Can two of us ever experience one and the same, single, numerically one thing, whether someone's body or even a writing pen?"

If the sense-data in my mind are numerically distinct from the sense-data in your mind, that is, if my sense-data and yours are only like each other, then my apple and your apple—or the pen I am seeing and the pen you are seeing—are two apples and two pens. I can never taste your apple or see your pen, and vice-versa.

Below are the opening lines from the private notebooks James used to record his perplexed reflections between 1905 and 1908, that is, during some of the time he was writing "A World of Pure Experience." Perry called them "The Miller-Bode Objections." The opening entry goes right to the above question:

> In my psychology I contended that each field of consciousness is entitatively a unit, and that its parts are only different cognitive relations which it may possess with different contexts. But in my doctrine that the same "pen" may be known by two knowers I seem to imply that an identical part can help to *constitute* two fields. Bode & Miller both pick up the contradiction. The fields are . . . decomposable into "parts," one of which at least is common to both; and my whole tirade against "composition" in the *Psychology* is belied by my own subsequent doctrine. How can I rescue the situation? Which doctrine must I stand by? . . . (Perry II:750; MEN:65)

"But in my doctrine that the same 'pen' may be known by two knowers . . . " There is the famous fudge word, "same." It is so handy that all of us use it. But we must develop an acute sensitivity to the fact that we often use it to mean *one thing*, as in "That is the same pen I was using yesterday." We often use it to mean *two similar things*, as in "Your pen is the same as mine." Once having acquired the required sensitivity, we can be on our guard against someone dodging an issue by semantic switchery, i.e., by using "same" and switching from one of its meanings to the other in order to side-step an either-or decision with a now-I'll-say-this-then-I'll-say-that equivocation. Such ambiguity—lack of decisiveness—is what challenges all of us who wish to unify James's best insights.

The first challenge for psychologists is accepting as a conclusion-premise the truth, "I do not have any direct knowledge of other people's bodies." As the last chapter noted, the better neuroscientists recognize that truth:

> Plato said that we are trapped inside a cave and know the world only through the shadows it casts on the wall. The skull is our cave, and mental representation is

all that we can know about the world. (Stephen Pinker, *How the Mind Works*, 1997, p.84.)

Russell applied this truth to the question of brains:

[. . .] when Dr. Watson watches rats in mazes, what he knows, apart from difficult inferences, are certain events in himself. The behavior of rats can only be inferred by the help of physics, and is by no means to be accepted as something accurately knowable by direct observation. . . To return to the physiologist observing another man's brain: what the physiologist sees is by no means identical with what happens in the brain he is observing. . . In a strict sense, then, he cannot observe anything in the other brain, but only the percepts which he himself has when he is suitably related to that brain. (B. Russell, *An Outline of Philosophy*, 1927, pp.140, 147)

When such truths are taken to heart, we see how fitting it was for G. Myers to place the following eye-catching segment—from an unsigned review written by James in 1877—near the front of his own lengthy presentation of James's thought:

Now, how are ideas [about brain function] to be understood or talked about without what introspection tells us of their formation from coalesced residua of motor and sensory feelings? In a word, brain physiologists would be still groping in Cimmerian darkness without the torch [of introspection] which psychology proper puts into their hands. The entire recent growth of their science may, in fact, be said to be a mere hypothetical schematization in material terms of the laws which introspection long ago laid bare. . . . But, whereas we directly see their [mental] process of combination in the mind, we only guess in the brain what it *may* be from fancied analogies with the mental phenomena. . . . Dr. Maudsley's bad temper about introspection is therefore not simply wrong, but monstrous. . . . His cerebral physiology is to a great extent a pure *a priori* attempt to make a diagram, as it were, out of fibres and cells, of phenomena whose existence is known to him only by subjective observation. (G. Myers, *William James: His Life and Thought*, pp.8-9; ECR:336-37)

Theories about the brain are a "mere hypothetical schematization"! Once again, test your grasp of the Jamesian view by critiquing the following from a leading neuroscientist:

For me, this is an easy question. I believe that animals have feelings and other states of consciousness, but neither I nor anyone else has been able to prove it. We can't even prove that other people are conscious, much less other animals. In the case of other people, though, we at least can have a little confidence since all people have brains with the same basic configurations.

How, then, Can I Be Certain About Anyone Else's Stream of Consciousness. If it is only by guessing or inference that anyone can learn about other persons' bodies, including their brains, *and* every fMRI, CAT, PET, or EEG machine, *and* every pencil-and-paper questionnaire, we are twice removed from their conscious experience. James had described the resulting problem in Chapter IX of *The Principles*. "The only states of consciousness that we naturally deal with are found in personal consciousnesses, minds, selves, concrete particular I's and you's." (PP I:226) The problem, then, is a personal one. "Given that I am *alone* with my own stream of consciousness, how can I—not we—be certain about anyone else's?"

The realization of our *aloneness* can—and should—evoke an emotional reaction. People in solitary confinement may have full confidence that the stone floor will continue supporting them, yet feel tortured by their separation from other humans. People with boundless wealth often suffer unbearable depression when they are cut off from this or that loved one. And most of us would experience fear if we found ourselves alone and lost, either in a great wilderness or at sea.

Fear. Is that the reason why even now, centuries after Descartes, most thinkers refuse to seriously question whether they have evidence for any self other than their own? If the 'bodies' of others are only visual sense-data in our own personal stream of consciousness, then we can only infer the existence and behavior of real human bodies. If we can only guess at the existence and behavior of others' bodies, our guesses about others' thoughts and experience are double inferences.

Fear is a perfectly rational feeling for anyone who suddenly realizes that not even her or his own 'felt body' is literally a flesh-and-blood body, that she or he has never seen another person, that from the beginning she or he has been constructing the thoughts and experiences attributed to others, just the same way every reader constructs the thoughts and experiences attributed to authors who, even if they are not, like James, long since dead, are at least asleep or thinking and experiencing other things than the 'words' suggest. (Is it still August 4, 2008?) Fear may be the first affect that is appropriate when the sudden realization of one's possible cosmic aloneness sweeps over one.

At least Bertrand Russell thought so. In this context, his views are helpful because he was more radical and daring in his declaration of naïve realism's (partial) falsity than James. Most memorable, perhaps, is what he wrote about solipsism in a 1943 comment regarding his own philosophic 'vision.'

> In some respects, my published work, outside mathematical logic, does not at all completely represent my beliefs or my general outlook. Theory of knowledge, with which I have been largely concerned, has a certain essential subjectivity; it asks "how do *I* know what I know?" and starts inevitably from personal experience. Its data are egocentric, and so are the earlier stages of its argumentation. I have not, so far, got beyond the earlier stages, and have therefore seemed more subjective in outlook than in fact I am. I am not a solipsist, nor an idealist; I believe (though without good grounds) in the world of physics as well as in the world of psychology. But it seems clear that whatever is not experienced must, if known, be known by inference. I find that the fear of solipsism has prevented philosophers from facing this problem, and that either the necessary principles of inference have been left vague, or else the distinction between what is known by experience and what is known by inference has been denied. If I ever have the leisure to undertake another serious investigation of a philosophical problem, I shall attempt to analyse the inferences from experience to the world of physics, assuming them capable of validity, and seeking to discover what principles of inference, if true, would make them valid. Whether these principles, when discovered, are accepted as true, is a matter of temperament; what should not be a matter of temperament should be the proof that acceptance of them is necessary if solipsism is to be rejected. (B. Russell, "My Mental Development," in *The Philosophy of Bertrand Russell*, ed. P. Schilpp, p.16)

James was keenly aware of the problem.

Solipsism: a Forty-Year-Long Problem for James. If an individual has no direct experience of or contact with any physical bodies or any conscious experience but her or his own, the obvious question is, "How can I even be certain anything else but my own virtual-reality 'world' exists?" If we call that "the solipsist challenge," then James wrestled with it for at least the forty years between the 1870's when he wrote his first notes regarding the problem and 1910 when he died.

Perry, in a chapter he titled "From Idealism to Phenomenalism," quoted extensively from an 1870's notebook of James (now published in *Manuscript Essays and Notes*) which contains thirty pages about the debate between idealists—Berkeley especially—claiming nothing can exist apart from our knowledge or experience of it, and realists insisting that they'll remain faithful to the common-sense view that realities, like desert flowers that come and go without being seen or thought about by any human, can exist as permanent unit-subjects independent of human experience. In Perry's words, James realized that "the Berkeleyan idealist can escape solipsism only by arguments or assumptions that contradict his idealism" (Perry I:577).

Years later, in his attempts to work out a radical-empiricist metaphysics or grand unifying theory, James was still wrestling with solipsism. Here, from 1904's "A World of Pure Experience," is the question and his answer:

> It is therefore not a formal question, but a question of empirical fact solely, whether, when you and I are said to know the 'same' Memorial Hall, our minds do terminate at or in a numerically identical percept. Obviously, as a plain matter of fact, they do *not*. Apart from color-blindness and such possibilities, we see the Hall in different perspectives. You may be on one side of it and I on another. The percept of each of us, as he sees the surface of the Hall, is moreover only his provisional terminus. The next thing beyond my percept is not your mind, but more percepts of my own into which my first percept develops, the interior of the Hall, for instance, or the inner structure of its bricks and mortar. If our minds were in a literal sense *con*terminous, neither could get beyond the percept which they had in common, it would be an ultimate barrier between them—unless indeed they became 'co-conscious' over a still larger part of their content, which (thought-transference apart) is not supposed to be the actual case. In point of fact the ultimate common barrier can always be pushed, by both minds, farther than any actual percept, until at last it resolves itself into the mere notion of imperceptibles like molecules or ether, so that, where we do terminate in percepts, our knowledge is only speciously completed, being, in theoretical strictness, only a virtual knowledge of those remoter objects which conception carries out. (*Writings* II:1178-79)

In an 1884 note, written between 1870 and 1904, James bluntly declared that Berkeley's idealist "Argt leads to solipsism." (MEN:199)

His critics saw that his radical empiricism did the same thing. B. H. Bode, in a 1905 review of James's "Pure Experience," took this as the outstanding sign of its inadequacy:

> That knowledge as a self-transcendent function, or as a reference to reality beyond itself, can be reduced to terms of immediate experience is a conviction that has motivated many a writer on philosophical topics. It is the source of Hume's protest against the complacent pretensions of rationalism, it is responsible for the 'permanent possibilities of sensation' advocated by John Stuart Mill, it motivates the opposition of neo-Kantianism against the claims of an experience-transcending

function such as the transcendental ego, and it lies at the basis of phenomenalistic doctrines such as those of Karl Pearson and Ernst Mach. . .

In this paper it is not proposed to determine whether the concept of pure experience has any validity whatever, or, more specifically, whether on the basis of epistemology we are entitled to postulate pure experience; the purpose is the more limited one of advancing certain reasons why the attempt to reduce everything to this one category must be considered futile. These reasons reduce down to what the writer considers to be the main difficulty of the position, viz., its solipsistic tendency. I shall confine myself to the position as stated by James in recent numbers of this journal. (B. H. Bode, "Discussion: 'Pure Experience' and the External World," in E. Taylor & R. Wozniak, ed., *Pure Experience: The Response to William James*, p.55)

But James's rejection of solipsism was similar to his rejection of determinism. In an often-quoted April 30, 1870, diary entry, he recorded the earlier decision, perhaps the most momentous will-to-believe decision of his life, one that he never went back on. It was a decision that appears and reappears throughout the lectures and writings of his last forty years.

I think that yesterday was a crisis in my life. I finished the first part of Renouvier's second *Essais* and see no reason why his definition of free will—"the sustaining of a thought *because I choose to* when I might have other thoughts"—need be the definition of an illusion. At any rate, I will assume for the present—until next year—that it is no illusion. My first act of free will shall be to believe in free will. (*Letters* I:147)

Evidence that he had solved the problem of solipsism once and for all in the same, decisive way comes from an 1884 note vis-à-vis solipsism:

Suppose . . . I refuse to assume the veracity of consciousness. Whilst admitting that a world of things and persons and a world of my own past thoughts appear to be revealed to my instant thought as other than [itself], suppose I still persist in regarding them as mere illusions; contained, as it were, in the thought's pocket, very much as a vast perspective view may be a mere image breathed on the windowpane in which it appears. This instantaneous solipsism, doubting all reality but that of the punctiform instant, is impregnable. But like an impregnable fort from which no sally can be made, we may if we like, turn our backs upon it with impunity. Let us now do so, and assume with Spencer that . . . a consciousness not self-transcendent in form is inconceivable; let us . . . not only admit this to be an irreversibly true description of the form of all consciousness, but let us believe that this form is veracious. We thus adopt the belief that an independent world exists of whose existence our instant perception is truly cognitive . . the object, whatever it be, is numerically other than the act by which we know it. (*Perry* I:579; MEN:180)

The second thing to recognize regarding James is that he was especially aware of how the challenge of solipsism related to writing a psychology text that would be valid, not just for his own stream of consciousness, but for everyone else's, too. To show how profoundly aware of the problem he was, we must now turn to the history of his wrestling with it.

The history will connect with the opening segment of this chapter re faith.

James and 'Psychology Valid for Everyone's Stream of Consciousness.' The problem of solipsism is what prompted James to tell an 1884 audience that the ultimate 'warrant' for calling anything "reality" is faith: "'Reality' has become our warrant for calling a feeling [or a thought] cognitive; but what becomes our warrant for calling anything reality? The only reply is—the faith of the present critic or inquirer." (*Writings* II:835)

What if the 'inquirer' is a psychologist? What is a psychologist's warrant for calling anything reality? It can only be the faith or belief of the psychologist who knows how far out on a limb he or she climbs when daring to speak of *everyone's* mind, consciousness, or experience 'in general.' From the moment he signed the contract to write a text on the 'empirical,' 'positivist,' or 'experimental' *science* of psychology, James wrestled with the problem of faith.

'The' All-Important Draft: Objects vs Things vs Realities. James told his publisher in 1878 that he could not finish his psychology text in less than two years. He took twelve. As explained in the first section of this chapter, his psychology was to explain, among other things, the mental states called "thoughts." But he knew that the great thinkers who preceded him disagreed about both thought and reality. He knew he'd have to make up his mind about how he would deal with that enormous problem.

After five years, he was still trying to make up his mind. For instance, around 1883-84, he tried to select a handful of terms and to use them with strict precision. We know this from an unused draft for his text's second chapter. It was tentatively titled "The Object of Cognition & the Judgment of Reality." The entire draft is now available in W. James, *Manuscript Essays and Notes*. It opens wide a window into James's mind. *Everyone who aspires to 'get into' James' mind should make a close study of it.*

The first presupposition of common sense with which we start is that of the existence of "objects" distinct both from the thinker & from the mental states by means of which he thinks them. That most of our thoughts do have such objects, no naturally-feeling man has any doubt; & in so far as they do have them, every naturally-feeling man thinks that they transcend their temporary subjective being & apprehend a reality whose existence is independent of their own. The reality may be a material "thing" or physical quality; it may be a spiritual fact such as a feeling in another mind, or a past feeling of the thinker himself; *what* it is is indifferent, so far as this mysterious fact of transcendency goes, which common sense believes the function of cognition to involve. (MEN:261)

"Thought," "object," "reality," and "thing." James starts with thought and uses three other terms—object, reality, and thing—for what thoughts are 'about.' In most cases, we think—believe!—that the object of our thought is a reality. It may be a thing, quality, spiritual fact, or a past feeling. The reality's existence is independent of our own. That is, we do not think brains, hands, or the moon cease to exist when we go to sleep. Thus "object" and "reality" seem to be synonyms. But not synonyms for "thing," at least not if "thing" refers only to what is physical. But then . . .

The word *Cognition* will be employed to denote the knowledge of realities exclusively, & not to cover cases of merely apparent knowledge, such as fictitious belief, error, or illusion. Reality thus becomes the warrant for our calling a feeling cognitive. But what becomes our warrant for calling anything reality? *Quis custodiet ipsum custodem?* The only reply is, the faith of the psychologist. At every moment of his life, he finds himself subject to a belief in some realities, even tho his realities of this year should appear his illusions of the next. . . . The most he claims is that what he says about cognition may be counted as true as what he says *about anything else.* If his hearers agree that he has assumed the wrong things to be realities, then doubtless they will reject his account of the way in which those realities become known. . . .

Since errors, illusions, & fictions are not cognitive in our sense, altho they have objects, it is clear that *object & reality* cannot be used as synonymous terms. We will keep the word object for use in the phenomenal sense exclusively, as equivalent to the mental content, deliverance or matter of consciousness alone, whether it reveal a reality recognized as such by us psychologists or not. The objects of error & fiction will then not be realities, for they will have no status or existence outside of the particular feelings in which they appear. Realities, on the other hand, unknown in any one's feeling, cannot be objects. Finally, the objects of genuinely cognitive feelings must either represent realities, or be the realities themselves,—later we shall have to find out which. (MEN:265-66)

It is wrong then to think "object" and "reality" are synonyms. A reality can be an object if it is known, but not if it is not known. If unknown, it can be a reality only. To say a reality is known is another way of saying it is the object of knowledge, and knowledge which is of reality will be called "cognition." If someone believes the object they are thinking about is a reality but later decides the object is not a reality, but only a fiction or an illusion, then the knowledge was not genuine cognition after all. It was only apparent knowledge.

Once we pick apart this draft and see what a tangle results from his effort to use such terms as object, thing, reality, thought, cognition, knowledge, apparent knowledge, faith, etc., with unwavering consistency, it sheds an enormous amount of light on two things.

First, it explains what he finally decided to do. The 1890 Preface to *The Principles of Psychology* tells us that he will assume certain 'data' uncritically. His all-important Chapter IX is explicitly and emphatically 'loose' and 'non-technical' at first. He writes, "we shall have to plunge *in medias res* as regards our terminology." Secondly, it explains why he repeatedly insisted that no 'natural science' which begins with dogmatic assumptions expressed with notoriously ambiguous everyday vocabulary should be viewed as the final truth, i.e., as 'science' in an unqualified sense. To count as genuine 'science,' those initial assumptions eventually must be critically re-examined and verified.

Where the 1883-84 Draft Finally Ended Up. The 1883-84 draft did not go to waste. On the contrary. First, he reworked it into an 1884 lecture entitled "The Function of Cognition." Then, he divided its main ideas in half and used it for two chapters of *The Principles*.

To see this, we need only compare the title of the draft, "The Object of Cognition & the Judgment of Reality," with the titles of Chapters XIX and XXI of *The Principles*. They are "The Perception of 'Things'" and "The Perception of Reality." Note the two terms, "Things" and "Reality." Unless James was deliberately using "thing" and "reality" to signify at least partially distinct concepts, those two chapters would have been redundant, two chapters on the same whatever! In fact, however, part of the draft became Chapter XIX, "The Perception of 'Things'," *with 'things' in quotation marks,* to indicate that it also included probable objects, illusions and hallucinations. The rest of the draft material became Chapter XXI, "The Perception of Reality," first published as a separate article in July 1889 with—note well!—the more appropriate title "The Psychology of Belief," aka "faith." It once more took up the draft's question about reality: "But what becomes our warrant for calling anything reality?" It gives, once more, the draft's answer, "The only reply is, the faith of the psychologist." The draft's thesis, 'His realities of this year may appear his illusions of the next,' when rephrased vis-à-vis *The Principles,* becomes "What he believes this year may belong in Chapter XXI, but next year it may belong in Chapter XIX."

Finally, in 1909 James published some of his essays in an anthology titled *The Meaning of Truth,* The very first one was the 1884 "Function of Cognition," slightly reworked!

A Later Attempt at 'Precision.*'* It is interesting to note that, in 1904, James attempted once more to do what he had attempted twenty years earlier in the unused draft of 1883-84. In 1904, he published "Does 'Consciousness' Exist?" Its opening sentence again uses "object" as a genus for two species, namely, "thoughts" and "things."

'Thoughts' and 'things' are names for two sorts of objects, which common sense will always find contrasted and will always practically oppose each other. Philosophy, reflecting on the contrast, has varied in the past in her explanations of it, and may be expected to vary in the future. (Writings II:1141)

Consciousness is the object James's thought was about when he asked, "Does 'Consciousness' Exist?" If it does, indeed, exist, is it a reality? Is it a thing? After recounting the doubts Kant cast on the idea of the soul as a spirit, James answered:

I believe that 'consciousness,' when once it has evaporated to this estate of pure diaphaneity, is on the point of disappearing altogether. It is the name of a nonentity, and has no right to a place among first principles. . .

To deny plumply that 'consciousness' exists seems so absurd on the face of it—

for undeniably 'thoughts' do exist—that I fear some readers will follow me no farther. Let me then immediately explain that I mean only to deny that the word stands for an entity, but to insist most emphatically that it does stand for a function. (*Writings* II:1142)

We now must add "entity" to our list of terms and wonder just how it relates to thoughts, things, objects, and realities. Other readers wondered, too. As G. Myers noted, readers of "Does 'Consciousness' Exist?", were more than a little perplexed by the claim that consciousness is not an entity. An entity? C. S. Peirce complained that James was making a huge 'case' out of nothing, since only some 'straw man' of James's imagination would hold that consciousness is an entity. Peirce then tried his hand at an answer, explaining that consciousness is 'real,' but adding that "the conception of the *real* is derived by a *mellonization* . . . of the constraint-side of the double-sided consciousness" (Perry II:430). When James replied that he couldn't understand a word of Peirce's reply, Peirce replied: "It is very vexatious to be told at every turn that I am utterly incomprehensible, notwithstanding my very careful study of language" (Perry II:431). A. N. Whitehead, who was insistent that the great challenge is to satisfy common sense, was happy to see James cut the legs from under Descartes and the scientific materialists, but felt puzzled by the word "entity":

The term 'entity,' or even that of 'stuff,' does not fully tell its own tale. The notion of 'entity' is so general that it may be taken to mean anything that can be thought about. You cannot think of mere nothing; and the something which is an object of thought may be called an entity. In this sense, a function is an entity. Obviously, this is not what James had in his mind. (A. N. Whitehead, *Science and the Modern World*, IX:144)

If there is to be any hope of unraveling the terminological tangles in James's thought, it will have to begin with a return to the matrix of everyone's subsequent, higher learning, namely, to common sense. When we do that, we find that it was a touch of genius that made James choose to put "thing" at the top of his list of common sense's magisterial concepts.

What Exactly Is a Thing? "What is a thing?" is behind our chapter titles, "Full-Bodied Sense-Data are Things" and "Images, too, are

Things." If quintalism is true, there are five different types of things. Apart from the similarity between sense-data and memory-images of them, the five types of things are radically different. The particulars referred to by the shorthand "persons, thoughts, images, sense-data, and subatomic bodies" are different kinds of particulars which really exist. If these claims are justified, the justification comes from two facts. We use "thing" for everything, and our use of it is guided by i) a deep-seated 'sense' of the difference between what really exists and what does not and ii) an equally deep-seated 'sense' of the difference between truth and error.

First, in our everyday, common-sense talk, we frequently use "thing" and "reality" interchangeably. A reality is a thing, and a thing is a reality. We often combine the two terms, as in "a real thing." However, we also distinguish the two, as when we refer to "imaginary things." Most of us believe that the things which appear in our dreams are only imaginary, e.g., such things as golden mountains. We can say that merely-dreamed-about things are unreal. We might add that they are not even things "in the proper sense of the term." Or we can turn around and insist that, though the things we dream about are imaginary and unreal, the dream itself is not imaginary or unreal. It is real. We may add that a dream is a real thing and that the dreamed-about golden mountain really was in our real dream.

Secondly, we are guided by a deep-seated 'sense' of reality in adjusting our everyday talk. Most often we think about what we are thinking about, rather than about our thinking. When talking with people who, we assume, have beliefs similar to ours about what does and what does not exist, we talk about imaginary things the same way we talk about real things. Literature teachers do not qualify everything they say. They do not begin every class with a reminder that, for instance, the imaginary Moor, Othello, was a fictitious character who never existed, created by the real writer, Shakespeare, who did. But even in everyday affairs, we often do have to think explicitly about such matters. Mothers must explain to children who wake from frightening nightmares that the figures in the dream are not real, that they do not really exist, that the child was only dreaming. Later, the child must learn what the story-teller means by "Let's pretend." Still later, we must deal with such human creations as imitation diamonds, fake fruit, artificial intelligence, each of which involves a genuine something-else, e.g., true zirconium, real pieces of shaped plastic, and ingenious electronics.

As we have seen, James devoted an enormous amount of thought to the question "What is a thing?" The fact that 'thing' was at the top of his list of common sense's most basic concepts by itself shows that the question "What is a thing?" was an important one for him. In "The Knowing of Things Together," he conveyed his sense of its importance.

"Things," then; to "know" things; and to know the "same" things "together" which elsewhere we knew singly—here, indeed, are terms concerning each of which we must put the question, "What do we *mean* by it when we use it?"—that question that Shadworth Hodgson lays so much stress on, and that is so well taught to students, as the beginning of all sound method, by our colleague Fullerton. And in exactly ascertaining what we do mean by such terms there might lie a lifetime of occupation.

For we do mean something; and we mean something true. Our terms, whatever confusion they may connote, denote at least a fundamental fact of our experience, whose existence no one here will deny. (CER:373; *Writings* 1:1058)

"And in exactly ascertaining what we do mean by such terms there might lie a lifetime of occupation." Perhaps not, if only we keep in mind that people use 'words' as cues and clues for what they have in mind. Go for the thoughts!

According to Jamesian quintalism, two things every word-user has are i) an inner model which consists of *images* (but not words) and ii) *thoughts* (also not words) which are correlated with each other. Whenever we read any author, we need to count how many items ('item' can serve as a neutral term) there are in that person's model of what-exists and how the items are class-ified thought-wise.

James's Decision: Different Faiths, Different 'Worlds.' Or Realities? In the unused draft for *The Principles'* second chapter, James had asked "What becomes our warrant for calling anything reality?" He had answered "The only reply is, the faith of the psychologist." He added that "At every moment of his life, he finds himself subject to a belief in some realities, even tho his realities of this year should appear his illusions of the next."

That sentence joins two crucial terms, "belief" and "reality," and implies that a person's cognition of realities might turn into merely apparent cognition of—of what, realities?—by next year. Now most of us, when we re-read the original, might try another way of formulating the problem that is closer to what we *usually* mean by "real" and "reality." In a sense, that is precisely what James did. He re-read his draft and decided it would not stand as written.

But he still did not revert fully to the common-sense, tacit meaning of "reality" as what-exists-independently-of-what-we-believe. Realities themselves, we know, do not turn into illusions! But when he converted the draft into a lecture given to the Aristotelian Society in December, 1884, James repeated the sentences about converting realities into illusions.

This first instalment of my thesis is sure to be attacked. But one word before defending it. 'Reality' has become our warrant for calling feeling cognitive; but what becomes our warrant for calling anything reality? The only reply is—the faith of the present critic or inquirer. At every moment of his life he finds himself subject to a belief in *some* realities, even though his realities of this year should prove to be his illusions of the next. (Writings II:835)

In *The Principles*, he rewrote the passage, but the 'thesis' is the same. After citing Kant's claim that "we must always step outside of it [a thing] in order to attribute to it existence," James continued:

The 'stepping outside' of it is the establishment either of immediate practical relations between it and ourselves or of relations between it and other objects with which we have immediate practical relations. Relations of this sort, which are as yet not transcended or superseded by others, are *ipso facto* real relations, and confer reality upon their objective term. *The fons et origo of all reality, whether from the absolute or the practical point of view, is thus subjective, is ourselves.* (PP II:296-97)

"The *fons et origo* of all reality . . . is ourselves." The font and origin of all reality is our faith, our belief, ourself. It is? Hardly! The difference between Kant and James, at least here, is that Kant generalizes and defines 'reality (as it appears)' as the entire race's 'naïve reality,' whereas James individualizes the process. For Kant, we all acquiesce in the same 'world (as it appears).' For James, we acquiesce in our own personally unique 'worlds.' It is here that James's famous (personal) will-to-believe thesis as well as the ladder-of-faith version of it connect with his description of 'reality.' In fact, numerous strands of James's thinking criss-cross here.

Chapter XXI is one of the most important of all for understanding James's mind. His decision to offer the world a vivid, concrete description of how our minds actually work and, while doing so, to set aside the question "What is the universe outside the perimeter of my experience and thought really like?" made it possible to show the connection between different people's different 'worlds' and their wills-to-believe. Here again is how he began Chapter XXI.

> Everyone knows the difference between imagining a thing and believing in its existence, between supposing a proposition and acquiescing in its truth. In the case of acquiescence or belief, the object is not only apprehended by the mind, but is held to have reality. Belief is thus the mental state or function of cognizing reality. As used in the following pages, 'Belief' will mean every degree of assurance, including the highest possible certainty and conviction. (PP II:283)

In one of that chapter's subsections, 'The Orders of Reality,' James described the process in which the learner who begins by being *entirely gullible*, grows to be a mature thinker whose belief-habits can become so ingrained that getting her or him to reconsider a long-rejected thought, even if it is true, is like getting a mule to do what it does not want to do. False beliefs, i.e., assented-to thoughts which are false, will not only seem true to the believer but, if they are woven into a highly-developed, well-integrated system of supporting beliefs, they will seem so self-evident that the believer will suspect that those unable to 'see the light' are motivated by bad faith, i.e., are guilty of culpable ignorance.

One of Chapter XXI's most important subsections is the one entitled 'The Many Worlds.' James knew that there are not literally many worlds. But to believers, the objects of their long-standing, deeply-ingrained belief-habits seem as real as Santa does to the child and as dragons threatening to swallow the sun during an eclipse seem to the aborigine adult. James, calling on his years of reading about the things believers believe in, classified them into a number of different 'worlds.' First, he divided them in two, viz., into the 'worlds' of realities and the 'worlds' of fancies and illusions. Then he offered a more refined seven-fold classification of 'worlds':

> The most important sub-universes commonly discriminated from each other

and recognized by most of us as existing, each with its own special and separate style of existence, are the following:

1. The world of sense, or of physical "things" as we instinctively apprehend them, with such qualities as heat, color, and sound, and such "forces" as life, chemical affinity, gravity, electricity, all existing as such within or on the surface of things.

2. The world of science, or of physical things as the learned conceive them, with secondary qualities and "forces" (in the popular sense) excluded, and nothing real but solids, fluids and their "laws" (i.e., customs) of motion.* [Note*: "I define the scientific universe here in the radical mechanical way. Practically, it is oftener thought of in a mongrel way and resembles in more points the popular physical world."]

3. The world of ideal relations, or abstract truths believed or believable by all, and expressed in logical, mathematical, metaphysical, ethical, or aesthetic propositions.

4. The world of "idols of the tribe," illusions or prejudices common to the race. All educated people recognize these as forming one subuniverse. The motion of the sky round the earth, for example, belongs to this world. That motion is not a recognized item in any of the other worlds; but as an "idol of the tribe" it really exists. For certain philosophers "matter" exists only as an idol of the tribe. For science, the "secondary qualities" of matter are but "idols of the tribe."

5. The various supernatural worlds, the Christian heaven and hell, the world of the Hindu mythology, the world of Swedenborg's *visa et audita*, etc. Each of these is a consistent system, with definite relations among its own parts. Neptune's trident, e.g., has no status of reality whatever in the Christian heaven; but within the classic Olympus certain definite things are true of it, whether one believe in the reality of the classic mythology as a whole or not. The various worlds of deliberate fable may be ranked with these worlds of faith—the world of the *Iliad*, that of *King Lear*, of the *Pickwick Papers*, etc.]

6. The various worlds of individual opinion, as numerous as men are.

7. The worlds of sheer madness and vagary, also indefinitely numerous. (PP II:291-93)

So, even though "Everyone knows the difference between imagining a thing and believing in its existence," that only means that we all construct two opposing mental pigeonholes labeled "What exists" (aka "Reality") and "What does not exist" (aka "Illusion"). The problem is that those with rival worldviews disagree in their imposition or application or attribution of the two concepts. Like the eye-witnesses who inspect individuals in a police line-up and try to decide which "The one I saw" should be applied to, each of us must decide which of the 'things' or 'objects' present in our stream of consciousness gets which label. In other words, each of us gets to freely decide which pigeonhole the 'things' or 'objects' get assigned to. James concluded his "Many Worlds" list with this observation:

> *Every object we think of gets at last referred to one world or another of this or of some similar list.* It settles into our belief as a common-sense object, a scientific object, an abstract object, a mythological object, an object of some one's mistaken conception, or a madman's object; and it reaches this state sometimes immediately, but often only after being hustled and bandied about amongst other objects until it finds some which will tolerate its presence and stand in relations to it which nothing contradicts. (PP I:293)

But, it is not only our own objects which may shuttle back and forth between Chapter XXI and Chapter XIX. We assign others' objects to the 'worlds' of our own choice. That is, we may put another's reality under our illusion-concept and another's illusion into our reality-file.

Back to Common Sense: Things Exist or They Don't, Period!
Things do exist or they don't. Period! The influence of Kant in this important chapter is evident from the fact that James included in it the notoriously absurd effort by Kant to redefine 'real' and 'reality.' Kant had a valid and important point to make. If, for instance, we distinguish propositions (objects) from acts, then we can say, as James did, that an understood proposition remains unchanged regardless of whether we believe it, disbelieve it, or doubt it. What Kant actually wrote, though, is literally non-sense.

"The real," as Kant says, "contains no more than the possible. A hundred real dollars do not contain a penny more than a hundred possible dollars. . . . By whatever, and by however many, predicates I may think a thing, nothing is added to it if I add that the thing exists. . . . Whatever, therefore, our concept of an object may contain, we must always step outside of it in order to attribute to it existence." (PP II:296)

There simply are no possible dollars. A creative deity may be able to create what does not now exist, but creating does not consist in going to a celestial storeroom of possible essences, selecting one of them, and then adding a coat of 'realness' onto it. To make the point clear, we might reply rhetorically to Kant that a pocket with a hundred real dollars in it has 10,000 more pennies than any pocket with only a possible hundred dollars in it.

Common sense must retained here. We may have a pasture with brown cows on one side and black cows on the other, or we may find a pasture with only female cows on one side and male cows on the other, but only Lewis Carroll would try to amuse young readers or tweak the noses of older ones by taking a hint from G. E. Moore and writing of a pasture in which the real cows are on one side and the unreal but possible ones on the other. Even Aquinas, inspirer of much pseudo-problem theorizing about essence and existence, once at least captured the truth with the kind of clarity desperately needed here. "Before an essence gains existence, it is nothing, except possibly in the mind of the creator where it is not a creature but the creative essence" (*De Potentia*, qu.3, art.5, ad 2).

(English) Terms, Such As "Being," "Essence," "Existence," etc. Name Fictions. And so, too, do such German terms as *Sein, Dasein, Das Nichts*, etc. By embracing plain common sense, according to which Santa either exists or doesn't, we simply lop off whatever tons of mental clutter we may have accumulated during our years of studying Plato's essences, Aristotle's potency, St. Thomas' existence, as well as more recent theories about subsistence, inexistence, intentional existence, and so on.

James, for example, un-constructed the idea of 'possible existence' while he was wrestling with Royce's monism. In notes he once made for himself in response to Royce's argument in favor of idealism, James discussed the meaning of "possible chickens." At any given moment in world history, he insisted, the only chickens that exist are actual ones. Whoever refers to possible chickens should admit that "in the universe itself apart from us is *the egg*—nothing else." (MEN:205)

People disagree about all of these matters. Those who disagree may use the 'same' words whereas those who agree may use 'unsame' words. In every case, it is up to each of us first to interpret the words, then to willfully choose what we, as judge and jury of one, will assent to. All of the evidence any of us has regarding what is out beyond our own private 'field of experienced sense-data, imagery, and thoughts' must be found here, in this private 'field.'

But what should we think James meant by "faith" or "belief"? If 'the *fons et origo* of all reality is ourselves' (PP II:296-97), because our 'warrant for reality is our faith,' then it is hard to think of a more important question than "What did James mean by 'faith,' that is, 'belief'?"

Some Jamesian Premises Re Belief/Believing. The claim in this book is that a Jamesian quintalism is the right frame on which to hang all particular facts. We need to now gather together the particular ingredients in James's account of belief to see whether his account of belief fits the rest of his most basic premise-conclusions.

The first requirement is to distinguish what is the object believed and the act of believing it. What a person believes—the object of faith—is best thought of as a proposition. A proposition or judgment (object) is distinct from our adopted attitude (act) toward it. Though James rejected the old picture of propositions being made of parts, i.e., separate concepts or ideas, he often found the picture useful, just as we all do. Such is the case here.

> The commonplace doctrine of 'judgment' is that it consists in the combination of 'ideas' by a 'copula' into a 'proposition,' which may be of various sorts, as affirmative, negative, hypothetical, etc. But who does not see that in a disbelieved or doubted or interrogative or conditional proposition, the ideas are combined in the same identical way in which they are in a proposition which is solidly believed? *The way in which the ideas are combined is a part of the inner constitution of the thought's object or content.* (PP I:286)

QU: "*That* is an apple?" AN: "That *is* an apple!" The same proposition, different adopted attitudes. That example should help make James's point clear. Once the principle is grasped and held onto as a premise for further conclusion-premises in our circularly-argued system, other points which he made are more easily understood. These further principles should be thought of as dealing with propositions-as-wholes.

First, we can understand a 'same' proposition later which we understood earlier. We can also understand other propositions which are inconsistent with it. We then have a choice of attitudes toward the rival propositions. We must not be lulled into forgetting about the propositions-as-wholes when James refers to things such as candles, horses, and the like. "Apple" is not a proposition. "That is an apple" is.

That we can at any moment think of the same thing which at any former moment we thought of is the ultimate law of our intellectual constitution. . . . *The whole distinction of real and unreal, the whole psychology of belief, disbelief, and doubt, is thus grounded on two mental facts—first, that we are liable to think differently of the same; and second, that when we have done so, we can choose which way of thinking to adhere to and which to disregard.* (PP:290)

Sentences which express complete thoughts are often quasi-hybrids that express both a proposition and a thinker's attitude. "Is that an apple?" expresses a proposition plus a waiting-for-an-answer attitude. Unless the respondent is lying, "Yes, that's an apple" expresses a proposition to which she or he has adopted an attitude of belief, consent, assent, acceptance, etc. (The different names are only clues to the thought, and the 'same' thought can be expressed with any one of those names.) "No, that is not an apple" expresses a proposition to which the respondent has adopted an attitude of disbelief, refusal, dissent, rejection, etc. But the 'content' of the three propositions, one interrogative, one affirmative, and one negative, is the 'same.' The difference is not in the proposition or thought understood. The difference is in the attitude which the thinker-understander adopts.

Our attitudes or responses or reactions to the propositions or thoughts which we understand are intimately connected to the frequency with which we think them. Frequency forms habits. The 'great law of habit' thus governs our thinking, our understanding, and our believing as much as any of our other acts or activities. This is an important 'fact of experience' that James captured in one of his most inspired passages. Here is part of a longer passage:

The truth must be admitted that thought works under conditions imposed *ab extra*. The great law of habit itself—that twenty experiences make us recall a thing better than one, that long indulgence in error makes right thinking almost impossible—seems to have no essential foundation in reason. The business of thought is with truth—the number of experiences ought to have nothing to do with her hold of it; and she ought by right to be able to hug it all the closer, after years wasted out of its presence. The contrary arrangements seem quite fantastic and arbitrary, but nevertheless are part of the very bone and marrow of our minds. (PP I:552; "ab extra" = from without)

Few things are more important than habits for understanding James's keen interest in rival belief-*systems*. The great thinkers who have made advances in understanding our impossibly-complex experience go far beyond their growing-up common-sense, but they go in different directions. When they do, they reach entirely incompatible, contradictory conclusions on a variety of matters. The result is incompatible *systems* of beliefs or belief-*systems*. As usual, James calls our attention to the fact that disagree'rs can at least return to their common-sense conviction that seeing is believing.

Each thinker, however, has dominant habits of attention; and these practically elect from among the various worlds some one to be for him the world of ultimate realities. From this world's objects he does not appeal. Whatever positively contradicts them must get into another world or die. The horse, e.g., may have wings to its heart's content, so long as it does not pretend to be the real world's horse—*that* horse is absolutely wingless. For most men, as we shall immediately see, the 'things of sense' hold this prerogative position, and are the absolutely real world's nucleus. Other things, to be sure, may be real for this man or for that—things of science, abstract moral relations, things of the Christian theology, or what not. But even for the special man, these things are usually real with a less real reality than that of the things of sense. They are taken less seriously; and the very utmost that can be said for anyone's belief in them is that they are as strong as his 'belief in his own senses.' (PP II:293-94)

"These things are usually real with a less real reality than that of the things of sense." As we saw in the preceding chapter, that claim represents the common core of James's two 'visions.'

Now the merely conceived or imagined objects which our mind represents as hanging to the sensations (causing them, etc.), filling the gaps between them, and weaving their interrupted chaos into order are innumerable. Whole systems of them conflict with other systems, and our choice of which system shall carry our belief is governed by principles which are simple enough, however subtle and difficult may be their application to details. *The conceived system, to pass for true, must at least include the reality of the sensible objects in it, by explaining them as effects on us, if nothing more. The system which includes the most of them, and definitely explains or pretends to explain the most of them, will, ceteris paribus, prevail.* It is needless to say how far mankind still is from having excogitated such a system. But the various materialisms, idealisms, and hylozoisms show with what industry the attempt is forever made. (PP II:311-12)

". . . our choice of which *system* shall carry our belief." The key word is "choice." Or "belief." We choose what we will believe. We choose entire *systems* of beliefs: materialism, idealism, or hylozoism. Repeated choices become habits. But, once we emerge from out helplessly gullible stage, we become judge and jury of one in deciding what we will-to-believe. Here is more of James's inspired passage:

> The great law of habit itself—that twenty experiences make us recall a thing better than one, that long indulgence in error makes right thinking almost impossible—seems to have no essential foundation in reason. The business of thought is with truth—the number of experiences ought to have nothing to do with her hold of it; and she ought by right to be able to hug it all the closer, after years wasted out of its presence. The contrary arrangements seem quite fantastic and arbitrary, but nevertheless are part of the very bone and marrow of our minds. Reason is only one out of a thousand possibilities in the thinking of each of us. Who can count all the silly fancies, the grotesque suppositions, the utterly irrelevant reflections he makes in the course of a day? Who can swear that his prejudices and irrational beliefs constitute a less bulky part of his mental furniture than his clarified opinions? It is true that a presiding arbiter seems to sit aloft in the mind, and emphasize the better suggestions into permanence . . . (PP I:552)

We do this 'emphasizing' with acts of free-will believing.

James: Belief, Attitude, and Will. At the end of chapter XXI, James discussed several related subjects. Besides habits of attention, they are: free-will, the effects of nature on us, our ability to effect changes in nature, emotions, conversion, God, and duty. Recalling his 1870's deliberate choice of belief in free-will vs belief in determinism, and looking ahead to the core of his outlook vis-à-vis moral responsibility, it is worth-while to give a few moments of attention to his ideas about belief.

> [. . .] Now the important thing to notice is that this difference between the objects of will and belief is entirely immaterial, as far as the relation of the mind to them goes. All that the mind does is in both cases the same; it looks at the object and consents to its existence, espouses it, says 'it shall be my reality.' It turns to it, in short, in the interested active emotional way. The rest is done by nature. . . . *Will and Belief, in short, meaning a certain relation between objects and the Self, are two names for one and the same* PSYCHOLOGICAL *phenomenon.* All the questions which arise concerning one are questions which arise concerning the other. The causes and conditions of the peculiar relation must be the same in both. The free-will question arises as regards belief. If our wills are indeterminate, so must our beliefs be, etc. The first act of free-will, in short, would naturally be to believe in free-will. (PP II:320-21)

The difference between the objects of *will* and *belief* is "entirely immaterial," meaning, entirely unimportant. In fact, James denies that there is a difference! In fact, James used a third term for that 'relation of the mind to its objects' was "*attitude*." Common-sensically, we are not our willings or believings, nor are we thought-about-objects. When we habitually assent to or acquiesce in those 'objects,' the result is a habitual *attitude*. In 1990, a panel of speakers helped to celebrate the centenary of James's *Principles of Psychology*. One of the lectures included a reading of James's impassioned defense of each human's private, 'subjective' experience as the place where truly important history is found. If we think of belief and unbelief, assent and dissent, as matters of *attitude*, then—according to James—they are the very stuff of world history. Here is part of the passage that came from Lecture XX of his *Varieties of Religious Experience* series.

> A conscious field *plus* its object as felt or thought of *plus* an attitude towards the object *plus* the sense of a self to whom the attitude belongs—such a concrete bit of personal experience may be a small bit, but it is a solid bit as long as it lasts; not hollow, not a mere abstract element of experience, such as the 'object' is when taken all alone. It is a *full* fact, even though it be an insignificant fact; it is of the *kind* to which all realities whatsoever must belong; the motor currents of the world run through the like of it; it is on the line connecting real events with real events. (Writings II:447)

". . . It is of the kind to which all realities whatsoever must belong . . .", even though one person's 'realities' are another person's 'illusions,' even though one person's 'realities' of this year may be 'unrealities' next year.

As noted above, there are problems with James's framework. His major life-decisions, if we can make any true judgments about them, were demonstrations of what "believe" ought to mean. Over and over, he described it in amazingly accurate ways. But *not* when he tried to 'define' it in Chapter XXI of *The Principles*!

James vs Hume vis-à-vis Belief. Given the importance of a true understanding of belief, a vigorous protest must be lodged against James's quasi-endorsement—in *The Principles*' Chapter XXI—of Hume's utterly mistaken account of what believing is. On page 295 James cited several lines from Sec.V, Pt.II, of Hume's *Enquiry Concerning Human Understanding*. Hume had begun with this admission:

Nothing is more free than the imagination of man; and though it cannot exceed that original stock of ideas furnished by the internal and external senses, it has unlimited power of mixing, compounding, separating, and dividing these ideas, in all the varieties of fiction and vision.

James ignored these lines of Hume which present the model of idea-atoms, the model James attacked frequently and strenuously. James skipped to lines that describe belief, not as our power over our thoughts, but as the power of ideas over us. Here are the lines James selected and rearranged, beginning with his (James') most egregious error:

[. . .] Hume's account of the matter was then essentially correct, when he said that belief in anything was simply the having the idea of it in a lively and active manner:

"I say then, that belief is nothing but a more vivid, lively, forcible, firm, steady conception of an object, than what the imagination alone is ever able to attain. . . . It consists not in the peculiar nature or order of ideas, but in the *manner* of their conception, and in their feeling to the mind. I confess, that it is impossible perfectly to explain this feeling or manner of conception. . . Its true and proper name . . . is *belief*; which is a term, that every one sufficiently understands in common life. And in philosophy, we can go no farther than assert, that *belief* is something felt by the mind, which distinguishes the ideas of the judgment from the fictions of the imagination. It gives them more weight and influence; makes them appear of greater importance; inforces them in the mind; gives them a superior influence on the passions, and renders them the governing principle of our actions." (PP II:295)

That account is decidedly *not* 'essentially correct'! Belief, as an act which each of us can exercise freely with respect to any proposition whatever, even one that initially 'feels' like an utterly 'dead option,' is the very heart of James's system, so far as its ethical or moral dimensions are concerned. In fact, the first of his *Varieties* lectures takes dead aim at the far-reaching implications of any such 'passive' view as Hume's. Belief is not something passively felt by the mind. It is something actively done by the person.

At first, of course, our 'believing' *is* passive. As James noted, we are not in control of our assenting and dissenting in our early years. *We are born defenseless and gullible.* James used the example of a child who might innocently put a hand into a candle's flame, not knowing what to expect after doing so. He justly inserted Spinoza's rumination that a boy who has no data that contradict a thought that a horse exists will not doubt it. (Once again, believing relates us to propositions, not to candles or horses, which are the 'content' of thoughts.) But it is not long before every normal learner has more than enough data needed to suspend assent if those data are brought to the learner's attention and shown to contradict the proposition previously 'acquiesced in.' However, those data often are not noticed or attended to. That is why, therefore, James chose in *The Principles* to go as far as possible—but not all the way!—to pretend with Hume that all states of consciousness are, in a sense, passively produced by the unseen brain.

There was, however, one issue on which James openly declared that he would reject that pretense, namely, in relation to our free-willing and morality. (See Ch. XXVI of *The Principles*, "Will.") Furthermore, how wrong it was for James to ever suggest that Hume's account was "essentially correct" should be glaringly obvious when we examine another paragraph in which Hume used an example to make certain that we would understand his view of 'believing.' How far off the mark Hume was should be immediately evident to anyone who has ever read and become so absorbed in a novel or play that the characters 'feel' far more real and vivid than any really-believed-in non-acquaintance.

This definition will also be found to be entirely conformable to every one's feeling and experience. Nothing is more evident, than that those ideas, to which we assent, are more strong, firm, and vivid, than the loose reveries of a castle-builder. If one person sits down to read a book as a romance, and another as a true history, they plainly receive the same ideas, and in the same order, nor does the incredulity of the one, and the belief of the other, hinder them from putting the very same sense upon their author. His words produce the same ideas in both; though his testimony has not the same influence on them. The latter has a more lively conception of all the incidents. He enters deeper into the concerns of the persons: represents to himself their actions, and characters, and friendships, and enmities: he even goes so far as to form a notion of their features, and air, and person. While the former who gives no credit to the testimony of the author, has a more faint and languid conception of all these particulars, and, except on account of the style and ingenuity of the composition, can receive little entertainment. (D. Hume, *A Treatise of Human Nature*, Bk. I, Pt. III, Sec. 8)

Do the names of Benjamin Paul Blood or John Pentland Mahaffy conjure 'a more lively conception' than Santa Claus, Snow White, Romeo and Juliet, or Kristin Lavransdatter do? How absurd! Yet most people, when told, "The first two are names of people who really lived and whose names are listed in the index to James's *Manuscript Essays and Notes*," will most likely assent—without any emotion or felt liveliness—to that proposition, even though they have no idea whatever of who those men were, when they lived, etc. On the other hand, every normal person can have *very* lively conceptions of fictitious characters in novels—or plays or movies—whose unreality they never once doubt or disbelieve.

Once more, the 'problem of semantics' confronts us here. We already know that many or most 'words' or 'names' even in 'the same' language have more than one meaning, i.e., are frequently used to signify different ideas. We use 'bat' to signify both the small mammal and the piece of baseball equipment. However, when we ask what materialists and phenomenalists mean by "a bat flew from the belfry," we find that they mean utterly different things even though both would point to 'the same' entry in the dictionary. This author recently heard a well-known philosopher state unblushingly that Hume believed in God, but not 'as a personal being.' That is like saying that pantheists who substitute "God" for "the universe as a whole" do not fit the everyday concept signified by "atheist."

Non-word 'words' are mere clues. To discover what people believe, we must resort to the count-and-classify rule.* The consequences of not following that principle of interpretation are impossible to over-estimate. Whoever thinks it harmless to take Hume's formula-analysis of 'believe' as meaning 'to feel strongly' and to substitute it for what James had in mind when he wrote "My first act of free will shall be to believe in free will" can probably convince her- or himself that Hume's substitution of 'constant conjunction' for 'cause' was harmless, too. James vigorously attacked that idea of Hume's. He should have blasted his idea of belief. (*See *William James on Common Sense*.)

The difference between what Hume and James believed "belief" should mean constitutes an unbridgeable gulf between Hume's 'world' and that of James, at least while the latter was composing Chapter XXVI ("Will"), "The Will to Believe" (both words in one title), "The

Dilemma of Determinism," the last of his 1890's *Talks to Teachers*, "The Energies of Men," etc. Note. The last, a 1906 Presidential Address to the American Philosophical Association (!), is especially noteworthy vis-à-vis James's attitudes regarding the burgeoning 'scientific' psychology. End note.

Section Two: My Own Consciousness. Here, then, we arrive at the final problem for psychologists. If, as James at one time insisted, the psychologist has direct access only to his or her own experience and therefore must take on faith the 'reality' of other persons' experiences, how is the psychologist to know what is the nature of his or her own experience?

Take, for example, what he wrote in Chapter XXVI.

> *Will and Belief, in short, meaning a certain relation between objects and the Self, are two names for one and the same* PSYCHOLOGICAL *phenomenon.* All the questions which arise concerning one are questions which arise concerning the other. The causes and conditions of the peculiar relation must be the same in both. The free-will question arises as regards belief. If our wills are indeterminate, so must our beliefs be, etc. The first act of free-will, in short, would naturally be to believe in free-will. (PP II:321)

How can we know what goes on in our own stream, the only one any of us has access to? It turns out that, here too, we have system'atic choices. Which one we will will-to-believe is up to each of us who, 'like a presiding arbiter, seems to sit aloft in the mind, able to emphasize the better suggestions into the permanence of habit.' With this question, "How can I know what goes on in my own experience?", we return to the announced topic of this chapter, namely, images and imagining.

How Do I Know What Goes On In My Own Mind? That is the ultimate, bottom-line question for all genuinely scientific psychological knowledge, that is, for all true and adequately verified knowledge, by any individual, of what 'goes on' in his or her own private experience.

As we have seen in Chapter I, James insisted on some occasions that the only answer to "How can I know what goes on in my mind?" is "By introspection." He was never so insistent on that answer as he was in "The Methods and Snares of Psychology," Chapter VII of *The*

Principles. "Introspective Observation is what we have to rely on first and foremost and always."

The trouble with that answer is that i) it is sheer metaphor and ii) it is literally false. It is a metaphor based on our common-sense idea that we can literally look at physical roses, stars, etc., with our eyes. But we cannot turn our eyes around and look into our mind. The value of the metaphor is that it helps to *understand* the thought—if we assent to it—that we are directly conscious or aware of some entities (sense-data and images) that are not physical and not outside our private, inner stream of consciousness. But it is literally false, because what the metaphor suggests is that all introspecting is like or similar to the *direct awareness* of a TVF, in part or in whole that looking gives us. It isn't.

> And, with that last thought, "It isn't," we come to Jamesian quintalism's *huge readjustment* of James' most persistent belief, his faith that somehow his two-item, radical-empiricist framework could accommodate all of his brilliant insights, all of his most tightly-held beliefs. To do that, we need at least a four- or five-item framework.

The readjustment was described in the Preface to this text. James tried to squeeze his philosophy into a two-item framework of percepts and concepts. *That two-item organizing skeleton must be expanded to include five items.* Besides persons and subatomic particles, the stream of conscious experience itself consists of three different types of objects: full-bodied sense-data, memory-images of them, and most importantly, complete thoughts.

The best way to describe our relation to those three types of objects in English is as follows. We are *directly aware of* (James's preferred term is "feel") the panoramas of color, the wrap-around sounds, the twinges of pain we experience. We are *directly aware of,* even feel, memory-images or 'faint copies' (Hume's term) of them. But we can only *understand* thoughts.

To show how Jamesian quintalism is the only right framework for learning the true nature of our own conscious experience, we once again use the process of elimination. As usual, we begin with our common-sense philosophy, with its convictions about the outer world and its convictions about inner experience, e.g., tickles, pains, and so on. We create a framework that has room for and can 'put order into' all of our common-sense convictions. Once we discover that this framework is not acquired by looking—we never observe either the outer realities or any but the most obvious inner ones, such as sense-data—we must recognize that all psychologies must be created by the imagination. The final stage is reached when we discover the truth behind the metaphor of 'creation by the imagination'! That is, the final step is to see through the 'creating' model in order to reach the pinnacle of insight.

Psychologies Are "Imaginative Creations." If our aborigine ancestors had no explicit theories about imagining and believing, and no explicit theories about truth and falsity, but only tacit, implicit 'senses,' then how did it come about that a psychologist, e.g., James, could write a 1400-page text that *explicitly* treats—in depth!—so many topics: thought, introspection, attention, conception, comparison, discrimination, association, reasoning, sensation, imagination, emotion, will, and necessary truths?

The first answer to be eliminated is *looking*. We cannot look outward and see thought, introspection, attention, etc. Nor can we look inward and see them. Call those lookings "extrospection" and "introspection," and eliminate both of them.

Test this for yourself. Close your eyes, concentrate on what is 'going on' in your mind, and see how many of the things named in that paragraph you notice. Unless you are different from James and everyone else, you will find only what Hume found when he 'looked inward.' But you won't even find what he thought* he found. (*Hume claimed there is nothing in the mind except impressions and ideas. If he hadn't acquired those two ideas (!) from the sense impressions he got from reading [seeing non-word 'words'] and listening [hearing non-word 'words'], he'd never have dreamed of saying "Wow, I never noticed this before, but there are only two types of things in my mind, impressions and ideas.")

However, you *may* get a start at noticing things which are not obvious at first if, like Hume, you are given hints in the form of a word-bearing or name-bearing question, such as, "Don't you have a lot of *memories* of people you've known, places you've been, things you've seen, etc.?" Once again, try looking to see if you can see a memory. If it was not by introspection, then how did James acquire all of those ideas about his own private stream of consciousness?

At this point in the elimination-process argument (similar to the one in the preceding chapter), we revert to the idea introduced in earlier segments of this chapter, viz., imagination. We can say that James 'created' all of those ideas with his imagination. But it was *an imagination stirred into action by his reading 'words' or 'names' for those ideas.* That is, in the same way that Newton created ideas of angles, vectors, circles, ellipses, force, gravity, etc., while reading-scanning those words or names in books by Euclid, Ptolemy, Copernicus, Galileo, Descartes, Kepler, and so on, James created ideas of ideas, thoughts, objects, impressions, sense-data, etc., while reading-scanning those words or names in books by older psychologists, ranging from Hippocrates to Helmholtz, from Socrates to Swedenborg.

James Knew All the Great Psychologies . . . in General. James was truly a scholars' scholar. He read everything worth reading about the human psyche. He was already reading Kant and other 'heavy hitters' long before he took a job teaching physiology. Only those blinded by the wonderful myth called 'science' could possibly read James's writings and not realize how absurd it is to think he was first just a physiologist, later became a psychologist, and finally learned enough to rise to the level of a philosopher.

The reason for emphasizing that point is simple. Whoever has not learned the history of 'psyche-science' as James did—and that means beginning with Plato and Aristotle, continuing with Descartes, and coming as far forward as Kant and Hegel—that is, whoever has not discovered their discoveries, whether by reading texts in the original languages, translations of those texts, or competent 'second-hand' summaries of them, is like someone who professes to be an astronomer but who knows nothing about the heavens except what aborigines know by looking up at the sky or what contemporaries learn by reading the Book of Genesis.

For anyone born after 1908 to know current theories about the heavens, he or she had first to spend five or six years acquiring their common-sense philosophy, then learn—mostly by reading—what recent researchers well-educated in Euclid's geometry, Newton's physics, Rutherford's atom, etc., have discovered. The current habit of imagining that the long list of discoveries about the psyche, discoveries made in the last twenty-five centuries, are less important than the long list of discoveries about the heavens is, unfortunately, one of the greatest impediments students face when they try to acquire a good education in 2008. To understand the human psyche is more important and infinitely more complex than understanding modern theories about the heavens, which—to repeat—would not exist were it not for the great minds of such thinkers as Euclid, Ptolemy, Copernicus, etc.

The We-Create-to-Discover Model for Psychology. At the very beginning of this volume, it was stated that *all psychology-containing, grand-unifying theories are created by imagining.* Once that thesis is understood, it is easy to verify. Pretend that reading prompts readers' imaginations to create necessary ideas, then consult history in the form of records available in every up-to-date, modern library. That history will reveal the slow development of models to be used in exploring the human psyche.

We can begin at the end. With James. Consider part of an 1884 note regarding Ferrier and Berkeley which was cited in the previous chapter:

> The neatest phrase, perhaps, for expressing the ambiguity is: "The world can't be tho't of except *as* thought of." The *as* here may refer to the act of thinking or to the object of the thinking. It may mean *when* thought of; and be true, but insignificant. Or it may mean, *under the appearance of being thought of;* when it is significant, but false. (Perry I:578)

"The *as* here may refer to the act of thinking or to the object of the thinking." Where did James get his ideas of acts as 'things' distinct from objects? The answer, in metaphorical shorthand, is easy. James inherited them from his predecessor psychologists who inherited them from Descartes who inherited them from the Medieval Schoolmen who inherited them from Aristotle who borrowed parts of his model from Plato who may or may not have inherited them from Socrates.

Aristotle's five-part model is the just-right, explicit framework for 'putting order' into our everyday-thinking, *common-sense* ideas about human knowledge. It is still being used by modern advocates of St.

Thomas' Aristotelian-type psychology. Our attention, then, must turn to Aristotle's model.

Aristotle's Five-Basic-Concepts Psychology. Aristotle's model is perfect for understanding common sense. When we speak of 'consciousness' or 'experience,' we must begin where all further theorizing begins, namely, with the already-massive foundation whose essentials we somehow 'come by' by the time we are five or six. Common-sensically, we know people exist. And, even if no one else exists, each of us can say "I exist." That is something we understand most clearly while we are awake. Ordinarily, though, it never occurs to us to question whether other persons exist. We feel quite certain they do, for the very simple reason that we sense them. When it is dark and we cannot see them, we can hear them. Or we can reach out and feel them.

When he ruminated on thousands upon thousands of facts such as those, Aristotle naturally tried to put order into his thinking by using various ideas his predecessors, especially his mentor, Plato*, had put forth. In time, he settled on the five particularly useful concepts which seemed to 'fit' those thousands of particular facts available in his memory. (*This is an important point. Aristotle did not start out, as we say, 'from scratch.' He got many, if not most, of his ideas 'from' his great teacher, Plato.)

In every case, Aristotle began with the *agent* or *actor* that performs *acts* or activities. Human agents are like all other agents in many respects. We can be stationary or moving, just as rocks are. We can grow, just as trees and plants do. We can see, hear, feel, and remember, just as dogs which bury bones in the back yard do. But, Aristotle noticed, we can perform acts that are different and unique. We can create theories—even about creating theories—and reason to new truths. Reflections such as those gave Aristotle his first two concepts for his model: agents and acts.

The other three concepts in his model are power or faculty, habit, and object. The concept of *power* or faculty is one we use constantly, usually without ever giving it a name. We talk of people who go blind as having 'lost their sight' or as having 'lost their power to see.' It is a short step from there to the notion that different kinds of agents are born with certain powers which later on they can use, develop, quit using, even lose. Humans are born with two legs which constitute their power to walk. Infants who do not walk already possess the ability, the power, or the faculty. When they exercise that power by actually walking, a *habit* develops. Aristotle generalized this last idea, extending it to the entire process of learning. Learning is a process whereby an agent performs certain acts made possible by its innate power, and repetition of those acts creates modifications of the powers, which modifications are called habits.

It is easy to distinguish powers from habits. Butterflies cannot play the piano, neither can infants. But the former do not even have the power or ability to 'tickle the ivories,' whereas the latter do. And, after the young Rubenstein has repeated the acts often enough, he will have the enviable habit we call a skill. Babies cannot think. But that is not because they lack the raw power. If they did, they would no more become mature and think than a butterfly does. But they do lack the habit called "knowledge." James is famous for his treatment of habit. Most important of all is his use of the idea behind "thought habit," which is shorthand for his slightly lengthier shorthand-*generalization* cited above, "Twenty experiences make us remember a thing better, and long indulgence in error makes right thinking almost impossible" (PP I:552), whose 'content' is thousands of particular, daily facts such as one's swift recall of spouse's, siblings', best friends' names, as opposed to failures to remember what lunch consisted of on this date a year ago, what that day's headline was, what . . . Still, Aristotle was the first to treat intellectual learning under the heading of habit. (*Categories*, ch.8)

Object is the last of the five concepts. It is the most obvious, but also the most tricky and troublesome of the five concepts when used to understand humans' knowledge. Chapter I has already presented a summary of Aristotle's common-sense notion that distinctions are needed when we ask "What do I see?", "What do I hear?", "What do I smell?", and so on. At first, we are tempted to answer in terms of material things such as people, rooms, books, buildings, trees, apples, and so on. Aristotle cautioned that it is more precise to say that we see the *colors* of things, hear their *sounds*, etc. By recalling thousands of everyday facts and then discriminating similarities and differences, Aristotle found that a three-fold classification into proper objects, common objects, and incidental objects worked best. Since we assume that we today see, hear, smell, taste, and feel in the same way that people in Aristotle's day did, what worked best then can be presumed to work best for us. At least so far as our naïve-realism is concerned.

Those Five Concepts Are Created, Not Observed. Recall again that James once insisted that the only way to know the stream of experience is by introspection, and that introspection is "looking into our own minds and reporting what we there discover." Pause for a moment and see whether or not, if you look into your mind, you can find an agent, some powers, several acts, various habits, and an object or two!

If that's absurd, consider another example that shows even more obviously how absurd it is to think our psychology is based on the naïve just-look-inward or just-reflect *model* as an explanation for the origin of psychological models. Where do such ideas as conscious, preconscious, subconscious, subliminally conscious, unconscious, and so on, come from?! Can anyone who is unconscious look inward to notice the state of unconsciousness? Clearly, such ideas are, in the Kant-James-and-Einstein model, created for the purpose of discovering how our minds or brains—both?—work. *At first*, a two-item model is all we need. Either we are awake and conscious, or else we are asleep and unconscious. *Later*, when we have become used to the facts we describe as 'dreaming while we are asleep,' we need a tri-partite model. There is wide-awake consciousness, there is the dreaming type of sleep, and there is the total lack of consciousness we call dreamless sleep, total and absolute coma, even death. *Later still*, particularly in and after his *Varieties of Religious Experience* lectures, James began to appeal—as other thinkers did—to such things as subliminal consciousness, a subconscious self, and so on.

Transition: Removing James' Ambiguities. James, we know, did not rest content with common sense. He later fastened on the system he called "radical empiricism." The result is that his writings challenge every reader's ability to deal with constant ambiguities.

In his naïve-realist mode, James referred to books, brains, etc., as objects. He retained part of common sense when he adopted Berkeley's adoption of Aristotle's thesis that, properly speaking, we sense color, sound, etc., now referred to as "secondary qualities." He did the same when he adopted Berkeley's decision to detach those qualities from such 'incidental sensibles' as substances.

In his radical-empiricist mode, he adopted Berkeley's good habit of taking those outward-seeming qualities and relocating them inside the mind. At the same time, however, he adopted Berkeley's bad habit of mentally grouping the secondary qualities into idea-clusters signified by the old thing-words, e.g., "apple," "the room you are in," "the book you are reading," "Memorial Hall," "tigers in India," and so on. Worse yet, he became so insistent on the partless unity of each moment's total stream of conscious experience and treated it as a single, unified 'object,' that he usually failed to acknowledge the *always*-distinctness of such sense-data as color, sound, and so on. In a few places, however, he did write more accurately about each distinct aspect of humans' conscious experience. This reconstruction relies on *selecting* the better, but scattered analyses.

Our guide for the *selecting* is certain general convictions and certain tacit 'senses' that permeate the massive common-sense philosophy each normal learner acquires in a gradual, unforeseen, unplanned, unself-conscious way, during the 'duration' between birth and the age of five or six. First on the list is that things are what exist. First on the list of specific things are persons. What are the acts persons perform? First on the list for psychologist-*theorists* are thinking, believing, pretending, telling the truth, lying, etc.

As for the tacit 'senses,' they are available when called for. The child of five who still believes in Santa does not need a lesson in ontology to understand that there is a problem if Susie down the street says "There's no Santa Claus." (Being vs nonbeing) The child of five understands if we ask, "You know, don't you, what the difference is between just pretending that you are asleep and being really and truly asleep?" (Conscious vs unconscious) A child who has knocked Mom's favorite lamp off the table has sufficient common sense to feel a twinge of guilt when, in answer to "Who broke the lamp," she or he answers "Nobody did, it just fell." (Caused vs uncaused) These are the 'facts' of everyday experience that pursuers of psychological wisdom must begin with, reexamine, and account for.

Here, then, we agree with the verdict James announced in "The Function of Cognition," namely, "If our hearers agree with us about what are to be held 'realities,' they will perhaps also agree to the reality of our doctrine of the way in which they are known." (*Writings* II:836) What that means begins as follows. Like everyone else, we acquired and still remember the common-sense view of realities. Details of that philosophy were described at length in the previous volume, *William James on Common Sense*. This follow-up volume uses that foundation as a quasi-floating platform for 'constructing' a Jamesian quintalist belief-system. According to quintalism, the only realities in the entire universe are persons, subatomic particles, and the three types of things that can be noticed in every human stream of consciousness that is like ours. That is, those are the only kinds of things that really exist.

Quintalism is a radically pared-down worldview. If nothing except persons, full-bodied sense-data, memory-images of them, ongoing thoughts (objects, not acts), and smaller-than-atom-sized bodies exist, then stars, clouds, horses, brains, etc., do not exist. Neither do nations, societies, cultures, markets, corporations, money, etc. Not even language.

But we do have thoughts about all of those and thousands of other 'things.' And the most convenient way to think about those 'things' is by adopting the image or model James suggested, namely, that those 'things' are "contained, as it were, in the thought's pocket." Call them "the mental content, deliverance, or matter of the understood-thought." Hundreds of those 'things' are convenient fictions or pragmatic concepts, hundreds more are indispensable constructs, though hundreds more are useless distractions requiring the decisive application of Ockham's Razor.

Keep this rule in mind, then. There are only three questions that must be answered completely in order to know all that is worth knowing. The first is "What exists?" The quintalist answer is firm. The second is, "What do things that exist do?" Acts or doings do not exist, though concepts of them are indispensable. The third is, "Why do those things do what they do?"

As for "What exists?", it is obvious that imaginations are not on that quintalist list. Imaginations do not exist. Images, however, are. Images exist.

5. 'Merging' Imagining and Thinking

Imagination: A Pragmatic or Useful Fiction. With this section of Chapter II we return to section 5 of Chapter I, where a list of quotations referring to such fictions as personality, society, culture, numbers, etc., was offered. They illustrate the point that various academic 'disciplines' have fictions built into their basic assumptions. Those fictions may not exist, but they often serve as useful shorthand in thinking about existents, that is, about things that do exist.

The way to *'analyse fictions till existents are reached'* was illustrated with a single specific example, the 'mental illness' fiction. On the one hand, schizophrenia and other fictions do not exist as such. But, on the other hand, persons and the three tributaries of their 'streams of conscious experience' do exist.

So here. There are no such things as faculties, powers, acts, habits, or even language. But there are persons, the full-bodied sense-data and images they are aware of, and most importantly the thoughts that they understand.

More to the point here, there is no such thing as 'the imagination.'

Analyzing "Imagination" Till Existent Thoughts Are Reached. There are no imaginations floating around like butterflies that can be caught with the right kind of net. However, there are human beings who can imagine. The way to understand what "who can imagine" means, is to understand that *imagining is thinking*.

In the same way that the motions of our two legs are described by different names, such as walking, sauntering, skipping, running, etc., understanding thoughts or thinking can be described by different names. When we are thinking of things that happened in the past, that thinking can be renamed "remembering." When we are thinking of things that will or may happen in the future, that thinking can be renamed "anticipating." When we are thinking about things that we believe exist now, that thinking is what is usually just called "thinking." And when we are thinking about things that never did happen, are not happening, and will never happen, we call that thinking "imagining."

Other forms of thinking to which we add those qualifications we call "connotations" are given such names as "pretending," "assuming for the sake of argument," "hypothesizing," "predicting," "asserting," "doubting," "denying," "inferring," "deducing," "reasoning," "abstracting," "reifying," and so on.

If we convert those *verbs* to *nouns*, the converting yields such 'reification' names as pretense, assumption, hypothesis, prediction, assertion, doubt, denial, inference, deduction, reasoning, abstraction, reification, and so on.

How to Analyse 'A Thought' by Adjusting Aristotle's Model. Thoughts will be the subject or topic of the following chapter. That chapter is the highlight of this book, because it will explain in detail the greatest of James's insights. However, in order to begin the transition from inadequate models for psyche-science or psyche-logy to a way of 'seeing' beyond models (an impossibility?), it will help to begin the process of fully analyzing imagination and imagining into understanding thoughts and their 'contents.'

To do that 'more fully analyzing,' it is necessary to adjust Aristotle's model just a bit. Instead of picturing our self (agent) intellectually knowing (act) a thing (object), we break the object into two and preface the second with a preposition. That is, instead of "I intellectually know my hand," we begin using "I (agent) understand (act) this complete thought (object) about my hand (object)."

By adopting this slightly adjusted model, it is easy to take account of the fact that, when we merely imagine things that do not exist, we need not fall into the trap Parmenides fell into when he concluded that 'nothing' cannot be thought or talked about since it does not exist. If we think about Santa Claus and agree that no such 'being' exists, it is clear that we 'have something very definite before our mind.' We are neither unconscious nor are we thoughtless when we think that thought. Or, rather, understand that thought! Recall the part of James's 1883-84 draft which was cited on an earlier page:

> Since errors, illusions, & fictions are not cognitive in our sense, altho they have objects, it is clear that *object* & *reality* cannot be used as synonymous terms. We will keep the word object for use in the phenomenal sense exclusively, as equivalent to the mental content, deliverance or matter of consciousness alone, whether it reveal a reality recognized as such by us psychologists or not. The objects of error & fiction will then not be realities, for they will have no status or existence outside of the particular feelings in which they appear. (MEN:265-66)

Instead of "content, deliverance or matter of consciousness," we can use the even more picturesque metaphor James used in another note that also was cited earlier. The object or content of the understood thought is 'in the thought's pocket.'

> Whilst admitting that a world of things and persons and a world of my own past thoughts appear to be revealed to my instant thought as other than [itself], suppose I still persist in regarding them as mere illusions; contained, as it were, in the thought's pocket, very much as a vast perspective view may be a mere image breathed on the windowpane in which it appears. (Perry I:579)

In each case, then, we (the agent-persons) are understanding (act) thoughts (objects) which are *about* this or that 'thing' which may or may not exist. To help get used to this improved model, we can apply it to imagination and imagining.

Many Complete Thoughts, but a 'Same Topic.' James's best description of "a thought" is "the meaning of a complete sentence." Written 'complete sentences,' like words and names, can be analyzed into such physical things as ink marks or into parts of TVFs, i.e., as parts of visual sense-data. In the latter case, thought must be understood in relation to full-bodied sense-data and memory-images of them, that is, in relation to the two types of existent things that it is distinct from, that it is correlated with, and that, together with them, can be imagined! as making up one single 'thing,' the 'stream of consciousness.'

However, one of the vitally important features of our thoughts is that we can think many thoughts about one and the same thing or topic. This was one of James's most important insights. Here is how he began his presentation of it in Chapter XII, "Conception," in a section titled, "The Sense of Sameness."

> "*The same matters can be thought of in successive portions of the mental stream, and some of these portions can know that they mean the same matters which the other portions meant.*" One might put it otherwise by saying that "*the mind can always intend, and know when it intends, to think of the Same.*"
>
> This *sense of sameness* is the very keel and backbone of our thinking. (PP I:459)

Applied. Till now, this chapter (if chapters existed) has been about the need for imagination. One 'generic' concept of need, but three 'specific' needs. But it is also possible to think that it, along with the previous chapter, is about the stream of consciousness. Or more specifically, about James's best thoughts about that stream (singular). Or about James's best thoughts about all human streams of consciousness (plural). In other words, it is possible to take a large number of thoughts, expressed by a large number of complete sentences, and to give several different answers to the question, "What is this chapter about?" Compare that to the question, "What is the one subject that James's *Principles of Psychology* is about?" The *one* subject?!

P. S. An outstanding illustration of the human ability to gather together or amass many thoughts about 'the same thing' is the gift resting here on my desk, a gift received many years ago from a colleague. It is an eight-hundred-pages-long collection of sentences whose topic is *The World of the Imagination, Sign and Substance*, by Eva T. H. Brann. Its topic(s) is imagination and images.

"*The* Imagination?" Did James believe imaginations exist? The answer is that, whether or not he believed imaginations in the plural existed, it is clear that he did not believe in the existence of 'the' Imagination. In Chapter XVIII of *The Principles*, he wrote,

> Until very recent years it was supposed by all philosophers that there was a typical human mind which all individual minds were like, and that propositions of universal validity could be laid down about such faculties as 'the Imagination.' Lately, however, a mass of revelations have poured in, which make us see how false a view this is. There are imaginations, not 'the Imagination,' and they must be studied in detail. (PP II:49-50)

Yet even though he denied that there is any 'the' imagination (singular), he did not deny that there are individual imaginations (plural). But that, too, is literally false. There are people who understand and assent to thoughts about things that do not exist, etc. Nevertheless, James's words point to a vitally important truth that had been hammered into him in 1865 by Louis Agassiz while the two were together on a biological expedition to the Amazon.

Generalizations vis-à-vis Particulars. One of the most important things James ever learned was the difference between generalizations and the particular, plural facts or details which can be 'summed up' with them.

No one sees farther into a generalization than his own knowledge of details extends, and you have a greater feeling of weight and solidity about the movement of Agassiz's mind, owing to the continual presences of this great background of special facts . . . (W. James, *Letters* I:65)

"No one sees farther into a generalization than his own knowledge of details extends." Evidence for the depth and permanence of James's conviction on this score is found in the fourth of his *Pragmatism* lectures, in which he told his audience that the problem of 'the one and the many' was the most profound of all. It is also found in a related outburst near the beginning of the seventh lecture:

It never occurs to most of us even later that the question 'what is *the* truth?' is no real question (being irrelative to all conditions) and that the whole notion of *the* truth is an abstraction from the fact of truths in the plural, a mere useful summarizing phrase like *the* Latin Language or *the* law. (*Writings* II:591)

James thus joins Descartes in reversing a tradition in Western thought, a long-standing tradition inaugurated by Socrates, Plato, and especially Aristotle. They held that scientific knowledge 'rises above' knowledge of individuals. To know all there is to know about a single, i.e., individual, rose would not count as science. First, the rose itself is in constant change, and to be true science, the knowledge would have to be updated each hour. Second, there would be no guarantee that knowing all about this particular rose would be of any help in knowing about any other rose.

That is part of what lies behind James's insistence that there is no *the* truth, no *the* Latin Language, and no *the* Imagination. If all you know is one truth, what can you know about truth in general? Etc.

And yet, did he not title the sixth of his *Pragmatism* lectures "Pragmatism's Conception of Truth"? Is there only one pragmatism? Arthur Lovejoy claimed he'd been able to find thirteen of them. Did all thirteen have only one conception of truth? James himself had at least two different ideas of truth. Truth? Or truths? But wait? How many things is this paragraph about? Paragraph or sentences? Sentences or words? Words or letters? Letters or ink marks? Ink marks or molecules of ink? Ink or black colors? Colors or color?

Once we begin to rethink every one of our beliefs, we find ourselves in a swirl of questions that have no well-flagged, absolutely final question. If someone is different from everyone else, that person is unique. If everyone is different from everyone else—and isn't that the truth?—everyone is unique. But if everyone is unique, doesn't that make everyone the same as everyone else—at least in that respect—and, therefore, not unique? Did the Cretan tell the truth who said, "All Cretans are liars"? But did the Cretan mean Cretans always lie?

The Remedy for Such *Ad Infinitum* (Endless) Series of Questions. The remedy, believe it or not, is one of the things that all philosophers or scientists aim at, viz., decisive unification, plus mindset-switching at the appropriate junctures. As James explained in "The Sentiment of Rationality," those individuals desire to reduce the plural facts of the world to some kind of simplicity comparable to the musician's "resolving a confused mass of sound into melodic or harmonic order."

Who does not feel the charm of thinking that the moon and the apple are, as far as their relation to the earth goes, identical; of knowing respiration and combustion to be one; of understanding that the balloon rises by the same law whereby the stone sinks; of feeling that the warmth in one's palm when on rubs one's sleeve is identical with the motion which the friction checks; of recognizing the difference between beast and fish to be only a higher degree of that between human father and son; of believing our strength when we climb the mountain or fell the tree to be no other than the strength of the sun's rays which made the corn grow out of which we got our morning meal? (WB:65-66; *Writings* I:506)

The thesis of this text is that, with the help of James's best descriptions of the nature of ongoing thought—and there are many of them, anyone can 'feel the charm,' or better the exhilaration, of recognizing the ultimate similarities between all of the universe's countless individual things. That recognition will, in turn, open the door to the endless riches of James's thought.

Those ultimate similarities can be found in the quintalist generalizations.

The Quintalist Generalizations: Massive Reduction. From here on, what James advised himself must be understood as this author's advice to himself. That advice was part of the All-Important Draft referred to earlier: "The most he [the author] claims is that what he says about cognition may be counted as true as what he says *about anything* *else*. If his hearers [readers] agree that he has assumed the wrong things to be realities, then doubtless they will reject his account of the way in which those realities become known. . . ." (MEN: 265)

This book, like James's *Principles of Psychology*, generalizes. It generalizes about 'everything else.' Each reader (e.g., you), as judge and jury of one, will have to be his or her own arbiter for what he or she will will-to-believe and will will-to-disbelieve. The generalizations here are: persons, sense-data, (memory-)images, thoughts, and subatomic particles.

"Sense-Data" is a generic term. There are colors, sounds, tastes, etc., but they are radically different from each other. Deaf people can see colors but not hear sounds, whereas blind people can hear sounds but not see colors. But colors and sounds are alike insofar as they are objects of direct awareness or, as James would say, 'knowledge by acquaintance.' What a huge step toward unifying one's worldview can be taken by seeing how similar are colors (which, by the way, are radically different from each other!), sounds (ditto), tastes, and other *things* which the norm'l person directly experiences!

"Image," too, is a generic term. We are accustomed to thinking of physical images, such as photographs, paintings, statues, drawings, and so on. Those are *visual* images, copies that are like or similar to original things that were or could be seen (unless they are originals themselves!), things that re-present or represent the original, seen things (ditto). In modern times, there are *auditory* images, in the sense that there are vinyl recordings, tape-cassette recordings, compact-disk recordings, etc., of sounds.

The images that are parts of a stream of consciousness, though they are not physical, are called "images" because they are copies (Hume's term) that are like or similar to—or that re-present—original seen, heard, tasted, smelled, and felt *things*, i.e., sensed givens or sense-data.

Finally, if this computer program counted correctly, you have just had twenty-six thoughts go through your mind as you read this section that was 'announced' by "The Quintalist Generalizations: Massive Reduction." Though you have scanned only shaped and arranged black figures, all sorts of images have been drawn into your stream of consciousness, along with an evolving, ongoing thought which, though partless, can be imagined or thought of as having parts which, in English*, are called "concepts" or "ideas." (*An important qualification, since it is estimated that there are three to ten thousand other languages; even in English, the parts are given different names by different thinkers.)

The preceding thoughts can now be summarized or generalized with a single sentence: each mature, norm'l person's stream of consciousness is 'made up' of three types of existent things, namely, full-bodied sense-data, memory-images of previously-experienced sense-data, and thought(s).

Add "persons" and "smaller-than-atom-sized bodies" to those three items, and all the 'things' that we humans have thoughts about can be analyzed into or reduced to one or more of those five mental classes, categories, file-cases, or pigeon-holes created for thinking about things, entities, items, beings, etc.

The mental picture conjured by the preceding, when compared to our usual, everyday thinking about this endlessly complex universe, is well described as "a massive reduction."

Reducing Imagining to Understanding Thoughts. This entire chapter has been constructed on the premise that there are three types of items in the mature person's stream of consciousness. The most crucial part of that stream is thought.

To see how true this is, a person who has read this chapter can pause for a few moments and ask, "What has been going on while I've been reading?" The answer is plain. Readers see a flow of black figures that awaken a constant flow of imagery associated with those figures, and the two flows are accompanied by a flow of thought(s).

Dozens, hundreds, even thousands of different answers, each part of one of the dozens, hundreds, even thousands of different belief-systems, have been created in the past by different thinkers who have tried to understand human knowledge.

James, brilliant psychologist that he was, took it as a given fact that each person has a philosophy (see Lecture I of *Pragmatism*) and that there are many rival or contradictory philosophies or belief-systems. If we imagine that those worldviews are created by human imaginations, it helps to appreciate the fertility of the human imagination, a fertility attested to by the thousands of novels, the thousands of movies, and the thousands of TV soap operas produced every single year.

What a gigantic proof of the unlimited fertility of the human imagination. That is, of human thought.

P. S. What animals display an ability to do anything remotely similar? What beast, bird, or insect alive today knows anything more about the cosmos than any of its remote ancestors? The only persons who do not appreciate the uniqueness of the human person are those whose imagination has not yet expanded enough to take in the full glory of itself!

6. More About Images As Such

The Topic Now Will Be Images. Until Descartes' revolutionary discovery, theories about the mind's images were meager in the extreme. That is because images were thought of rather simply as snapshot copies of sensed things. Because it was assumed that the sensed things were stars, the sun, clouds, trees, animals, people, etc., images were assumed to be faint mental copies of stars, the sun, clouds, trees, animals, people, etc.

After Descartes showed that we do not sense stars, etc., those who continued to believe that all our knowledge begins with experience—Locke, Berkeley, and Hume are the most famous—inaugurated more detailed research to see how the learning process works. The image or picture that guided their inquiries into the thickets of inner experience is the view that original ideas or images are faint copies of sense-impressions. That model led by inexorably logical reasoning to Hume's conclusion that most of what we grow up thinking we know is illusion, reached by 'mixing, compounding, separating, and dividing' faint copies that do not get us 'outside our mind.'

A Major Role of Imagery: One-Space-One-History Models. Inner models, 'composed' of images, are accompaniments to our thoughts. It is convenient to refer to the models or images as 'vehicles' for thought. In fact, in some sense, it is convenient to think of 'clarifying our thoughts' as partly referring to 'clarifying our inner model.' For instance, recognition of the role of imagery in the form of inner models and maps helps to more clearly delineate the differences between rival belief-systems, that is, rival worldviews or 'philosophies.' We can now notice, for instance, how one materialist who hears "consciousness" immediately calls up on the screen of imagination an inner model focused on behaving organisms, how a different materialist conjures a picture of a brain, and how a dualist uses a model of both a brain-possessing organism and an immaterial consciousness.

We begin with the fact there are more and less inclusive concepts, analogous to maps which vary in how much they represent. Different maps will be needed in order to pinpoint any given individual existent. Someone asks "Where do you live?" We begin our answers with 'the Big Picture,' then zoom in: "In the universe," "In the Milky Way," "On a planet in the solar system," "In North America," "In the United States," etc. As for the United States, a map showing the entire surface of the planet will suffice. But a more detailed map will be needed for "In Massachusetts," another for "On Salisbury Street," etc.

In similar fashion, a thinker's answers to "What is that?" can range from the utterly general "It's clearly some thing" to the utterly specific "It's the first copy of the Bible printed on the Gutenberg Press during the middle of the fifteen century."

It is when we zoom back out to the most inclusive map that we find different thinkers. When they switch from their common-sense map to their 'professional' mindset, they give radically divergent answers to the question, "What reality or realities do all of your concepts and/or models represent?" If we can identify a writer's fullest answer to "What exists, period?", we can begin the task of constructing our own version of that individual's philosophy. The most general classes of philosophies are: materialism ("The universe contains only stars, planets, etc."), idealism ("The universe contains only immaterial realities"), and dualism ("The universe contains both material and immaterial realities"). Quintalism is closer to dualism than to either materialism or idealism. The reason why materialists, idealists, and dualists—if they have sufficient time and intellectual capability—can understand one another's divergent worldviews is because all higher learning begins with and can be traced back to common sense.

In the prequel, *William James on Common Sense*, it was explained that, in addition to the one-space model, we must construct a one-history time for what things do. For instance, new-born learners learn only gradually . . .

A Gradually Increasing Stream. Here is a picture or model to help understand the time-perspective of human learning. It amends James's "great blooming, buzzing confusion" image. That is, the stream of consciousness is initially made up of distinct sense-data: color-fields, sounds, pinches, and so on. They are as distinct from each other at the beginning as they are later on. It is simply that, so far as thought-ful *understanding* of those differences is concerned, the infant's 'world' might just as well be a big, sometimes buzzing, occasionally booming, confusing jumble.

Only gradually do vast stocks of associated memory-images accumulate and, in time, start getting selectively evoked by the from-the-start-discrete sense-data, even by from-the-start discrete 'parts' of sense-data. Thus, if the newborn's own 'hand' and another's 'hand' are simultaneously in its total visual field, it will not automatically associate what it feels with its own seen 'hand' rather than with the other's only-seen 'hand.' That is, the association of discriminated parts of the visual field with the discriminated parts of the body-image is not immediate but takes time. (Dr. V. S. Ramachandran's use of mirror images to treat amputees by breaking locked-in associations was noteworthy enough to be reported in the 3-28-95 *New York Times*.)

It takes even more time for those 'special' sounds later called "words" to evoke distinct, associated memory-image clusters that Berkeley would say *are* stars, clouds, forest-animals, lake-fish, etc. In time, the child's always-present 'body' sense-data will cluster sufficiently to be discriminated from the intermittent sense-data of (other) persons, animals, plants, minerals, and so on. That will lead to the 'out-there' vs 'in-here' division of the 'universe' into what James called "the not-me and the me." (****An all-important note must be appended here. Only after the child has first learned by itself, from inside, to discriminate its self from non-its-self selves can mythical 'society'—in the person of those other, not-its-self individuals—'program' the infant to create 'its self' (really its self-concept), 'its culture,' 'its social world,' etc.)

Decisions. As our learning progresses, our inner models 'contain' more and more items which can be conjured by a simple 'language prompt.' The 'language-prompts' we receive from others play a major role in our creation of new items. 'Conceptual analysis' or, in Socrates' terms, 'the examined life' allows us to make new decisions about which 'things' represented by items in our inner model really exist and which do not. When we decide some do not, we reduce the number of things we believe in. This down-sizing analysis is referred to as "applying Ockham's Razor" and "reductionism." As noted above, Jamesian quintalism is a form of reductionism, though far less radical than James's radical empiricism.

When dealing with things we've always pictured as three-dimensional, the process is simple. We decide Santa and his toyshop don't exist? We clear him and it from our picture of the North Pole. Hell doesn't exist? We fill in that hollowed-out, flame-filled area far below our feet.

However, in the case of non-dimensional, purely theoretical or abstract items,, e.g., space as such, time as such, imagination as such, the removal may involve no more than switching from assenting to a thought to denying it, e.g., from believing "Space exists" to denying "Space exists."

But each time we boldly decide that such-and-such does not exist, we must be equally careful to decide what does. For instance, consciousness as such does not exist. We remove from our model any thing with that name. But people do exist, people are consciously aware of sense-data and images that do exist, and people consciously understand thoughts that exist. We make certain that those are retained in our inner model. Similarly, sensations do not exist as such. People do, however, and people are aware of colors, sounds, and other sensed objects. There are no minds. It may be convenient to mark out an area near brains and to use it to represent a place where sense-data, images, and thoughts exist, but the only things 'there' are sense-data, images, and thoughts, no literal 'mind' container. There are no free wills. But there are people who freely will to believe or not to believe that persons, sense-data, images, thoughts, and subatoms exist. Etc.

A Notice. Whoever wants to explore the topic of images will find no guide better than James. However, there is one qualification that must be added, one caution. James did not always respect a clear-cut distinction between concepts and images or, as the next chapter will explain in more detail, between the thoughts we understand and the images which accompany them. There are some passages where his failure to distinguish is egregious. Probably none, though, surpasses the beginning of the second paragraph he wrote about reasoning for the chapter on that topic in *The Principles of Psychology*, namely, "Much of our thinking consists of trains of images suggested one by another, of a sort of spontaneous revery of which it seems likely enough that the higher brutes should be capable" (PP II:325). Our thoughts may be accompanied by trains of imagery, but the two are utterly distinct from each other. Unless, of course, we use "thinking" as a hybrid form of shorthand for two radically different phenomena.

Initial Vagueness. This text, then, makes a sharp theoretical distinction between images (and sense-data), on the one hand, and concepts or thoughts, on the other. But that sharp distinction is initially vague. James gave a considerable amount of attention to the vagueness in areas of the stream. For instance, he wrote about it as early as 1878 when he published "Brute and Human Intellect." He copied much of the essay into Chapter XXII of *The Principles*, including the following passage:

> All our knowledge at first is vague. When we say that a thing is vague, we mean that it has no subdivisions *ab intra*, nor precise limitations *ab extra*; but still all the forms of thought may apply to it. It may have unity, reality, externality, extent, and what not—*thinghood*, in a word, but thinghood only as a whole. In this vague way, probably, does the room appear to the babe who first begins to be conscious of it as something other than his moving nurse. (PP II:343-44; *Writings* I:924)

Because James was not in the habit of always sharply discriminating his concepts of sense-data, images, and thoughts, he was not always in the habit of distinguishing the vagueness of each from the vagueness of the others. And yet, by the time we are old and experienced enough to have acquired our common-sense philosophy, it is easy for us to understand that there are distinct vaguenesses. There is vagueness in sense-data: e.g., when we are in the midst of a dense fog, objects can appear with outlines which are at first very fuzzy and vague. There is vagueness in our images: e.g., when we close our eyes and try to picture a 999-sided figure alongside a 1000-sided figure, both appear rather vaguely as circles. Finally, there is vagueness in our unclear, indistinct thoughts: e.g., when we first encounter James's essays about radical empiricism, our thoughts are bound to be more than a little vague!

Until we have developed the requisite number of concepts, we can hardly *not* fail to notice things which later on will seem obvious and obviously distinct. At first, equipped with only our somewhat jumbled common-sense conceptual framework, we think of the 'things' we sense as if they are single, partless wholes. To grasp James's thinking, we must later try to understand what he meant when he wrote in "The Knowing of Things Together" (1894) that "things have no other nature than thoughts have." If it takes time to distinguish accidents from substances, e.g., the color, shape, and size of a stick from the stick's substance, what five-year old would understand right away what James meant by saying that the stick chased by the dog "has no other nature than thoughts have"? How can anyone's journey of discovery leading from their five-year-old's mindset to one like James's begin with anything but vagueness? What else but still-unremoved vagueness explains why some 'philosophers' refuse to recognize the clear reality of images?

Images: a Test for Metaphysicians' Grand-Unifying Modeled-Theories. All of us must be metaphysicians in the sense of deciding *what exists*. Like James, Jamesian quintalists put "images" on their existents-list. The pre-quel to this text, *William James on Common Sense*, already discussed images at considerable length. The term will be used most often in this text to refer to what thinkers in the past have used it for, namely, mental copies, inside our mind, of the objects we have sensed. As explained earlier, everyone learns what a copy is. Pictures and photographs are referred to as copies in relation to the things they are pictures or photos of.

One of the most astonishing features of human experience is that we can look at something and then, with our eyes closed, conjure an inner picture or copy of what we saw. Once we notice this, we can begin distinguishing external, physical copies, and internal, mental images.

It was also noted earlier that visual images, i.e., copies of what we have seen, are not the only inner images. We can also hear a sound and later, when everything is silent, conjure a faint 'echo' of what we heard. By expanding the concept of images, we can group faint reproductions of sounds, tastes, smells, pains, tickles, and other sensed 'objects,' together with visual copies, all under "images." There are, then, visual, auditory, gustatory, olfactory, and other types of mental images.

Nevertheless, images are strange, and not everyone agrees that they exist. Many recent thinkers argue that "image" names a reification or logical fiction at best, a self-induced illusion at worst. They apply Ockham's Razor to images, the same way Watson and behaviorists applied it to every kind of private, inner mental state. True, we are accustomed to using such expressions as "I can see his face as if he was right in front of me" or "I can practically hear the sound of his voice" even when we know there is no literal seeing or hearing going on. But what *is* literally going on? The answers of image-deniers range from "It is remembering" or "It is having a disposition to recognize" to "It is an activation of certain neurons."

Given that thinkers from Plato who died in 347 B. C. to James who died in 1910 A. D. have believed images exist, why would anyone deny it? There is no single answer. Image-deniers have as many reasons or motives for not believing in images as they have theories about what is literally going on. Resistance to giving up long-standing materialist beliefs is one of the most common. Another is that, if images do exist, they do not fit into any normal category of 'things that exist.' They are strange indeed.

For instance, consider one of the most undeniable kinds of image, an after-image of the noonday sun. If we stare at the sun for just one or two seconds and then look at something else, the vivid after-image will 'block out' whatever we look at. James describes some remarkable experiments that can be done by anyone experiencing it. (See PP II:231) If we carry out those experiments, we will notice that the 'size' seems to change from tiny to huge and back. Does it make any sense to say that one and the same after-image can have different sizes? Does that after-image have another side, or only the one 'facing' us? How far is the after-image of the sun 'up here' from the wiggling of our toes which seems to be 'down there'? Are images in 'physical space' or is there another space, one that some thinkers call "perceptual space"? If images really do exist, should we call them "things"? Are they things the way stars and planets are things which, common-sensically, we think were in existence long before there were humans to look up and see them? That is, where are images when we are not conjuring them up from . . . .? From our memory? Is that a place? From our brain? Do brains exist? Should we classify images as attributes, properties, or qualities, and say they modify us while we are inspecting or introspecting them? On and on could go the questions.

Images are indeed strange. But by the time we finish understanding James, it will be clear that everything is strange. *This whole world is unexpected, astonishing, and, yes, mysterious.* That is why the strangeness of images is a silly reason for denying their existence. What isn't? As the phrase goes, "There are more things in this world, Horatio . . .'

Back for a moment to 'metaphysics.' Those who deny that images as such exist can clearly understand questions about them. How or why? According to the Rorty Rule, upon which this entire interpretation of James is based, they must. Otherwise, how would they know the difference between "Images exist" and "No, they don't"? If deniers do understand those questions, however, is it not obvious that they can think about *what-does-not-exist* (images) as easily as Parmenides did when he denied that such a thing is possible? And if we can think about a non-existent image on two successive days, where was 'it' during the night between the two days? Is it any wonder that, when he pondered such imponderable mysteries, Parmenides decided the only way to drown out such troubling thoughts was to insist that they made no sense? As we have seen, James wrestled mightily with such questions which go to the very core of our everyday ideas about truth and error. As well as to the core of all those other theories we label "science," "philosophy," "theology," and "psychology."

Acquired Clarity in Thinking About Images. One reason some people deny the existence of images is the fact that they have not thought it worthwhile to study them. (Can anyone imagine Watson spending time pondering after-images?) For those who do devote time and effort to studying their own images in order to learn whether the older psychologists, from Plato to Descartes, understood them, there are two invaluable revisions James made to 'traditional thinking' about them.

First is his realization that images are extended but not—as Descartes' theory maintained—material. The vivid after-image of the sun is clearly spread out in two dimensions. (For more on James's revision, see *William James on Common Sense*.) His second revision corrected the traditional notion that images are exact, not vague copies, a correction he credited to Huxley and Taine, but which he set forth prominently at the beginning of *The Principles*'s chapter dealing with images. Though Hume was the target of his criticism, Hume himself had merely repeated what he had been taught (by his reading).

Hume was the hero of the atomistic theory. Not only were ideas copies of original impressions made on the sense-organs, but they were, according to him, completely adequate copies, and were all so separate from each other as to possess no manner of connection. Hume proves ideas in the imagination to be completely adequate copies, not by appeal to observation, but by *a priori* reasoning . . .

The slightest introspective glance will show to anyone the falsity of this opinion. Hume surely had images of his own works without seeing distinctly every word and letter upon the pages which floated before his mind's eye. His dictum is therefore an exquisite example of the way in which a man will be blinded by *a priori* theories to the most flagrant facts. (PP II:45-46)

Once again, James's insights into vagueness are quite obvious once drawn to our attention. All of us begin life as infants for whom the distinctness of seen colors vs heard sounds vs felt pinches, etc., is matched by an utter lack of distinctness so far as *understanding* or *theory* is concerned. However, as our learning progresses, we can acquire utterly clear and distinct ideas. Among them should be clear and distinct ideas of utterly faint and vague images as contrasted with vivid and sharp images. How much farther our learning goes depends on opportunities offered and efforts made. There's so much to analyse. James summed up the challenge on one of the pages in his chapter on "The Stream of Thought."

[. . .] Here, again, language works against our perception of the truth. We name our thoughts simply, each after its thing, as if each knew its own thing and nothing else. What each really knows is clearly the thing it is named for, with dimly perhaps a thousand other things. It ought to be named after all of them, but it never is. Some of them are always things known a moment ago more clearly; others are things to be known more clearly a moment hence. Our own bodily position, attitude, condition, is one of the things of which *some* awareness, however inattentive, invariably accompanies the knowledge of whatever else we know. (PP I:241)

"Dimly"—that is, vaguely—"a thousand other things." Why not a million? The next chapter will delve further into the unspeakable complexity of each moment's passing thought.

But James's reference to our normally unnoticed awareness of our own body-image sense-data offers an opening for mentioning a few more details about our images of those somatic sense-data and all of our other images.

Images Are Where Their 'Originals' Were. Our 'body sense-data' are clearly 'felt' in different places. But so, too, are our other sense-data. Getting a solid grip on this sense-datum insight is a prerequisite for getting a solid grip on the full truth about images. The reason is this. Images are in the exact same location that sense-data are in. The 'faint' visual images are where visual sense-data or color-fields are. 'Faint' auditory images are where auditory sense-data or sounds are. 'Faint' tactile images are in the same place as tactile sense-data or pressures, etc., are. To know 'where to look' for images, then, it is necessary to know 'where to look' for sense-data. That is the reason for the pages devoted earlier to the need to get beyond a 'purely intellectualistic' or abstract theory concerning what we sense.

An overwhelming surprise awaits everyone who has grown up never doubting common sense's naïve realism. That surprise is the 'spaciousness' of one's mind. We are used to looking around us, thinking that the things we sense are far off horizons: far off mountains, endless stretches of ocean, far off stars in a dark night sky. We are used to feeling small and insignificant in such vast stretches of space. What and where is our mind? It is some small, unseen area beneath our hair-covered scalp. If images exist, where are they? In the same tiny area.

But when the insight finally 'hits home' that what we have been seeing are not horizons, mountains, oceans, stars, etc., and that what we have been hearing are not distant rumbles of thunder or roars of jet engines, etc., but are rather parts of a holographic 'world' distinct from whatever never-seen and never-heard bodies inhabit the pitch-dark and dead-silent spaces physicists picture to themselves, we marvel that our 'mind' is spacious enough to contain all these spread-out, sensuous, data-givens.

We ask again, "Where are images?" Where are those things which, in Hume's vivid vocabulary, are 'faint copies'? Once we suddenly stop implicitly mis-taking what is thought of as a book and stop saying 'This *visible* book is sending (invisible) light to my (invisible) retinas and sending (invisible) impulses to my (invisible) brain to create (invisible) sensations in my tiny (invisible) mind,' and begin to explicitly take what is sensed as the *visible* end-product effect of a physical (invisible) book sending (invisible) light to (invisible) retinas sending (invisible) nerve impulses to an (invisible) brain," there is no overlooking the fact that the total visual-field is quite spacious. Sense-data do not feel as if they are packed like sardines into a tiny box called 'the mind.' Now, with a field of experience that seems as spacious as the universe, we can notice that the faint-copy images of those sense-data appear in just the same places as the sense-data 'originals.'

A few reflections will make it easier to understand this point about images. Notice that, when we try to conjure a visual image of something we have seen, the image does not materialize down near our toes but in the place we all call 'right before my eyes.' Jacques Barzun, in *A Stroll with William James*, related a memorable anecdote apropos of this usually overlooked fact so crucial for James's theory of expectancy at the end of *William James on Common Sense*.

[. . .] But born teachers—who are fewer perhaps than born poets—when the demand comes, and despite their reluctance and disapproval, cannot help explaining, coaching, tutoring, enlightening.

The ways of accomplishing this are endless. James's was the spontaneous—after long preparation. Each hour might bring forth a new perception, a new formulation. Woodbridge, himself a philosopher of note, has recorded how James would startle the group. "I recall a remark of William James's to the effect that we do not see out of the palms of our hands or from the middle of our backs. Such obvious remarks were characteristic of him and often more instructive than pages of forced reasoning. . . . One may now meditate for hours, for days." (J. Barzun, *A Stroll*, pp.277-78)

That passage draws attention to the fact that, not only are images where the original sense-data were, those images are also related to our body's orientation in space. Left, right, up, down, back, front, right-side-up, upside-down, and so on, are glued to the 'feel' we have for our total phenomenal 'body.' It takes but little reflection to notice how natural it is for us to use references to distinct spatial directions. On the one hand (the left one?), there is the past which is behind us (it is?), while on the other hand (right?), the future is ahead of us (oh, sure!). We reason to ever higher levels of generalization, though our thinking becomes ever deeper as we mature. Such images as those are far more specific than more general but equally familiar ones. Everyone 'knows' that the North Pole is at the top of the world and the South Pole down under. And of course everyone 'knows' that to point 'straight up' means pointing to the sun when it is just passing overhead. It is always interesting to wonder whether the South Pole would be at the top of the world if natives of South Africa and not Europeans had produced the bulk of Western literature. If they had, would the Australians refer to us as living 'down under'?

The easiest cases for noticing that images are where their originals were are cases involving vivid images of pains. Among our most vivid sensations are our aches and pains. Whoever has had an exceptionally painful experience of the 'physical' rather than emotional variety of pain is likely never to forget it, particularly if she or he has kept the memory of the pain alive by often referring to it. Suppose, for instance, someone has stepped on a nail, then been taken to the hospital and received a 'tetanus shot' directly into the open wound in the foot. So vivid may be the 'memory-image' of that pain that, years later, it is tempting to say "I can practically feel it, still!" When we see "headache" several times in "Professor Pratt on Truth," which is the Chapter-VII essay in *The Meaning of Truth*, the non-word "headache" takes our attention to the area we would describe as "behind and above my eyes" and not to our right hip where we might have felt the pain if it had been caused by an irritated nerve at the base of our spine.

Incidentally, the crucial distinction between images and thoughts can be illustrated nicely by reference to present images of earlier pain. We can think-together every sort of ache and pain—headaches, toothaches, sore arms, stomach cramps, big-toe gout, and so on—and refer to every sort simultaneously with the shorthand "pain," as when we say "No one likes pain." Careful reflection, using memories evoked by the previous paragraphs, should help to notice that any present sense-datum pain we are feeling is distinct both from all present 'memory-images' of no-longer-felt pains and from present thoughts of pain(s) 'in general.'

Reading and Our 'Bodily" Orientation. But the foregoing facts pale when compared to the following. 'Word' images play a huge role in our thinking, especially in the thinking we do while reading. If the 'meaning' of the non-word 'words' were on the page which we are reading, then why is it that the speed and facility with which we read is so severely diminished when we turn the book upside down? If the spatial orientation of a book were something absolute, that is, a feature of the world as it is in itself, independent of our stream of consciousness, then why does turning the book around have such an effect? What's more, why is it that having the book upside down relative to the room in which we are reading makes no difference whatever in the speed and facility with which we read *if we stand on our head*—so that we are upside down ourselves—while reading the upside-down book? This links with different habits, acquired in different 'cultures,' of writing (and reading) from right to left rather than from left to right. It links with da Vinci's backwards notebook-writing. Etc. All such facts relate also to Kant's gloves example to show that space is a form of 'subjective' sensibility, a notion suggested to him by both Berkeley's and Hume's explorations.

Once we learn to attend-to-and-notice images, our awareness of what is going on in our 'world' allows us to increase the scope of our worldview so that it embraces as many facts about 'inner' goings-on as about 'outer' ones. But it is important to constantly practice our noticing. James's *Principles* and *Briefer Course*, as well as numerous passages in his other works, offer attentive readers rich opportunities for such attending-and-noticing. As Woodbridge concluded, "One may now meditate for hours, for days."

Postscript. Research by 'cognitive-scientists'—e.g., R. Shepard and L. Cooper —has called attention to additional facets of experience which fit James's notion of a One-Space inner model of outer reality. The child is born without it. Sensations begin. Image clusters accumulate. Later, we use images to map the image-clusters. Word-sounds become attached to various parts of the map-images. Mental experiments with images can be timed with watches. M. Levine studied a type of experience familiar to everyone who has used roadmaps. The easiest way to use a roadmap is to turn it so that its N, E, S, or W matches the direction we are headed in. With the map in this position, it is easy to decide whether to go right or left the next time we must turn. One of Levine's experiments requires us to imagine that someone asks how to get to location X when getting there requires a right or left turn or both. Why is it so much easier to give directions when X is up ahead of us and not behind us? (*Science News*, 3-19-83.)

'Modern Philosophy' Theories About Qualities, Sense-Data, and Images. Images are strange. In relation to our growing-up notion of 'thing,' it is tempting to say that they are downright weird. Our common-sense notion of 'things' and their 'attributes' does not prepare us at all for images.

Nevertheless, willy-nilly, we all become common-sensical naïve realists as we are growing up. James turned to Aristotle and the scholastics for common sense's 'magisterial concepts.' Substance and accident are two of them. After Aristotle mentally surveyed thousands of 'facts' he had learned, he concluded that, instead of saying we sense such things as men, horses, etc., it is more exact to say that we sense only such surface qualities as their color, shape, size, etc. He called the things 'substances' and their qualities 'accidents.' The English word 'substance,' like its Latin ancestor, signifies that the men, horses, etc., stand under or support the qualities which, like color, shape, etc., cannot exist independently.

In the eighteenth century, John Locke launched an attack against the notions about substance held by his predecessors, especially Descartes. Descartes claimed that he had a clear and distinct idea of substance. Locke said it was no more clear than the idea of 'something, I know not what.' Berkeley discarded the concept from his belief-system. He decided that, so far as men's bodies, horses' bodies, apples, books, etc., were concerned, he needed only the ideas of accidents or qualities. James, in his third *Pragmatism* lecture, took account of Locke's exposé of the obscureness of the 'substance' concept and adopted Berkeley's view of material 'things' as 'groups of sense qualities united by a law.'

But colors, sounds, etc., when they are conceived within the

Berkeleyan-Jamesian framework, are conceived very differently from those identical colors, sounds, etc., when conceived within the common-sense framework. Our naïve-realist view of them is that they do not depend on us any more than the things to which they belong depend on us. According to our growing-up philosophy, the blue of the sky, the song of the nightingale, and the scent of the rose are as much part of nature as the sky, the nightingale, and the rose, are. Put another way, the sky is as blue when we are not looking at it as it is when we are. The nightingale's song is equally sweet with or without an audience. Switching to the Berkeley-James view, though, means realizing that colors, sounds, scents, etc., are part of our inner 'world' and that they evaporate as soon as we no longer are experiencing them. The reason Einstein asked, "Does the moon exist only if I look at it?", was to challenge the Berkeley'an view of quantum theorists.

If the qualities are not part of physical things, what are they? We believed that the color could not be detached from the sky and bottled, that the bird's song was motion of its throat muscles, that the fragrance needs a rose or some other thing to be the fragrance of, and so on. Sense-data, on the other hand, are detached from things. They are things themselves. But what kind of things? The blue which is flush up against me is not hard or soft, the headphone music permeating my head cannot be touched, the scent I smell cannot be passed around to others, etc.

Recent theorists have tried desperately to avoid frankly admitting the reality of odd sense-data. Some have said that 'I see blueness' means 'I immaterially or intentionally become blue.' Others want to convert to adverbs, e.g., 'I see blue-ly.' Still others analyse sensing blueness as being suddenly beset with an urge to believe something is blue. Some have hypothesized that sense-data are sufficiently similar to material things to say that, till they are sensed, we should call them 'sensibilia' (sense-able things) and that we should call them 'sense-data' only while they are being sensed. Two valuable anthologies offering the various theories about sensing were published in the 1960's: *Perceiving, Sensing and Knowing*, edited by R. J. Swartz, and *Perception and the Physical World*, edited by R. J. Hirst.

Perhaps the most relevant comment on the oddness of sense-data came from the pen of W. H. F. Barnes who did not believe in them.

[. . .] Many philosophers . . . have produced arguments to show that we never perceive physical objects, and that we are in fact subject to a constant delusion on this score. As these arguments are by no means easily refuted and are such as any intelligent person interested in the matter will sooner or later come to think of, they are well worth considering. Moreover, certain modern philosophers claim to show by these arguments not only that we do not perceive physical objects but that what we do perceive is a different sort of thing altogether, which they call a sense-datum. They are obliged to invent a new term for it because no one had previously noticed that there were such things. This theory is obviously important because it not only claims to settle the doubts which we cannot help feeling when we reflect on our perceptual experience, but it makes the astonishing claim that we have all failed to notice a quite peculiar kind of entity, or at least have constantly made mistakes about its nature. (W. H. F. Barnes, "The Myth of Sense-Data," in *Perceiving, Sensing, and Knowing*, ed., R. J. Swartz, pp.138-39)

True. But tricky and easily-misleading. That is the verdict we must pass on Barnes' report. He is right about the "constant delusion on this score." The things we sense are not physical objects, e.g., bananas. That means that "what we do perceive is a different sort of thing altogether" from a physical object. An immaterial field of colors is different from a table with a bowl of bananas on it. Of course, Aristotle too had noted that a more careful description of what we visually perceive or see is proper-object 'colors,' not 'physical objects.' As James said, it is what we say (i.e., think) about what we sense that is true or false, not what we sense. We must not be misled, therefore, by "we have all failed to notice a quite peculiar kind of entity." We've all noticed them, just not their real and strange nature. Who, for instance, fails to notice the color and shape of that they think is a banana? What we fail to notice is how incorrectly we have classified the things we see, inasmuch as we have classified what we see as independent things 'out there' rather than as ephemeral effects produced 'in here.' Barnes' final phrase, though, is a fitting summary. We truly "have constantly made mistakes about its nature," meaning by 'it' every sense-datum we ever experience.

It must be confessed that, were it not for the enormous mass of directly-observed facts that convincingly vindicate James's decision that 'science' and 'philosophy' have shown that the things we sense are not the things we common-sensically think of when we hear "apple," "book," "room," and so on, we would join those who are so puzzled by the odd nature of total visual fields, wrap-around sounds, located aches and pains, etc., that they will go to any length to hang on to naïve realism.

But that enormous mass of experiential evidence is not imaginary. Not only are there after-images of the sun which are bright enough to override whatever else is in the 'foveal' area of the visual field (James wrote that after-images could be classified as sensation: cfr. PP II:44), not only are there tinnitus ear-ringings which can be heard when we are in a room where all is silent, and not only are there phantom pains which hurt far more than slight scratchings from a pin, but the ordinary person can at any time cross her or his eyes and get the equivalent of a double-exposure photo. Russell, when he abandoned neo-Hegelian idealism, returned to naïve realism and, in his words, "rejoiced in the thought that grass is really green, in spite of the adverse opinion of all philosophers from Locke onwards." Nevertheless, as his later works amply show, he was, again in his words, not "able to retain this pleasing faith in its pristine vigour" (B. Russell, *My Philosophical Development*, pp.62-63).

As stated earlier, if sense-data are odd, images are odd, too. The reason images are odd is because they seem to differ in only one major respect from sense-data: they are less vivid, that is, fainter. If we wonder whether visual-field sense-data have a far side to them, we must wonder the same thing about visual images. In fact, the two concepts, that of sense-data and that of images, melt into one another at the weak and strong ends of their spectra, respectively. That is, there are innumerable situations in which what we experience is 'on the borderline,' so that we are not certain we 'really see something' or have merely awakened an image, not certain there is a 'real noise' or that we are simply imagining it, etc.

How should we deal with the oddness of sense-data and images? We must deal with them the same way we deal with everything we can think distinctly about. We create classification systems so that we can think-together things which are alike in this or that respect as well as discriminate them from things which they are not alike in 'said' respect. What we find is that, in a sense, everything can be compared to every other thing and fitted into some category with it. Even Dumbo and Bambi can be classed as "Disney fictions." This comparing and categorizing can itself be classed as "(phenomenologically) describing."

That is preferable to "abstracting or intuiting essences." Essences do not exist.

The preceding observations do little more than recapitulate much of what has already been presented. Far more could be said, and far more would have to be said if every critic with a different approach was responded to in detail. However, enough has been said to indicate how a Jamesian quintalist will approach the issues just referred to. She or he will acknowledge that, the farther we 'dig into' the meanings of our statements about images and sense-data, that is, into our thoughts about them, or rather the more we try to create clear and distinct pictures to 'go with' our thoughts, the more vague the 'content' becomes.

And so, as James noted, all of us at some point stop analyzing. This fact is significant. It can and will be analyzed farther in the next chapter. But, so long as we do not allow ourselves to get mired down in endless goings-deeper into what it means, a quick survey of all the thinkers James was familiar with proves that his statement "All of us at some point stop analyzing" is both intelligible and true. That is what we understand. That is what we can trust.

The best way to bring this section to a close is with a passage from James, the radical empiricist, which illustrates his typical approach. There is the flux and there is what we learn to 'say' about it.

Where, then, do we feel the objects of our original sensations to be?

Certainly a child newly born in Boston, who gets a sensation from the candle-flame which lights the bedroom, or from his diaper-pin, does not feel either of these objects to be situated in longitude 72° W. and latitude 41° N. He does not feel them to be in the third story of the house. He does not even feel them in any distinct manner to be to the right or the left of any of the other sensations which he may be getting from other objects in the room at the same time. He does not, in short, know anything *about* their space-relations to anything else in the world. The flame fills its own place, the pain fills its own place; but as yet these places are neither identified with, nor discriminated from, any other places. That comes later. For the places thus first sensibly known are elements of the child's space-world which remain with him all his life; and by memory and later experience he learns a vast number of things *about* those places which at first he did not know. But to the end of time certain places of the world remain defined for him as the places *where those sensations were*; and his only possible answer to the question *where anything is* will be say '*there*,' and to name some sensation or other like those first ones, which shall identify the spot. Space *means* but the aggregate of all our possible sensations. There is no duplicate space known *aliunde*, or created by an 'epoch-making achievement' into which our sensations, originally spaceless, are dropped. They *bring* space and all its places to our intellect, and do not derive it there.

By his body, then, the child later means simply *that place where* the pain from the pin, and a lot of other sensations like it, were or are felt. It is no more true to say that he locates that pain in his body, than to say that he locates his body in that pain. Both are true: that pain is part of what he *means by the word body.* Just so by the outer world the child means nothing more than *that place where* the candle-flame and a lot of other sensations like it are felt. He no more locates the candle in the outer world than he locates the outer world in the candle. Once again, he does both; for the candle is part of what he *means* by 'outer world.' (PP II:34-35)

Transition: 'Inner Speech.' This lengthy chapter on images and sense-data can serve as preparation for the next chapter by drawing attention to one more vital role played by imagery. That is, by drawing further attention to a role played by images of 'words.' As with any sense-data, we form images of audible-sound 'words,' images of visible-cipher 'words,' images of visible-gesture 'signs,' images of tactile-tracing 'words,' etc. We call these images "inner speech." But specific images, from visual to tactile, all fit under the genus-concept labeled "images."

7. Inner Speech: Transition to Chapter III

"Is Thought Possible Without Language?" From an early age, James gave considerable attention to the role of language in human experience. That is because he was giving much attention to the challenge that Darwin's theory of evolution posed to traditional theories about the huge gap between human intelligence and whatever intelligence, if any, 'lower' (than human) animals showed. In reflecting on that question, it was to be expected that he would give thought to the traditional view that "Man is known again as 'the talking animal'; and language is assuredly a capital distinction between man and brute." (PP II:355-56; *Writings* I:936).

But, even for a naïve realist, there are two special categories of things visible and audible for which the non-word "language" is a reminder. There are those sensed things which, we might say, constitute sensed language. For most people, such sensed things are the only type or category of which they are aware. To understand what James writes about thought, however, it is necessary to become extremely familiar with the images referred to as "inner speech." He often refers to 'words' which exist in memory only, in the form of images of sensed 'words.' The following passage from his chapter on "The Stream of Thought" is a typical example.

> [. . .] An exceptionally intelligent friend informs me that he can frame no image whatever of the appearance of his breakfast table. When asked how he then remembers it at all, he says he simply '*knows*' that it seated four people, and was covered with a white cloth on which were a butter-dish, a coffee pot, radishes, and so forth. The mind-stuff of which this 'knowing' is made seems to be verbal images exclusively. But if the words 'coffee,' 'bacon,' 'muffins,' and 'eggs' lead a man to speak to his cook, to pay his bills, and to take measures for the morrow's meal exactly as visual and gustatory memories would, why are they not, for all practical purposes, as good a kind of material in which to think? In fact, we may suspect them to be good for most purposes better than terms with a richer imaginative coloring. The scheme of relationship and the conclusion being the essential things in thinking, that kind of mind-stuff which is handiest will be the best for the purpose. Now words, uttered or unexpressed, are the handiest mental elements we have. Not only are they very *rapidly* revivable, but they are revivable as actual sensations more easily than any other items of our experience. Did they not possess some such advantage as this, it would hardly be the case that the older men are and the more effective as thinkers, the more, as a rule, they have lost their visualizing power and depend on words. This was ascertained by Mr. Galton to be the case with members of the Royal Society. The present writer observes it in his own person most distinctly.
>
> On the other hand, a deaf and dumb man can weave his tactile and visual images into a system of thought quite as effective and rational as that of a word-user. *The question whether thought is possible without language* has been a favorite topic of discussion among philosophers. Some interesting reminiscences of his childhood by Mr. Ballard, a deaf-mute instructor in the National College of Washington, show it to be perfectly possible. A few paragraphs may be quoted here. (PP I:265-66)

After copying into his text two pages from the deaf Mr. Ballard's report of his 'wordless' wonderings and thoughts about the origin of the world, wonderings prompted by his observations of the origin of successive birthings of new trees, animals, and humans, James commented:

> Here we may pause. The reader sees by this time that it makes little or no difference in what sort of mind-stuff, in what quality of imagery, his thinking goes on. The only images *intrinsically* important are the halting-places, the substantive conclusions, provisional or final, of the thought. Throughout all the rest of the stream, the feelings of relation are everything, and the terms related almost naught. These feelings of relation, these psychic overtones, haloes, suffusions, or fringes about the terms, may be the same in very different systems of imagery. (PP I:269)

Sensed 'Language.' "Language" is shorthand. In the same way that Berkeley and James used "apple" as shorthand for a group of sense-data rather than for material substances that grow on trees, "language" is shorthand as well. For naïve realists, it is used to refer simultaneously to a variety of physical things. Chief among them are air-molecule vibrations caused by human vocal cords. We refer to those physical things as "spoken language." But it is also used as a generic category for lines in the sand, marks on slate, chalk marks on the blackboard, ink marks on parchment and papyrus, pencil marks on paper, contrails in the sky, smoke puffs from a distant fire, flashes of light from a semaphore, the kind of 'natural signs and pantomime' gestures Mr. Ballard says he and his family used, and so on.

For Berkeley or James, of course, the visible ciphers, 'l-a-n-g-u-a-g-e,' should have evoked an associated auditory image of the 'spoken' sound* which, in turn, was associated—as a 'name,' 'label,' or 'handle'—with selectively grouped memory-images of the sense-data which, for Berkeley and James, replace the 'things' listed above (e.g., sensed air-molecule vibrations, lines in the sand, etc.). More simply, phenomenalists must convert concepts of physical 'language' into concepts of correlated sense-data. (See Chapter I of *William James on Common Sense*.)

But, whether as physical things or as sense-data, words and language as such do not exist. In the same way a kiss is just a kiss, sounds are just sounds, lines in the sand are just lines in the sand, ink marks are just ink marks, etc. Quintalists believe only five types of things exist. None of the five is words. Whoever thinks some extra type of reality is present, over and beyond the items just referred to, is either hearing ghosts in the sounds or seeing ghosts in the ink marks. This seems to be what Ryle and so many others did.

Inner Speech: Simply More Images. The real challenge is to see how the various sense-data and images we call 'words' serve our thinking. What did James have in mind when he wrote about 'words' as if they were distinct from "visual and gustatory memories" or "tactile and visual images'? What did he mean by saying that "they are revivable as actual sensations?" Why did he say that the only intrinsically important images are at the halting places, and then reduce the other images to the level of unimportance?

Once we begin to notice, then to pay ever closer attention to the 'inner words' that form part of our stream of consciousness, we may become convinced that thought without words is impossible. If we do, there is only one phrase to describe the account that Helen Keller gave of her discovery that certain tactile sensations were not just haphazard and annoying tactile sensations. The phrase would have to be 'almost too good to be true.' Perhaps it was. Here, though, as abridged in the April, 1956, issue of *Readers Digest*, is Helen's account of her momentous discovery:

> Here was a small human being who at the age of 19 months had moved with appalling suddenness not only from light to darkness but to silence. My few words wilted, my mind was chained in darkness, and my growing body was governed largely by animal impulses. . . A sorrier situation never confronted a young woman with a noble purpose than that which faced Annie Sullivan. I recall her repeated attempts to spell words—words which meant nothing—into my small hand. But at last, on April 5, 1887, about a month after her arrival, she reached my consciousness with the word "water."
>
> It happened at the well house, where I was holding a mug under the spout. Annie pumped water into it, and when the water gushed over onto my hand she kept spelling w-a-t-e-r into my other hand with her fingers. Suddenly I understood. Caught up in the first joy I had known since my illness, I reached out eagerly to Annie's ever-ready hand, begging for new words to identify whatever object I touched. Spark after spark of meaning flew from hand to hand and, miraculously, affection was born. From the well house there walked two enraptured beings calling each other "Helen" and "Teacher."
>
> Those first words that I understood were like the first warm beams that start the melting of winter snow, a patch here, another there. Next came adjectives, then verbs, and the melting was more rapid. Every object I touched was transformed. Earth, air, and water were quickened by Teacher's creative hand, and life tumbled upon me full of meaning. . . In a few days I was another child, pursuing new discoveries through the witchery of Teacher's finger-spelling.
>
> Teacher would not let the world about me be silent. I "heard" in my fingers the neigh of Prince, the saddle horse, the mooing of cows, the squeal of baby pigs. She brought me into sensory contact with everything that could be reached or felt—sunlight, the quivering of soap bubbles, the rustling of silk, the fury of a storm, the noises of insects, the creaking of a door, the voice of a loved one. To this day I cannot "command the uses of my soul" or stir my mind to action without the memory of the quasi-electric touch of Teacher's fingers upon my palm. (H. Keller, Teacher; in *Readers Digest*, April 1956, pp.217-18)

Helen Keller's images 'of' tactile sensations—"To this day I cannot 'command the uses of my soul' or stir my mind to action without the memory of the quasi-electric touch of Teacher's fingers upon my palm"—are the direct equivalent of the auditory images or images of heard sounds which are often the most noticeable inner things accompanying the normal person's thinking. In the same way that children prattle aloud to themselves, Helen wrote that she experienced strong urges to 'write' to herself.

And in telling that story Helen, in her seventies, was reminded of how she had "sinned in another way, by spelling constantly to herself with her fingers, even after she had learned to speak with her mouth." Helen asserts that it was she herself who determined to stop spelling to herself before it became "a habit I could not break, and so I asked her [Annie] to tie my fingers up in paper. She did it, but she was sorrowful at the thought of my deprivation. In fact, she cried. For many hours, day and night, I ached to form the words that kept me in touch with others, but the experiment succeeded except that even now, in moments of excitement or when I wake from sleep, I occasionally catch myself spelling with my fingers." (J. P. Lash, *Helen and Teacher*, 1980, p.235)

In Vol. II of *The Principles*, James refers to the case of Laura Bridgman, a deaf-mute whose experience was in some respects similar to that of Helen. Laura's mentor was Dr. Howe, and in the same way that a considerable amount of tactile 'speaking' was done before Laura made the connection, the moment came for her as it had for Helen. James links this fact to a point he made more than once, viz., each child must 'learn from inside' what the 'extra, language sounds' mean.

In the human child, however, these ruptures of contiguous association are very soon made; far off cases of sign-using arise when we make a sign now; and soon language is launched. The child in each case must make the discovery for himself. No one can help him except by furnishing him with the conditions. But as he is constituted, the conditions will sooner or later shoot together into the result.

The exceedingly interesting account which Dr. Howe gives of the education of his various blind-deaf mutes illustrates this point admirably. He began to teach Laura Bridgman by gumming raised letters on various familiar articles. The child was taught by mere contiguity to pick out a certain number of particular articles when made to feel the letters. But this was merely a collection of particular signs, out of the mass of which the general purpose of *signification* had not yet been extracted by the child's mind. Dr. Howe compares his situation at this moment to that of lowering

211

a line to the bottom of the deep sea in which Laura's soul lay, and waiting until she should spontaneously take hold of it and be raised into the light. The moment came, 'accompanied by a radiant flash of intelligence and glow of joy'; she seemed suddenly to become aware of the general purpose imbedded in the different details of all these signs, and from that moment her education went on with extreme rapidity. (PP II:357-58)

Cognitive Therapy and Inner Speech. Inner speech has become a staple for 'cognitive therapy.' Albert Ellis and others have publicized the fact that we have 'tape recordings' running through our minds and that, quite often, they carry negative thoughts. When the emotional effects of negative inner speech become disruptive enough in a person's life, a cognitive therapist can assist the person in noticing and then changing those inner tapes. In his 1977 work, *Cognitive-Behavior Modification*, D. Meichenbaum makes a case which directly connects to our focus here. Not simply for recognizing the reality of inner speech, but for recognizing the importance of what is being argued for in this work.

I have been making the case that inner speech plays an important role in being able to influence the client's behaviors, but this is only half the story. There is the second important function of inner speech, and that is to influence and alter what I call the client's *cognitive structures*.

Let us explore why the construct *cognitive structure* is required in an explanation of behavior change. Consider the following questions and observations. What shapes the content of the client's internal dialogue; that is, why does an individual emit one set of self-statements rather than another? If internal dialogue has meaning, where does this meaning come from? For example, in the prologue I included a quote from Sokolov's book *Inner Speech and Thought*, which illustrated the implicit need for some construct such as cognitive structure. To quote Sokolov once again:

> "Inner speech is nothing but speech to oneself, or concealed verbalization, which is instrumental in the logical processing of sensory data, in their realization and comprehension with a *definite system of concepts and judgments.*"

The phrase to be highlighted is "a system of concepts and judgments." The meaning system or "structure" that gives rise to a particular set of self-statements and images must be taken into consideration in the change process. (*Op. cit.*, p.211)

Language: James's Unfinished Business. James, who wrote so masterfully of the distinct components of our varied streams of conscious experience, also frequently ignored the distinctions he had written about. One of the most blatant illustrations is found in his would-be summing-up, *Some Problems of Philosophy*, in his first chapter on percept and concept.

> The concept 'man,' to take an example, is three things: 1, the word itself; 2, a vague picture of the human form which has its own value in the way of beauty or not; and 3, an instrument for symbolizing certain objects from which we may expect human treatment when occasion arises. Similarly of 'triangle,' 'cosine,'—they have their substantive value both as words and as images suggested, but they also have a functional value whenever they led us elsewhere in discourse. (*Writings* II:1012-13)

What is the "it"? One thing or three? What are the "they" which have value as words, images, and functions? How can we possibly get a clear answer if we inspect that paragraph and try to count-and-classify the things James had in mind? Concepts? Do concepts exist? Is 'concept' shorthand for three things? His next paragraph continued this way:

> There are concepts, however, the image-part of which is so faint that their whole value seems to be functional. 'God,' 'cause,' 'number,' 'substance,' 'soul,' for example, suggest no definite picture; and their significance seems to consist entirely in their *tendency*, in the further turn which they may give to our action or our thought. We cannot rest in the contemplation of their form, as we can in that of a 'circle' or a 'man'; we must pass beyond. (*Writings* II:1013)

We must 'pass beyond.' There are no concepts. They do not exist. They have no image-parts, they have no tendencies, they have no functions. There are no "they" to have such things. But how could we ever discover what does exist if we did not have the ability to pretend that our stream of consciousness is made up of sense-data which mean nothing (they just are), of images which mean nothing (they, too, just are), and of something 'more,' that is, something different from sense-data and images, that is, if we could not imagine ourselves having concepts of sense-data distinct from our concepts of images and now concepts of the extra, additional things whose nature we must study, namely, thoughts? Concepts may not exist, but we cannot do without the concept of 'concept.' Words do not exist, either, but how could we ever learn what is really going on without the concept of 'words'?

[. . .] The whole universe of concrete objects, as we know them, swims, not only for such a transcendentalist writer [Emerson], but for all of us, in a wider and higher universe of abstract ideas, that lend it its significance. As time, space, and the ether soak through all things, so (we feel) do abstract and essential goodness, beauty, strength, significance, justice, soak through all things good, strong, significant, and just.

Such ideas, and others equally abstract, form the background for all our facts, the fountain-head of all the possibilities we conceive of. They give its 'nature,' as we call it, to every special thing. Everything we know is 'what' it is by sharing in the nature of one of these abstractions. We can never look directly at them, for they are bodiless and featureless and footless, but we grasp all other things by their means, and in handling the real world we should be stricken with helplessness in just so far forth as we might lose these mental objects, these adjectives and adverbs and predicates and heads of classification and conception. (Writings II:57-58)

These lines from the *Varieties'* chapter on "The Reality of the Unseen" form a fitting conclusion to this chapter on images. It is now time to move on to the most elusive of all the constituents of our streams of conscious experience, thoughts. Apples may not exist, but sense-data do. Inner-speech words may not exist, but images do. Concepts may not exist, but thoughts do. And we who understand such thoughts as these do. And maybe, but only maybe, subatomic bodies do. Unseen.

CHAPTER III

Complete Thoughts, Not Concepts

"The reader who has made himself acquainted with Chapter IX will always understand, when he hears of many ideas simultaneously present to the mind and acting upon each other, that what is really meant is a mind with one idea before it, of many objects, purposes, reasons, motives related to each other, some in a harmonious and some in an antagonistic way." (W.James, *Principles of Psychology* II:528, n*)

1. Thought: the Hardest Thing to Think Clearly About

A Mystery Full of Paradox. Thinking 'straight' about understanding thoughts is the most difficult task of all. By comparison, thinking about persons, images, and sense-data is easy thinking. Yet thinking correctly about persons, images, and sense-data is far more difficult than thinking about bodies. Even if bodies do not exist, they are as easy to think about as Santa Claus or Ivanhoe are.

What is not easy is to think about our thoughts about Santa and bodies and the act of understanding which we must exercise even as we understand. The claim here is that James did it best. Even he did not always do it perfectly. One reason for the contradictions in his writings is that he tracked down more of thought's paradoxical dimensions than anyone else, but was not able to reconcile all of them. We can never avoid paradoxes, but we can eliminate the contradictions.

What Is A Thought? Thoughts are what humans understand. There is never more than one thought being understood by any human being at a time. But, although that one, single thought must be thought of as being a single thought, it must also be thought of as being many thoughts in one. How many thoughts in one? Always far more than anyone can possibly count.

An Experiment. Why far more than can be counted? Well, in order to understand any of the thoughts in the preceding paragraph, it is necessary to have a worldview which is a vast system of beliefs

215

that should 'fit together.' The sheer number of the beliefs and what 'fitting together' consists of are obvious once noticed. Experiments will demonstrate what that means. Consider each paragraph below as one experiment.

Thoughts are lovely things. I cut one this afternoon and brought it into my study. It is rather small, like a skyscraper, fits right on the corner of my Rolls Royce here. I would love to eat it, but I'd also like to have it, too. Is there anybody who would not like to do that with a thought?

Thoughts are terribly expensive. I have four thoughts, one for each month of the year. I had to save up my allowance for six minutes to have enough to buy all four. During that time, I ate nothing but bread and water, barely enough to keep me alive. I lost eighty pounds during that time.

The birds filled the tree-tops with their morning thoughts, making the air moist, cool, and pleasant is a sentence James remembered reading once in a report of some athletic exercises in Jerome Park, and he used it as an illustration of strung-together words that make no sense, much the same way those others do not.

Enough. Incidentally, James used "song" rather than "thought" for the previous paragraph, and he inserted quotation marks before The birds and after and pleasant. His illustration is found on page 263 of *The Principles*, Vol. I, and the point he used the sentence to illustrate was "if words do belong to the same vocabulary, and if the grammatical structure is correct, sentences with absolutely no meaning may be uttered in good faith and pass unchallenged." A sophist might quibble and insist that the first half of his example, "The birds filled the tree-tops with their morning song" does make sense and add that, even if the birds had nothing to do with it, the words referring to the air's being moist, cool, and pleasant add to one's picture of a delightful summer morning experience. After all, James himself referred in a footnote to the fact that children listen with "rapt attention" to word-strings *only* "half of which they do not understand" (PP I:264, note). Only, he didn't stress "only."

Another Experiment. Our ability to conjure a mental picture that 'makes some sense'—even if it is not the sense the speaker or writer intended—is remarkable. Cryptographers are often able to discover the sense even when the speaker or writer does not intend them to, a fact that we must keep in mind as we try to understand what a thought is. Suppose the original paragraph were re-written with a nonsense word, i.e., a non-word, inserted in place of "thought." What makes "thought" better than any of the following?

Xs are what humans understand. There is never more than one x being understood by any human being at a time. But, although that one, single x must be thought of as being a single x, it must also be thought of as being many xs in one. How many xs in one? Always far more than anyone can possibly count.

Blics are what humans understand. There is never more than one blic being understood by any human being at a time. But, although that one, single blic must be thought of as being a single blic, it must also be thought of as being many blics in one. How many blics in one? Always far more than anyone can possibly count.

Grues are what humans understand. There is never more than one grue being understood by any human being at a time. But, although that one, single grue must be thought of as being a single grue, it must also be thought of as being many grues in one. How many grues in one? Always far more than anyone can possibly count.

For Instance. Suppose we substitute some of the words which James often used when he wrote about the stream of consciousness and wanted to convey his ideas. Do the following paragraphs mean the same thing with the substitutions?

Concepts are what humans understand. There is never more than one concept being understood by any human being at a time. But, although that one, single concept must be thought of as being a single concept, it must also be thought of as being many concepts in one. How many concepts in one? Always far more than anyone can possibly count.

Objects are what humans understand. There is never more than one object being understood by any human being at a time. But, although that one, single object must be thought of as being a single object, it must also be thought of as being many objects in one. How many objects in one? Always far more than anyone can possibly count.

Things are what humans understand. There is never more than one thing being understood by any human being at a time. But, although that one, single thing must be thought of as being a single thing, it must also be thought of as being many things in one. How many things in one? Always far more than anyone can possibly count.

Facts are what humans understand. There is never more than one fact being understood by any human being at a time. But, although that one, single fact must be thought of as being a single fact, it must also be thought of as being many facts in one. How many facts in one? Always far more than anyone can possibly count.

Propositions are what humans understand. There is never more than one proposition being understood by any human being at a time. But, although that one, single proposition must be thought of as being a single proposition, it must also be thought of as being many propositions in one. How many propositions in one? Always far more than anyone can possibly count.

Enough. What is the point of the preceding? It is to emphasize that we must use 'words,' i.e., sense-data, to go beyond them in order to discover the writer's mindset-context for what he or she writes. (Non-word) 'words' and thoughts are utterly distinct, and the former are mere clues to the latter.

In fact, James used many different words when he was trying to explain the stream of thought (the title he chose for *The Principles*), stream of consciousness (the title he chose for *Briefer Course*), or field of experience (a phrase he often used in *The Varieties of Religious Experience*). It must not be thought for an instant, though, that James was insensitive to vocabulary. Quite the opposite is true. As Chapter II explained, he was remarkably sensitive to it. What's more, in Chapter VII of *The Principles*, "The Methods and Snares of Psychology," he devoted several paragraphs to "A Question of Nomenclature" (PP I:185-87).

The point has now been reached where the claim that 'thoughts' can be used to replace many of James's terms must be explained further and then, using positions which James himself advocated on one occasion or other, must be defended. The thesis of this chapter was stated in its third paragraph: "Thoughts are what humans understand." That word, "thought" is the best name for the objects of the non-sensory, intellectual knowing that we'll use "understand" for. Thoughts-as-objects are radically different from sense-data and images. The adoption of this thesis paves the way to an enormous simplification and thereby to an enormous clarification.

Aristotle's Five-Concept Grid (Again). We begin by recalling Aristotle's five-concept grid to use as a psychological model. Knowing *agents*, by means of their knowing *powers*, exercise *acts* of knowing, whose *objects* are what is known. Repeated exercise of some powers, such as memory, imagination, and thinking, results in increased knowledge which both Aristotle and James classed under "*habit*."

That set of concepts (seemingly) grows out of our original view of reality, to which James gave the name "common sense [philosophy]." One of the most obviously real things, according to common sense, is one's own self, as Descartes finally noticed. Hence the first of Aristotle's concepts to adopt is that of *agent*. In this case it is the agent to whom James, in a diagram he presented in Chapter VII, gave the title "The Psychologist" (PP I:184). Each of us must be our own psychologist, because each of us has direct access to only one sample of consciousness, our own.

After the human agent, the idea of *act or activity* is the most important of the five concepts. The question we must ask is simply, "What kinds of things do we do?" James adopted a two-part classification for the acts we humans perform. There are the physical or bodily activities. We walk, talk, eat, drink, digest food, grow, reproduce, breathe air, and so on. We also do things which do not appear to be physical or bodily. We see, we hear, we smell, we taste, we feel, we experience emotions, we desire, we think, we decide, and so on. These latter type of activities are called 'conscious activities,' because they are done most noticeably when we are conscious or awake. True, we also dream while we are not awake, and dreams seem to involve certain of the activities we carry out while awake. Since conscious acts exercised while we are awake are difficult enough to deal with, however, it is well to try and get our thinking clear about them before turning to more puzzling matters.

It seems plausible that the next idea, that of *power*, faculty, ability, etc., was created originally in relation to bodily actions. We walk, run, jump, and skip with our legs. We pick up, hold, move, throw, and manipulate things with our arms and hands. We eat, drink, and speak with our mouth. It was only natural that the model would eventually be extended to our conscious acts. We see, look, glance, and observe with our eyes. We hear, listen, and harken with our ears. We also taste with our tongue, smell with our nose, feel with our skin, and so on. As our ancestors began noticing that we do such additional things as think, remember, imagine, discover, question, doubt, decide, etc., they followed the pattern already set. The reason we can perform a particular type of act is because there is a particular part of us related to the act. We remember with our memory, we imagine with our imagination, we think with our mind, etc. Hence all of us who grow up using English get in the habit of referring to people with good or bad memories, creative or poor imaginations, first-rate minds, strong wills, etc. Powers are modified by repeated acts which produce *habits*. Skill, virtue, knowledge, vice, depravity, etc., are examples of habits.

The notion of *objects* arises quite effortlessly from thinking about the most obvious of all our conscious activities, namely, sensing. "Sensing" is shorthand for seeing, hearing, smelling, tasting, and so on. At first, we simply use 'things' as a generic form of shorthand to refer to what-we-see-and-hear, etc. We see the covers of books, we hear words, we smell coffee and smoke, we taste our food, and we feel the smooth texture of a book's pages. All of those are things. But it takes only a little bit of further thought to discover why Aristotle said "each sense has its own specialty which it alone, and no other sense, can know." Thus, sight knows color, hearing knows sounds, smell knows odors, and so on.

Three Kinds of Objects. In this restructuring of James's thought, three types of objects are most important. *Sense-data* are the first type, and Chapter I sketched some of the discoveries our ancestors made when they began more carefully examining certain common-sense convictions. Yes, we see the sun, but we always thought that the sun's color stayed the same. How can we explain the fact that it looks dazzlingly white at noon but soft peach at certain sunset times? Yes, we hear birds and thunder, but why do we hear thunder at the same instant we see the lightning on some occasions, but hear it several seconds later on others? Yes, we smell the limburger cheese while it's on the table, but why do we still smell it after it's been taken to another room? These and thousands of other puzzling everyday experiences which few of us are curious enough to study in a systematic way led our more curious ancestors to try and explain them. By now, there are many rival-system explanations. Chapter I examined four, ruled out three, and settled on the survivor. In effect, it used parts of the naïve-realist portion of our common-sense philosophy to eliminate others in order to find a view that 'covers' everything. But there is a steep price to pay, viz., the realization that we must now confront "the challenge of solipsism." We may be able to retain our non-sensory beliefs about the sun, birds, etc., and especially other people, but we must surrender our naïve view that we can ever sense them.

Images are the second type of object. To discover the truth about our sense-objects, we had to remember a vast number of past seeings, hearings, smellings, and so on. If we did not, we would never realize that we have actually seen different colors 'of the sun,' that we have often seen lightning and heard thunder simultaneously but often heard them separated by varying intervals of time, that we often smelled limburger cheese as strongly after someone ate it as when it was still on the table, etc. Involved in those memories are images, the second of our 'mental objects.' We can 'visualize' ourselves walking along a path we can see, hearing the birds singing in the trees overhead, feeling the cool moist morning air on our face, and so on. We can recall such real natural scenes and real movie or TV scenes. We can later use these images to 'create' scenes that never occurred.

This chapter will focus on a third type of objects, *thoughts*. These are represented by the middle two areas of James's diagram. He labeled them "The Thought Studied" and "The Thought's Object," respectively. For all of the reasons marshaled in the previous chapters and for the reasons now to be presented, this 'readjustment' of James's thought rests on a sharp distinction between sense-data and images on the one hand and thoughts on the other. James did not treat the term 'thought' as consistently as we intend to do. At times he uses "thought" for thoughts, but other times he uses "thought" to include sense-data and images. Therefore, whenever James refers to "thought" or "thought's object," great care must be exercised to translate what he writes so that it fits this tri-partite model. When James writes sentences whose meaning seems to be at odds with this model, we must see if the fact he is trying to bring out can be reformulated to 'fit.' When it cannot, we must simply declare that Homer nodded.

This third type of object is known by a special act called "understanding." It is distinct from awareness and attention. As has been noted already, James recognized the role that images play in our thinking, images which take the form of maps, models, diagrams, etc. It is inevitable, therefore, that we will use images or pictures when dealing with the act that puts us into 'relation' to thoughts. But such terms as 'relation,' 'contact,' 'access,' and so on, express metaphors. Less confusion results if we return regularly to the term "understand." Also, "understand" should be understood the way we take it in passing. Its 'etymological roots' should be ignored.

2. Thought: the 'Water' Flowing Around Sense-Data and Images

Four Preliminary Theses. In order to gain an insight into what an understood "thought" refers to in this text, especially in relation to sense-data and images, *four preliminary theses will be presented.* The first relates to James insistence that we must not be misled by images or metaphors when we try to understand thought. The second presents James's greatest insight, namely, that thoughts are the meanings of complete sentences. The third thesis is that non-word 'words' relate directly to images, not to the thought that constitutes their enveloping environment. Finally, it is thought that provides our ultimate freedom, namely, the freedom to believe what we will.

First: We Use Images and Metaphors to Think About Thoughts. All of our theories, i.e., thoughts, about thought are inescapably metaphorical. The reason is that all of our theories or thoughts, whether about thoughts or anything else, must 'ride atop' the imagery we have been describing as maps, models, pictures, diagrams, word-lists, etc. But the two—thoughts and images—are radically distinct. The reason we must recognize this fact is because, unless we do, we are bound to become seduced, then trapped by unnoticed fictions.

The preceding paragraph, for instance, should create a picture. There are thoughts, and they ride imagery, as we ride a horse or bike. On top are the thoughts, below are images of various types. The two things are distinct, and we must not confuse them. But till we connect that picture with our actual, ongoing experience, it may be that we understand very little except a bare skeleton of a thought which is so vague that, if pressed to 'explain in detail' what it means, we may find ourselves tongue-tied. In fact, if we go to the library, we would find that different thinkers who might agree with the bare formula would give radically different 'explanations' of what it means. Other thinkers would disagree entirely with the formula.

The claim here is that every thinker who tries to explain thought uses such imagery as pictures or diagrams. In the *Republic*, Plato drew a picture of the human soul as having three parts to it, the desiring, the spirit or spirited, and the reasoning parts, and in the *Theatetus*, he invokes the picture of birds in a bird-cage to describe the mind and its ideas or thoughts. Aristotle explains knowledge with an elaborate model of forms which are found both in things and in the mind which knows the things. St. Augustine built his theology of the Father-Son-Holy-Ghost Trinity on the idea that a knower 'speaks' an inner 'word' that can reflect itself. St. Thomas, too, used the 'mind speaks words' image for thinking, which explains why the title chosen for the volume of Bernard Lonergan's essays on St. Thomas's theory of intellectual knowledge is *Verbum: Word and Idea in Aquinas*. The scholastics added details to create a very complex model of knowing which always requires a '*species impressa*' (an 'impressed likeness'), plus a '*species expressa*' in situations where the outside object is not presently accessible to the senses. Hegel relied heavily on the picture of a big, growing, evolving organism, viz., the Geist or World-Spirit or World-Mind, etc., as well as on a picture of states as mid-level persons or organisms.

In 1903-04 James began writing a technical text-book to sum up his worldview. His first idea was to call it *The Many and the One*. That title conjured a picture which he explained by saying that he wanted to show how the plurality of things comes together into a unity. One of his introductions for that work was going to be titled "Philosophies Paint Pictures." One of his most vivid presentations of that thesis can be found in the first of the *Pluralistic Universe* lectures he gave in 1908.

[. . .] No philosophy can ever be anything but a summary sketch, a picture of the world in abridgment, a foreshortened bird's-eye view of the perspective of events. . . . All philosophers, accordingly, have conceived of the whole world after the analogy of some particular feature of it which has particularly captivated their attention. Thus, the theists take their cue from manufacture, the pantheists from growth. For one man, the world is like a thought or a grammatical sentence in which a thought is expressed. For such a philosopher, the whole must logically be prior to the parts; for letters would never have been invented without syllables to spell, or syllables without words to utter. (*Writings* II:633; see MEN 91-2 for his Dec. 9, 1905 note on his own use of imagery)

With the next few paragraphs, James gives examples of the way well-known thinkers' philosophies are shaped by different dominant metaphors. There is now a considerable amount of literature constructed on the picture of worldviews being constructed on pictures. For instance, Stephen Pepper wrote an entire book, *World Hypotheses and Root Metaphors*, to explain how the various metaphysical systems build on different pictures. Nelson Goodman's *Ways of Worldmaking* describes doing on a large scale what Alfred J. Ayer's theory of logical constructions describes doing on a small scale. Wittgenstein's *Tractatus* offers what some call "a picture theory of language" to explain theory. Various 'schools' of structuralism invite us to see shapes, structures, and frameworks of all sorts everywhere.

But thoughts and theories are not images or pictures. The images merely help to understand the thoughts and theories. James's unused draft for a chapter in *The Principles of Psychology*, the one discussed in the preceding chapter, included a warning about the images used in theorizing about the *relation* of thought(s) to the objects they are 'about.' He himself pictured the objects as being 'in the pocket' of the thought.

In his unused draft, he listed three possible pictures of that relation. We can i) picture the mind taking the object into itself (his own picture of the object 'in the thought's pocket'), ii) picture the mind reaching out and touching the object, or iii) picture the object sending representations of itself to the mind. (See MEN:286-87)

Consider, for instance, the supernova which Ian Shelton discovered on the night of February 23, 1987. One metaphor pictures bringing the star into the mind. Another describes the mind reaching out to the star. A third pictures the star sending re-present-ations of itself to earth and to Ian Shelton's mind. Those alternatives were all created by thinkers trying to unravel the mysteries of 'knowing' after years of knowing and thinking which are far too complex to be captured by *any* picture!

Still, we need pictures and images. Each of them can help to capture just how mysterious thought is, and why it—not the brain—is the final frontier in achieving a truly grand unifying theory of everything. Supernova 1987A did not travel to Ian Shelton's mind, Ian Shelton's mind did not literally stretch out trillions of miles to touch a now-vastly-changed star (if stars exist), nor do the ripples of light radiating in every direction for the last 160,000 years bear any 'representational' resemblance to the star. But whoever pauses to reflect on the thought, "If there was a supernova blast thousands of years ago and trillions of miles away, I can think about it right now and, if this thought is true, I can know something," can use those three models, see how inadequate each one is, and become captivated, as James was, by the greatest mystery in the universe.

That is, those three pictures may help us meditate on what an infinite mystery knowing really is. But understanding a thought, even the thought that 'knowing is an infinite mystery,' cannot ever be 'captured' by any imagery. In fact, it is only by noticing more fully the imagery we are using that we can reach the pinnacle of insight into the 'more' that is understanding a thought. It is more than sensing and more than imaging. But it will be our common-sense idea of 'thinking about some thing' that presents the greatest obstacle, because we rarely realize that it, too, rides on a picture.

The psychologist's attitude towards cognition will be so important in the sequel that we must not leave it until it is made perfectly clear. *It is a thoroughgoing dualism.* It supposes two elements, mind knowing and thing known, and treats them as irreducible. Neither gets out of itself or into the other, neither in any way *is* the other, neither *makes* the other. They just stand face to face in a common world, and one simply knows, or is known unto, its counterpart. This singular relation is not to be expressed in any lower terms, or translated into any more intelligible name. Some sort of *signal* must be given by the thing to the mind's brain, or the knowing will not occur—we find as a matter of fact that the mere *existence* of a thing outside the brain is not a sufficient cause for our knowing it: it must strike the brain in some way, as well as be there, to be known. But the brain being struck, the knowledge is constituted by a new construction that occurs altogether *in* the mind. The thing remains the same whether known or not. And when once there, the knowledge may remain there, whatever becomes of the thing. (PP I:218-19)

"This singular relation is not to be expressed in any lower terms, or translated into any more intelligible name." That sums up the much longer 'warning' James wrote into his unused draft of 1883-84. Knowing is not a physical taking-in, not a physical stretching across a gap, nor being offered a substitute object. Still, so long as we do not forget what we 'more literally' believe, there is no reason to avoid metaphors, analogies, similes, comparisons, etc. In the present chapter whose topic is thought or thoughts, the best literal formula ('expressed' in English non-words!) to which all metaphors and comparisons are to be reduced will be "I understand the thought *that* such-and-such."

The next section will explain, i.e., further describe, this critically important formula.

Second: A Thought Is the Meaning of a Complete Sentence.
The heart and soul of James's best answer to "What is a thought?" uses 'language' as its foil.

A thought is the complete meaning of a complete sentence.

This chapter first approached thought in relation to one type of act, viz., understanding, performed by one type of agent, viz., humans. *Thoughts are what humans understand.*

This second approach locates thoughts in relation to language. *A thought is the meaning of a complete sentence.* Just as the first approach was made possible only by using Aristotle's five-concept model, this second approach is possible only by virtue of complex 'language' constructs. We can think without having such non-word 'words' as "language," "sentence," "word," "name," "verb," and so on, but we would never be able to learn what James discovered about thinking i) if we did not have non-word 'cues'—e.g., "mom," "mothers," "parents," etc.—to serve as tags for the items in our complex inner model and ii) if we did not have an added set of created 'language concepts'—e.g., "words," "names," "sentences," etc.—to serve as tools for using the non-word sounds and color patterns as sensible foils for purely intelligible thought(s).

That James succeeded in noticing the nature of the non-sensible, purely intelligible thought(s) is the crowning triumph of his *Principles of Psychology*. He was aided, of course, by the writings of his great predecessors with whom he partly agreed and at times vehemently disagreed.

On the one hand, he agreed with a basic conclusions reached, not just by the empiricists, Locke, Berkeley, and Hume, but also by the rationalists, Descartes and Leibniz: we have no direct access to anything beyond the perimeter of our own experience. It might be better to say that we have no direct access to anything except our own individual mind's contents. This means that we must rely entirely on those contents in order to form and test 'from inside' all our theories about whatever lies beyond those contents.

In dealing with those predecessors writings, James had to contend with the wide variety of terms used by those predecessors when they tried to put their thoughts about those contents 'into writing.' Locke said that ideas made up the contents of his mind. In order to keep clear on the distinction between thought and language, it is more accurate to say that Locke used the name "idea" for everything he thought minds contain, from thoughts, ideas, and memories to emotions, desires, and everything else. He did invent extra mental classifications for those contents, but "idea" was the one generic (English) name he used to 'cover' them all. Berkeley had two names for his mind's contents: "ideas" and "notions." Hume used a third vocabulary: he divided the mind's contents into impressions and ideas. But, like Locke, he also used a more general or generic name to distinguish the mind's contents from, say, stars and butterflies. "Perceptions" served the generic purpose for Hume that "idea" served for Locke.

The names are secondary, however. The important question is, "What sort of things did they think those mental contents were?" Locke was a mind-body dualist the way Descartes was, with the result that he treated all the contents of the mind as immaterial. He did not make a radical distinction between images and concepts. The medieval scholastics did. They regarded concepts as well as the judgments composed of concepts as *purely* immaterial things, in contrast to both the things we sense and our images of them which have some *admixture* of matter. Berkeley, who denied the existence of all matter, followed Locke in regarding everything in the mind as nonphysical. He distinguished ideas from notions on the ground that ideas are in a sense 'sensory' and related to what we regard as apples, trees, books, etc., whereas notions are of purely spiritual or non-sensory things such as souls and God. Hume is very different. Instead of discussing physical and non-physical beings, he focused on the difference in the mind's contents, which are either vivid (impressions) or faint (ideas). But what Hume called "ideas," the scholastics called "images," which means that when Hume had the idea that he was talking about thought, he was thinking about images. And all three of these authors used only 'English' to express their ideas. Or thoughts.

In other words, the 'words' that various thinkers use are merely cues and clues to their thoughts (meanings). It is necessary to use those clues in order to construct an adequate model of their belief-systems in order to decipher what ideas their non-word 'words' refer to.

As for James's vehement disagreements with his forebears, they focused on another issue. Whereas Locke, Berkeley, Hume, and others tended to view ideas—both those which are contemporaneous and those which are time-sequential—as separate individual entities, James preferred to say that, at any given moment, the mind's contents make up a single, total, unified whole and to emphasize that each moment's total thought grows so smoothly from those behind it, that those allegedly 'behind' are subsumed, taken up, or integrated into the next moment's new thought. The contrast is best seen by comparing Hume's most famous formula for consciousness with that of James. Hume described the contents of the present moment as "a bundle of [discrete] perceptions," placing the accent on the plural rather than the singular, and on the distinctness of consciousness' parts rather than on their intimate connection. James's way of stressing what impressed him the most about consciousness, namely, its unity and partlessness, was to replace "bundle of perceptions" with "stream of thought" (in *The Principles*) and the now famous phrase, "the stream of consciousness" (in *Psychology: Briefer Course*).

James's accent on the unity of thought, that is, *on entire thoughts as wholes*, is the most important feature of his thought. Nowhere did he explain his thought as clearly as he did in Chapter IX of *The Principles*, and nowhere in that chapter did he express himself as well as he did in the following passage.

> We have been using the word Object. *Something must now be said about the proper use of the term Object in Psychology.*
>
> In popular parlance the word object is commonly taken without reference to the act of knowledge, and treated as synonymous with individual subject of existence. Thus if anyone ask what is the mind's object when you say 'Columbus discovered America in 1492,' most people will reply 'Columbus,' or 'America,' or, at most, 'the discovery of America.' They will name a substantive kernel or nucleus of the consciousness, and say the thought is 'about' that—as indeed it is,—and they will call that your thought's 'object.' Really that is usually only the grammatical object, or more likely the grammatical subject, of your sentence. It is at most your 'fractional object;' or you may call it the 'topic' of your thought, or the 'subject of your discourse.' But the *Object* of your thought is really its entire content or deliverance, neither more nor less. It is a vicious use of speech to take out a substantive kernel from its content and call that its object; and it is an equally vicious use of speech to add a substantive kernel not articulately included in its content and to call that its object. Yet either one of these two sins we commit, whenever we content ourselves with saying that a given thought is simply 'about' a certain topic, or that that topic is its 'object.' The object of my thought in the previous sentence, for example, is strictly speaking neither Columbus, nor America, nor its discovery. It is nothing short of the entire sentence, 'Columbus-discovered-America-in-1492.' And if we wish to speak of it substantively, we must make a substantive of it by writing it out thus with hyphens between all its words. Nothing but this can possibly name its delicate idiosyncrasy. And if we wish to *feel* that idiosyncrasy we must reproduce the thought as it was uttered, with every word fringed and the whole sentence bathed in that original halo of obscure relations, which, like an horizon, then spread about its meaning. (PP I:275-76; see also *Writings* I:1009-10)

"And if we wish to speak of it substantively, we must make a substantive of it by writing it out thus with hyphens between all its words." This idea is so important that James's suggestion that we have some reminder of it will be adhered to in what follows. However, instead of using hyphens *inside* the sentence, we will often use the word "that" to precede the sentence whose meaning is the complete thought. And, instead of using quotes, we will simply italicize the word *that*. That is, Columbus-discovered-America-in-1492 will often be replaced by *that* Columbus discovered America or by *that* Columbus-discovered-America.

A warning. The thought is not 'the entire sentence'! It is the partless meaning 'of' the many-word sentence. The thought is not uttered, the words are. The thought is not relations *surrounding* the sentence's meaning; it *is* the sentence's meaning.

Certain passages in James's writing are superior to others. This chapter will focus on what this interpreter regards as James's best descriptions of thought. As previous chapters have explained, James's radical empiricism did not incorporate a strict distinction of thought from sense-data and images as this text does. The preceding description of thought, as an object distinct from all other objects, must be viewed as the best that James or anyone else ever offered. So, when other passages of his conflict with the central thrust of this one, priority will be given to this. Those who read James's conflicting statements will naturally give priority to those which fit into their own grand view of things, a psychological fact that accounts for competing interpretations of 'James's thought.'

James's works are filled with passages, each of which shed light on one facet or another of human thought, easily the most complex and multi-faceted thing experienced by us in the entire universe. The preceding passage offers us a beautifully concretized way of handling a thing utterly mercurial, multi-faceted, and ever-changing. The next passage may be even clearer about the relation between the idea, total object, or meaning, and the distinct words of the sentence.

This latter author [Egger] seems to me to have kept at much closer quarters with the facts than any other analyst of consciousness. But even he does not quite hit the mark, for, as I understand him, he thinks that each word as it occupies the mind *displaces* the rest of the thought's content. He distinguishes the 'idea' (what I have called the total *object* or meaning) from the consciousness of the words, calling the former a very feeble state, and contrasting it with the liveliness of the words, even when these are only silently rehearsed. "The feeling," he says, "of the words makes ten or twenty times more noise in our consciousness than the sense of the phrase, which for consciousness is a very slight matter." And having distinguished these two things, he goes on to separate them in time, saying that the idea may either precede or follow the words, but that it is a 'pure illusion' to suppose them simultaneous. Now I believe that in all cases where the words are *understood*, the total idea may be and usually is present not only before and after the phrase has been spoken, but also whilst each separate word is uttered. It is the overtone, halo, or fringe of the word, *as spoken in that sentence*. It is never absent; no word in an understood sentence comes to consciousness as a mere noise. We feel its meaning as it passes; and although our object differs from one moment to another as to its verbal kernel or nucleus, yet it is *similar* throughout the entire segment of the stream. The same object is known everywhere, now from the point of view, if we may so call it, of this word, now from the point of view of that. And in our feeling of each word there chimes an echo or foretaste of every other. The consciousness of the 'Idea' and that of the words are thus consubstantial. They are made of the same 'mind-stuff,' and form an unbroken stream. Annihilate a mind at any instant, cut its thought through whilst yet uncompleted, and examine the object present to the cross-section thus suddenly made; you will find, not the bald word in process of utterance, but that word suffused with the whole idea. (PP I:280-82)

There is, then, a single thought or total meaning, and it is present throughout the uttering of the distinct words. That is the reason for the formula adopted here, namely, that a thought is the (single, total, partless) meaning of a complete sentence. That formula is a two-sided coin. Its flip side is that the thought is not like a long string of sausage links, with a separate meaning for each word in the word-string called 'a sentence.' Thoughts are not 'made of' images or even concepts. Concepts do not exist. That is why they are not on the quintalist's list of things which exist. James used several diagrams in *The Principles'* Chapter IX to make certain his view of the unity of a sentence's meaning was as clear as he could make it.

A feature of this second passage is its reference to the 'inner speech' which was emphasized at the end of the previous chapter. More will be said about inner speech later in this chapter. But the phrase "even when these [the words] are only silently rehearsed" should be underscored, for they are extremely important and relate to the question, "Can there be thought without language?"

James relied on our ability to attend to 'language' in order to draw attention to many features of conscious experience which would otherwise go unnoticed. For instance, whether we are taking in the words or expressing them, thoughts and words create expectancies* regarding each other. (*See the last chapter of *William James on Common Sense*.) Words we hear or read lead to expectations of new thought-meanings that will continue the 'train of thought,' and our train of thought conjures the next of the words needed to 'express' them.

[. . .] One may admit that a good third of our psychic life consists in these rapid premonitory perspective views of schemes of thought not yet articulate. How comes it about that a man reading something aloud for the first time is able immediately to emphasize all his words aright, unless from the very first he have a sense of at least the form of the sentence yet to come, which sense is fused with his consciousness of the present word, and modifies its emphasis in his mind so as to make him give it the proper accent as he utters it? Emphasis of this kind is almost a matter of grammatical construction. If we read 'no more' we expect presently to come upon a 'than'; if we read 'however' at the outset of a sentence it is a 'yet,' a 'still,' or a 'nevertheless,' that we expect. A noun in a certain position demands a verb in a certain mood and number, in another position it expects a relative pronoun. Adjectives call for nouns, verbs for adverbs, etc., etc. (PP I:253-54)

As he wrote this passage, James's attention shuttled from thoughts evoking 'words,' then to 'words' evoking expectancies of grammatically correct 'words,' and even to 'words' evoking expectancies concerning meaning. The paragraph-experiments at the beginning of the chapter illustrate how words lead us to expect new thoughts that 'make sense' and of how our expectations are not met when, like skyscrapers, the blues won't fit on the tidbit of our desk. Word-strings may be grammatically correct, but grammatical non-sense. "That is one thing up with which I will not put," "To is the numeral which is next two too," and "Both the man neither his wife used the car yesterday" help us notice other types of awakened expectancies. James later used 'words' to draw attention to the expectation-raisings which can be experienced by someone who is bilingual.

[. . .] Our understanding of a French sentence heard never falls to so low an ebb that we are not aware that the words linguistically belong together. Our attention can hardly so wander that if an English word be suddenly introduced we shall not start at the change. Such a vague sense as this of the words belonging together is the very minimum of fringe that can accompany them, if 'thought' at all. Usually the vague perception that all the words we hear belong to the same language and to the same special vocabulary in that language, and that the grammatical sequence is familiar, is practically equivalent to an admission that what we hear is sense. But if an unusual foreign word be introduced, if the grammar trip, or if a term from an incongruous vocabulary suddenly appear, such as 'rat-trap' or 'plumber's bill' in a philosophical discourse, the sentence detonates, as it were, we receive a shock from the incongruity, and the drowsy assent is gone. (PP I:262)

Warning. Unless the preceding chapters' analyses are kept in mind here, we will be unable to untangle James's extremely rich meanings. Elsewhere, when he closed in on details, he sharply distinguished words from meanings, words from images, sharp images from vague images, images from thoughts or meanings, and so on. Here, in this chapter, he tends to fuse them all together. The most obvious explanation is the one he gave in an overly conciliatory letter he wrote to a reviewer who apparently objected to Chapter IX's neglect, perhaps even its practical denial, of separate 'ideas':

> [. . .] I cannot, however, [see] why you should *object* to my formulation, for even if our thoughts *are* compounds of 'ideas,' they are at least superficially and practically also all that I say they are, namely integral pulses of consciousness with respect to the multitude of facts of which they may take cognizance in a single passing moment of time. All you ought to accuse me of is *insufficiency*, not error. But I freely admit that in the vehemence of my argumentation in the chapter on the 'Stream of Thought,' I seem to be contending for the unity more as an ultimate and definitive truth than as a peculiarly advantageous methodological assumption. That chapter was really written as a bit of popular description. (Perry II:102-03)

Though his ninth chapter does make bowing concessions to this distinction here and to that distinction there, it is practically one long concatenation of illustrations selected for one overarching purpose, viz., to create in the minds of his readers a super-acute awareness of the commingling-into-unity of every separate strand of everyday consciousness. With his reference to the effect of 'rat-trap' and 'plumber's bill' in a serious, philosophical treatise, he even takes note of those whose thinking is compartmentalized 'discipline-wise.' When he gave his *Pragmatism* lectures, he drew that audience's attention to the probable reaction they would have, if he suddenly began uttering piercing shrieks and acting like a maniac. If you like, you old fart, you can read his entire second *Pragmatism* lecture as a treatise on the way a person's past experience has built up an enormous freight load of expectancies about the future, in every possible respect. What we are shocked by when we come across it in a 'serious' academic treatise causes nary a blink of our eye if our eyes scan it in a 'novel.' When Socrates told his judges that the unexamined life is not worth living, he may not have realized how long a reexamination of every nook and cranny of one's mindset would take. James would have.

As noted earlier, he also draws attention to the way our train of thought evokes a chain of words. When the words don't come, we experience a mental log-jam:

> In all our voluntary thinking there is some topic or subject about which all the

members of the thought revolve. Half the time this topic is a problem, a gap we cannot yet fill with a definite picture, word, or phrase, but which, in the manner described some time back, influences us in an intensely active and determinate psychic way. Whatever may be the images and phrases that pass before us, we feel their relation to this aching gap. To fill it up is our thought's destiny. (PP I:259)

This fact, that we can concentrate on our thinking and trust that the words will just 'come,' is perhaps best illustrated when we are in the process of learning to speak a foreign language. At first, we quite noticeably 'think in our native language' and have to 'mentally translate' from our old language to the new one. Such facts take us to those passages in which James noted that, even as we watch the theater performance, or proofread a term-paper, or just read a book, many of the 'words' that pass through our mind with the rest of the stream of 'stuff' are supplied from our own memory and do not 'come' from the players' mouths or the print on the page.

For example, when we listen to a person speaking or read a page of print, much of what we think we see or hear is supplied from our memory. We overlook misprints, imagining the right letters, though we see the wrong ones; and how little we actually hear, when we listen to speech, we realize when we go to a foreign theatre; for there what troubles us is not so much that we cannot understand what the actors say as that we cannot hear their words. The fact is that we hear quite as little under similar conditions at home, only our mind, being fuller of English verbal associations, supplies the requisite material for comprehension upon a much slighter auditory hint. (TT:110-11; *Writings* I:802)

A sentence. A complete sentence. To understand this second introductory thesis, it is essential to be clear about what is meant here. The concept (we need this useful fiction) of 'a complete sentence' is probably the most important concept for everyone who intends to learn what Aristotle and later thinkers called 'logic.' It is essential to realize that, *since every system is circularly reasoned*, our views on one basic topic have to be adjusted to fit our views on all other basic topics. Two jurors can have similar common-sense philosophies and disagree vehemently about whether or not Lizzie Borden, Sacco & Vanzetti, Bruno Hauptmann, Julius and Ethel Rosenberg, etc., were guilty as charged. But two persons who approach morality as differently as Friedrich Nietzsche and Martin Luther King did would never agree even on what "guilty" means. So here, unless we are clear about the meaning of "sentence," our touchstone for talking with precision about thoughts (as much as such a thing is possible!), using the concept of 'a complete sentence' as the window onto a thought will go awry.

'A complete sentence' will be taken here the way young school children are taught to take it. A complete sentence is one which expresses a complete thought. It is well to recall that no grammarians or logicians first learn grammar or logic and only then proceed to the next step, learning how to use language. No one learns their native tongue the way so many of us were taught to learn Latin and French, viz., by first memorizing vocabulary and studying the rules of grammar, etc. The reason Aristotle, Hegel, Frege, etc., had such different approaches to logic is because they were able to study vast numbers of sentences and create hypothetical models to explain how humans 'reason.' Not one of them, of course, would be caught dead beginning a treatise on logic with a sentence like the one James used in his chapter on reasoning: "Much of our thinking consists of trains of images suggested one by another, of a sort of spontaneous revery of which it seems likely enough that the higher brutes should be capable" (PP II:325). Reasoning is not manipulating images!

Suppose, then, that we begin as everyone must, with common sense. A complete sentence is one which expresses a complete thought, and a complete thought is the one, partless meaning of a complete sentence. By the time we reach fifth grade, we have a 'sense' of what is meant by 'a complete sentence,' and it is the misuse of that 'sense' which has led so many students of 'logic' astray in their thinking about thinking as reasoning. The reason is because the 'inventor' of logic, Aristotle, was interested (as many of us are) in knowledge that is true and utterly certain. Today, we call such knowledge "science." A complete thought in the context of logic, then, is one that is either true or false. A complete sentence is one which expresses a thought which is either true or false. Since only one type of sentences, those known as declarative, declares something to be true or false, the logicians evicted the other three classes of sentence, viz., exclamatory, imperative, and interrogative from the realm of logic. There is a bit of good common sense in this practice. But . . .

But, if we look more closely, isn't it obvious that it is only a bit? And a somewhat small bit at that?! Walk up to a child and begin asking questions. "Susie, three blind mice. Is that true or false?" How about the following? "Susie, some students. Is that true or false?" Or "Oh, my gosh!" Finally, "After you have put on your jacket and boots to go out and play in the back yard with your brother and sister who've already gone out, please close the door behind you as quietly as you can, so as not to wake up your mother who came home from work very late last night and who needs her rest"? Now, think about all the sentences people speak during the course of a day, and try to figure out what percentage of them a logic professor who is interested only in true or false declaratives would have to exclude. Do you see why someone like James, who kept one eye fixed on real-life facts while he tried to enunciate timeless generalizations about them, might be a better authority on thought than the logicians? *Have you been noticing how many of the sentences in this paragraph are declarative sentences?* Was Socrates a genius or not, insofar as he noted that each one of us acts only as an external catalyst to 'draw out' (the root of 'e-duc-ate') knowledge which the person we speak to must already possess? See the *Meno* for his demonstration of 'teaching with questions.' See the *Phaedo* for the way he used that idea to argue for personal immortality.

What is the point? The point is that, to understand thought, we must look for it in its most natural setting, namely, as the meaning of everything we say. At least. There is no limit to the 'appearances' a complete sentence can take. Probably the most famous sentence in all of philosophy, certainly the most revolutionary in its implications, has only six letters and looks like a single word. Its Latin appearance is "*Cogito*," and its English counterpart is "I am thinking." If a complete sentence is one that expresses a complete thought, we might ask whether "Cogito" is a sentence with one or three words. School children learn quickly how to handle that problem. In some cases, the subject of the sentence is 'understood.' That is, it is not spoken or written. "Don't got a lot of money" might have the subject "I" merely understood, and "A mighty fine man, that son of yours" has the verb "is" unspoken or tacit. A professor who has corrected only half of the class's exams might reply simply "Some" to a query, "Did any of us pass the exam?" (The logic text will explain that 'some' in that sentence may mean 'some but not all' or 'some and possibly all.') And a grammar school child might offer "Oh, my gosh!" as a complete-sentence answer, and a correct one, to the exam question, "Give one example of an exclamation." Whoever keeps those few ideas in mind can agree perfectly with a conclusion about logic offered by Alfred N. Whitehead at the end of his Ingersoll lecture on immortality, delivered in April, 1941, nearly forty-four years after James delivered his:

> The conclusion is that Logic, conceived as an adequate analysis of the advance of thought, is a fake. It is a superb instrument, but it requires a background of common sense.
> To take another example: Consider the "exact" statements of the various schools of Christian theology. If the leaders of any ecclesiastical organization at present existing were transported back to the sixteenth century, and stated their full beliefs, historical and doctrinal, either in Geneva or in Spain, then Calvin, or the Inquisitors, would have been profoundly shocked, and would have acted according to their habits in such cases. Perhaps, after some explanation, both Calvin and the Inquisitors would have had the sense to shift the emphasis to their own beliefs. That is another question which does not concern us.
> My point is that the final outlook of philosophic thought cannot be based upon the exact statements which form the basis of special sciences.
> The exactness is a fake. ("Immortality," sec.XIX)

What's more, those who know how radically Whitehead's and Russell's thinking careers diverged after they completed their famous, joint treatise on logic entitled *Principia Mathematica,* in 1913, will understand how right Whitehead was when he made the above comments in 1941. That reflection will also help us form some estimate of the relative merits of James's thought about thought versus that of C. S. Peirce.

We can therefore sum up this digression (!) on the proper way to understand what 'a complete sentence' means by saying that a complete sentence is one which expresses a complete thought. By importing all that we common-sensically take for granted, we can say that an enormous amount of a sentence's full meaning is tacit, unspoken, merely understood, and that different logicians will therefore 'translate' or analyse an everyday sentence in line with her or his own theoretical framework. (This explains why different interpreters give divergent interpretations of what, for example, James meant here or there.) If we think of a 'proposition' as the meaning of a complete sentence which is either true or false, and if we link that to the idea that every proposition has a contrary or contradictory proposition in opposition to it, we can change the name of 'proposition' to 'proposal' and say that *every thought is one of several possible proposals offered to a human agent for a free response.* The response, as discussed in Chapter II, may be assent, dissent, or suspended judgment. For instance, the paragraph before this one proposed two thoughts: "James towered over Peirce in understanding thought" vs "Peirce was the better logician."

Most of the meaning/thought is tacit. What precisely is that 'enormous amount of the sentence's meaning'? In order to understand what it is and how to 'access it,' we can reinterpret an everyday experience James used several times to illustrate 'vague but precise thoughts.' In the passage cited earlier about our encountering gaps in our thinking, James made a reference to what he had "described some time back." He referred there (on page 259) to what he had written on page 251. Here is the earlier passage. (It can also serve as an introduction to the third thesis.)

Suppose we try to recall a forgotten name. The state of our consciousness is peculiar. There is a gap therein; but no mere gap. It is a gap that is intensely active. A sort of wraith of the name is in it, beckoning us in a given direction, making us at moments tingle with the sense of our closeness, and then letting us sink back without the longed-for term. If wrong names are proposed to us, this singularly definite gap acts immediately so as to negate them. They do not fit into its mould. And the gap of one word does not feel like the gap of another, all empty of content as both might seem necessarily to be when described as gaps. When I vainly try to recall the name of Spalding, my consciousness is far removed from what it is when I vainly try to recall the name of Bowles. Here some ingenious persons will say: "How *can* the two consciousnesses be different when the terms which might make them different are not there? All that is there, so long as the effort to recall is vain, is the bare effort itself. How should that differ in the two cases? You are making it seem to differ by prematurely filling it out with the different names, although these, by the hypothesis, have not yet come. Stick to the two efforts as they are, without naming them after facts not yet existent, and you'll be quite unable to designate any point in which they differ." Designate, truly enough. We can only designate the difference by borrowing the names of objects not yet in the mind. Which is to say that our psychological vocabulary is wholly inadequate to name the differences that exist, even such strong differences as these. But namelessness is compatible with existence. There are innumerable consciousnesses of emptiness, no one of which taken in itself has a name, but all different from each other. The ordinary way is to assume that they are all emptinesses of consciousness, and so the same state. But the feeling of an absence is *toto coelo* other than the absence of a feeling. It is an intense feeling. The rhythm of a lost word may be there without a sound to clothe it; or the evanescent sense of something which is the initial vowel or consonant may mock us fitfully, without growing more distinct. . . .

The truth is that large tracts of human speech are nothing but *signs of direction* in thought, of which direction we nevertheless have an acutely discriminative sense, though no definite sensorial image plays any part in it whatsoever. Sensorial images are stable psychic facts; we can hold them still and look at them as long as we like. These bare images of logical movement, on the contrary, are psychic transitions, always on the wing, so to speak, and not to be glimpsed except in flight. Their function is to lead from one set of images to another. (PP I:251-53)

When he penned these lines, James had not yet discovered—really discovered!—the importance of common sense and its One-Space, One-Time inner map-model of 'cosmic geography' and 'universal history.' Once we have thoroughly grounded ourselves in his later insight, we can use it to remove whatever unnecessary or extra mystery there is in the kind of phenomenon James refers to here.

It is here that the foundation laid in Chapters II and III of *William James on Common Sense* must be relied on, particularly the discussion in Chapter III of the way an apparently stable worldview emerges from an unstable stream of experience. To show the difference, suppose we erase the picture of our vain search for a forgotten name as the picture of a 'felt' gap or absence. Suppose we replace it with a picture of our mind filled with our inner model of the world. By virtue of a near-infinite network of associations, we have zoomed in to a very precise area of that model. We know all sorts of things which we are not trying to recall, such as the name of a distant galaxy, another planet, a favorite elephant, etc. Someone who sees us struggling for a person's name may say "Tell me where you know her from or what she did," etc. If we want their help, we may say "It was my third grade teacher." If our assist'er asks "Was it Sister Celine?", the sounds we hear are gone instantly. Only the memory of them remains. We may think/know instantly, "No, that is the wrong name." Or we may need a moment for a second, continuing thought.

What we are doing then is comparing the suggested sound 'of' the teacher's name with a not-quite-recalled-sound in a very small, precise area in our vast inner model. James himself offered this better analysis in another chapter of *The Principles*:

The writer of these pages has every year to learn the names of a large number of students who sit in alphabetical order in a lecture-room. He finally learns to call them by name, as they sit in their accustomed places. On meeting one in the street, however, early in the year, the face hardly ever recalls the name, but it may recall the place of its owner in the lecture-room, his neighbors' faces, and consequently his general alphabetical position; and then, usually as the common associate of all these combined data, the student's name surges up in his mind. (PP I:568)

The same comparing-acts take place constantly. To replace 'transcendent relations of ideas to realities' as the image for explaining the truth of ideas or thoughts, James invoked 'transitions and terminations' which consist in comparing memory 'videos' with actual sense-data sequences, e.g., taking a walk to Memorial Hall to compare what we recall to what we see. There are other types. Students use questions on an exam sheet to begin a search for the relevant items in their inner model so they can fill the 'gap' in the exam booklet. The proofreader is checking the seen 'ciphers' against remembered spellings. And, yes, if we are given instructions to fetch 'five red apples,' we will be trying to match activated memory-images against what we see. Counting to five can be done by simply matching memorized sound sequences with items seen and/or felt, though small-enough 'groups' forming visual gestalts instantly recall the correlated sound-memory sometimes called 'a numeral.'

There are, of course, no red apples, no color-charts, no drawers, etc., as James and Russell realized. Not everyone agrees with them, only those who are willing to be daring in the negations that rigorous thinking points to. James was a daring thinker who believed some like-minded thinkers would have followed him in his negation of consciousness as an entity if they had been as daring as he. Our daring follows him in some, perhaps most things, but we refuse to follow him all the way to some conclusions, and we take his own insights farther to others. For instance, once we realize that words as such do not exist, we must re-think the meaning of that most indispensable clue to a complete thought, namely, the meaning of "a sentence."

Third: Non-Word 'Words' Associate Directly With (Other) Images, not With Thoughts. Three types of things 'make up' the totality of what we experience. Images can be viewed as things sandwiched between the flux of sensed objects and the thoughts whereby we interpret that flux. It became customary long ago to think of images in relation to sensed objects. The first thing we notice about images, once we begin to notice them, is that they are like or similar to the things we sense. Whoever walks into a dark space—a cave, a movie theater, etc.—after looking at the sun knows that the dancing disk that lingers is not the sun which is still up in the sky but an 'image' of the sun. Recalled later, that image is immeasurably fainter. So much fainter are images that modern thinkers—for whom the recognition of images as genuine realities in their own right would be theoretically disastrous—convince themselves they are fictions suggested by our misuse of words.

But they have things backwards. Thinkers who are ready to deny images are convinced that the words we misuse are real. As has been argued, though, words are the fictitious entities. They do not make up a fourth component of the 'world' as we experience it. 'Words' are either sense-data or images. As sense-data, they are sounds we call "voices," parts of color-fields which we call "writing" and "gestures," and for Laura Bridgman, Helen Keller, and Joe Bonham (in D. Trumbo's novel, *Johny Got His Gun*) tactile sense-data. The images we call "inner speech" are—correspondingly—auditory, visual, and tactile images. But all of these are sense-data or images, not words.

What we grow up calling "words" are sense-data and images that have been singled out, put into a special mental pigeonhole, and given a new, second name, "words." The basis for distinguishing them from other sense-data and images is most easily grasped if we divide the entire combined class of sense-data and images into two mental-class 'species' which we name "natural" and "conventional." Into the 'natural' class we put all those which beasts would experience if no 'language-using' humans existed. Into the 'conventional' category go the others already classified in our common-sense philosophy as 'words' which, we say, make up language. Once again, both species are 'governed' by the same discrimination-and-association laws.

The thesis here is that *heard and seen 'words'—sense-data—are not attached directly to thoughts*. They correlate with thoughts only by virtue of their ties with the vast and intricate criss-crossing networks of inner imagery which they evoke. They are first tied to more simple image-clusters. Their conventionality comes from the fact that, in different countries, different sounds and ciphers are associated with similar clusters. "Water," "acqua," "agua," "eau," "wasser," etc., are different, but the basic images of similar sensations which they conjure are similar. This is why 'translation' from one 'language' to another is possible. The person able to speak two, six, or sixteen diverse 'languages' does not need two, six, or sixteen distinct inner models of reality. Or concepts of water.

'Word'-images attach directly to images, not directly to thoughts. If they attached to thoughts directly, how could we explain how we who 'know' only English can learn the theories of the Greek-writing Plato, the Latin-writing St. Augustine, the French-using Descartes, and the German-using Kant, etc. How could we explain the even more wonderful fact of bi-lingualism? How could we explain why the Rorty Rule makes it possible to 'translate' one thinker's English into another's use of English?

In other words, there are many ways of 'saying the same thing' or 'putting something into words.' Anyone can pause and think of dozens of examples of using different word-sense-data for similar images to accompany the same thought. For instance, "The New York Yankees will be here in Cleveland to play the Indians tomorrow night," "The Yankees are in town for a night game tomorrow," "New York and Cleveland will play under the lights tomorrow," "The Yanks and Indians clash at Jacob's Field tomorrow at 7:30 pm," etc., should suffice to get the general idea across. (Is it induction when a dozen illustrations are provided, but deduction when the generalization is offered first and then particulars are offered as minors and conclusions, as in "There are many ways of saying the same thing: 'NY is in Cleveland tomorrow' is one way to say something; therefore there are many ways of saying 'NY is in Cleveland tomorrow'"?)

Big differences in words can coexist with slight differences in thought. But tiny differences in words may signify gigantic differences in worldviews. As answers to the question, "How many gods are there," the mere prefixing of an 'N' to the word "ONE" indicates such a radical difference in meaning that a larger one is hard to imagine. This adds to the evidence that 'words' attach more directly to the imagery 'making up' our stable-seeming inner model rather than to thoughts. "He is in the house" vs "He is on the house," "I went to the scene" vs "I went by the scene," etc., are other illustrations.

Thus, whether we believe in words but not images or in images but not words has far-reaching consequences so far as choosing an adequate worldview is concerned. If we choose to believe in both or choose to regard one as real and the other as merely a useful, even indispensable fiction, there are other far-reaching consequences. For instance, there are different consequences to James's view of conjunctions and prepositions and our view. Ours is that non-word 'words' attach directly to stable-model imagery. James's view offers another choice.

James adopted an unusual view of conjunctions and prepositions in order to stress the inadequacy of the 'static concepts' tradition. The attention of traditionalists is on what James called the 'substantive' elements of sentences. Those 'substantive' elements are singled out because they appear to correspond to the 'substantive' things which we think, common-sensically, make up the world. There are people. People like Columbus have a reality of their own. There are places. Places like America have a reality of their own. And, we say, there are fixed dates in history. Dates like the year 1492 have a reality of their own. If we approach consciousness looking for mental counterparts for those enduring or fixed realities, it is natural to picture 'images' and/or 'concepts' as enduring or fixed ideas which have a relation to the enduring things which they 'represent.' Once our thinking becomes fixated by that picture, we tend to overlook other obvious features of experience 'as it presents itself in its own nature.' One feature is the unbroken continuity of ongoing thought.

James criticized that natural oversight as the major flaw in traditional psychologies. While in London in 1883, he composed a lecture for a small group, then worked it into an article with the title "On Some Omissions of Introspective Psychology." In it he offered an alternative to the 'static' approach to knowledge which viewed it as assembling those pre-acquired units, images and concepts, into thoughts which were then thought to reflect reality if assembled correctly. His replacement was the dynamic image of a "wonderful stream of consciousness." His focus was away from discrete parts of thought with their relations to outer realities, and onto experience itself. It was to highlight his replacement image of a stream that he introduced his unusual view of conjunctions and prepositions. If nouns are the names of things, verbs the names of actions, adjectives names of things' qualities, and adverbs names of actions' qualities, what are the other words names of? They are the names of relations connecting the otherwise discrete, static parts of experience itself. Conjunctions and prepositions represent the continuity of each moment's conscious experience as it flows into the next moment's. Here is the passage as it later appeared in Chapter IX of *The Principles*.

> We ought to say a feeling of *and*, a feeling of *if*, a feeling of *but*, and a feeling of *by*, quite as readily as we say a feeling of *blue* or a feeling of *cold*. Yet we do not: so inveterate has our habit become of recognizing the existence of the substantive parts alone, that language almost refuses to lend itself to any other use. The Empiricists have always dwelt on its influence in making us suppose that where we have a separate name, a separate thing must needs be there to correspond with it; and they have rightly denied the existence of the mob of abstract entities, principles and forces, in whose favor no other evidence than this could be brought up. But they have said nothing of the obverse error . . . of supposing that where there is *no* name no entity can exist. All *dumb* or anonymous psychic states have, owing to this error, been coolly suppressed; or, if recognized at all, have been named after the substantive perception they led to, as thoughts 'about' this object or 'about' that, the stolid word *about* engulfing all their delicate idiosyncrasies in its monotonous sound. Thus the greater and greater accentuation and isolation of the substantive parts have continually gone on. (PP I:245-46)

In the original article, he added that the worst feature of the old introspectors' omissions was portraying a thought as a 'manifold' that can be broken into parts that are 'discrete.' (See *Writings* I:990-91)

"Discrete." That word accents the static, fixed, and—especially—*separate* elements of thought. James himself routinely emphasized the stability and fixed nature of our knowledge. Stability was the keynote of his recognition of our One-Space, One-History, inner models. The inner model has 'items' tagged with language's 'substantive terms,' and those relate to our ability to form unchanging, even eternal! (shorthand) concepts cognitive of the 'sameness' of those items. (See Chapter II concerning "Many Complete Thoughts, but a 'Same Topic'.") Here, however, James's goal is to emphasize the fact that the whole ongoing 'stream' evolves smoothly from one moment to the next. Our challenge is to not-deny either stability or change, but to find some way of reconciling the two. By thinking.

Fourth: It is thought that provides our ultimate freedom. Namely,

244

the freedom to believe what we will. The way to reconcile stability and change is by thinking the right thoughts. Thinking trumps everything: sense-data, words, images, habits, etc. One thought can even trump other thoughts. This was a major theme in his 1881 address which he entitled "Reflex Action and Theism."

[. . .] The real world as it is given at this moment is the sum total of all its beings and events now. But can we think of such a sum? Can we realize for an instant what a cross-section of all existence at a definite point of time would be? While I talk and the flies buzz, a sea gull catches a fish at the mouth of the Amazon, a tree falls in the Adirondack wilderness, a man sneezes in Germany, a horse dies in Tartary, and twins are born in France. What does that mean? Does the contemporaneity of these events with each other and with a million others as disjointed, form a rational bond between them, and unite them into anything that means for us a world? Yet just such a collateral contemporaneity, and nothing else, is the real order of the world. It is an order with which we have nothing to do but to get away from it as fast as possible. As I said, we break it: we break it into histories, and we break it into arts, and we break it into sciences; and then we begin to feel at home. We make ten thousand separate serial orders of it, and on any one of these we react as though the others did not exist. We discover among its various parts relations that were never given to sense at all (mathematical relations, tangents, squares, and roots and logarithmic functions), and out of an infinite number of these we call certain ones essential and lawgiving, and ignore the rest. Essential these relations are, but only *for our purpose*, the other relations being just as real and present as they; and our purpose is to *conceive simply* and to *foresee*. Are not simple conception and prevision subjective ends pure and simple? They are the ends of what we call science; and the miracle of miracles, a miracle not yet exhaustively cleared up by any philosophy, is that the given order lends itself to the remodelling. It shows itself plastic to many of our scientific, to many of our aesthetic, to many of our practical purposes and ends. (WB:119-20; PP II:635, n; *Writings* I:545-46)

The real order of the world "is an order with which we have nothing to do but to get away from it as fast as possible"? Yes, our mind is such that it allows us to theorize or, in James's terms, conceptualize, and this is doing more than simply record or copy the order of our impressions.

[. . .] I am not sure, for example, that all physiologists see that it [the reflex theory of the mind] commits them to regarding the mind as an essentially teleological mechanism. I mean by this that the conceiving or theorizing faculty—the mind's middle department—functions *exclusively for the sake of ends* that do not exist at all in the world of impressions we receive by way of our senses, but are set by our emotional and practical subjectivity altogether. It is a transformer of the world of our impressions into a totally different world—the world of our conception; and the transformation is effected in the interests of our volitional nature, and for no other purpose whatsoever. Destroy the volitional nature, the definite subjective purposes, preferences, fondnesses for certain effects, forms, orders, and not the slightest motive would remain for the brute order of our experience to be remodelled. But, as we have the elaborate volitional constitution we do have, the remodelling must be effected; there is no escape. (WB:117-18; *Writings* I:544-45)

We do more than simply 'copy impressions.' We model and remodel experience. We 'transform' the world of our impressions. All of us learners begin by creating for our 'world of impressions' what will be the foundational model used for most purposes during the rest of our lives, namely, our common-sense model. And all of us transform that common sense in certain important, though not initially in radically anti-common-sensical ways. The more numerous of these ways are called "cultural"; the ways which are more idiosyncratic are called "personal." Finally, some of us also remodel our worldview quite radically into materialism, sharp dualism, idealism, neutral monism, etc.

The transforming is the work of thinking and thoughts. The challenge is to select the true thoughts—when and if they come—in preference to other thoughts which are false. It is also to select better thoughts over less appropriate ones. We judge by thinking, that is, by understanding the alternatives (with the help of our stable inner models), and then deciding what fits best with experience and with the rest of our preferred overall philosophy, worldview, etc.

Thinkers who find contradictions within common sense seek better worldviews. *'Finding contradictions'* is understanding thoughts which conflict with each other. Finding better worldviews is also understanding thoughts. It is only by finding better thoughts that we can reconcile the contradictions, real and apparent, in earlier thoughts, beginning with our common-sense beliefs. Hume admitted to inescapable confusion, but he sought a specious calm in a re-turn or turning back to first-thought naïve realism combined with a turning away from second-thought efforts to resolve the contradictions at the heart of naïve-realism. Not James. If a phrase can capture the opposite mentalities of Hume and James, it is that Hume was willing to live with theory-schizophrenia, and James was not. To the end, James persisted in trying to forge radical empiricism into a coherent grand unifying theory. By reasoning.

James was rational, a rationalist even! It was by reasoning that he tried to show that, to know the inner nature of reality, the flux of perception has more value than the use of 'winged concepts' or intellectual reasoning.

We disagree. The rest of this section will be devoted to explaining why his brilliant descriptions of the nature of ongoing thought, found in Chapters IX and X of *The Principles of Psychology*, should be used to trump those wrong-direction theorizings of James's last years.

We present that 'explanation' as a series of decisions.

Decision #1. To begin with, thoughts give us, the agents, control over the way we think about our selves (us). Common-sensically, everyone believes *that* she-or-he-is-the-one-individual-born-so-many-years-before-today-and-who-has-understood-thousands-upon-thousands-of-thoughts,-each-an-object-of-an-act-exercised-by-the-one-agent. We can create a rival model of the universe with nothing but floating islands of ever-changing 'streams of consciousness' or 'fields of experience,' i.e., with no perduring agent-selves who understand (i) *that* I-who-understand-a-present-changing-thought-am-not-that-thought as well as (ii) *that* both-"I"-and-"the-present-changing-island-of-thought-called-mine"-are-names-for-the-same-thing.

The difference is this. The common-sense model has 6.7 billion agents-as-such, plus 6.7 billion distinct thoughts-as-such, whereas the 'islands' model has only 6.7 billion items called by two different names. James went wrong when he, a free agent, opted for the latter view from the time he wrote the conclusion of Chapter X of *The Principles* ("The I which knows . . . is a Thought, at each moment different from that of the last moment"; PP I:401) till he wrote the second footnote in "Does 'Consciousness' Exist?" ("In my 'Psychology' I have tried to show that we need no knower other than the 'passing thought'"; *Writings* II:1142). Apart from the fact that the agent-self does not have any experience of itself whatever, James never gave any sound reason to reject the common sense view we rely on in our everyday, 'practical' lives. Just because I, an agent-self, am not evidence for anything but am the transcendent agent who must weigh the evidence found in my field of conscious experience only means I serve no purpose as evidence. As a committed rationalist, I am the being who looks for evidence of my existence, my nature, and my purpose for being.

Decision #2. 'We-understand-thoughts' is the correct, three-item formula. It is vitally important to understand that formula in the light of Aristotle's five-concept analysis. 'We understand thoughts' fits an agent-act-object pattern. This requires several semantic alterations vis-à-vis much of what James wrote. In Chapter IX of *The Principles*, James used a stripped-down model consisting of 'thought' and 'its object.' But a careful reading will show that his meaning is often unclear and just as often shifts. Of course, 'thought' is a word used by all of us for different things, e.g., the past tense of an action-verb, 'think,' or the thing which comes to us and which we understand. James even used it for the knower and the knower's state of mind, as in this passage which was quoted earlier.

The psychologist's attitude towards cognition will be so important in the sequel that we must not leave it until it is made perfectly clear. *It is a thoroughgoing dualism.* It supposes two elements, mind knowing and thing known, and treats them as irreducible. Neither gets out of itself or into the other, neither in any way *is* the other, neither *makes* the other. They just stand face to face in a common world, and one simply knows, or is known unto, its counterpart. This singular relation is not to be expressed in any lower terms, or translated into any more intelligible name. Some sort of *signal* must be given by the thing to the mind's brain, or the knowing will not occur—we find as a matter of fact that the mere *existence* of a thing outside the brain is not a sufficient cause for our knowing it: it must strike the brain in some way, as well as be there, to be known. But the brain being struck, the knowledge is constituted by a new construction that occurs altogether *in* the mind. The thing remains the same whether known or not. And when once there, the knowledge may remain there, whatever becomes of the thing. (PP I:218-19)

"Thing known," "signal given by the thing to the mind's brain," "existence of a thing outside the brain," "the thing remains the same whether known or not," etc., all betray the fact that James did not write this paragraph with an eye on his analysis of "Columbus discovered America in 1492"! This is where our own thoughts and their supporting imagery must be sharper. *We do not understand things.* *We understand thoughts about things. (*This requires a gestalt shift, since thoughts themselves are things; but they are not persons, signals, brains, or unchanging things outside the brain.)

In other words, the agent-self 'does many things,' i.e., exercises many acts vis-à-vis many different objects. I am directly aware of sense-data and images. Sense-data and images do not have objects. They do not know, I do. They are objects of my acts, they are directly sensed, felt, experienced by me, etc. I also understand, and that act has only one type of object, namely, thoughts or meanings. Once it is realized that the objects I see, the objects I hear, etc., are intra-psychic effects produced by unsensed sources 'ab extra,' it is advisable to change the terms from "I see color" to "I am directly aware of color." That way, the connoted reference to eyes is removed, in order to adjust to the fact that there is no little man inside with an extra pair of eyes to look at the color-fields or TVFs.

There is another difference between sense-data and images on the one hand and thoughts on the other. I can 'direct my attention' at any of the former, but I cannot point my attention at a thought in the same way. I can attend to all the intra-psychic sense-data and images, including inner-speech, and—in light of all that—I can be quite certain that more! was going on, viz., that I was also thinking. But it is less misleading just to say "I can only notice *that* there-is-more-than-sense-data-and-images, and I am certain I not only understand what this means but also that I assent fully to it." If we conjure images to help think about thoughts, the images are used to help know in what direction lies that which we can notice only by means of a thought.

James's analysis of "Columbus discovered America in 1492" now falls into place perfectly. We must, as he insisted, avoid confusing two items, viz., the meaning-thought in our mind and 'substantive things,' such as Columbus, America, 1492, etc., outside our mind. But we must make further useful- or pragmatic-fiction distinctions or use a more complex model to help keep our thinking clear. Where James was content for the most part to deal with two items, thoughts (in the mind) knowing and things (outside) known, we work with (i) the agent-self who (2) understands (3) thoughts (4) 'about' the 'content' of the thoughts in the mind, all of which are distinct from whatever (5) outside things exist. If I am thinking *that* the-sun-exists, the object is the total meaning in my mind which is different from the total meaning in other cases, such as when I am thinking *that* the moon exists. The thought and what it is 'about' (its content) are best viewed as two ways of describing one thing, namely, the thought I am understanding. In the case of "the sun exists," the thought-plus-its-content 'in my mind' is distinct from the sun, assuming that the sun exists. (It doesn't.)

Those of us who adopt 'representationalism' as a provisional, interim theory think of thoughts as if they are pieces of glass which act as mediums between us the lookers and the object-things out beyond the glass. Relevant to this is a note that James inserted into the syllabus he drafted for a very late 1906-07 course. (The term "representationalism" will be inserted to indicate which part of his note refers to this helpful, interim theory.)

> A useful distinction is that between epistemological and ontological idealism. Epistemological idealism says: "I know nothing but my own ideas." This opinion, consistently held, would amount to "solipsism":—nobody seriously defends it. Epistemological realism [representationalism] says: "I know, *through* my ideas, other realities." *Ontological* idealism may then define these other realities as spiritual entities (panpsychically, for example). Ontological realism on the other hand, defends them as something material, unknowable, or at any rate non-psychical. (ML:424)

"I know, *through* my ideas, other realities." In a sense, I do, but only if they exist. I don't, if they don't. Since none of us has *direct* access to anything but our 'ideas' [thoughts-plus-their-content], sense-data, and images, we find ourselves confronted with the challenge of solipsism. Even so, however, there simply is no better picture than this. If we believe we see the sun, and if that 'belief' (assented-to-thought) is true, then we know *that* we-see-the-sun, and we can 'say' we know us, our seeing, and the sun, 'in and through' that thought.

Jamesian quintalists, then, are radical in viewing the universe as constituted of person-agents, the sense-data and images which they are directly aware of and can attend to directly, the thoughts-plus-their-content which they understand, and possibly sub-atoms. Though unflinching in their refusal to do any further 'reducing,' quintalists also unflinchingly refuse to add any other kinds of things. Any other 'things' which we think of with our endless stream of thoughts are to be regarded merely as 'contents' of existing thoughts. This means that most things we grow up believing in and that academic experts write about are fictions, i.e., we must recognize those beliefs as real thoughts whose 'content-items' are not matched by numerically-exact, correlative realities.

Decision #4. "Things which do not exist." Is it not a contradiction to believe that we can think about things which do not exist? Parmenides decided it was, but he seems to have allowed such illusions to pass as illusions or 'the way of opinion.' But can illusions be real? Can appearances be realities? To deal with such issues, we must cling to our model, analyse the relevant details, and make our talk fit our thought.

If we start with the last item, namely, *appearances*, it is clear that the word is used for a thought about things that either exist or don't exist. Writers have used many 'words' as synonyms for 'sense-data,' e.g., appearances, phenomena, proper sense objects, secondary qualities, and so on. When such terms are substituted for 'sense-data,' then *appearances* are real things. If sense-data were not real, they could not 'appear' or be directly known by us. Other times, 'appearance' and 'illusion' involve a false belief about something or someone, e.g., "Contrary to all appearances, he was quite selfish" or "Magicians create the illusion of a rabbit being suddenly created from nothing." In such cases, appearances and illusions do not exist, but the false-belief thoughts really do. But what about Santa Claus, Ivanhoe, darkness, and nothingness?

Parmenides declared that non-being cannot be, cannot be thought, and cannot be named. His logic seemed impeccable. If non-being ever came to be, it would not be non-being. There cannot be thought when there is not some thing being thought of, because thinking about nothing is not thinking. Whence it follows that it cannot be named, because there is no 'it' to be named. But the trap Parmenides fell into is clear if we examine his statements and see that he has named 'non-being' several times, and that either his statements were devoid of meaning or else he succeeded quite handily in thinking about non-being, even if he was right to believe it does not exist. Even Plato and Aristotle were unable to solve this paradox.

James's formula is the only one that succeeds in satisfying our common sense. It is easy to understand, e.g., *that* the-sun-does-not-exist-and-therefore-is-not-a-being, just as it is easy to understand *that* Santa-does-not-exist. This does not make the sun or Santa into a being or a non-being. We should avoid the nouns 'being' and 'non-being' (except when writing poetry or when our meaning is easily understood) and substitute "The sun exists" for "The sun is a being" and substitute "Santa does not exist" for "Santa is a non-being." Then we decide which of those thoughts we will assent to. If I assent to "The sun exists" and there is no sun, my thought is false. If I assent to "God does not exist" and there is a deity, my thought is false. If I assent to "Space and time exist" and they do, my thought is true. If I assent to "Neither space nor time exist" and they do not, my thought is true. If I say "Images exist, concepts do not, but the concept of 'concept' is, like so many other concepts, e.g., those of space and time, a useful and even indispensable pragmatic-fiction" and such is the case, my thought is true. Etc.

As mentioned, we can also describe every thing that a thought appears to be about as the thought's content. Ivanhoe is the 'content' of a real thought. Scott's thoughts 'about' Ivanhoe were real. Our thoughts about Scott's real thoughts are real. But if Scott, like Ivanhoe, never existed, then both are our real thoughts' content and only that. (Thoughts provide 'an open area' where the 'unveiling' of 'possible truth' can happen.)

Decision #5. QU: How ought we to think about acts? AN: By clinging to the thesis that there are only three wholly basic questions: What exists?, What does whatever exists do?, and Why? Acts are not on the list of things that exist. People exist and people are aware, attend, understand, and wilfully decide. Thoughts are real, but they do not really do anything, since it is we who 'do' to them, namely, understand them. Sense-data and images also 'do nothing,' and it is we who are aware of and attend to them. If bodies exist, we can say they stand still vis-à-vis each other or get farther apart from or closer to each other. Motion-as-such does not exist, only the bodies which we say, misleadingly, do those 'things!' The topic of reifications was discussed earlier, so we need only insert a reminder here. But...

But, just because acts do not exist, only agents who act, this does not mean we can reduce our five-concept model of agent, power, act, habit, and object to four by eliminating acts. In order to know 'about' the selves we cannot turn and look at, we must follow the old adage, "By their deeds you will know them." I must infer what kind of thing

I am—i.e., how to classify me vis-à-vis the things I am like and those I am not like—by using as evidence what-I-do. I am not only aware of sense-data as I was at birth. Now that I have a common-sense belief system which I understand, I am aware of sense-data and I can do something in addition to being aware of sense-data: I can understand the thought *that* I-am-aware-of-sense-data. My 'concepts' of such acts are needed.

In fact, it is convenient to even reify acts and to speak about awareness, attention, understanding, decision, etc. And this convenience helps me to take my complete thoughts and to 'see' if they are verified by my total experience. Only, as James noticed, when we do this, we liken cognitive acts to physical processes, such as grasping, seizing, etc., a danger we must always guard against. What follow are a few analogies to point attention to just one type of act, viz., awareness, followed in each case by an insistence on the difference between the analogy and the reality.

First, sense awareness can be compared to *acquaintance.* This is a favorite analogy of James's. In *The Principles'* Chapter XVII, "Sensation," he used several terms for the act whose objects are "simple qualities or attributes like hard, hot, pain" (PP II:3). At one point he wrote "Sensations, then, first make us acquainted with innumerable things, and then are replaced by thoughts which know the same things in altogether other ways" (PP II:6). He ought to have said, "Sensing [act] is when we are acquainted with sense-data that we can then or later have thoughts about." Only if we start thinking that apples, trees, squirrels, etc., are 'groups of sense-data' the way Berkeley and James, in his radical empiricist mood, thought, can we say that "Sensation makes us [!} acquainted with innumerable things besides sense-data." As for "replaced by," it falsely suggests that awareness and thinking cannot go on at the same time.

For that reason, simple awareness is better compared to simple *contact.* It is natural to say that our senses put us in direct contact with the objects sensed. We see things directly, with no visible intermediaries, hear things directly, and so on. But seeing in the common-sense sense is not literally contact. Our eyes do not reach out and touch stars. And there is all the difference in the world between one thing touching another and one thing being aware of the other. Our head is in direct contact with the pillow we are sleeping on, but our head does not feel it. The legs of the chair we sit on are in direct contact with the floor, but who would be tempted to say that the legs of the chair sense or feel the floor? (Or vice-versa!) Once we discover that what we see is not the stars but an intrapsychic visual field, 'direct contact' comes closer to being literally true. Color fields, sounds, etc., are 'flush up against us.'

Another favorite analogy is that of *presence*. Like contact, the idea of presence is a spatial one, but presence allows for some spatial separation in a way that contact does not. We picture things which are 'present' to each other as being in roughly the same location in space. The scholastics, champions of common sense, held that sensing requires the presence—and existence—of whatever object is sensed. A thing cannot be in some place unless it first of all *is*, period! But something can be and be present without being known. We can think of a cabbage in the midst of a cabbage patch, surrounded by other cabbages, all of them present with the one in their midst. But would anyone say that the cabbages which are 'present' with the one in the center are also known by it or that they are aware of it? For us to simply be, period!, either in the presence of other things or not, would be no better than not-being. A person who was born, lived twenty-five years in a total comatose state surrounded by the bed, the bedroom walls, people, etc., and then died, might as well have never existed.

Keeping our wits here is quite difficult. James used action-nouns freely, as we all do. Hence our care—when it is important for removing objections that rise so easily—to keep in mind the precise distinctions needed to think clearly about these matters. Thinking is the key. We cannot see, look at, hear, smell, taste, or feel our awareness of colors, sounds, etc. Locke was wrong about the mind looking back and watching itself perform mental acts. Being unable to sense awareness or any other mental act, we really cannot picture them with faint-copy images of what we have (not) sensed. But we can think about acts—or about our self acting—by understanding thoughts. We use models which we can picture in order to understand more clearly thoughts of things we cannot picture. I understand *that* I-can-understand-all-of-the-thoughts-'expressed'-by-the-preceding-sentences. Having understood them, I am now in a position to respond in whatever way I freely choose.

Decision #6. The fact that we can freely choose to assent, dissent, or suspend our judgment on the above points means that we—not society and not our old habits—are in control of our beliefs.

Decision #7. Our thousand-thoughts-in-one give us that freedom to believe what we will. Thinking trumps everything: sense-data, 'words,' images, habits, 'society,' and even other thoughts. Earlier, a reference was made to James's great difficulty in reconciling stability and continuity. In the great compositions of the last five years of his life, namely, *Pragmatism, A Pluralistic Universe,* and *Some Problems of Philosophy,* he struggled to construct a system with fixed concepts of just two types of ingredients, the concept of a continuous, unbroken flow of perceptual experience and the concept of distinction-creating concepts needed for constructing a conceptual system. That two-concept model was one-item too short to embrace his best insights. It excluded the most important continuity of all, the one he had so brilliantly written about in Chapters IX and X of *The Principles of Psychology.* There are no such things as concepts, but there are ongoing, thousand-thoughts-in-one thoughts which have more continuity than the sense-data which he referred to as "the perceptual flux." In our imagination, we can pretend that a complete thought can be broken into concepts, but that is pretending.

First, since neither stability nor change name things that exist, these two opposing 'concepts' should be taken the way all 'fiction-concepts' should, as tools that can be 'used' in any way that helps us understand reality better. Of course, we must try to keep the thoughts in which we 'use' these concepts as consistent with the rest of our beliefs as possible, but it is simply not possible to 'wrap our mind' around the phenomenon of our conscious experience. Not only does experience elude 'capture' in our words, but—what is worse—our words which are not words will invariably give the appearance of paradox and contradiction. We simply do our best, therefore, to 'notice' what is going on and to use 'words' to evoke the best thoughts we can.

Next, in order to sharpen the line between thoughts and the other components of conscious experience, we must review the distinction. It is a line James often blurred. In discussing continuity as opposed to stability, it is critically important to see that the continuity of thought is a separate continuity from the continuity of sense-data or imagery, because thought is separate or distinct. Getting our thoughts clear requires the use of the tri-partite model rather than either of the two which James made the most use of, namely, his idea that "consciousness" names an originally-one, amorphous type of 'stuff' which he called "thought" in *The Principles* or "pure experience" later, and his other idea that "experience" has two components, viz., percepts and concepts. The importance can be stated quite simply. *There are different continuities to take into account.*

There is one type of continuity which seems directly observable. It is the continuity of sense-data and images. Movie-like sense-data constantly change, as do the images they evoke, yet we (often) detect no more 'breaks' between one and the next than we observe while watching a movie. But there is also continuity in the partless meanings or thoughts that we understand. This continuity cannot be observed but only known through self-referential thought.

In Chapter IX of *The Principles*, James treats the stream of thought almost as if it is the continuity of a single stuff. That simply doesn't work. Later, he used his two-part, percept vs concept, format for analysing the stream. The result was that he tended to visualize concepts and words as cut-up, non-continuous entities used to 'deal' with the only really continuous stuff, the perceptual flux. Thus change was ascribed only to the percepts or the perceptual stuff, and stability only to the concepts. Hence, in *A Pluralistic Universe*, he viewed fixed concepts as inadequate to capture flowing percepts, and as liable to 'falsify' experience as to be true of it. However, once we are equipped with his earlier, better insight into the continuity of thought, we should deny the reality of concept-parts. The concepts and words he so strongly distrusted in *A Pluralistic Universe* were both fictions. They are therefore non-existing obstacles to recognizing that there is more than one type of continuity.

Using the three-part model, we can read his 1883 article, "On Some Omissions of Introspective Psychology," as describing thought or meaning as water that flows around and through the relatively more discrete sense-data and images. Though the latter are involved in his description, we can notice that he is trying to direct our attention to a 'more' which is elusive but which, once we notice it, is known to be very real. That 'more' is the thousand-thoughts-in-one, ongoing thought which can be pictured also as an enveloping environment for everything else.

Here is the relevant passage as inserted into Chapter IX of *The Principles*.

[. . .] It is in short the re-instatement of the vague to its proper place in our mental life which I am so anxious to press on the attention. Mr. Galton and Prof. Huxley have . . . made one step in advance in exploding the ridiculous theory of Hume and Berkeley that we can have no images but of perfectly definite things. Another is made in the overthrow of the equally ridiculous notion that, whilst simple objective qualities are revealed to our knowledge in subjective feelings, relations are not. But these reforms are not half sweeping and radical enough. What must be admitted is that the definite images of traditional psychology form but the very smallest part of our minds as they actually live. The traditional psychology talks like one who should say a river consists of nothing but pailsful, spoonsful, quartpotsful, barrelsful, and other moulded forms of water. Even were the pails and the pots all actually standing in the stream, still between them the free water would continue to flow. It is just this free water of consciousness that psychologists resolutely overlook. Every definite image in the mind is steeped and dyed in the free water that flows round it. With it goes the sense of its relations, near and remote, the dying echo of whence it came to us, and dawning sense of whither it is to lead. The significance, the value, of the image is all in this halo or penumbra, that surrounds and escorts it,—or rather that is fused into one with it and has become bone of its bone and flesh of its flesh; leaving it, it is true, an image of the same *thing* it was before, but making it an image of that thing newly taken and freshly understood.

What is that shadowy scheme of the 'form' of an opera, play, or book, which remains in our mind and on which we pass judgment when the actual thing is done? What is our notion of a scientific or philosophical system? Great thinkers have vast premonitory glimpses of schemes of relation between terms, which hardly even as verbal images enter the mind, so rapid is the whole process. We all of us have this permanent consciousness of whither our thought is going. It is a feeling like any other, a feeling of what thoughts are next to arise, before they have arisen. This field of view of consciousness varies very much in extent, depending largely on the degree of mental freshness or fatigue. When very fresh, our minds carry an immense horizon with them. The present image shoots its perspective far before it, irradiating in advance the regions in which lie the thoughts as yet unborn. Under ordinary conditions the halo of felt relations is much more circumscribed. And in states of extreme brain-fag . . . (PP I:254-56; *Writings* I:1002-03)

The second paragraph offers several hints of the vastness James had in mind. We no longer try to 'notice' just the meaning of the most recent complete sentence. We try to recall the 'sense' we have of, say, an opera we attend, with its characters, the gamut of their thoughts and feelings, all the visual effects such as the costuming and action, all the orchestral and vocal effects, our own intellectual and emotional reactions to what we witness. James invites us to re-capture what we experience after the curtain has come down and we perhaps sit there—oblivious of the now opera-less theater—'feeling the impact of the whole thing.' Which now shall we call "the experience"? The three-hours-long, flowing experience? Or the all-at-once summing-up at the end? We need both concepts, and yet—assuming we did not fall fast asleep or suffer comatose moments—there was no 'break' between those 'parts' of one, flowing, intensely alert experience, viz., the three-hours-long taking-in and the recapitulating feeling-the-impact.

Parenthetically, in order to be clear about the vastness of a thought, James added a footnote to that second paragraph. He calls upon Mozart for support:

> Mozart describes thus his manner of composing: First bits and crumbs of the piece come and gradually join together in his mind; then the soul getting warmed to the work, the thing grows more and more, "and I spread it out broader and clearer, and at last it gets almost finished in my head, even when it is a long piece, so that I can see the whole of it at a single glance in my mind, as if it were a beautiful painting or a handsome human being; in which way I do not hear it in my imagination at all as a succession—the way it must come later—but all at once, as it were. It is a rare feast! All the inventing and making goes on in me as in a beautiful strong dream. But the best of all is the *hearing of it all at once*." (PP I:255, n.)

Many of James's descriptions are powerfully evocative of the full glory of 'a passing thought.' But the description he composed for his seventh *Pluralistic Universe* lectures, the one entitled "The Continuity of Experience," is perhaps even better than the last. First, it is more inclusive. Also, it allows us to 'read into' his reference to "a little awareness of his body" our awareness of the whole panoply of presently incoming sense-data which are concurrent with the thinking that 'flows around and through them.' Thirdly, this later description presents the whole as having a verbalized meaning [of a sentence] at its center. Still, 'adjustments' must be made. Above all, his view of 'bad' concepts and words should be replaced by a 'good' stream of unbroken thought whereby we are able to understand continuous experience.

[. . .] Every smallest state of consciousness, concretely taken, overflows its own definition. Only concepts are self-identical; only 'reason' deals with closed equations; nature is but a name for excess; every point in her opens out and runs into the more; and the only question, with reference to any point we may be considering, is how far into the rest of nature we may have to go in order to get entirely beyond its overflow. In the pulse of inner life immediately present now in each of us is a little past, a little future, a little awareness of our own body, of each other's persons, of these sublimities we are trying to talk about, of the earth's geography and the direction of history, of truth and error, of good and bad, and of who knows how much more? Feeling, however dimly and subconsciously, all these things, your pulse of inner life is continuous with them, belongs to them and they to it. You can't identify it with either one of them rather than with the others, for if you let it develop into no matter which of those directions, what it develops into will look back on it and say, 'That was the original germ of me.'

[. . .] All real units of experience *overlap*. Let a row of equidistant dots on a sheet of paper symbolize the concepts by which we intellectualize the world. Let a ruler long enough to cover at least three dots stand for our sensible experience. Then the conceived changes of the sensible experience can be symbolized by sliding the ruler along the line of dots. One concept after another will apply to it, one after another drop away, but it will always cover at least two of them, and no dots less than three will ever adequately cover *it*. You falsify it if you treat it conceptually, or by the law of dots.

What is true here of successive states must also be true of simultaneous characters. They also overlap each other with their being. My present field of consciousness is a centre surrounded by a fringe that shades insensibly into a subconscious more. I use three separate terms here to describe this fact; but I might as well use three hundred, for the fact is all shades and no boundaries. Which part of it properly is in my consciousness, which out? If I name what is out, it already has come in. The centre works in one way while the margins work in another, and presently overpower the centre and are central themselves. What we conceptually identify ourselves with and say we are thinking of at any time is the centre; but our *full* self is the whole field, with all those indefinitely radiating subconscious possibilities of increase that we can only feel without conceiving, and can hardly begin to analyze. The collective and the distributive ways of being coexist here, for each part functions distinctly, makes connexion with its own peculiar region in the still wider rest of experience and tends to draw us into that line, and yet the whole is somehow felt as one pulse of our life,—not conceived so, but felt so. (*Writings* II:760-62)

The decision to seize on his 1890 'Columbus-discovered-America-in-1492' picture of 'meaning as a partless whole' in preference to his other models for thought and thoughts is, once again, a pivotal decision for this entire text. In the same way that we can pretend there is a Santa or an Ivanhoe, even if there is none, we can pretend that fleeting images make up a truly stable, perduring inner model, even if they do not. We can pretend a thought or meaning is 'made up' of distinct concepts, even if we believe it is not. We have choices. We can choose to side with James who increasingly viewed only the perceptual flux as genuinely continuous and conceptual thought as breaking it up, or we can decide to believe there are two continuities, a lesser one referred to as 'the perceptual flow of sense-data and imagery' and the far vaster one of thought-meanings by means of which or through which we can understand so much 'about' everything.

Rather than write more about two types of continuity vs only one type, let a single illustration suffice. Consider James's reference to "a little awareness of my own body." Suppose there are two selves, one of whom we describe as having a 'female' body and the other a 'male' body. Both selves will experience two feet-percepts, two leg-percepts, two arm-percepts, one face-percept, etc. As life goes on, however, slow continuous differences in the body-percepts will become apparent. Included in this reflective comparison must be such facts as female menses, pregnancies, birth pains, menopausal hot flashes, etc., which are integral parts of the one self's 'awareness of my own body' but not of the other's. But, unless we choose to be male or female chauvinists, we must believe that both the 'female' and the 'male' selves can slowly learn to understand the thoughts or meanings evoked by all of this paragraph's words equally well. The 'laws' of logic, grammar, spelling, mathematics, association, discrimination, etc., 'govern' the female and male thought-processes equally. The continuous 'body' percepts are radically different from the continuous thoughts whose 'flow' can be understood and thought, but not observed directly.

Moreover, only the second continuity makes possible any thoughtful recognition of the first. For that reason, we must register a flat-out "Wrong!" in relation to what James said in parts of his *Pluralistic Universe* lectures. We must applaud his insight into the problem, "How can any of us become aware of experience, its richness, and above all its continuity?" First, we can agree entirely with the insight he had earlier when he said that born-blind people can learn to use the word 'color' in all sorts of intelligible ways but will never know what color-as-such is unless they experience it. (PP II:7) We can add examples of our own to his: no one will ever know what dizziness is who has never felt it.

Even if two people both insist that they know the difference between the taste of a banana and that of a peach, neither will ever have any way of proving that her or his two tastes are exactly like the other's two, etc. We can agree that his *Pluralistic Universe* listeners may have gotten the right 'sense' from his advice for overcoming vicious intellectualism which prizes abstractions over experience.

But we cannot agree that his pictures of the relation between thought and perceptual experience always got things right. This sixth lecture passage from *A Pluralistic Universe* most certainly got things wrong. Unbelievably wrong.

> Thought deals thus solely with surfaces. It can name the thickness of reality, but it cannot fathom it, and its insufficiency here is essential and permanent, not temporary.
>
> The only way in which to apprehend reality's thickness is either to experience it directly by being a part of reality one's self, or to evoke it in imagination by sympathetically divining some one else's inner life. But what we thus immediately experience or concretely divine is very limited in duration, whereas abstractly we are able to conceive eternities. Could we feel a million years concretely as we now feel a passing minute, we should have very little employment for our conceptual faculty. We should know the whole period fully at every moment of its passage, whereas we must now construct it laboriously by means of concepts which we project. Direct acquaintance and conceptual knowledge are thus complementary of each other; each remedies the other's defects. If what we care most about be the synoptic treatment of phenomena, the vision of the far and the gathering of the scattered like, we must follow the conceptual method. But if, as metaphysicians, we are more curious about the inner nature of reality or about what really makes it go, we must turn our backs upon our winged concepts altogether, and bury ourselves in the thickness of those passing moments over the surface of which they fly, and on particular points of which they occasionally rest and perch. (*Writings* II:745)

"Could we feel a million years concretely as we now feel a passing minute, we should have very little employment for our conceptual faculty." This sentiment shows how far off the mark his final two-part model had become. With only (sensible) experience and no thought, James would never have had a moment's suspicion that there is more than sense experience. He would never have had a moment's suspicion *that* there is experience, period! With only experience and no thought, he would never have had more than a newborn's mute or dumb enjoyment of any sense pleasure. With only the flux of sense or perceptual experience and no thought, he would never have had a play to attend, an opera to enjoy, a Santayana system to understand.

In other words, with only experience, his consciousness would never have been anything more than the 'most moving' experience his 'experienced' dog ever 'felt.'

> Take our dogs and ourselves, connected as we are by a tie more intimate than most ties in this world; and yet, outside of that tie of friendly fondness, how insensible, each of us, to all that makes life significant for the other!—we to the rapture of bone under the hedges, or smells of trees and lamp-posts, they to the delights of literature and art. As you sit reading the most moving romance you ever fell upon, what sort of a judge is your fox-terrier of your behavior? With all his good will towards you, the nature of your conduct is absolutely excluded from his comprehension. To sit there like a senseless statue, when you might be taking him to walk and throwing sticks for him to catch! What queer disease is this that comes over you every day, of holding things and staring at them like that for hours together, paralyzed of motion and vacant of all conscious life? (TT:150; *Writings* I:841-42)

Can anyone imagine James wanting to trade places with his dog?! It was not experience alone, but his magnificent ability to think profound thoughts about it that made it possible for James to think the thoughts behind those words from his "On a Certain Blindness in Human Beings" talk to students. It was not experience alone, but thought that made it possible for him, despite his disclaimer, to imagine the pleasures dogs may experience with bones under hedges or smells of trees and lamp-posts and to imagine what exclamatory sentences about walks and sticks a dog might utter, perhaps under its breath, if it had the thought needed to use such 'words.' No, even a million years lived concretely but without thought would have left his 'world' as impoverished as if they were reduced to a single minute.

And what about "sympathetically divining some one else's inner life"? True, only someone who has experienced emotion and understood thoughts can do it. But how could James have dreamed for an instant that such a thing—in effect, overcoming what he once called "the most absolute breaches in nature" (PP I:226)—could be achieved with nothing but dumb, 'animal' experience?! If, as many believe, genuine altruism requires an ability to 'place ourselves in the shoes of another,' the way James described it in "On a Certain Blindness," why is it that beasts, said to experience concretely, cannot do that and, consequently, live lives untouched by the least smidgeon of moral quality? How is it that, on the other hand, someone with no additional concrete experience might, while merely scanning the word-filled pages of *To Kill a Mockingbird, Black Like Me*, be moved by the evoked thoughts to 'sympathetically divine someone else's inner life'? Finally . . .

Finally, who would trade a million years of concrete experience with 'very little employment for her or his conceptual faculty' in exchange for a normal lifetime which offers opportunities to read and understand the thousands of pages of James's works? Jacques Barzun, who was no more than three years old when James died, learned of him as we must, through his writings, yet the pleasure he derived from those books which are closed tight to even the smartest dog that ever lived was such that he felt moved to write *A Stroll With William James* in gratitude.

The legitimacy of these protests is confirmed by a passage from James's 1883-84 unused draft:

> . . . The endowing him [an imaginary statue] with a mere repetition of *sensations* for a million years, would leave him no wiser at the end than he was at the beginning. . . . But it is hard to believe it the exclusive rule in any sort of organism, because it is impossible to see of what use consciousness would be at all when reduced to such an incoherent rope of sand. (MEN:275-76)

Enough then for this 7th decision. The problem of reconciling experience's flow with its appearance of stability is a problem that can only be understood by means of thoughts which also flow. The sought-for resolution of the problem must be sought, not in more sense experience, but in further thoughts. The needed thoughts must become habitual. They must also be the right ones. As James noted, "twenty experiences make us remember a thing better, long indulgence in error makes right thinking almost impossible." Let this last introductory thesis, viz., that "It is thought that provides our ultimate freedom, namely, our freedom to believe what we will," conclude with a fact James drew attention to in Chapter IX of *The Principles,* just as he had drawn attention to it in 1883 in "On Some Omissions of Introspection."

> Suppose three successive persons say to us: 'Wait!' 'Hark!' 'Look!' Our consciousness is thrown into three quite different attitudes of expectancy, although no definite object is before it in any one of the three cases. Leaving out different

actual bodily attitudes, and leaving out the reverberating images of the three words, which are of course diverse, probably no one will deny the existence of a residual conscious affection, a sense of the direction from which an impression is about to come, although no positive impression is yet there. Meanwhile we have no names for the psychoses in question but the names hark, look, and wait. (PP I:250-51; see also *Writings* I:998-99)

Pasteur had a name for these "psychoses" or states of mind. He would have called them by one name, "a prepared mind." Ask the average college freshman to discuss "The value of hark, look, and wait for understanding human thought." Then ask James who had a mind prepared by years of experience which no college freshman has yet acquired. It consisted of an unimaginably large volume of memories, not merely accumulated like beads on a chain, but 'organized' and 'catalogued' by criss-crossing associations as well as by theoretical generalizations whose scope ranged from few ("the sounds you've heard in the last two minutes") to many ("the number of kinds of things that exist"). If someone pointed to a sentence in a book and said "Look," James would not merely have done what a dog or illiterate child would do, turned his eyes and seen merely some printed ciphers. What we call 'reading' evokes. Whoever is unmindful of what is there to be evoked in any given person's mind will never understand the full glory of a 'passing' human thought. Whoever wants a brief overview of what's there will find it in James's *Talks to Teachers*, especially Chapter XIV on 'the apperceptive mass.'

Were the potential consequences of overlooking James's better paragraphs on the full glory of a 'passing thought' not so far-reaching, it would be unnecessary to highlight the above disagreements. Confronting the challenge James faced, namely, to find a way of conveying—evoking—vital insights about thought which cannot be 'put into words,' forces us to be more prolix than many readers, even we, would prefer. Nevertheless, there is no other way to fully open the treasure of James's vision than by means of words, words, words which are not words.

Transition. To grasp the glory of thought as it really is 'in itself,' we must catch it in its real-life context. All of us are learners, and real-life learning is both a year-to-year and a moment-to-moment process of growth. The process can be analysed from all those angles which James discriminated: as a process of discriminating, comparing, associating, conceptualizing, sensing, remembering, perceiving time and space and things and reality, etc. Those are the names of acts, but acts do not exist. They are, then, the names for 'theoretical constructs' which are useful, even indispensable, for understanding our selves and all the facets of our conscious experiencing.

In the next section, we must try to acquire a stable understanding of the process of change whereby one's acquired stable worldview changes radically to a new one. We will focus on an example of a year-to-year learning process which, as always, took place in moment-to-moment fashion, the only fashion there is. Like museum visitors who can 'take in' the full outline of a tapestry which no ant crawling over it can do, we can often 'take in' more of what 'real life' is really like if we 'step back' in imagination and think of it the way James did when he wrote the following:

> [. . .] Often we are ourselves struck at the strange differences in our successive views of the same thing. We wonder how we ever could have opined as we did last month about a certain matter. We have outgrown the possibility of that state of mind, we know not how. From one year to another we see things in new lights. What was unreal has grown real, and what was exciting is insipid. The friends we used to care the world for are shrunken to shadows; the women, once so divine, the stars, the woods, and the waters, how now so dull and common; the young girls that brought an aura of infinity, at present hardly distinguishable existences; the pictures so empty; and as for the books, what was there to find so mysteriously significant in Goethe, or in John Mill so full of weight? Instead of all this, more zestful than ever is the work, the work; and fuller and deeper the import of common duties and of common goods. (PP I:233-34)

The phenomenon James captured with this prose is what we will call "changing our mind." Everyone changes her or his mind. In tiny, insignificant ways that we might not even notice. In huge, very significant ways that we notice a lot. Is there any way we can think in a generalized fashion about all such changes? Our answer is that James's theory about partless thought evolving in continuous fashion not only offers a way to generalize about mind-changing, but also offers a way to notice how many different components must be kept in view in any effort to isolate and notice the barely noticeable but most important 'more' which is thought itself.

3. Insight Into The Many-in-One Intellectual Act of Insight

Prepared Minds Can Re-Prepare: Kuhn & Conversions. Suppose you are a student taking your first course in a new subject, 'philosophy.' You know nothing about the subject. You approach it the same way you would approach your first course in any new and never-before-studied 'subject,' e.g., physics, chemistry, biology, psychology, sociology, etc. You might pay little attention when the instructor assures the class that the text is 'solid' and the author 'reliable.' Fresh from courses in which you've never doubted that the teachers 'know their material' or that those who write text-books are as 'knowledgeable' as teachers, it would never occur to you that text-books are not solid. That is why you might have given no thought to the 'philosophy' professor's reassuring comments about the two-volume textbook you will be using for the next three years during which your 'major' subject will be this totally new, difficult subject called 'philosophy.'

Only later, when—like Thomas Kuhn—you had learned a lot more of the West's intellectual history, would you begin to realize what was 'behind' your instructor's words that first day of class. What Kuhn said in the preface to his revolutionizing work, *The Structure of Scientific Revolutions*, one that hit the non-public 'public' at just the right time, relates perfectly to the difference that more learning can make vis-à-vis the words we hear. The difference can be revolutionary. It may be similar to the difference that occurs when jurors with minds shaped by testimony carefully selected to prove the accused guilty, are exposed to testimony selected with equal care to prove the accused, if not innocent, is at least not certainly guilty either.

The essay that follows is the first full published report on a project originally conceived almost fifteen years ago. At that time I was a graduate student in theoretical physics already within sight of the end of my dissertation. A fortunate involvement with an experimental college course treating physical science for the non-scientist provided my first exposure to the history of science. To my complete surprise, that exposure to out-of-date scientific theory and practice radically undermined some of my basic conceptions about the nature of science and the reasons for its special success. (T. Kuhn, *The Structure of Scientific Revolutions*, 2nd ed., p.v)

Given that there are no group minds or even any groups of any kind, the only real revolutions that take place are few and far between. All intellectual revolutions are individual persons' revolutions. There are two types of learners, older ones who have gotten set in their habits of thinking in terms of one model or paradigm and those whose thought-habits are still malleable. Kuhn's word "revolution" was shorthand for what happens when more and more younger thinkers drift into a new way of thinking which relies on a new model, till they eventually make up the bulk of the older thinkers who have gotten set in the habit of thinking in terms of the by-now-old 'new' model or paradigm. The reason that genuine revolutions are few and far between is because very few of the old timers switch habits. They don't revolt. And the young never were fixed in the old habits, so they are not really revolting either. Only a few—Kuhn?—undergo major theoretical conversions. That is why some wag said that the old paradigms perish one funeral at a time.

That entire description is, of course, an exercise in generalization about thinkers, and no one sees farther into a generalization than his knowledge of details extends. But the position here is that there are no groups, only individual thinkers who have each personally learned everything they know by personal sensing, personal remembering, and personal thinking. Kuhn himself tended to think in group terms. Dewey, who thought in terms of a fiction named 'individualism' more than in terms of individuals, may—by many individuals—be lumped with James in their mental pigeonhole labeled 'pragmatists,' but the direction of this exposition is away from Kuhn and Dewey, and in the direction of James, the pluralist.

The kind of 'revolution' Kuhn described in his preface was the intensely individual type that a Jamesian pluralist would take note of. It was part of Kuhn's life-long learning career. Like everyone, he began by acquiring a common-sense philosophy. That served as his jumping-off point for acquiring the stable knowledge of facts, formulas, and theories which were to qualify him for a terminal degree in physics. Then he learned new facts which did not fit into the general 'model' he had constructed in his mind and labeled with the name 'science.' His preface goes on to mention several other 'theory modules' which he learned later, somewhat in isolation from each other, but which—by the time he wrote the preface—had fused in his mind into a far larger 'vision' of which they had become subsidiary 'parts.' Besides works by historians such as A. Koyré, E. Meyerson, H. Metzger, and A. Maier, Kuhn mentions J. Piaget's studies of "the various worlds of the growing child" as well as "the process of transition from one to the next," the gestalt psychologists' studies of perceptual switches, B. Whorf's ideas about language shaping people's worldviews, W. Quine's work on the "analytic-synthetic distinction," and so on. An individual's learning career, though described in summary fashion, is lived on a day to day, hour to hour, etc., schedule, that is, the way James described his father's life: "how long all these things were in the living, but how short their memory now is?"

A Jamesian Conversion: Introduction. James wrote a great deal about the competing visions of rival thinkers. In some sense, his psychology may be said to have dealt with the shaping of those rival views, for he did write a great deal about the shaping of habits, the importance of habits, and the tenacity of habits. But, at first sight, it seems he gave little attention to the ways in which people change their thought habits radically enough to constitute a 'revolution.' *Pragmatism* seems on the surface to be about a method for allowing rival thinkers to co-exist with mutual understanding rather than an invitation to convert to a set of new beliefs.

But there is one work in which he paid more than a little attention to radical shifts in people's mindsets. That work is *The Varieties of Religious Experience*, and three of its lectures specifically address the issue. Lecture VIII is entitled "The Divided Self, and the Process of Its Unification," and the two following lectures are both entitled "Conversion." When people hear the word "conversion," they normally think that it has to do with religion. But the idea fits any major type of turn-about, whether in life-style or in beliefs. Hence, what Kuhn experienced personally and what some of James's subjects experienced can be viewed as two species of a single genus. 'Scientific revolutions' and 'religious conversions' both fit under 'changes of base,' 'mind changings,' 'gestalt shifts,' 'alterations of viewpoints,' etc.

It may help to understand more clearly what is being referred to in these pages as 'the full glory of a passing thought' if a conversion regarding, not the 'philosophy of science,' but the 'philosophy of thought' is described. Imagine a years-long process of acquiring a common-sense philosophy, of using it as a door into the vast 'world' of scholastic philosophical theory, including a theory of intellectual knowledge, and then a sudden conversion from that to a view quite similar to the one James presented in parts of *The Principles'* ninth chapter.

Concepts as Thoughts' Parts: The 'Intellectualist' Tradition. Suppose that the very first subject in your two-volume philosophy text was logic. The reason for starting with logic was the traditional belief that logic is a tool which teaches us how to think scientifically. Suppose that the very first topic you learned about in logic was the theory of concepts: their nature, their acquisition, and their use. "Concept" is the name for ideas of things. Coming to the study of 'philosophy' with a ready-made worldview, you simply assumed, without question, all the common-sense beliefs you had 'acquiesced' in from as far back as you could remember. You already believed in people, horses, numbers, amounts, parents, children, aunts, nieces, colors, and so on. Therefore, when you learned about the various categories of concepts which Aristotle presented in his short work entitled "Categories," which forms Part One of his *Organon* (Greek for 'The Tool')—such categories as substances (people and horses), quantity (numbers, amounts, etc.), relation (parent-child, aunt-niece, etc.), quality (color, etc.), and so on—the new 'logic' concepts were only more generic concepts to help organize your old concepts of things whose existence no one, least of all a student new to 'philosophy,' would ever dream of questioning.

From the outset, you would be led ever so gradually to learn the basic assumptions that James protested so strenuously against and to then get in the habit of building all of your subsequent 'philosophical' theorizing on the foundation of those assumptions. It is worth noting—in relation to James's thesis that a thought is the meaning of 'all the words' in a complete sentence—that Aristotle's logic begins with the model James rebelled against, namely, separate words, especially words used to name 'substantive' things. Aristotle's opening paragraph is about word-names whose meanings are equivocal or more-than-one.

Things are said to be named 'equivocally' when, though they have a common name, the definition corresponding with the name differs for each. Thus, a real man and a figure in a picture can both lay claim to the name 'animal'; yet these are equivocally so named, for, though they have a common name, the definition corresponding with the name differs for each. For should any one define in what sense each is an animal, his definition in the one case will be appropriate to that case only. (Aristotle, "Categories"; trans. E. M. Edghill, in *Basic Works of Aristotle*, ed., R. McKeon; paragraph 1.)

Reflection on the preceding paragraphs will show that we can think about our thinking, and we can think about that thinking about thinking. If we assume that thinking builds on concepts, it is natural to think of common sense as acquiring concepts of the real world and to think of 'philosophy' or 'psychology' as acquiring concepts of the process whereby we acquire concepts and use them to think scientifically. At various times, James relied on this picture, as when he explained common sense in terms of a list of 'magisterial concepts' or when he explained how the mind operates, in chapters with such noun-titles as discrimination, comparison, association, conceptualization, and so on.

This retrospective theory sounds fine. We do all of our earliest learning with no idea of what we are doing. Specifically, learners acquire concepts of people, horses, large servings of spinach, small servings of dessert, and so on, and we learn with no awareness of the learning going on, without needing instruction in how to learn, without ever having heard the word "learn." In fact, we do many things without knowing what we are doing and without any instruction. We start breathing the moment we are born and do it later when we are asleep, we digest while we are asleep, we build muscle while we are asleep, and we grow while we are asleep. We do all those things without being aware of doing them. We see, hear, and feel, we remember images of what we see, hear, and feel, we form concepts of what we see, hear, and feel, and we do all those things before we have any concepts for "see," for "hear," for "feel," for "remember," or for "have concepts." The only difference is that we do these things while we are awake and conscious. Later, we 'begin philosophy' and learn new concepts—'substance' (for people, horses, spinach, etc.), 'vegetative life,' 'sense activities,' and so on—which allow us to build a higher level of concepts to put order into our lower-level concepts. We learned these higher-level concepts without ever hearing 'higher level,' without any instructions in how to form 'higher-level concepts,' etc. Now, years later, having studied rival theories, including the theories of James, we can use still higher-level concepts to describe how we use less higher-level concepts to put order into our lower-level concepts which we are said to have acquired between our birth-date and our fifth birth-anniversary.

> **This third section is an attack on the truth of the entire 'concept' story, from beginning to end. There are no concepts. There never were.**

Suppose, though, that when the theory that we form concepts of the things which make up reality and that we store those concepts in our mind was proposed, we simply accepted it. In James's terms, we 'acquiesced' in it. It seemed to make perfectly good sense. When it was later explained that concepts in our soul's mind are distinct from images which pertain more to the senses and therefore the body, that too seemed obvious enough to accept without question. Animals have images of sticks, bones, and bushes which they have sensed, but animals have no abstract concepts and therefore cannot reason. Hence they have no need of language to express thoughts composed of abstract concepts.

Abstract concepts. Suppose that, among the theories we learned later is the one called 'abstraction.' Abstraction is the name of the process whereby we form the concepts in our mind. Abstraction presupposes much sense experience and a considerable build-up of memories of what we have sensed. The memories consist of images of things sensed. For instance, we become acquainted with numerous people, ranging from parents to strangers on streets and in supermarkets. From this build-up of memory-images of people, we extract what they have in common, namely, rational animality, and leave behind such things as their different ages, heights, sex, etc. Because such abstracted concepts 'fit' all human beings, they are referred to as "universals." James discussed abstraction and universals in Chapter XII of *The Principles*, "Conception."

Universal concepts are the heart and soul of Aristotle's treatment of 'syllogisms' which is the heart and soul of Aristotle's logic. 'Syllogism' stands for 'a simple piece of thinking' which uses two propositions called 'premises' to reason that a third proposition called 'a conclusion' is true. For instance, we can use the premises (a) *that* all-things-made-from-matter-are-mortal and (b) *that* all-animals-are-made-from-matter as reasons for concluding (c) *that* all-animals-are-mortal is true. The propositions are constructed with three universal concepts, viz., 'things made from matter,' 'mortal things,' and 'animals,' and as James noted in Chapter XXII of *The Principles*, it is possible to create a picture of the so-called 'form' of our bit of reasoning, i.e., our syllogism.

> If we glance at the ordinary syllogism—
> M is P;
> S is M;
> S is P
> —we see that the second or minor premise, the 'subsumption' as it is sometimes called, is the one requiring the sagacity . . . (PP II:331-32)

The later parts of Aristotle's logic text, *The Organon*, deal with the various forms and rules for reasoning correctly. But the notion of universal concepts is at the core of the entire project. Chapter XIX of Book II of "Posterior Analytics" is devoted to an account of the process whereby, from our experience, we acquire universal concepts.

> Let us now restate the account given already, though with insufficient clearness. When one of a number of logically indiscriminable particulars has made a stand, the earliest universal is present in the soul: for though the act of sense-perception is of the particular, its content is universal—is man, for example, not the man Callias. A fresh stand is made among these rudimentary universals, and the process does not cease until the indivisible concepts, the true universals, are established: e.g., such and such a species of animal is a step towards the genus animal, which by the same process is a step toward a further generalization. (Aristotle, "Posterior Analytics," trans., G. R. G. Mure; Bk.II, ch.19)

The sharp line which Aristotle, following Plato, drew between the individual or particular things we know with our senses and the universal or abstract concepts we form with our intellect, eventually led to a problem. If the concepts which we 'put together' to form complete thoughts or judgments symbolized by complete sentences are universal, and if universal concepts apply equally to all of the individuals from which they have been extracted, which is to say that they do not apply to this or that individual rather than another, then how is it that we actually spend most of our lives thinking and reasoning about this or that single individual? In fact, a frequently used syllogism found in many logic texts goes as follows: "All men are mortal; Socrates is a man; therefore Socrates is mortal." How can our intellect know anything about Socrates since it has never had any contact with him? Or with Mom or Dad or Sis, etc.? Unlike the later monists whom the pluralist James battled against, the medieval schoolmen did not deny the genuine reality of the individual beings amidst whom we must spend our everyday, common-sense-ruled lives. Nor did they deny our ability to know them. Faced with what they took to be facts, they sought an explanation.

To solve this problem, the scholastics looked to 'imagination' where images are stored. They pictured the imagination as the 'common meeting ground' between the intellect which knows only universal essences and the senses which know singular existents. This move seemed logical, since it is from accumulated images that the intellect originally acquires its concepts. St. Thomas's *Summa Theologiae* presents the problem and its solution. (James, in Chapter I of *Some Problems of Philosophy* [see *Writings* II:989], praised Aquinas's works, saying that they produce on the reader an impression of "almost superhuman intellectual resources.") Having absorbed the theories about logic, reasoning, the abstraction of universal concepts, and so on, you understood why St. Thomas would declare that "Our intellect cannot *directly and primarily* know what is singular in material things" (*Summa Th.*, I, qu.86, art.I, c; emphasis added). You would also be able to understand in a vague way why he answered "No" to the question, "Does the intellect actually understand just by means of intelligible species it has within itself, without turning to phantasms?" ("Phantasms" stands for what "images" stands for in this text.) In other words, can the intellect, when it is in operation and actually functioning, understand just by means of the concepts it has acquired and retained within itself, or can it make use of its concepts only if there is a sensory-image accompanying its act of understanding?

Aristotle, regarded by Aquinas as "The Philosopher!", had written that "To the thinking soul images serve as if they are contents of perception . . . That is why the soul never thinks without an image"

(Aristotle, *On the Soul*, 431a 14-5). Hence, when Aquinas went into the question in some detail in his *Summa*, he concluded that "In its present state of life, in which it is joined to an impress(ion)able body (*passibili corpori*), the intellect cannot do any actual thinking without turning to phantasms" (*Summa Th.*, I, qu.84, art.7 c). If the intellect later returns to the phantasms or images from which it originally derived its concepts, it will discover there the images of Mom, Dad, Sis, etc., and uncle Socrates. Hence, it is through the particular images, or images of particulars, that the intellect is able to know about particular beings altogether outside the psyche. This will happen when the intellect turns from being occupied solely with the purely immaterial conceptualized essences and glances downward to the imagery stored 'below' in the less-immaterial imagination which gets its material from bodily senses which have direct contact with material bodies.

Without the least suspicion that it was happening, though, your study of universals would be taking you at least part way in the direction of James's thesis that a thought is the meaning of all the words in the complete sentence. If asked to prove that universal concepts exist, your immersion in scholastic thought would train you to appeal to *meaning*. How do we know, for instance, that 'man' signifies a universal concept that applies to every man, woman, and child? The answer goes back to language and the words used in propositions. If I study what I mean when I say that "Socrates is a man" and that "Plato is a man," I know that the word "man" which is used in each sentence *means exactly the same thing or stands for the same concept*. This focus on the meaning of general terms goes back to Socrates who first noticed the importance of requiring definitions, and the idea of definition is central to the first two paragraphs of Aristotle's "Categories." James, though his approach to meaning was—typically and fortunately—that of a pluralist who emphasized different shades of meaning in each individual sentence we utter, also stressed the sameness—even the eternal sameness!—of some meanings. Here is a passage from his Chapter XII, "Conception." It refers to meanings, same meanings, different meanings, and, most importantly, thought.

The sense of our meaning is an entirely peculiar element of the thought. It is one of those evanescent and 'transitive' facts of mind which introspection cannot turn round upon, and isolate and hold up for examination, as an entomologist passes round an insect on a pin. In the (somewhat clumsy) terminology I have used, it pertains to the 'fringe' of the subjective state, and is a 'feeling of tendency,' whose neural counterpart is undoubtedly a lot of dawning and dying processes too faint and complex to be traced. The geometer, with his one definite figure before him, knows perfectly that his thoughts apply to countless other figures as well, and that although he *sees* lines of a certain special bigness, direction, color, etc., he *means* not one of these details. When I use the word *man* in two different sentences, I may have both times exactly the same sound upon my lips and the same picture in my mental eye, but I may mean, and at the very moment of uttering the word and imagining the picture know that I mean, two entirely different things. Thus when I say: "What a wonderful man Jones is!" I am perfectly aware that I mean by man to exclude Napoleon Bonaparte or Smith. But when I say: "What a wonderful thing Man is!" I am equally well aware that I mean to *in*clude not only Jones, but Napoleon and Smith as well. This added consciousness is an absolutely positive sort of feeling, transforming what would otherwise be mere noise or vision into something *understood*; and determining the sequel of my thinking, the later words and images, in a perfectly definite way. (PP I:472)

Enlarging the Role of Imagery. Such was the scholastics' focus on concepts and reasoning that their view of imagery was paltry, even piddling, by comparison. Suppose, therefore, that some time after you finished logic you read a book in which Jacques Maritain, a modern follower of St. Thomas, used the role of images to create a bridge between logical science and creative poetry. The spur for his work, entitled *Creative Intuition in Art and Poetry*, was undoubtedly the fact that his wife was a poetess whose art involved intelligence but also dealt extensively with sensible particulars. Maritain saw that art and poetry had to somehow be explained by the same 'theory of the soul' or 'psyche-logos' which he had already used in his book, *The Degrees of Knowledge*, to explain scientific reasoning. Maritain had a poetic inspiration of his own and created a model that would explain both 'non-rational' art and 'rational' reasoning. The following passage comes from *Creative Intuition in Art and Poetry* which grew out of the 1952 Mellon Lectures in the Fine Arts which Maritain delivered at Washington's National Gallery of Art. Once, after apologizing for a "rather chill irruption of Scholastic lecturing," he went on with more of it:

[. . .] There are two things in this structure of our intellectual activity which play an essential role: the Illuminating Intellect and the intelligible germ or impressed pattern. And philosophical reflection is able to establish, through the logical necessities of reasoning, the fact of their existence, but they totally escape experience and consciousness.

On the one hand, our intellect is fecundated by intelligible germs on which all the formation of ideas depends. And it draws from them, and produces within itself, through the most vital process, its own living fruits, its concepts and ideas. But it knows nothing either of these germs it receives within or of the very process through which it produces its concepts. Only the concepts are known. And even as regards the concepts, they cause the object seen in them to be known, but they themselves are not directly known; they are not known through their essence, they are known only through a reflective return of the intellect upon its own operations; and this kind of reflective grasping can possibly not occur. There can exist unconscious acts of thought and unconscious ideas.

On the other hand, and this is the fundamental point for me, we possess in ourselves the Illuminating Intellect, a spiritual sun ceaselessly radiating, which activates everything in intelligence, and whose light causes all our ideas to arise in us, and whose energy permeates every operation of our mind. And this primal source of light cannot be seen by us; it remains concealed in the unconscious of the spirit.

Furthermore, it illuminates with its spiritual light the images from which our concepts are drawn. And this very process of illumination is unknown to us, it takes place in the unconscious; and often these very images, without which there is no thought, remain also unconscious or scarcely perceived in the process, at least for the most part.

Thus it is that we know (not always, to be sure!) what we are thinking, but we don't know how we are thinking; and that before being formed and expressed in concepts and judgments, intellectual knowledge is at first a beginning of insight, still unformulated, a kind of many-eyed cloud which is born from the impact of the light of the Illuminating Intellect on the world of images and which is but a humble and trembling incoation, yet invaluable, tending toward an intelligible content to be grasped. (J. Maritain, *Creative Intuition in Art and Poetry*, Ch. Three, sec.9)

Suppose that Maritain's image of "a kind of many-eyed cloud which is born from the impact of the light of the Illuminating Intellect on the world of images" strikes deep into your psyche, already primed to approach human experience with the sharpest possible distinction between three radically distinct types of entities, viz., the physical bodies whose colors, sounds, shapes, sizes, etc., we sense, the singular phantasms or images which in the imagination are combined so as to reflect the way the sensed features are joined outside in physical bodies, and finally the universal concepts in the soul-owned spiritual or immaterial intellect. Of course, besides helping to see the connection between the 'creative' thinking which artists do and the 'logical' thinking that philosophers, theologians, and scientists do, Maritain's image of an inner 'many-eyed world of images' would also open a back door to let in, later on, the empiricists' explorations of images and the laws of association which knit images together in thousands of criss-crossing patterns. At the time, however, you would have no idea that you were acquiring a 'separate lesson' or 'theory module' that was a large step on a journey to an entirely different view, one that would replace the approach to knowledge as science-based-on-universal-logic with an approach to real-life thinking influenced as much by chance associations created by unique, individual experiences as by universal logic.

Noticing Inner Speech and Silent Thought. Socrates, Plato, and Aristotle in olden days, as well as behaviorists, logical positivists, and linguistic analysts in recent times, all focused on speech that is audible or writing that is visible. The ancients thought of sensed words as signs for unsensed thought. Most of the recent thinkers discussed earlier viewed words as visible signs for other visible things, mostly for visible behavior. When neither the words nor the behavior appears to be visible, many recent thinkers try to save their theory by means of such 'dei ex machina' or deus-ex-machinas as covert speech-behavior, e.g., vocal-muscle twitches, or even more esoteric entities which they name "dispositions to behave." These last two inventions pay tribute to the fact that ancient thinkers noticed, namely, that even when someone else is talking, listeners can think silently. In a way that perhaps parallels Ryle's pronouncement that children learn to prattle aloud before they learn to 'prattle silently to themselves,' the Greeks took the word "logos" which stood for audible speech and used it to refer to thought as the soul's inner discourse. They pictured thinking as the soul talking to itself.

Suppose that, when you began studying logic and concepts, you simply never asked yourself whether thought is possible without words. True, you never doubted that people who lie can think two things silently and say only one out loud. True, you knew from a young age that your mind could 'wander' by thinking about distant things while you were saying the words of your prayers out loud. Had you thought about it, you might have admitted immediately that the same thing happened when you were singing, e.g., while 'joining in' with the national anthem before the basketball game begins. But such pieces of knowledge were tucked away in different parts of your mind and, much as you thought about words and thought, you never asked yourself whether silent thoughts could occur without words.

Suppose that one day, by accident, you noticed something that started you toward believing that all thinking involves words. You noticed that, when your mind is otherwise still (for example, just before you fall off to sleep at night), calling a single 'word' up from memory seems to bring with it many other 'words' and 'ideas.' If you mentally pronounce the word "man," it is as if your mind instantly prepares to think all sorts of thoughts associated with that word. This fits with the scholastic theory of universals. It means that you can use the concept in any proposition that has the word 'man' in it. "A man is a rational animal," "A man is a mortal being," "A man may be born almost without hair, grow to have thick dark hair by twenty, but be nearly bald by fifty," "A man is usually bigger and stronger than a woman," and so on. But, just as it is possible to focus on general propositions, it is also possible to turn attention to the "many-eyed cloud" of images which are the present residue of your long years of life-experience. You can begin to think of this or that particular person—family member, friend, etc.— of whom you have dozens upon dozens of 'memory videos.'

If later on you were to study philosophy at the graduate level, you would begin learning various theories about thought, such as Plato's theory of essences, Descartes' theory of innate ideas, Kant's idea of a mind pre-equipped to 'put order' into sense phenomena by means of certain types of judgments, and especially Husserl's ideas about essences, eidetic intuition, and meaning. You might find yourself returning to your earlier theories about the intellect which abstracts universal concepts from sense experience and which then needs to 'return' to images in order to think again about those specific individual beings. At the same time, as you studied recent theories concerning the relations between language, meaning, and thought, you might also turn your attention to those inner 'words' and what happens when you pronounce just one.

James wrote often about the relation of thought to words. He frequently used the experience of reading as a point of contact between himself the author of the words and the reader who would later scan those words to learn about James's thought. He noted that, even when there is little else that is 'observable' in the mind, as when the thoughts are vague but definitely distinct from other vague thoughts, there still are words accompanying the thought. In the 1884 essay, "On the Function of Cognition," for instance, he wrote:

> In the whole field of symbolic thought [as opposed to percepts] we are universally held both to intend, to speak of, and to reach conclusions about—to know in short—particular realities, without having in our subjective consciousness any mind-stuff that resembles them in even a remote degree. We are instructed about them by language which awakens no consciousness beyond its sound. . . . As minds may differ here, let me speak in the first person. I am sure that my own current thinking has *words* for its almost exclusive subjective material, words which are made intelligible by being referred to some reality that lies beyond the horizon of direct consciousness . . . (*Writings* II:847)

The only words anyone can detect while she or he is alone, thinking silently or musing, are those which we are calling inner speech. Though James did not always place as much emphasis on inner speech as he did there, he did discuss it with remarkable insight in Chapter XVIII, "Imagination." In a passage which anticipates John Watson's and Gilbert Ryle's notions about covert speech as felt vocal-cord muscle-twitching, James made the following observations.

> Most persons, on being asked *in what sort of terms they imagine words*, will say 'in terms of hearing.' It is not until their attention is expressly drawn to the point that they find it difficult to say whether auditory images or motor images connected with the organs of articulation predominate. A good way of bringing the difficulty to consciousness is that proposed by Stricker: Partly open your mouth and then imagine any word with labials or dentals in it, such as 'bubble,' 'toddle.' Is your image under these conditions distinct? To most people the image is at first 'thick,' as the sound of the word would be if they tried to pronounce it with the lips parted. Many can never imagine clearly with the mouth open; others succeed after a few preliminary trials. The experiment proves how dependent our verbal imagination is on actual feeling in lips, tongue, throat, larynx, etc. . . .
>
> The open mouth in Stricker's experiment not only prevents actual articulation of the labials, but our feeling of its openness keeps us from imagining their articulation, just as a sensation of glaring light will keep us from strongly imagining darkness. In persons whose auditory imagination is weak, the articulatory image seems to constitute the whole material for verbal thought. Professor Stricker says that in his own case no auditory image enters into the words of which he thinks. Like most psychologists, however, he makes of his own personal peculiarities a rule, and says that verbal thinking is normally and universally an exclusively motor representation. *I* certain get auditory images, both of vowels and of consonants, in addition to the

articulatory images or feelings on which this author lays such stress. And I find that numbers of my students, after repeating his experiments, come to this conclusion. There is *at first* a difficulty due to the open mouth. That, however, soon vanishes, as does also the difficulty of thinking of one vowel whilst continuously sounding another. What probably remains true, however, is that most men have a less auditory and a more articulatory verbal imagination than they are apt to be aware of. (PP II:64-65)

Readers whose native language is English are at an advantage in trying to notice and begin attending closely to inner speech. That is because of the lack of consistency in the correlation of written to spoken 'language,' i.e., of seen ciphers to heard sounds. What reader has never read about red things? For instance, is "read" pronounced like reed or red? How many readers, familiar with wreak, wreathe, and write, would object if told that there is a word spelled "wrede"? Why not write wreding and writing? Twice in *The Principles*, James used "pas de lieu Rhône qu' nous" as an unfamiliar way to 'write' the sounds representable by a perfectly 'intelligible' English sentence. Most of us are baffled at first when told that ghoti is simply an unfamiliar 'spelling' for the name of what Catholics used to eat on Friday before it became so expensive. So, though it may be thought tough ghor ghoreigners to learn how to pronounce English riting, still, threw enuf practice it becomes so much a second-nature habit that we have to work hard to notice the complexity of what goes on while we wreed. Though hard at first, noticing inner speech can increase to the point where, in Egger's terms, it seems to make "ten or twenty times more noise in our consciousness" than the words' meaning.

Noticing inner speech is simply part of noticing images generally, a matter discussed in the previous chapter. Inner speech is a species of imagery. That is why no one can hope to fathom the full reality of what constitutes her or his 'stream of experience' or 'field of consciousness' who does not begin to notice the many-eyed world of imagery which is an enormously thick 'layer' between the sense-data and evoked thoughts, and whose parts seem to 'respond' instantly to sense-data triggers.

The noticing can be done, however. James's voluminous writings testify to that, for he did it. His concrete appreciation for the richness of the stream of consciousness, a richness all of us grow up oblivious to and most of us die still oblivious to, shines through in a passage from Chapter IX of his *Talks to Teachers*, the abridged version of his abridgment of his *Principles*. Here is what he wrote to support the bold claim that we can "start from any idea whatever," and discover that "the entire range" of our ideas are at any given moment "potentially" at our disposal. What he wrote is especially apt in relation to the earlier discussion about 'inwardly pronouncing just one word' and noticing what the remembered sound calls up from the depths of memory to the surface of awareness:

[. . .] If we take as the associative starting-point, or cue, some simple word which I pronounce before you, there is no limit to the possible diversity of suggestions which it may set up in your minds. Suppose I say 'blue,' for example: some of you may think of the blue sky and hot weather from which we now are suffering, then go off on thoughts of summer clothing, or possibly of meteorology at large; others may think of the spectrum and the physiology of color-vision, and glide into X-rays and recent physical speculations; others may think of blue ribbons, or of the blue flowers on a friend's hat, and proceed on lines of personal reminiscence. To others again, etymology and linguistic thoughts may be suggested; or blue may be 'apperceived' as a synonym for melancholy, and a train of associates connected with morbid psychology may proceed to unroll themselves. (TT:69; *Writings* I:762)

For James, obviously, the single word "blue" conjured all those thoughts! Can there be thoughts and theories without words, then? Some of the things called up by the single word "blue" will be in the form of images. But many of the things James mentioned are 'scientific' or 'philosophical' subjects, often things entirely invisible and intangible. Can we know them without words? We can begin with theories about light waves, the spectrum, lenses, retinas, nerve impulses, and others in which theoretical models are required, and ask whether those theories would be possible without language. How much 'symbolic' thought, e.g., arithmetic, algebra, geometry, trigonometry, etc., would be possible without what James called 'symbols.' How far would Ptolemy, Copernicus, Galileo, or Newton have gotten without mathematics? Ballard, the deaf person James wrote about and whose testimony about his pre-linguistic thinking James discussed, may have had thoughts about the origin of the world. If he tried to be specific about whatever wondering he did—and did without the 'gestural' symbols he confessed to using—would he have been able to get beyond, say, images of fertility goddesses giving birth, etc.? Would he ever have reached the lofty views which some of the Hebrew prophets reached, those thinkers who opposed images as incapable of 'capturing' the concept of a formless deity? We may be able to do some thinking without words, but just how much of what we now think could we think without them?

Except, words do not exist, though linguists, grammarians, logicians, semanticists, and other experts have filled shelf upon shelf with collections of pages filled with ciphers (all of this is expressed while reverting to common sense as the mindset-context) which evoke thoughts ranging from the tiniest of details to the broadest of generalizations. Access to what is allegedly but mistakenly thought to be 'contained' in those pages is available in only one way for those devoid of telepathic power, namely, by reading. And so, we come to the core of this reinterpretation of James, the claim that the best way to understand thought is to understand what goes on as we 'read.'

A Sudden Conversion. Suppose finally that one day you were 'introspecting' as James tells us he often did. Suppose you were concentrating on what happens while you are reading. You imagine that you are reading a passage which is a description of one, single, 'same' thing. Writers who imagine that they are 'phenomenologically describing' something seem to believe they are holding an item 'before their mind' and simply writing down what they mentally 'see.' You read samples of their phenomenological descriptions. To imitate them, you try to mentally inspect just a single object. Suppose the object, topic, or subject you choose is reading. James once gave a minimalist account of this familiar but enormously complex activity. It is found in an early essay, "The Function of Cognition." Reading it will pave the way to understanding a true 'conversion experience.'

Let an illustration make this plainer. I open the first book I take up, and read the first sentence that meets my eye: 'Newton saw the handiwork of God in the heavens as plainly as Paley in the animal kingdom.' I immediately look back and try to analyze the subjective state in which I rapidly apprehended this sentence as I read it. In the first place there was an obvious feeling that the sentence was intelligible and rational and related to the world of realities. There was also a sense of agreement or harmony between 'Newton,' 'Paley,' and 'God.' There was no apparent image connected with the words 'heavens,' or 'handiwork,' or 'God'; they were words merely. With 'animal kingdom' I think there was the faintest consciousness (it may possibly have been an image of the steps) of the Museum of Zoölogy in the town of Cambridge where I write. With 'Paley' there was an equally faint consciousness of a small dark leather book; and with 'Newton' a pretty distinct vision of the right-hand lower corner of a curling periwig. This is all the mind-stuff I can discover in my first consciousness of the meaning of this sentence . . . (*Writings* II:848)

One day, as you like James are trying to notice what 'reading' is, it suddenly dawns on you that you are not thinking and writing about just one thing, namely, reading. You are thinking an entire 'train' of thought, i.e., thinking with sentence after sentence rather than just one word. The sentences name dozens of things. You realize that when you read, you are not simply scanning a page with a single word written over and over. It is not a page covered with 'reading,' 'reading,' 'reading,' 'reading,' and more 'reading's.

Suppose further that, as you noticed that fact, a suggestion suddenly flashed across your mind: "To know what 'thought' is, just pay attention to the meaning." Slowly, like an iceberg looming out of a thick fog, a new idea—plus a picture—took shape in your mind, and, as you tried it out this way and that, it became clearer and clearer till you were convinced. What idea? That you should stop thinking about concepts, about concepts put together into concept-pairs called 'propositions,' about 'concept-pairs' being referred back to the many-eyed cloud of images, about abstract essences vs singular existents, about judgments linked to judgments to form syllogisms, about science vs philosophy vs theology vs everyday knowledge, etc. That you should stop thinking that way and begin to concentrate on meaning in relation to words and imagery, that is, on meaning as 'more' than what you are already aware of. How much meaning is involved? *The meaning of all the words* as they pass through your mind and dredge up imagery from memory the way a fishing net brings fish up from the ocean depths. Thinking while you read, you become convinced, is understanding a flow of meaning evoked by the non-word 'words' your eyes scan. Thinking while you write is having a world-ful of meaning evoking non-word 'words' that will 'capture' your meaning. Either way, though, thinking is understanding the meaning of the words. Of all of them.

Confronted with this new conviction, you would immediately begin to reconstruct your entire scholastic 'conceptual framework.' It might be years before you 'iron out' all of the wrinkles remaining in your official or professional 'philosophy.' It might be only during that long reconstructive period that you began to understand the real depth in James's thought. It might also be that your initial insight into partless meaning posed the greatest obstacle in the reconstruction process, and that it was not until you learned more about theoretical fictions—useful pretending—and then saw a way to combine that with James's practice of breaking up the endless flow of words into discrete sentences, that you were able to 'get a handle' on your insight. True, what we understand as we read is the partless meaning of all the discrete words which make up the phrase in the phrase-containing clause in the clause-containing sentence. The fuller context is the sentence-containing paragraph, the paragraph-containing section, the section-containing chapter, the chapter-containing book, the book-containing *Works*. We also must think of the one-sentence, passing thought *as if* it has all the 'parts' James mentioned in the mental picture he drew in his seventh *Pluralistic Universe* lecture, including the center which is the currently-being-verbalized 'part.' ("Self" here = "Thought.")

[. . .] In the pulse of inner life immediately present now in each of us is a little past, a little future, a little awareness of our own body, of each other's persons, of these sublimities we are trying to talk about, of the earth's geography and the direction of history, of truth and error, of good and bad, and of who knows how much more? . . .

[. . .] My present field of consciousness is a centre surrounded by a fringe that shades insensibly into a subconscious more. I use three separate terms here to describe this fact; but I might as well use three hundred, for the fact is all shades and no boundaries. . . . What we conceptually identify ourselves with and say we are thinking of at any time is the centre; but our *full* self is the whole field, with all those indefinitely radiating subconscious possibilities of increase that we can only feel without conceiving, and can hardly begin to analyze. (*Writings* II:760-61

This model helps us learn not to think that what we 'have in mind' is a tiny bit of meaning related to a few uttered sounds. But it also fits the fact that we are able to respond to what we understand, and our response begins with the 'part' related to those few uttered sounds or written ciphers. We can wilfully believe this 'part' of the total thought-meaning, wilfully reject that 'part,' wilfully choose to postpone a decision on those two contradictory 'parts' of the flow of meaning, dive in to analyse further what this or that 'word' or 'phrase' brings to mind.

By pretending to break up the one total, really partless flow of meaning into 'parts,' and by pretending that each most-important present 'part' of the total flow is the 'part' which correlates with what we pretend is a single very discrete-part-ful 'sentence,' we are able to create just the right model.

The 'just right' model is simple but complex. This planet is populated by 6.7 billion agent-self-humans. As soon as any of us has experienced enough *sense-data*, a flow of memory-images will begin to accompany the flow of sense-data. As soon as enough *image-memories* are acquired and catalogued by criss-crossing associations with 'words,' thoughts will begin to come to us as well. The *thoughts* should be thought of as one proposal after another of something to be passively acquiesced in, wilfully believed, wilfully rejected, filed away for future consideration, etc. As here...

Years might pass while a full system-reconstruction takes place. It would, however, be simply one part of your life. You would continue to experience what seems like a world of stars above, earth below, mountains and oceans and cities all around, a world which you lose consciousness of when you close your eyes in sleep each night and which is still there when you wake again in the morning. During the day, you would apparently 'go about business as usual,' using your common-sense mindset. You would continue walking through piles of dry leaves in autumn and deep snow in winter, enjoying Thanksgiving and Christmas dinners, moving heavy furniture when you change 'where you live,' etc. Were the conversion-scenario described here factual, you could do what Kuhn did. In his preface, he described the process whereby he became 're-prepared' enough to write *The Structure of Scientific Revolutions*. You, too, could later give a brief description of your conversion and the subsequent restructuring process. As you looked back, you would think, "So long the living, so short the telling." Those are words James used in a letter to his wife after his father died in 1882. They help think about learning and mind-forming and mind-changing and phenomenologically-describing the way such things really happen so that we can choose theories that conform better to real-life experiences, such as, for instance, the end-of-the-opera experience described earlier.

[...] Father's boyhood up in Albany, Grandmother's house, the father and brothers and sister, with their passions and turbulent histories, his burning, amputation and sickness, his college days and ramblings, his theological throes, his engagement and marriage and fatherhood, his finding more and more of the truths he finally settled down in, his travels in Europe, the days of the old house in New York and all the men I used to see there, at last his quieter motion down the later years of life in Newport, Boston and Cambridge, with his friends and correspondents about him, and his books more and more easily brought forth—how long, how long all these things were in the living, but how short their memory now is. What remains is a few printed pages, us and our children and some incalculable modifications of other people's lives, influenced this way or that by what he said or did. . . . (Letters II:221)

A Speeded-Up Picture of Thinking. Our clearest thinking is assisted by the use of clear models. Here, then, is a picture to replace the old, slow-motion, 'thinking is a one-by-one assembling of distinct ideas and propositions' model. It is a picture to use for the 'thinking is understanding a flow of meaning(s)' model that blends with James's *Principles of Psychology* model. It is a 'normal-speed model' of thinking.

We picture ourselves standing on the bank of a fast-flowing stream. Out beyond the bank, the water rushes by. But, floating on the surface of the water, is a large, inflated balloon. It is more or less 'stationary,' that is, it does not rush downstream with the water. It is supported by the water which flows beneath it and, if the flow were cut off, the balloon would sink to the stream-bed. But, even though the balloon remains before us, moving neither up- nor downstream, it is definitely affected by all the variations at the surface of the stream. When the water rises in a sudden wavelet, the balloon rises. When a trough comes, the balloon takes a dip. The balloon is continually spinning and bouncing, turning this way and that, as the water churns beneath it. Yet, once again, the balloon itself does not move along downstream. It floats above the water and remains more or less 'just there.'

Let the stream represent the stream of images conjured by visually scanning rows and rows of 'word' ciphers. The stream of imagery 'flows' so smoothly that we do not even notice it until we kumuh kross holy uneks-peck-tud ciphers. If we come upon pas de lieu Rhône qu' nous, we might have to study it for some time before we finally, in James's terms, 'twig it' or 'get it.' ("Twig it" can be found in PP I:253 and Writings I:1001; "pas de lieu Rhône qu' nous" in PP I:442 and II:80.) That is, in some cases bathi carries us along smoothly with only first thoughts, whereas other times sarnoe must be exercised in difficult second thoughts as, for instance, when we must stop to decipher the word-scrambles, bathi and sarnoe. Reading involves logic, but it is simultaneously dependent entirely upon the contingencies of language. Reading a difficult text can be a mixture of first-thought bathi and second-thought sarnoeing.

Note. It is extremely critical to keep 'first thought' thinking in mind. Twentieth-century, linguistic-turning thinkers were fond of Berkeley's claim that language is not always for the purpose of 'communicating ideas.' We use words to raise passions, deter actions, and so on, he—and they—said. Imagine trying to do any of those things if the listener had no clue to the meanings or thoughts?! The idea of army doctors using English to insult foreigners (e.g., Koreans), all the while smiling and evoking smiles from those being insulted, familiar to today's movie and TV viewers, puts the lie to Berkeley's and their damaging error, an error committed even by Peirce and Dewey, who often wrote as if thinking—read 'reasoning'—kicks in only when habits fail to 'carry us through.' End of note.

Let the balloon represent thought. Or let the balloon be a cloud (of meaning). A cloud might serve even better than a balloon, since it would give less definiteness to the outline or shape of the thought. But whether balloon or cloud, that is only an image and must be corrected immediately. James described the 'passing thought' as a 'halo,' 'an overtone,' above all, as something we cannot get a direct look at. But we can notice it as an overflowing 'fringe' surrounding the sense-data and images which we can, if we choose, be directly aware of and attend to, even though we cannot directly 'look at' the thought-meaning.

The sense of our meaning is an entirely peculiar element of the thought. It is one of those evanescent and 'transitive' facts of mind which introspection cannot turn round upon, and isolate and hold up for examination, as an entomologist passes round an insect on a pin. In the (somewhat clumsy) terminology I have used, it pertains to the 'fringe' of the subjective state . . . (PP I:472)

We can notice. Then we can think *about* it and understand why it was so hard for James to find the right 'words' for his insight into the unnoticed and ignored 'flow' of our conscious life. First, even if the 'outer' universe were what common sense holds it to be, a collection of distinct substances, the most obvious of all obvious facts is that our waking experience does not feel like one slice of consciousness succeeded by another slice, then by another, then another, and so on. Besides, our conscious experience seems wholly transparent. We are not conscious of consciousness. As we read, we may be wholly absorbed, but we are aware of many other things we pay no attention to. That is why we know the answers to later questions: "Were you just now swimming or reading?", "Were you doing it in the jungle or a living room?", etc. It may take "A penny for your thought" to make us even notice that we are thinking at all.

But, when we later pause to create a model to explain our day-to-day waking life, our model may—like so many—be one that hides the truth more than it reveals it. This is what James complained about in "On Some Omissions" and, later, in Chapter IX of *The Principles*, where he admitted the convenience of the 'discrete parts' model, but only as a useful device for 'analyzing' thought:

> [. . .] no two 'ideas' are ever exactly the same, which is the proposition we started to prove. The proposition is more important theoretically than it at first sight seems. For it makes it already impossible for us to follow obediently in the footprints of either the Lockian or the Herbartian school, schools which have had almost unlimited influence in Germany and among ourselves. No doubt it is often convenient to formulate the mental facts in an atomistic sort of way, and to treat curves as if they were composed of small straight lines, and electricity and nerve-force as if they were fluids. But in the one case as in the other we must never forget that we are talking symbolically, and that there is nothing in nature to answer to our words. *A permanently existing 'idea' or 'Vorstellung' which makes its appearance before the footlights of consciousness at periodical intervals, is as mythological an entity as the Jack of Spades.* (PP I:236; see *Writings* I:991)

An aside. James's references to the pretence at the base of calculus, electricity, etc., show not only his familiarity with the science of his day, but presage his theory of pragmatic 'truth,' i.e., the convenience or usefulness of literally false hypotheses.

Only One Changing Thought Exists at a Time. "The total idea or meaning is present not only before and after the words are spoken but whilst each separate word is uttered" is James's best description vis-à-vis words. No more important formula exists for trying to understand thought, even though there are no words. We may later conclude, after much badgering by colleagues and authors, that thoughts can occur without the specific imagery we refer to as 'spoken and written words,' but for now we will work with the hypothesis that no thoughts are as clear and distinct as those 'expressed' by words, whether spoken, written, or silent.

"Each moment's thought or meaning is one thing." This chapter began with an expanded version of this shorter, telescoped answer to the question, "What is a thought?" The longer version of the answer given there bears repeating:

> **What is a thought? Thoughts are what humans understand. There is never more than one thought being understood by any human being at a time. But, although that one, single thought must be thought of as being a single thought, it must also be thought of as being many thoughts in one. How many thoughts in one? Always far more than anyone can possibly count.**

To see how we can avoid committing the error James complained so vociferously against, namely, changing thought into a 'manifold,' breaking it into bits, and calling its bits 'discrete,' it may help to see how James sometimes suggested we deal with *counting*. The issue here is another of the many one-and-many problems he discussed in the fourth of his *Pragmatism* lectures. Whatever solution we adopt, it will be convenient to pretend that we have three concepts signified by the non-name names, 'none,' 'one,' and 'more than one (many)' and that they are names for distinct concepts which we can apply when and where we choose. In the final chapter of *The Principles*, James offered some thoughts on numbers which we can adapt for thinking about thoughts.

Number seems to signify primarily the strokes of our attention in discriminating things. These strokes remain in the memory in groups, large and small, and the groups can be compared. The discrimination is, as we know, psychologically facilitated by the mobility of the thing as a total. But within each thing we discriminate parts; so that the number of things which any one given phenomenon may be depends in the last instance on our way of taking it. A globe is one, if undivided; two, if composed of hemispheres. A sand-heap is one thing, or twenty thousand things, as we may choose to count it. We amuse ourselves by the counting of mere strokes, to form rhythms, and these we compare and name. Little by little in our minds the number-series is formed. This, like all lists of terms in which there is a direction of serial increase, carries with it the sense of those mediate relations between its terms which we expressed by the axiom "the more than the more is more than the less." That axiom seems, in fact, only a way of stating that the terms do form an increasing series. (PP II:652)

In the midst of this paragraph on numbers, James noted that there is an element of arbitrariness in the way we answer questions about numbers. "The number of things which any one given phenomenon may be," he wrote, "depends in the last instance on our way of taking it." Does "brain" refer to nothing real, to one real thing, or to many real things? Is a human being one thing or does "a human being" refer to two things, a body and a soul? Is a stream of consciousness nothing real (materialists), one thing (James?), or is "a stream of consciousness" the name for three types of changing things (quintalism)? Is a thought one thing? Or is it many things jammed together? Or is there no it, so that "a thought" is the name for many things jammed together? "None," "one," and "many," we can generalize, can be taken as word-signs for concepts that can be 'imposed' wherever and whenever we will. After we have created them.

When we impose them, however, the sharpness of our thinking must not be allowed to blur under the influence of old common-sense habits. We can practice our sharpness on James's examples, namely, on "A globe is one, if undivided; two, if composed of hemispheres" and on "A sand-heap is one thing, or twenty thousand things, as we may choose to count it." Before the globe is divided, we can pretend it has two halves (right and left), four halves (right and left, top and bottom), four quarter-parts, and so on. But it is never 'composed' of those parts, because they do not exist, they are only imagined. Once the globe is divided, it no longer exists, so again 'it' is not composed of anything. Where there was an undivided globe, there are now two whole things, each half as large as the original globe. If the two become re-fused into one globe, there is no longer 'they' but only 'it,' and it is now twice as large as either of the two whole 'halves' or half-as-large wholes were. Similarly, James's use of "it" to refer to "a sand-heap" must be changed to "them." There are no sand-heaps, only (common-sensically) twenty thousand—or more or less—whole grains of sand. Or molecules. Or atoms? No, subatoms. 'Group' concepts are 'projections.'

[. . .] The mind-stuff theory, in short, is unintelligible. Atoms of feeling cannot compose higher feelings, any more than atoms of matter can compose physical things! The 'things,' for a clear-headed atomistic evolutionist, are not. Nothing is but the everlasting atoms. When grouped in a certain way, we name them this 'thing' or that; but the thing we name has no existence out of our mind. (PP I:161)

Each thought, then, is one thing, not a group of things. We cannot explore thoughts unless we think of them as if they have many 'parts' or facets and then explore those facets somewhat independently. But the process of 'breaking' the whole into imaginary parts and exploring them comes only after we have been thinking for a long time.

James offered many pictures of thoughts viewed through a many-parts model. One of the best even describes its temporally-sequential parts. It is probably as good as any description of a passing thought we are likely to come across. However, it is not in Chapter IX on "The Stream of Thought," but in the summary of Chapter X on "The Consciousness of Self." He called that passing thought "I" and "the self," but what he actually described was a thought, i.e., a single, partless, changing thing 'in which' he pretended to discern parts. Of course, common sense regards the real self as not part of a thought, as James knew. The real self is only 'pointed to' by a 'sense' which in his later *Varieties*' description James said is one of the 'plusses' found in the field of experience or thought. Still, by keeping in mind all that has been reviewed in the previous pages of this 'adjustment' of James's overall thought, we can use what he wrote in order to learn what he thought a 'passing thought'—which is *not* really a self!—is:

[. . .] The consciousness of Self involves a stream of thought, each part of which as 'I' can 1) remember those which went before, and know the things they knew; and 2) emphasize and care paramountly for certain ones among them as '*me*,' and *appropriate to these* the rest. The nucleus of the '*me*' is always the bodily existence felt to be present at the time. Whatever remembered-past-feelings *resemble* this present feeling are deemed to belong to the same *me* with it. Whatever other things are perceived to be *associated* with this feeling are deemed to form part of that me's *experience*; and of them certain ones (which fluctuate more or less) are reckoned to be themselves *constituents* of the me in a larger sense,—such as the clothes, the material possessions, the friends, the honors and esteem which the person receives or may receive. This me is an empirical aggregate of things objectively known. The *I* which knows them cannot itself be an aggregate, neither for psychological purposes need it be considered to be an unchanging metaphysical entity like the Soul, or a principle like the pure Ego, viewed as 'out of time.' It is a *Thought*, at each moment different from that of the last moment, but *appropriative* of the latter, together with all that the latter called its own. All the experiential facts find their place in this description, unencumbered with any hypothesis save that of the existence of passing thoughts or states of mind. . . . (PP I:400-01)

"It is a Thought, at each moment different from that of the last moment, but appropriative of the latter, together with all that the latter called its own." That is a description of an ongoing or evolving thought, not a self. Of course, the short-term-memory 'part' of a thought will be appropriative of certain details about the past and the long-term-memory 'part' appropriative of others. And if, as James claimed, "All the experiential facts find their place in this description, unencumbered with any hypothesis save that of the existence of passing thoughts or states of mind," then the present total thought also has a 'part' which constitutes the sense of expectancy which was discussed in Chapter III of *William James on Common Sense*.

But the Time-Parts of Thought Are Pure Non-Parts. There is *only one ongoing, changing thought* being understood by anyone at a given time. James described thoughts in terms of two entirely different types of imaginary parts, spatial and temporal. It is one thing to imagine that, because our acquired belief-system includes, as 'content,' an "awareness of our own body, of each other's persons, of the earth's geography," those can be called 'parts' of the passing, *ongoing* thought. This 'content' remains, no matter what happens to the outside realities (if they ever existed), and it remains in the present. But when James describes the present thought, distinct from "that of the last moment," he is talking about two things, one of which does not exist and never did. And, if we imagine the present thought and the thought which will only come in the next moment, we are dealing again with a thing that, like the previous thought, does not exist and never will. It is one thing to think of a present, *ongoing* thought as having different parts the way we can picture the uncut globe presently having two halves.

Chapter III of the prequel has already addressed the question of time and how to think as accurately as possible with the concepts of past, present, and future, the so-called parts of time. That analysis must now be applied to James's notion of 'the passing thought' which, in his radical empiricist mood, he called 'the self.' Because James did not select the same conclusions about 'time' as we have, there is no way of knowing how he would have responded to the reflections which will follow in a moment. Before applying our—actually only slightly different—theory of time to James's notion of a passing thought, we may recommend it by recalling his disagreement with Hume.

James regarded the disagreement between himself and the empiricists, especially Hume, as momentous. He objected to Hume's claim that a continuous thought is 'made up' of discrete, pre-existing perceptions. The disagreement here is equally or even more momentous. Most of all, because—as James discussed in the last two chapters of his never-finished *Some Problems of Philosophy*—this issue relates to the replacement of the common-sense notion of 'cause and effect' by Hume's anti-common-sense notion of 'invariable concomitant succession.' What James may not have noticed is that Hume never observed so much as a single succession or sequence of perception-events.

Another Hume'an Error. Every thought being understood at any time—whether in the course of reading or in the course of listening to a lecture, etc.—is a particular thought. The topic of a particular thought can be a particular thought or many particular thoughts 'collectively.' There is no thinking or thought in general. Every thought is also an ongoing thought, and every ongoing thought is thought by a real person at a particular moment in her or his life. To find out what a real thought is, as opposed to an imaginary thought, it is best to think a particular thought about an actually real, particular thought. And no one can be absolutely sure about any actually real, particular thought other than the one she or he is thinking at the moment in question. Whoever reads these pages can look at the calendar to know exactly how many years, months, and days it has been since she or he was born, and then look at a clock or a watch to know exactly how many hours, minutes, and seconds it has been since the alarm went off this morning, i.e., to know what exact moment in her or his life it is at the moment of reading this very word of this very sentence. This is another of those thoughts which merits a second thought:

293

No one can be absolutely certain about any actually real, particular thought other than the one she or he is thinking at the moment in question. Whoever reads these pages can look at the calendar to know exactly how many years, months, and days it has been since she or he was born, and then look at a clock or a watch to know exactly how many hours, minutes, and seconds it has been since the alarm went off this morning, i.e., to know what exact moment in her or his life it is at the moment of reading this very word of this very sentence. It is, of course, later than when the similar 'words' in the previous paragraph were read, just as it is later since I wrote them, etc.

That is what must be kept in mind if we determine to push to its limit what James thought about humans' conscious experience, particularly thoughts. We recall his constant rejection of the empiricists' belief that our knowledge is a putting-together of discrete ideas and/or images. Their belief was worse than the older tradition which viewed thinking as putting together discrete concepts into discrete judgments which can be put together into discrete syllogisms. Both camps erred in imagining that images and concepts are timeless entities, like still-shot photographs that can be spread out on a table, inspected, and then put into a permanent album, to be viewed on special occasions. Time, passing time, must be brought into our theories in a radical way. Our everyday, common-sense sense of time. Our sense of past, present, and future. And our certainty that only what exists now, and now, and . . . exists.

For instance, how is it possible that anyone can think of the past which never has existed or been observed? Or about the future which has never existed or been observed? For Hume, "all our ideas or more feeble perceptions are copies of our impressions or more lively ones" (*Enquiry*, Sec. ii). If that were true, he might—if he could have remembered it— claim to have gotten the idea of a billiard ball by looking at a billiard ball, but he would not have gotten the idea of a tree from a billiard ball. Where then did he get his ideas of the past which, unlike a billiard ball, is never 'there' to be observed. We may have a present memory of past events, but we can't compare that memory with the actual past which nowhere exists. Where did he get his idea of the future? We may have a present anticipation of future events, but we can't compare that anticipation with the actual future which nowhere exists. In fact, how can anyone get the idea of the present by looking at a billiard ball? Or how can we get an idea of motion by observing a billiard ball which is never in more than one location at any given instant? Chapter I has already dealt with the question, "What are the things we sense?", hence there is no need to repeat it here.

Remembering is not observing. We never observe anything but what we observe, and we never observe the past, the present, or the future. Remembering is not the same thing as observing, which is why students who remember observing the textbook last night often fail the exam they are observing today. Empiricists—as well as all of us when we are not careful—think our confidence is based on sensing. "Seeing is believing," we say. But in fact it is memory that we base our confidence on, confidence in our present memory, not our present observing. Jurors are told they must render a verdict relative to a crime 'in the past' they will never observe. But their verdict will be based on their ongoing memory of all the evidence 'taken in' during the minutes and hours of over-and-done-with courtroom-observing. Darwin and others write to tell us about the history of this planet's past and the past of entire species, a past none of them observed, therefore a past none of them remembers but only infers. Physicists tell us all sorts of things about the universe's past, a past none of them observed, therefore none remembers but only infers.

And so, in order to grasp the full implications of these simple facts, we must take our common-sense beliefs about time, sensing, remembering, and creating theories about things we have never observed, and then combine them with James's acute sense of the passing-and-gone-before-we-can-describe-it nature of our observings. As was noted earlier, 'remembering' is shorthand for 'understanding thoughts *that* such-and-such-happened-in-the-past.' To appreciate the importance of memory requires far more reflection than we normally give it, reflection on the naïveté of youth, the desperation of amnesia, the vacuousness of terminal senility, and all of the strange permutations of memory James cited in his psychology. Or, we might ponder the question, "If God created Adam and Eve instantly as nubile youths, could God have also created for them fifteen-year-old-type memories of past years and made them believe they had lived during all that time?" Or this: "Without relying on memory, how could I prove the entire universe is not just fifteen minutes old?"

And so, we reflect on Hume's brilliant insight into our assumptions about cause and effect. He was utterly right to say that we never observe causal power or force being transmitted from one billiard ball to another. He was even right to note that we ascribe 'identity' in areas where we have observed no identity. In fact, much of Hume's exposé, in Part IV of the first part of his *Treatise*, of the falseness of our naïve-realist assumptions about experience is as brilliant as James's.

But why did Hume not critique his confidence that there was meaning in his use of the 'ideas' of past, present, and future, even though he used them to reason as logically as anyone ever has that logical reasoning cannot be trusted? According to him, our ideas of cause and effect should be retitled 'ideas of constant concomitance of events similar enough to be called the-same.' By his own admission, no one can simultaneously observe events which occur only sequentially. Where did he acquire his idea of either simultaneity or sequence? If "all our ideas or more feeble perceptions are copies of our impressions or more lively ones," how could he even pretend to have such ideas? Einstein launched the journey to modern-physics fiction in Chapter VIII of *Relativity: the Special and General Theory*, entitled "On The Idea of Time in Physics," by questioning the very meaning of the word "simultaneously." Who can be certain she or he has observed two lightning strikes simultaneously? But if they are not simultaneous, they must be sequential. Would Hume have replied to Einstein that he could tell when two events he observed were simultaneous and when they were temporally sequential? And would he not have had to rely on the accuracy of his memory if he said which one he had observed on any given occasion?

Again and again, we must remind ourselves that the past does not exist. Whoever wishes to can look everywhere, but she or he will never observe the past. All of space is filled up with things which presently exist. According to the Rorty Rule, Hume understood the meaning of whatever complete sentences he might have uttered, but he never literally uttered a complete sentence. By the time a second word was on his lips, nothing remained of the first. There might have been a new, present image 'of' something, viz., of the first, which no longer existed. How could Hume ever have justified his decision to be a moderate skeptic rather than a complete and total skeptic if he had taken seriously his premises about the contents of our minds being discrete, atomic ideas, some of them originals and some merely copies?! How would he know which were which? He said the faint ones were the copies. How did he learn that? As for the future, even he never claimed to have observed it.

Simplifications. Our early 'sense' of time comes with our common-sense worldview. That any of us can understand such thoughts as those preceding this one is a fact which more than merits the name 'mystery.' The fact that all of us with common sense can understand them is an even greater mystery. And we do understand. St. Augustine's answer to "What is time?", namely, "As long as no one asks, I know; as soon as I want to explain it, I don't," is not something only a mystic can understand. He only described in a clever way what all of us feel. Even as children, we encounter such teasing statements as "Tomorrow will never come." That certainly seems to follow from the fact that I will go to sleep tonite and, if asked what day it is when I wake in the morning, I will know that the answer is "today" and not "tomorrow." There never was and never will be a day which is called "tomorrow." Tomorrow remains forever trapped in the future which, for the same reason, will never arrive to exist in the only part of time that could possibly be real, namely, the present. Ordinary people are knowledgeable enough to become confused by the juxtaposition of such thoughts, just as they are knowledgeable enough to understand what the psalmist meant when he wrote "For a thousand years in thy sight are but as yesterday when it is past, or as a watch in the night" (Ps 90:4) and what the author of 2 Peter 3:8 meant with his embellishment, "With the Lord one day is as a thousand years, and a thousand years are as one day," and what the scribe of Ecclesiastes 3 meant with his poignant poem, "For everything there is a season and a time for every purpose under heaven; a time to be born, a time to die. . . ."

Our task then is to take our common-sense notions of One-Time cosmic history, make liberal use of fictions and models, while refusing to become trapped by the fictions. We must then unmask dozens of previously accepted theories as fictitious, castle-in-the-air constructions originally created to clarify basic common-sense convictions. Once those fictions are reduced to size, we can begin to see wholly different ways of approaching thought and the issues related to it.

The Kepler of Psychology. Ever since Plato adopted the metaphors of "morphé" and "eidos" to explain intellectual knowledge, they have shaped most subsequent thinking about thinking and reasoning. Those metaphors combine the ideas of shape, form, and something that can be seen. The English words "idea" and "idol" are descended from the ideas referred to by the Greek terms. The history of subsequent theorizing about ideas, universals, and concepts provides abundant evidence for the claim that knowing was compared to looking, and that the medium for knowing was thought to consist of mental copies of things known. Chapters IX and X of James's *Principles of Psychology* achieved a breakthrough by deliberately replacing the 'looking' analogy with the tactile analogy of 'feeling,' and by replacing the idea of 'copies' with such items as 'meaning,' 'fringe,' 'halo,' etc.

The best way to fully appreciate James's history-making breakthrough is to compare it to that of Kepler (1571-1630). Once ancient Greek thinkers concluded that heavenly bodies, such as the sun, moon, planets, and stars, revolved around the earth in roughly circular orbits, mathematically-trained astronomers 'saw' nothing but circles, circles, circles, when they looked up at the sky. Copernicus replaced the earth-centered model with a sun-centered one, but he remained under the spell of the circles tradition. Even Galileo, who broke the spell of Aristotle's four-elements theory of natural-vs-violent motion, remained under the circles spell. It took Kepler years of patient, manual calculation to discover that an elliptical model worked better than the circles model. When he did, the logjam created by new discoveries that could not be aligned with the old theories was broken and the smooth course of progress resumed.

If Kepler broke the spell of circles, circles, circles that exerted a chokehold on astronomers and physicists, James showed how to break the spell of concepts, concepts, concepts that exerted a chokehold on those who tried to understand human thought, whether they classified their psychological theories as philosophical or empirical.

Beyond Nominalism. James's thinking is often dismissed as nominalism. In a strict, literal sense, "nominalism" (*name'ism*) would mean that thinking is talking or using names, and that thinking about things in general is using general terms to talk about things. "Nominalism" is used more loosely to refer to those who think a train of thought is a sequence of images (*imagism*) or a concatenation of concepts which do not literally match anything in the real world (*conceptualism*). Even C. S. Peirce, whom James credited as the author of the pragmatist theory of meaning, accused him of nominalism. For instance, in a 1904 letter, Peirce complained to James:

> . . . You and Schiller carry pragmatism too far for me. I don't want to exaggerate it, but keep it within the bounds to which the evidences of it are limited. The most important consequence of it, by far, on which I have always insisted . . . is that under the conception of reality we must abandon nominalism. That in my opinion is the great need of philosophy. . . . I also want to say that after all pragmatism solves no real problems. (Perry II:430)

But James's Chapter IX and X description of partless thought does not represent a fall from the height of insight reached by early non-nominalist psychologists. Nor did he descend to conceptualism, imagism, or literal nominalism. On the contrary, after rising to the height reached by earlier researchers, *James went beyond them* and reached the pinnacle of insight described in this chapter. A partless complete thought is utterly distinct from images and words, and it is only by means of complete, partless thoughts that we can think about both real things, such as persons and thoughts, and about unreal things, such as concepts.

Insight: 'Seeing' the Many in One. First, we can see that the varieties of humans' conscious experiences are not simply varied but are also 'essentially the same.' They are as similar in general as they are different in details. James's interest in abnormal psychology, psychics, hypnosis, alternating personalities, mysticism, etc., was driven by his conviction that all experiences fitted somewhere on the same spectrum or under a common genus. After recounting, in the sixteenth of the *Varieties of Religious Experience* lectures, his own rare experiment with an 'altered state of consciousness,' he commented at length on that conviction.

[...] One conclusion was forced upon my mind at that time, and my impression of its truth has ever since remained unshaken. It is that our normal waking consciousness, rational consciousness as we call it, is but one special type of consciousness, whilst all about it, parted from it by the filmiest of screens, there lie potential forms of consciousness entirely different. We may go through life without suspecting their existence but apply the requisite stimulus, and at a touch they are there in all their completeness, definite types of mentality which probably somewhere have their field of application and adaptation. No account of the universe in its totality can be final which leaves these other forms of consciousness quite disregarded. How to regard them is the question,—for they are so discontinuous with ordinary consciousness. Yet they may determine attitudes though they cannot furnish formulas, and open a region though they fail to give a map. At any rate, they forbid a premature closing of our accounts with reality. Looking back on my own experiences, they all converge towards a kind of insight to which I cannot help ascribing some metaphysical significance. The keynote is invariably a reconciliation. It is as if the opposites of the world, whose contradictoriness and conflict make all our difficulties and troubles, were melted into unity. Not only do they, as contrasted species, belong to one and the same genus, but *one of the species*, the nobler and better one, *is itself the genus, and so soaks up and absorbs its opposite into itself.* This is a dark saying, I know, when thus expressed in terms of common logic, but I cannot wholly escape from its authority. I feel as if it must mean something, something like what the hegelian philosophy means, if one could only lay hold of it more clearly. (*Writings* II:349-50)

"Not only do they, as contrasted species, belong to one and the same genus . . ." But which of the species, though, is the important one? Which is the one that we will choose as our own 'supreme genus' because it captures the 'sameness' in all the rest? Our choice? It is named in the very phrase James used while expressing his conviction about forms of consciousness converging "towards a kind of insight.'

'Insight' is the key word to explore at the end of this second section entitled "Insight into the many-in-one intellectual act of insight." When James delivered the first of his "Mysticism" lectures in 1902, he began with insight, a common, everyday experience, in order to build up gradually to 'mystical experience' and thereby make it seem less bizarre, less 'discontinuous' with 'normal, rational consciousness.'

[. . .] The range of mystical experience is very wide, much too wide for us to cover in the time at our disposal. Yet the method of serial study is so essential for interpretation that if we really wish to reach conclusions we must use it. I will begin, therefore, with phenomena which claim no special religious significance, and end with those of which the religious pretensions are extreme.

The simplest rudiment of mystical experience would seem to be that deepened sense of the significance of a maxim or formula which occasionally sweeps over one. "I've heard that said all my life," we exclaim, "but I never realized its full meaning until now." (*Writings* II:344)

James's *Varieties* is filled with accounts of insight experiences. But a first-hand account from Viktor Frankl's *Man's Search for Meaning* may be the most appropriate to cite here, both because it depicts the full nature of an insight, viz., the long period of experience-accumulating followed later by a climactic 'vision,' and also because its 'content value' is of general interest.

In spite of all the enforced physical and mental primitiveness of the life in a concentration camp, it was possible for spiritual life to deepen. Sensitive people who were used to a rich intellectual life may have suffered much pain (they were often of a delicate constitution), but the damage to their inner selves was less. They were able to retreat from their terrible surroundings to a life of inner riches and spiritual freedom. Only in this way can one explain the apparent paradox that some prisoners of a less hardy make-up often seemed to survive camp life better than did those of a robust nature. In order to make myself clear, I am forced to fall back on personal experience. . . .

We stumbled on in the darkness, over big stones and through large puddles, along the one road leading from the camp. . . . Hardly a word was spoken; the icy wind did not encourage talk. Hiding his mouth behind his upturned collar, the man marching next to me whispered suddenly: "If our wives could see us now! I do hope they are better off in their camps and don't know what is happening to us."

That brought thoughts of my own wife to mind. And as we stumbled on for miles, slipping on icy spots, supporting each other time and again, dragging one another up and onward, nothing was said, but we both knew each of us was thinking of his wife. Occasionally I looked at the sky, where the stars were fading and the pink light of the morning was beginning to spread behind a dark bank of clouds. But my mind clung to my wife's image, imagining it with an uncanny acuteness. I heard her answering me, saw her smile, her frank and encouraging look. Real or not, her look was then more luminous than the sun which was beginning to rise.

A thought transfixed me: for the first time in my life I saw the truth as it is set into song by so many poets, proclaimed as the final wisdom by so many thinkers. The truth—that love is the ultimate and the highest goal to which man can aspire. Then I grasped the meaning of the greatest secret that human poetry and human thought and belief have to impart: The salvation of man is through love and in love. I understood how a man who has nothing left in this world still may know bliss, be it only for a brief moment, in the contemplation of his beloved. In a position of utter desolation, when man cannot express himself in positive action, when his only achievement may consist in enduring his sufferings in the right way—an honorable way—in such a position man can, through loving contemplation of the image he carries of his beloved, achieve fulfillment. For the first time in my life I was able to understand the meaning of the words, 'The angels are lost in perpetual contemplation of infinite glory.' (V. Frankl, *Man's Search for Meaning*, 2nd ed., pp.55-57)

The more familiar we become with the full range of James's thought, the more obvious it is that insight is the type of experience normal, non-mystical citizens must rely on to take them to an intellectual 'vision' of the grand scheme of things. Insights are what help learners 'see' more and more connections which allow them to 'put together' larger and ever-larger numbers of details so that they can make the discoveries and conversions which every learner must make on the way to that final, all-encompassing 'vision' which is the pinnacle of insight. First, the relatively uncomplicated insight into the fact that no one has ever gotten a single idea from any other human. Second, the radical insight-conversion away from naïve realism. Third, the insight that the challenge of solipsism is real. Etc.

In his essay, "A Pluralistic Mystic," James contrasted 'rotary motion' or 'dialectic' to the 'rectilinear mentality.' It captures the central difference between Plato's dialectic (see the *Republic*) and Aristotle's syllogism (see his *Analytics*). James advocated the 'round and round' dialectical model as opposed to the 'straight ahead' linear one. 'Insight' names the moment of success. Insight comes after our thoughts have 'gone round' many times, often without seeming to 'go ahead.' Insight is even better than the usual thesis-antithesis-synthesis interpretation of 'dialectic': often, as Kierkegaard insisted, it is an Ockham's-Razor either-or choice that is called for, not a both-and fudge. Still, both metaphors are correctives to the 'linear reasoning' model if we wish to think seriously about real-life learning.

[. . .] Dialectic thought of the Hegelian type is a whirlpool into which some persons are sucked out of the stream which the straightforward understanding follows. Once in the eddy, nothing but rotary motion can go on. All who have been in it know the feel of its swirl—they know thenceforward that thinking unreturning on itself is but one part of reason, and that rectilinear mentality, in philosophy at any rate, will never do. Though each one may report in different words of his rotational experience, the experience itself is almost childishly simple, and whosoever has been there instantly recognizes other authentic reports. To have been in that eddy is a freemasonry of which the common password is a "fie" on all the operations of the simple popular understanding. . . .

[. . .] Non-dialectic thought takes facts as singly given, and accounts for one fact by another. But when we think of "*all* fact," we see that nothing of the nature of fact can explain it, "for that were but one more added to the list of things to be accounted for. . . ." (*Writings* II:1296)

What better description of James's own real-life thinking can be imagined? If ever anyone's thinking returned again and again on itself, it was his. Just read his notes on the 'Miller-Bode Objections' to see how he circled around and around on what seems to naïve realists to be a silly question, namely, "Can two people see the same writing pen?" (The answer is "No.") His lack of success in finding the insight needed to reconcile the contradictory principles he had set forth at the very outset of those notes shows that, in the final analysis, insight is a gift.

Truth Must Be Sought Open-Mindedly. This text is being written with two beliefs in mind. First, *that* Jamesian quintalism so radically contradicts the naïve realism of common sense that it is hard to even take it seriously at first. Second, *that* what James wrote in that all-important but unused draft discussed in the previous chapter is 100% true: "The most he [the author] claims is that what he says about cognition may be counted as true as what he says *about anything else*. If his hearers [readers] agree that he has assumed the wrong things to be realities, then doubtless they will reject his account of the way in which those realities become known. . . ."

But there is only one way for any reader to find out whether or not Jamesian quintalism is true, and that is to open-mindedly 'try it out.' In the chapter of *The Principles* which he entitled "The Perception of Reality," James gave some advice about learning truths that at first— because of long-standing false thought-habits—seem absurd.

A practical observation may end this chapter. If belief consists in an emotional reaction of the entire man on an object, how *can* we believe at all? We cannot control our emotions. Truly enough, a man cannot believe at will abruptly. Nature sometimes, and indeed not very infrequently, produces instantaneous conversions for us. She suddenly puts us in an active connection with objects of which she had till then left us cold. "I realize for the first time," we then say, "what that means!" This happens often with moral propositions. We have often heard them; but now they shoot into our lives; they move us; we feel their living force. Such instantaneous beliefs are truly enough not to be achieved by will. But *gradually* our will can lead us to the same results by a very simple method: *we need only in cold blood* ACT *as if the thing in question were real, and keep acting as if it were real, and it will infallibly end by growing into such a connection with our life that it will become real.* It will become so knit with habit and emotion that our interests in it will be those which characterize belief. Those to whom 'God' and 'Duty' are now mere names can make them much more than that, if they make a little sacrifice to them every day. But all this is so well known in moral and religious education that I need say no more. (PP II:321-22)

What he was referring to were 'big' and 'far-reaching' beliefs, not mere trivia. In fact, it is quite obvious that James's whole theory of belief was shaped by what happened for him when he decided in 1870 that "my first act of free will shall be to believe in free will." It is interesting to compare what James wrote with the facts and the logic in Edwin Boring's highly paradoxical report about Francis Galton:

In spite of this very practical trend in Galton's psychology, he was also a good introspectionist. He argued, against the philosophers, that the report of a man as to what goes on in his own mind is as valid as the report of a geographer about a new country. He was himself an excellent observer of conscious as well as of objective events. By observing his own mind as he walked along the streets of London, he came to his first conclusions about the variety of its associative processes, and also as to the great extent with which unconscious processes occur in "the antechamber of consciousness." On the basis of such careful introspection, he also formed his own conclusion against the freedom of the will, noting how, in choice, ideas fluctuate until one of them dominates without any conscious act of will. This conclusion he reached independently of the introspective work of the German laboratories, but of course not without the influence of his predisposition toward deterministic science and away from current theology. He attacked the problem of the religious consciousness introspectively, for he put up a comic picture of Punch and made believe in its possession of divine attributes, addressing it "with much quasi-reverence as possessing a mighty power to reward or punish the behaviour of men toward it"; and he was finally rewarded by the acquisition of a superstitious feeling toward the picture and the possession in "a large share of the feelings that a barbarian entertains towards his idol." This result must have been a great triumph for a nature so little subject to superstition. Galton also tried a personal excursion into insanity. He undertook to invest everything he met, "whether human, animal, or inanimate, with the imaginary attributes of a spy"; and he succeeded in establishing in himself a paranoid state "in which every horse seemed to be watching him, either with pricked ears or disguising its espionage." (E. Boring, *A History of Experimental Psychology*, 2nd ed., pp.484-85)

Galton's research proved the truth of James's claim that a decision to practice certain thoughts and to reinforce them with action may result not just in a new habit, but in some genuine emotions consonant therewith. James's claim is further supported by what later came to be called 'behavioral therapy,' 'desensitization programs,' etc., all of which required willing clients who did their 'cold-blooded,' that is, deliberate, behaving and imaging while awake and thinking (two facts that behaviorists tried to ignore).

James dealt with these matters in far greater detail in his *Varieties* lectures on the topic of conversion. At the end of his discussion of conversion, he invited some in his audience to convert from their bias against sudden conversions.

> One word, before I close this lecture, on the question of the transiency or permanence of these abrupt conversions. Some of you, I feel sure, knowing that numerous backslidings and relapses take place, make of these their apperceiving mass for interpreting the whole subject, and dismiss it with a pitying smile as so much 'hysterics.' Psychologically, as well as religiously, this is shallow. It misses the point of serious interest, which is not so much the duration as the nature and quality of these shiftings of character to higher levels. Men lapse from every level—we need no statistics to tell us that. Love is, for instance, well known not to be irrevocable, yet, constant or inconstant, it reveals new flights and reaches of ideality while it lasts. These revelations form its significance to men and women, whatever be its duration. So with the conversion experience: that it should for even a short time show a human being what the high-water mark of his spiritual capacity is, this is what constitutes its importance,—an importance which backsliding cannot diminish, although persistence might increase it. As a matter of fact, all the more striking instances of conversion, all those, for instance, which I have quoted, *have* been permanent. (*Writings* II:236-37)

James's advocacy of good common-sense thinking about habit-formation and habit-alteration is a desperately needed corrective to current dogmas about the brain. Since it is so succinct and packs volumes into such beautiful, even poetic shorthand, the passage from James's *Principles* cited in the last chapter deserves recognition as one of James's most important insights:

> The truth must be admitted that thought works under conditions imposed *ab extra*. The great law of habit itself—that twenty experiences make us recall a thing better than one, that long indulgence in error makes right thinking almost impossible—seems to have no essential foundation in reason. The business of thought is with truth—the number of experiences ought to have nothing to do with her hold

of it; and she ought by right to be able to hug it all the closer, after years wasted out of its presence. The contrary arrangements seem quite fantastic and arbitrary, but nevertheless are part of the very bone and marrow of our minds. Reason is only one out of a thousand possibilities in the thinking of each of us. Who can count all the silly fancies, the grotesque suppositions, the utterly irrelevant reflections he makes in the course of a day? Who can swear that his prejudices and irrational beliefs constitute a less bulky part of his mental furniture than his clarified opinions? It is true that a presiding arbiter seems to sit aloft in the mind, and emphasize the better suggestions into permanence, while it ends by dropping out and leaving unrecorded the confusion. But this is all the difference. The *mode of genesis* of the worthy and the worthless seems the same. The laws of our actual thinking, of the *cogitatum*, must account alike for the bad and the good materials on which the arbiter has to decide, for wisdom and for folly. The laws of the arbiter, of the *cogitandum*, of what we *ought* to think, are to the former as the laws of ethics are to those of history. (PP I:552; *ab extra* = from without)

"The great law of habit itself." Ordinary, common-sense folk—all of us early in life and all of us later during our off-duty hours—are perfectly content with common sense. At such periods, we are not bothered by the facts which, as James insisted, "burst the bounds of common sense." At first, we are not as acutely aware of the 'psychological laws' which govern our real-life learning as James was. But every one of us without exception is an arbiter and jury of one, sitting aloft and presiding over what goes on in her or his mind. Only by willing-to-believe there may be errors in our thinking and there may be important things still to be learned can we avoid unjustified complacency and 'try out' foreign-to-us hypotheses.

[. . .] As I sit here, I think objects, and I make inferences, which the future is sure to analyse and articulate and riddle with discriminations, showing me many things wherever I now notice one. Nevertheless, my thought feels quite sufficient unto itself for the time being; and ranges from pole to pole, as free, and as unconscious of having overlooked anything, as if it possessed the greatest discriminative enlightenment. We all cease analyzing the world at some point, and notice no more differences. The last units with which we stop are our objective elements of being. Those of a dog are different from those of a Humboldt; those of a practical man from those of a metaphysician. But the dog's and the practical man's *feel* continuous, though to the Humboldt or the metaphysician they would appear full of gaps and defects. And they *are* continuous, *as thoughts*. It is only *as mirrors of things* that the superior minds find them full of omissions. And when the omitted things are discovered and the unnoticed differences laid bare, it is not that the old *thoughts* split up, but that *new thoughts supersede* them, which make new judgments about the same objective world. (PP I:489)

"My thought . . . ranges from pole to pole." From our God-like perch, we can see the world far below, with the river of time flowing from the far away past, through the present, on to the mist-hidden future. But the rival worldviews James never forgot must now be added between those 'poles.' Were we as omniscient as traditionalists believe God is, we would see, living on planet Earth below, millions of people with radically conflicting God's-eye worldviews. Not every presiding arbiter 'emphasizes the better suggestions into permanence'! Their thoughts may all 'range from pole to pole,' but what many of them see must be illusory 'worlds' of their own making, which 'making' consists of their willed assents, dissents, and fence-sittings vis-à-vis the thoughts that have been proposed to them over the course of a lifetime. As James noted in *The Principles*, not all the stages of 'insight' lead heavenward.

[. . .] these so-called 'transitions of reason' are far from being all alike reasonable. If pure thought runs all our trains, why should she run some so fast and some so slow, some through dull flats and some through gorgeous scenery, some to mountain-heights and jewelled mines, others through dismal swamps and darkness?—and run some off the track altogether, and into the wilderness of lunacy? (PP I:551-52)

The Unity of Consciousness. To grasp this unity, we begin with common sense, with a passage James used to make Fechner's panpsychism plausible. It is a rather unusual passage, because James rarely took explicit account of the fact that seeing colors, hearing sounds, and thinking about the two, are three distinct acts, with distinct objects, that occur simultaneously. "Our eyes know nothing of sound, our ears nothing of light, but, having brains, we can feel sound and light together, and compare them" (Writings II:703). That is imagery, to be certain, but it helps to grasp one of the most important of all James's great insights, his sense of 'the unity of consciousness.'

Long before James, Plato drew explicit attention to the unity of our own consciousness, a fact that all of us know 'tacitly.' To rebut Protagoras' claim that knowing is perceiving, Plato pointed out *that* seeing is perceiving colors and hearing is perceiving sounds, and *that* seeing does not perceive sounds nor hearing colors, and *that* we also

307

know both color and sound and know their difference. Obviously, there is more going on than sense-perceiving. (See his *Theatetus*, 184 ff.) To explain the same unification fact, Aristotle invented an internal faculty called the 'sensus communis.'

We, by recognizing that eyes, ears, and other organs and faculties are merely useful fictions, can arrive at the simple insight that it is we our selves who do it all: the being-visually-aware of colors, the being-audibly-aware of sounds, the comparing, the discriminating, the model-creating, and the naming. James's best example to illustrate the unified-manyness of word-using thought is one that sharply contrasts the number of words to the oneness of a thought.

> Take a sentence of a dozen words, and take twelve men and tell to each one word. Then stand the men in a row or jam them in a bunch, and let each think of his word as intently as he will; nowhere will there be a consciousness of the whole sentence. We talk of the 'spirit of the age,' and the 'sentiment of the people,' and in various ways we hypostatize 'public opinion.' But we know this to be symbolic speech, and never dream that the spirit, opinion, sentiment, etc., constitute a consciousness other than, and additional to, that of the several individuals whom the words 'age,' 'people,' or 'public' denote. The private minds do not agglomerate into a higher compound mind. (PP I:160)

This claim, which James spent a good deal of his fifth *Pluralistic Universe* lecture on, is obviously related to his claim about Columbus-discovered-America-in-1492. It relates directly to the issue of linear reasoning vs insight. No one who hears all twelve words shouted *simultaneously*, would get one thought, clear and easy to understand. We must hear them successively, not forgetting the first while hearing the second, or the second while hearing the third, etc. No one who sees all twelve words, jumbled!, with a single glance, will get the same clear thought as when sequence read they proper them in the. So intimate is the bond between the 'flow of time' and the 'laws of habit' involved in reading, that anyone who ignores it will never understand either. As we read, our eyes scan the words, but we pay no attentin to them unless word is misspelled or omitted, as 'attention' and 'a' were. The focal area of our field of consciousness while reading is the meaning of the read sentence, but context'd by the whole ongoing thought. Both linear scanning and much-at-once insight can occur simultaneously.

How Many Intellectual Acts Are There? With those thought-premises in mind, it takes but a moment to point out one great simplification or reduction they make possible with regard to theories about our intellect's operations.

For instance, *our concept of 'insight' is a construct.* Not every moment of reading results in what we ordinarily describe as an insight. We create the concept of insight *as a contrast to 'non-insight'* in order to help capture and remember the thought *that* sometimes a thought seems to be far more of a revelation than the thoughts we understand at other times. It does seem at times that we 'see' things more clearly or we 'see' more things at once, etc. But, if all thinking is simply (!!!) "understanding one partless, infinitely complex thought which evolves or changes from moment to moment," then insights and non-insights are far more alike than different. It may be—no, it is—a case of not noticing the immense learning that the average person, after five and before senility, 'wears so lightly' at all waking moments. Another way of conjuring a similar thought is to say that everyone equipped with the common-sense philosophy has a prepared mind. Perhaps not as prepared as Pasteur's, but one prepared for more and more 'everyday situations' as life and experience 'go on.' The twenty-year old will be readier for more insights than a five-year old.

If all questions fit under just three—What exists?, What do existent things do?, and Why?—and if there are only five types of existents, then most of our non-names for intellectual acts are names for fictions. But, in the same way that we use "walk," "skip," "jump," etc., to describe differences in what we do with the same two legs, we can use induction, deduction, abduction, material or formal implication, dialectic, linear reasoning, etc., as forms of shorthand for various facets of the one miracle, namely, understanding thoughts. James, who relished useful fictions, still warned those listening to the fourteenth of his *Talks to Teachers* against so-called 'experts' and their tendency to create useless, even obfuscating fiction-trivia.

In some of the books we find the various forms of apperception codified, and their subdivisions numbered and ticketed in tabular form in the way so delightful to the pedagogic eye. In one book which I remember reading there were sixteen different types of apperception discriminated from each other. There was associative apperception, subsumptive apperception, assimilative apperception, and others up

309

to sixteen. It is needless to say that this is nothing but an exhibition of the crass artificiality which has always haunted psychology, and which perpetuates itself by lingering along, especially in these works which are advertised as 'written for the use of teachers.' The flowing life of the mind is sorted into parcels suitable for presentation in the recitation-room, and chopped up into supposed 'processes' with long greek and latin names, which in real life have no distinct existence.

There is no reason, if we are classing the different types of apperception, why we should stop at sixteen rather than sixteen hundred. There are as many types of apperception as there are possible ways in which an incoming experience may be reacted on by an individual mind. (TT:112; *Writings* I:803)

Reading, Again. Reading offers the ideal means of studying thinking because it involves the most important issues. What do I see while reading? How much memory do I need to understand what I read? Where are my thoughts coming from as I read? What laws or regularities, especially the great law of habit, are detectable as I read? How do my ideas of time relate to all of the above? Trying to understand reading requires the right inner model as a scaffold for all of the insight-thoughts needed to 'see' how everything 'fits together.' We pause to ruminate about the right scaffold. The flow of thought changes dramatically. Or we can stop reading and *try* to put everything out of our mind altogether. But can we avoid thoughts about what we're *trying* to do? (If someone interrupts us and asks "What are you doing?", would we be at a loss for words?) We start reading again, and the flow resumes. This is one way to 'notice' our ongoing stream of thought.

But, whether we continue thinking or try to stop the flow of thought, the river of time moves on steadily, inexorably carrying us farther from the moment of birth and closer to the end of a journey. Did any lone, aloft-sitting, presiding arbiter ever have a keener hold on this fact, pluralistically interpreted, than James?

A Debt. A work particularly helpful for reflecting on the theme of insight followed by critical reflection followed by new insight, etc., in the learning process is Michael Novak's *Belief and Unbelief,* which extracts the best of Bernard Lonergan's *Insight.*

4. The 'Source' Question

Thoughts Come to Us' . . . But From Where? In his never-completed, was-to-be *magnum opus*, viz., *Some Problems of Philosophy*, the one great question James zeroed in on was, "Whence come the next ingredients in my effervescent, always novel, 'finite experiences'?"

In Chapter XIII, his focus narrowed even more to thoughts. He describes the fact that his hand writes words to capture his ongoing thought. He remarks on an aspect of that writing experience that is particularly significant.

> As I now write, I am in one of those activity situations. I 'strive' after words, which I only half prefigure, but which, when they shall have come, must satisfactorily complete the nascent sense I have of what they ought to be. The words are to run out of my pen, which I find that my hand actuates so obediently to desire that I am hardly conscious either of resistance or of effort. Some of the words come wrong, and then I do feel a resistance, not muscular but mental, which instigates a new instalment of my activity . . . (*Writings* II:1090)

This poses the ultimate causal question. The title of *Some Problems'* Chapter XIII is "Novelty and Causation." Chapters III to XII should be read as a build-up to it. This last finished chapter ends by bringing up the mind-brain relation and then leaving it dangling, because it is "such a complicated topic." At that point, James put down his pen for good on *Some Problems*, leaving the ultimate problem unsolved.

The truth is that we have direct access only to our private field of experience, that is, to an *effect*. We have no direct access to the *source* of any part of it! Writing in Chapter X of *The Principles* from the perspective that mental events accompany brain processes, James expressed the premise he had adopted for that work:

> That bald fact is that when the brain acts, a thought occurs. The spiritualistic formulation says that the brain-processes knock the thought, so to speak, out of a Soul which stands there to receive their influence. The simpler formulation says that the thought simply *comes*. (PP I:345)

James never 'officially' retracted that premise. Thought or thoughts simply come. But, from where?

Retracing the Road from Common Sense to "Thought Simply Comes." Or from physics to psychology. We acquire our common-sense philosophy during the days, months, and years between our birth and our fifth birth celebration. We begin acquiring it before we have any theory whatever about learning, that is, at a time when we have no theories about how to see, what to see, how to remember, what to remember, how to think, what to think about, and so on.

By the time we are five and have acquired the basics of our first overall worldview, we still have only the vaguest ideas about those things. Yes, we can play the game of Twenty Questions, which means we know enough about things in the 'physical' world to mentally distinguish or class-ify them into persons, places, minerals, vegetables, or animals. As for consciousness, the most explicit facts we know are *that* we see with our eyes, hear with our ears, smell with our nose, etc., as well as *that* people can tease us with statements which are untrue, *that* we often tell fibs to avoid punishment, and so on. But about the topics discussed in James's *Principles*, our five-year-old's knowledge is vague, sketchy, and almost 100% tacit or implicit.

But James eventually concluded that our common-sense worldview is simply inconsistent with 'science' and 'critical philosophy.' To understand him, it is vitally important to understand Chapter I of this text which summarized the tight reasoning which shows the inadequacy of common sense. But that reasoning had to begin with common sense. *Descartes' critique of common sense was an internal critique,* i.e., a critique showing that some basic common-sense convictions contradict other basic common-sense convictions. The different, rival philosophical systems constructed since Descartes result from different free will-to-believe decisions regarding which convictions to retain and which to surrender.

In other words, the train of thought leading from explicit Twenty-Question common sense to James's concluding thought that we have access only to a private stream of conscious experience began with common sense. For everyone, in fact, the reliable trail to the mind and consciousness must begin from (ideas of) the physical environment, proceed to the physics and physiology of the senses, and finally to the brain. Only then can we discover, with full confidence, that we have found the sole evidence for any certainty about what lies beyond our stream of consciousness, namely, that stream itself.

This brings us to the ultimate causal question. Thought or thoughts simply come. But, from where?

"The Brain" Was One of James' Two Most Referred-to Answers.

We cannot begin with common sense, as James did in *The Principles of Psychology*, and not find ourselves having to admit, first, that the only physical body we can possibly have any direct *causal* contact with is our own brain.

> THE RELATIONS OF MINDS TO OTHER OBJECTS
> are either relations *to other minds*, or to *material things*. The material things are either the mind's *own brain*, on the one hand, or *anything else*, on the other. The relations of a mind to its own brain are of a unique and utterly mysterious sort; we discussed them in the last two chapters, and can add nothing to that account.
>
> The mind's relations to other objects than the brain are *cognitive and emotional* relations exclusively, so far as we know. It *knows* them, and it inwardly *welcomes or rejects* them, but it has no other dealings with them. When it seems to *act* upon them, it only does so through the intermediary of its own body, so that not it but the body is what acts on them, and the brain must first act upon the body. The same is true when other things seem to act on it—they only act on its body, and through that on its brain. All that it *can* do *directly* is to know other things, misknow or ignore them, and to find that they interest it, in this fashion or in that. (PP I:216)

Our brain, if it exists, comes between us and every other physical body. It is like a funnel or like an import-export terminal. James based his 1400-page masterpiece, *The Principles of Psychology*, on that premise, most particularly with relation to what comes into our mind. In Chapter I, he postulated that "the brain is the one immediate bodily condition of the mental operations" (PP I:4). From then on, he found it difficult to conclude once and for all that the brain is irrelevant as a causal source of our stream of consciousness. Till the very end of his life, he continued to insist on the critical importance of settling accounts with 'the brain problem.'

(1890) The nature and hidden causes of ideas will never be unravelled till the *nexus* between the brain and consciousness is cleared up" (PP II:6).

(1890) The causes of our mental structure are doubtless natural and connected, like all our other peculiarities, with those of our nervous structure. Our interests, our tendencies of attention, our motor impulses, the aesthetic, moral, and theoretic combinations we delight in, the extent of our power of apprehending schemes of relation, just like our elementary relations themselves, time, space, difference and similarity, and the elementary kinds of feeling, have all grown up in ways of which at present we can give no account. Even in the clearest parts of Psychology our insight is insignificant enough. And the more sincerely one seeks to trace the actual course of *psychogenesis*, the steps by which as a race we may have come by the peculiar mental attributes which we possess, the more clearly one perceives "the slowly gathering twilight close in utter night." (PP II:688)

(1897) The first of these difficulties [re immortality] is relative to the absolute dependence of our spiritual life, as we know it here, upon the brain. One hears not only physiologists, but numbers of laymen who read the popular science books and magazines, saying all about us, How can we believe in life hereafter when Science has once for all attained to proving, beyond possibility of escape, that our inner life is a function of that famous material, the so-called 'gray matter' of our cerebral convolutions? How can the function possibly persist after its organ has undergone decay? ("Human Immortality," p.7; *Writings* I:1102)

(1907) All the consciousness we directly know seems tied to brains. (*Writings* II:702).

(1909) If we took these experiences as the type of what actual causation is, we should have to ascribe to cases of causation outside of our own life, to physical cases also, an inwardly experiential nature. In other words we should have to espouse a so-called 'pan-psychic' philosophy. This complication, and the fact that hidden brain-events appear to be 'closer' effects than those which consciousness directly aims at, lead us to interrupt the subject here provisionally. (*Writings* II:1093-94)

But Our Brain Can't Be the Source. As we have seen in Chapter I, James had good reasons to deny that our consciousness is caused by, or causes effects in, our own brain. In various places he stated those reasons.

First and foremost is the startling fact that none of us has any direct awareness whatever of our own brain, the only physical thing that *could* directly affect us. But theories about our brain are as much constructs as our hypotheses about anything else outside the perimeter of our private 'field' of experience. All of our evidence about our own alleged brain is found inside the three-tributaried stream of conscious experience of which our brain is supposedly the cause, and none of our inner evidence points directly to or reveals specific details about our brain!

This was a point James himself made early on. In 1877, the thirty-five-year old James wrote a book review in which he summed up an idea which he never relinquished: "The entire recent growth of their science [brain physiology] may, in fact, be said to be a mere hypothetical schematization in material terms of the laws which introspection long ago laid bare" (Cited by *Myers*: 8-9; also ECR:336).

Secondly, as Chapter I already noted, James drew attention to a contradiction between recent 'corpuscular' (atomic) physics and the physiologists' hypothetical schematization of the brain as a single entity.

> *The 'entire brain-process' is not a physical fact at all.* It is the appearance to an onlooking mind of a multitude of physical facts. 'Entire brain' is nothing but our name for the way in which a million of molecules arranged in certain positions may affect our sense. On the principles of the corpuscular or mechanical philosophy, the only realities are the separate molecules, or at most the cells. Their aggregation into a 'brain' is a fiction of popular speech. Such a fiction cannot serve as the objectively real counterpart to any psychic state whatever. (PP I:178)

Twenty years later, in 1909's *Some Problems of Philosophy*, he continued to emphasize the *lack* of correlation between experience and anything physical.

> So far as physical nature goes few of us experience any temptation to postulate real novelty. The notion of eternal elements and their mixture serves us in so many ways, that we adopt unhesitatingly the theory that primordial being is inalterable in its attributes as well as in its quantity, and that the laws by which we describe its habits are uniform in the strictest mathematical sense. These are the absolute conceptual foundations, we think, spread beneath the surface of perceptual variety. It is when we come to human lives, that our point of view changes. It is hard to imagine that 'really' our own subjective experiences are only molecular arrangements, even though the molecules be conceived as beings of a psychic kind. A material fact may indeed be different from what we feel it to be, but what sense is there in saying that a feeling, which has no other nature than to be felt, is not as it *is* felt? Psychologically considered, our experiences resist conceptual reduction, and our fields of consciousness, taken simply as such, remain just what they appear, even though facts of a molecular order should prove to be the signals of the appearance. Biography is the concrete form in which all that is is immediately given; the perceptual flux is the authentic stuff of each of our biographies, and yields a perfect effervescence of novelty all the time. . . . (*Writings* II:1058-59)

Thirdly, the case for 'the brain as source' got worse during the twentieth century. Electron microscopes (common-sensically speaking) have yielded evidence that the billions of neuronal cells are separated by gaps called "synapses." Then modern physics, as Eddington noted, undermined the idea of neurons as unified entities. Even if matter or physical bodies exist, it/they consist of discrete subatomic particles.

315

What Alternatives Are There to the Brain? Here, then, is our challenge. Naïve realism leads to the idea that our brains cause our streams of consciousness. But 'science' and 'critical philosophy' lead to the further conclusion that no brains as such exist, only groups of sense-qualities and (at best) subatoms. How then do we explain our ever-fresh experience, in which alone we find the desire to explain our ever-fresh stream of experience? More to the point, how can we account for the fact that we have these questioning thoughts? Can our brain be telling us that it does not exist? We look again at the question. We want to answer it. We start listing the possible answers. But where do the contradictory answers come from?

> . . . The end is defined beforehand in most cases only as a general direction, along which all sorts of novelties and surprises lie in wait. These words I write even now surprise me; yet I adopt them as effects of my scriptorial causality. Their being 'contained' means only their harmony and continuity with my general aim. They 'fill the bill' and I accept them, but the exact shape of them seems determined by something outside of my explicit will. (*Writings* II:1091)

"Something outside of my explicit will." James's suggestions about this 'something' varied. In his common-sense moments, he spoke of external objects causing an idea, as when he spoke of the clock creating our image of the clock by means of the processes we call sensation. Other times, he suggested that at least our common-sense philosophy is inherited from our ancestors. Occasionally, he invoked 'spontaneous' or 'random' mutations in the functioning of the brain as the cause of certain ideas. (John Dewey liked this third answer.) In many places, he speculated about each of us possessing a subliminal self as well as a self-conscious self.

But James also referred frequently to 'higher' selves or minds. It is time to explore that option.

"Higher Mind(s)" was James' Other Most-Referred-to Answer. A 'higher minds' theory was one which James referred to many times during his long writing and lecturing career. It needs only some fuller development for it to be seen as a viable explanation for our streams of consciousness. Since the idea played a large role in guiding the composition of his final lecture series, the 1908 *Pluralistic Universe* series, it is appropriate to begin with what he said then:

In spite of rationalism's disdain for the particular, the personal, and the unwholesome, the drift of all the evidence we have seems to me to sweep us very strongly towards the belief in some form of superhuman life with which we may, unknown to ourselves, be co-conscious. We may be in the universe as dogs and cats are in our libraries, seeing the books and hearing the conversation, but having no inkling of the meaning of it all. The intellectualist objections to this fall away when the authority of intellectualist logic is undermined by criticism, and then the positive empirical evidence remains. The analogies with ordinary psychology and with the facts of pathology, with those of psychical research, so called, and with those of religious experience . . . (*Writings* II:770-71)

Other minds greater than ours. James believed his faith in bodiless minds was true, which explains why he attended seances to see whether merely human minds survived death. More than that, however, James sought evidence for beings with mentality superior to ours, and it was in reports of peak religious experiences, viz., mystical experiences, that he felt he had found the best evidence that some of our experience does not come from our brain.

Here we must be bold, because James was consistently vague and often inconsistent. Recall the ideas he expressed in his Ingersoll lecture, "Human Immortality: Two Supposed Objections to the Doctrine." There, he described two ways of interpreting the role of the brain, viz., either as productive or transmissive. The second, transmissive, suggestion relates to an outside source of knowledge.

[. . .] On the production-theory one does not see from what sensations such odd bits of knowledge are produced. On the transmission-theory, they don't have to be 'produced,'—they exist ready-made in the transcendental world, and all that is needed is an abnormal lowering of the brain-threshold to let them through. In cases of conversion, in providential leadings, sudden mental healings, etc., it seems to the subjects themselves of the experience as if a power from without, quite different from the ordinary action of the senses or of the sense-led mind, came into their life, as if the latter suddenly opened into that greater life in which it has its source. The word 'influx,' used in Swedenborgian circles, well describes this impression of new insight, or new willingness, sweeping over us like a tide. All such experiences, quite paradoxical and meaningless on the production-theory, fall very naturally into place on the other theory. We need only suppose the continuity of our consciousness with a mother-sea, to allow for exceptional waves occasionally pouring over the dam. Of course the causes of these odd lowerings of the brain's threshold still remain a mystery on any terms. (*Human Immortality*:26-7; *Writings* I:1118-19)

The "mother sea" recalls a metaphor James used when he was inclined to believe that we may be 'in' God as in some medium which links us the way the sea links islands or the earth links the deep-rooted forest trees. To repeat, he rarely ventures far beyond metaphors, but the picture of an alternative to 'the brain as source' is clear. Here is a later but similar passage from the concluding *Pluralistic Universe* lecture:

Thus does foreignness get banished from our world, and far more so when we take the system of it pluralistically. We are indeed internal parts of God and not external creations, on any possible reading of the panpsychic system. Yet because God is not the absolute, but is himself a part when the system is conceived pluralistically, his functions can be taken as not wholly dissimilar to those of the other smaller parts,—as similar to our functions consequently. (*Writings* II:774-75)

An Even More Explicit Version. As Myers notes, James worked hard on Chapter XXI, "The Perception of Reality," of *The Principles*. (See Myers:507-09, n.14.). He published an earlier version of the chapter separately in 1889 under the title of "The Psychology of Belief." In a passage found in both the original version and in the revised version, James offered one third of the theory needed to fill the "Whence come our streams of consciousness?" gap in the quintalist view. As he made clear, James did not commit himself to the theory. He only described a hypothesis which—if true—would gratify both our intellectual and our emotional needs.

[. . .] It is undeniably true that materialistic, or so-called 'scientific,' conceptions of the universe have so far gratified the purely intellectual interests more than the more sentimental conceptions have. But, on the other hand, as already remarked, they leave the emotional and active interests cold. *The perfect object of belief would be a God or 'Soul of the World,' represented both optimistically and moralistically (if such a combination could be), and withal so definitely conceived as to show us why our phenomenal experiences should be sent to us by Him in just the very way in which they come.* All Science and all History would thus be accounted for in the deepest and simplest fashion. The very room in which I sit, its sensible walls and floor, and the feeling the air and fire within it give me, no less than the 'scientific' conceptions which I am urged to frame concerning the mode of existence of all these phenomena when my back is turned, would then all be corroborated, not de-realised, by the ultimate principle of my belief. The World-soul sends me just those phenomena in order that

I may react upon them; and among the reactions is the intellectual one of spinning these conceptions. What is beyond the crude experiences is not an *alternative* to them, but something that *means* them for me here and now. It is safe to say that, if ever such a system is satisfactorily excogitated, mankind will drop all other systems and cling to that one alone as real. Meanwhile the other systems co-exist with the attempts at that one, and, all being alike fragmentary, each has its little audience and day. (PP II:317; see also *Writings* I:1054-55)

This is almost perfect. But only almost. James suggests that the Higher Mind or Soul sends us phenomena, but leaves it to us to 'spin the conceptions' needed to explain the phenomena.

The second third of the needed theory is a recognition that we do not spin the conceptions. 'Thought simply comes.' Thoughts are proposed to us. Along with our sense-data and images 'of' earlier sense-data, the Higher Mind also begins at an early point in our learning career to send us thoughts, among which are those which we call 'our common-sense interpretations of the sense-data.' In fact, the same Agent creates conflicting thoughts for us which open our minds to 'science' and to the rival worldviews collectively referred to as 'critical philosophy.' Finally, the Higher Mind proposes not only our 'rational' thoughts, but also all "the silly fancies, the grotesque suppositions, the utterly irrelevant reflections" which James mentioned in his inspired 'great law of habit itself' passage. (PP I:552)

If we put all of those thoughts together, we find we are now free to explore a novel thesis which anyone can understand who is able to read James's works with a basic amount of comprehension. In its most condensed form, that thesis would hold that every tiniest facet of our three-tributaried river of conscious experience is presented directly by the Higher Mind (or Minds) to which James made occasional references. By supplying us, not only with sense-data and images, but also with conflicting or contradictory beliefs, the Beyond-Human Mind(s) also leave us free to choose or react by assenting, dissenting, or suspending judgment.

This gives us two thirds of what is needed to adequately and truly account for our experience.

Choosing Thoughts that are True. The last third of what we need is a clearer idea about evidence for what is true. Why do we regard anything—sense-data, logical consistency, consensus—as proof or evidence? This need, too, is met by one of James's best-known theories, one which he incorporated into the title of an early lecture-article, "The Sentiment of Rationality." A major theme of that essay and of his famous "Will to Believe" lecture-article is that *our passional nature* is relevant to our efforts to distinguish what is true from what is false.

Suppose that our belief-related feelings, passions, sentiments, etc., are part of a rational plan of the superhuman mind(s) to leave us free but not clueless. We already know that, for every affirmation, there is a contradiction. That is, our belief-options are almost limitless. But the thoughts which are proposed to us often come with feelings attached. The presentation of thoughts about possible facts which are contrary to long-standing, deeply-ingrained thought-habits tends to evoke feelings of annoyance, etc., while every thought of a new fact which supports those same old thought-habits tends to evoke a feeling of satisfaction. Recall what James wrote shortly before his death:

> [. . .] As I now write, I am in one of these activity situations. I 'strive' after words, which I only half prefigure, but which, when they shall have come, must satisfactorily complete the nascent sense I have of what they ought to be. The words are to run out of my pen, which I find that my hand actuates so obediently to desire that I am hardly conscious either of resistance or of effort. Some of the words come wrong, and then I feel a resistance, not muscular but mental, which instigates a new instalment of my activity, accompanied by more or less feeling of exertion. If the resistance were to my muscles, the exertion would contain an element of strain or squeeze which is less present where the resistance is only mental. If it proves considerable in either kind I may leave off trying to overcome it; or, on the other hand, I may sustain my effort till I have succeeded in my aim. (*Writings* II:1090)

Correlations between thoughts and feelings are complex. The Source does not operate in an ahistorical vacuum. Thoughts and feelings are proposed in ways that generally conform to the great law of habit*, according to which 'twenty experiences make us recall a thing better and long indulgence in error makes right thinking almost impossible' (PP I:552). James, in other words, would feel satisfactions and resistances vis-à-vis proposed thoughts which would be quite different from those which, say, Friedrich Nietzsche would feel vis-à-vis similar thoughts. (*James explored the topic of long-established thought-habits quite often. He went so far as to coin a phrase for the way in which each of us becomes 'wedded' quite early to certain belief-habits. The phrase was "old fogyism." James included it in the index for both *The Principles* and *Briefer Course*. His most humorous presentation of old fogyism is found in Chapter 14 of *Talks to Teachers*.)

That James had a theory about sentiment vis-à-vis our judgments, a theory that fits the need for a theory about evidence with almost uncanny perfection, together with his belated recognition of common sense, coupled with his radical-empiricist principle that everything we have direct access to—thoughts which do or do not meet the criterion of logical consistency, sense-data which constitute 'sense evidence,' even the things we call 'gut feelings,' 'eureka-type elation,' 'cognitive dissonance,' and 'subjective certainty'—is intrapsychic . . . all of this makes us feel (!) that such a confluence cannot be just a freak coincidence but points to the truth.

Still, we wonder. Does the 'explanation' really explain? Even if we were to accept James's view that there is a mind higher than ours, and even if that mind is the source of the effervescent novelty of our streams of consciousness, we are left completely in the dark as to how a mind or minds external to ours can create such a thing.

We Cannot See Causality; We *Can* Understand Thoughts 'About' It. We need a four-element model or picture to think about thinking and thought. First comes an *agent*, a thinker. Thinkers *act*, namely, they think. Thinking is understanding, and understanding has an *object*. Thinkers understand thoughts. Understood thoughts, which are objects of understanding, are about things which exist or do not exist. Those 'things' are a *subsidiary* type of object, in the pocket, as it were, of the *basic* objects of understanding, that is, the understood thoughts. This means that the phrase, "thought-objects," is ambiguous, and must always be further analyzed.

As James warned, we are tempted to water down such ideas (not names) as "think," by substituting such 'physical' metaphors as "grasp," "apprehend," etc., which metaphors are or conjure concrete images. (See MEN:286-87) True, trying to picture whatever it is we are trying to 'know better' is psychologically unavoidable. But it is also a trap. The only way to avoid falling into it is to detect the image-substitute and avoid using it as 'a final analysis.' The *final* analysis must always be "We think," "We understand thoughts that come to us," etc.

Why final? Because it is the only way that allows us to focus on whether or not the thoughts in question are logically consistent and whether they account for the available evidence, i.e., all three parts of our tri-partite stream of consciousness.

Again, pictures or images are not thoughts. This makes it vitally important, when asking "What is the source of the thoughts that come to me?", to avoid trying to picture the source-agent's causing-act. The causing in question cannot be seen, but thoughts 'about' it can be understood. (E.g., the thought-meaning of the preceding sentence cannot be seen, but the thought *that* causing cannot be seen can be grasped.)

In trying to weave James's history-making insight 'about' thought into a successful grand unifying theory that includes an insight 'about' thought's cause, our obstacle will always be the old 'looking' approach to understanding causation, the approach that invariably leads to 'mechanical' explanations. (James blasted Hume's analysis of "cause" in Chapter XII of *Some Problems*.) The fact that no one can watch a material brain producing immaterial sense-data was used by Berkeley to discard the idea that bodies produce ideas. Even when we try to picture—imagine—a deity 'creating' something, whether a garden, a sense-datum, or a thought, that effort is doomed from the start. Picturing a non-pictureable act of an invisible agent creating an invisible object, viz., an unpictureable thought, is trebly impossible.

A perfect illustration of the difference between a mechanical and a non-mechanical approach to causation is the now-dominant, 'scientific' approach to seeing. When expert neuroscientists today think about seeing, they instantly picture a long chain of cause-effect happenings. Galaxy-stars radiate light, light travels, light arrives and interacts with apples and other bodies, some frequencies are absorbed and the rest reflected, reflected light travels to eyes to activate optic nerves, optic nerves send 'signals' to the brain to activate its neurons to secrete and absorb neurotransmitters, etc. One long-ago colleague, 'backed into a corner' about this analysis of "seeing," claimed that "see" is shorthand for the entire process. Oh, sure. It takes million of years to see a distant galaxy. It took Ian Shelton 160,000 years to see Supernova 1987A!

Visual *experience* is none of those things. Instead of immediately conjuring an action-video of never-seen, inferred, causal mechanisms, we must first get a clear fix on what needs to be explained. That is, before trying to guess what causes the effects—TVFs—that constitute the objects of our visual experience, we must first notice the color-effects themselves. Then we should notice our thoughts: *that* we understand the thought *that* color fields appear and *that* we are aware of them. After learning the various rival-theory explanations (thoughts), we can confront them all with the *experienced, not-inferred* colors. We then eliminate the theories that do not 'fit,' and assent to the victorious survivor of the process of elimination.

In short, the desire to have pictures of acts we cannot picture or visualize is a temptation that must be resisted. Creating theories, like understanding the created theories, is not a visible process that can be mentally visualized. In these cases a theory which offers explanations that we *can* picture or visualize is evidence that such a theory is the wrong one. Such is the case with creating and understanding thoughts. This should be obvious, once we have grasped James's momentous discovery of partless thoughts.

What, then, is the *central* fact to be causally explained? Not our experience of sense-data and memory-images, but our understanding of thoughts. Here is *the ultimate self-reflexive thought*: "I understand the thought *that* I understand the thoughts that come to me." If each of us is an arbiter seeming to 'sit aloft' in the mind and to select which thoughts to accept as permanent, that means that each reader is his or her own judge and jury of one charged with answering this question: "Aren't you certain *that* you understand the thoughts coming to you?"

If anyone *doesn't* understand these thoughts, how can they decide *that* this or that thought is true or false?

A New Model: 'Things Are Told to Us' About What is Unexperienced. Instead of using visual images to *picture* the creation of thoughts, we can explore an alternative, auditory model: *Things are told to us.*

Things are told to us.

Understanding a thought is not putting a few concepts together and looking at the result. It is rather like having something told to us. Chapter I of *William James on Common Sense* was constructed around the ancient appearance-vs-reality distinction. There is a difference between the way things seem and the way they are. It seems that 'things are told to us,' but in fact we only hear sounds which, we later say (with Plato, Augustine, and Locke), activate our associative-memory processes. But still, it will always continue to seem that the thoughts that 'come to us' while others speak are coming *from* them, not our memory.

Apply that to reading. As we scan the rows and rows of tiny black marks, a stream of thoughts comes to us. But the thoughts obviously do not come from any author who is dead (James) or a living one occupied with other things than creating our thoughts. (Is it still August 30, 2008?)

Using half of that appearance-vs-reality distinction, we now hypothesize that, for instance, as we read (are you noticing?), *'things are being told to us' by the higher mind or minds James wrote about.* Our ultimate freedom with regard to what we are told is always the one James, almost obsessively, emphasized, namely, our will-to-believe: "My first act of free will shall be to believe in free will."

A Solution to "How Can Anyone Know That?", with 'that' referring to what exists out beyond the perimeter of our present-moment stream of consciousness. The solution begins with common sense. "Since I wasn't alive when Socrates was on trial, how can I know anything about it?" Or, "Since I cannot see your thoughts, how can I know what you are thinking?" Except when we are in the mood for second thoughts, we accept the 'words' of Plato's *Apology* for Socrates' trial, and others' words for what thoughts they are having, at least the ones we are willing to pay a penny for. When others' words tell us things we did not know, it is not uncommon to call those things "revelations."

Then we make the transfer. We may not have been present at the Big Bang or the origin of life or the fall of Jericho, but higher minds than ours may have been. We may not be able to see *others' present thoughts*, but higher minds than ours may be able to reveal them to us, especially if they are themselves the sources of those others' thoughts!

Thoughts about such matters can clearly 'come to us' while we read, else no reader could later write a paragraph such as this and no other reader could understand it. That last thought is the one for whose truth we have the best evidence of all. Once more, the generalizing thought for which we have the best and most direct evidence is *that* thoughts 'come to us' and we understand them.

We do not understand essences. We do not understand people. We do not understand acts. We do not understand events or processes. We do not understand how things do what they do. *We understand thoughts.* These thoughts which we understand are what need to be explained. If they come from any source at all, that source is as unseen as the source of our color-fields. Theories or thoughts about that source, e.g., sources that are persons who 'tell,' may be true and they may be false.

But we can understand them . . ., that is, the thoughts that come to us.

5. Mentality and Morality

'Mentality' and Purpose. Any reference to higher minds involves the notion of mentality. ("Mentality" is derived from the Latin term "mens," which is translated into English as "mind.") For that reason, a brief look at James's thoughts on the subject of minds and mentality is in order.

The preceding chapter discussed some of the basic issues James wrestled with while he was writing his 1890 masterpiece. It took him twelve years to fulfill his 1878 promise to the publisher, Henry Holt, to write a college textbook on the new 'scientific' or 'empirical' psychology. If we ponder what must have gone on in his mind during those twelve years, it helps to understand the way he finally decided to describe the 'scope of psychology' in Chapter I of *The Principles*.

"Psychology is the Science of Mental Life, both of its phenomena and their conditions" is the first line of that first chapter. What follows next are James's reasons for refusing to follow i) the medieval psychologists' science of mental life (they merely embellished the five-concept model proposed by Aristotle) or ii) the more recent idea-combining model proposed by Locke and his followers.

James then begins the task of conveying his own idea of what an experience-based science of mental life should focus on. He does it by contrasting the behavior of iron filings and bubbles to the behavior of frogs. What he draws from the contrast gives him his definition of "mentality":

> *The pursuance of future ends and the choice of means for their attainment are thus the mark and criterion of the presence of mentality* in a phenomenon. We all use this test to discriminate between an intelligent and a mechanical performance. We impute no mentality to sticks and stones, because they never seem to move for *the sake of* anything, but always when pushed, and then indifferently and with no sign of choice. So we unhesitatingly call them senseless. (PP I:8)

In the very next paragraph after writing this, James linked that notion of 'mentality' to purpose. (What he wrote is as worth reflecting on today as James thought it was in 1890.)

> Just so we form our decision upon the deepest of all philosophic problems: Is the Kosmos an expression of intelligence rational in its inward nature, or a brute external fact pure and simple? If we find ourselves, in contemplating it, unable to banish the impression that it is a realm of final purposes, that it exists for the sake of something, we place intelligence at the heart of it and have a religion. If, on the contrary, in surveying its irremediable flux, we can think of the present only as so much mere mechanical sprouting from the past, occurring with no reference to the future, we are atheists and materialists. (PP I:8)

The Principles was published in 1890. Ten years earlier, in "The Sentiment of Rationality" previously referred to, he had expressed the same conviction.

> Let us now turn to the radical question of life—the question whether this be at bottom a moral or unmoral universe—and see whether the method of faith may legitimately have a place there. It is really the question of materialism. Is the world a simple brute actuality, an existence *de facto* about which the deepest thing that can be said is that it happens so to be; or is the judgment of *better* or *worse*, of *ought*, as intimately pertinent to phenomena as the simple judgment *is* or *is not*? (WB:103; *Writings* I:533)

If 'mentality' is central to James's view of the world because it

326

is central to his ideas about morality, then we must be certain our understanding of mentality is clear. In what remains of this third and most important chapter about James's best thoughts about thought, then, the meaning of "mentality" in relation to ends and means will be further—but briefly—explored.

First of all, there is no conscious planning, no deliberate ends-and-means strategizing, without thought. But there can be no full grasp of the complexity of conscious, deliberate planning without a full grasp of the non-existence of any but present, ongoing thoughts. Early on, there is i) only a present plan and a present anticipation of future means; later on, ii) only a present memory of early planning, experience of current means-taking, present expectancy of more to come; finally, iii) only an experience of the goal attained, coupled with memories of earlier plans and efforts.

In short, there is no point in discussing whether or not there is thought 'behind' this universe of ours—and certainly no point in discussing whether the agent doing the cosmic thinking is our thought-provider—unless we are clear on what we mean by "thought" on both a human and a cosmic scale.

Planned = Deliberate. As any competent juror must clearly understand, there is a great difference between saying some being gives evidence of being conscious and some being gives evidence of being able to pursue foreseen future ends and to deliberately choose the means for reaching them. The latter may be impossible without being conscious, but being conscious is possible without the latter. Any juror who did not understand that distinction tacitly but precisely would not be competent to serve in a trial where the central issue is whether a victim's death was a *deliberate* murder (the conclusion or verdict the prosecuting attorney will construct syllogisms to prove) or an *unintended* accident which led to a fatal accident (as the defense attorney will create syllogisms to prove).

To understand even more clearly the distinction between mere consciousness and being able consciously to pursue ends or goals, i.e., between merely being awake and having wide-awake reasons for our acts, it helps to recall the difference between awareness of sense-data and images, on the one hand, and understanding thoughts, on the other. Newborn infants are conscious, but we do not hold them responsible for their actions. What they do, they do not do deliberately. Some 'schools' of moral and ethical theory hold that humans are not capable of moral right and wrong until they have i) reached 'the age of reason,' i.e., become knowledgeable enough to think about future ends and to act in view of them, and ii) acquired a 'sense' that some ends and means are right and others wrong.

Moreover, there are degrees of knowledge. We do not judge adolescents to be as morally praise- or blame-worthy as adults who are older and more knowledgeable. No one can understand such matters who is incapable of at least a tacit grasp of the different quantities of intelligence, experience, knowledge, and strength of will which we expect from humans whose ages and natural abilities differ widely. Jurors who are required to understand legal distinctions between aggravated assault, manslaughter, murder in the second and first degree, and so on, must be equipped with just such a grasp. This is common sense.

Aristotle held that only humans have reason. But ever since Darwin pulled together a mass of alleged facts—all based on pre-scientific naïve realism—to argue that every contemporary species of living thing is a descendent of primitive life forms which, in turn, 'evolved from' inanimate matter, the thinkers James referred to as atheists and materialists have looked for signs of mind in non-human organisms. Today, there are lengthy discussions of what is referred to as "artificial intelligence," allegedly found in the functioning of computers. By adding James's notion that we must inquire into mentality on a cosmic scale, we can see that the idea of mentality cuts across everything, from the tiniest atom and its behavior all the way up to the universe as a whole and the processes displayed in it. The challenge is to clarify our original common-sense notions on these matters and then to not lose sight of them while reexamining other youthful convictions or while weighing the merits of rival systems offered as better explanations of the universe than 'mere' common sense.

The Turing Test. In his classic, 1950 essay, "Computing Machines and Intelligence," Alan Turing proposed a test which he thought would be relevant to the question, "Can a machine duplicate what we call 'thinking' when humans do it?" Suppose all we have as evidence for understanding the meaning of "thinking" and of "mentality"—or the lack of it—is our experience of own stream of consciousness, and that all we have as evidence for mentality in anything else is teletype, whereby we can 'send' questions and 'receive' printed answers. Could we tell, just from words, whether their unseen source was human or only what we now call a 'computer'? Turing's proposal has become famous as the Turing Test. He explained his own position as follows:

> It will simplify matters for the reader if I explain first my own beliefs in the matter. Consider first the more accurate form of the question. I believe that in about fifty years' time it will be possible to program computers, with a storage capacity of about 10^9, to make them play the imitation game so well that an average interrogator will not have more than 70 per cent chance of making the right identification after five minutes of questioning. The original question, "Can machines think?" I believe to be too meaningless to deserve discussion. Nevertheless I believe that at the end of the century the use of words and general educated opinion will have altered so much that one will be able to speak of machines thinking without expecting to be contradicted. (*Op. cit.,* sec.6)

Suppose that, in order to clarify James's idea of mentality in relation to 'a passing thought,' we use James's works in place of typed answers to typed questions. Can anyone tell whether, to produce those works, there had to have been thoughts about ends/goals, plus selections from ever-changing menus of optional means, which selections were made with an eye on earlier-chosen ends/goals? Or was the composition of James's works done without any thought 'about' ends and means? 'Ends' and 'means' denote two theoretical fictions constructed to help us keep clear about different facets of our complex streams of thought, much the way 'true' and 'false' are constructs to help discriminate thoughts which give us insight into what exists, what existents do, and why, from thoughts which do not. In fact, even 'truth' and 'proof' signify mental constructs created to help us discriminate alleged relations of thoughts to reality from the conscious factors we rely on to decide which thoughts have the desired relations to reality and which do not.

As noted earlier, the constructs signified by 'end' and 'means' necessarily involve the theoretical fictions of time and its 'parts,' namely, past, present, and future. The scholastics, whom James regarded as fairly authoritative vis-à-vis the explicitation of many or most tacit presuppositions of our early common-sense philosophy, incorporated the notions of time into their theorizing about ends and means. The end, they noted, is first time-wise in relation to intention or planning but last time-wise in actual attainment or execution. Means, on the other hand, are time-wise first in execution and time-wise last in intention or planning. Quite simply, when a thought comes to us about something desirable but not instantly attainable, we have a choice: shall we try to obtain it or shall we forget it? If we elect to go for it, we must then give some thought to how we can obtain it. Having selected a course of steps which must be taken in order to achieve our end some time in the future, we begin by actually taking the first step. The steps to the goal are intermediate—time-wise they come between the goal-choice and the goal-achievement—and so we call them 'mediums' which we shorten to 'means.' But, the important thing is that, since there is never a past thought, only a present memory incorporated into a present, ongoing thought, and since there is never a future thought, but only a present anticipation integrated with the present memory into a present, ongoing thought, even the notion of human 'mentality' as James described it requires a god-like human agent able to both 'rise above' time in order to 'see' past, present, and future 'in' a single, ever-changing thought as well as to be 'in' the present which, if any part of time existed, would be the only real, non-imaginary one.

Once we analyse and clarify our common-sense views, we are ready to apply the Turing Test to James's works. Is there evidence of mentality in James's works or was the 'performance,' i.e., the inscribing of hundreds of pages of ink marks, done 'not for the sake of anything,' but only 'indifferently and with no sign of choice'? In fact, we need only *The Principles of Psychology* for our test. In June, 1878, James signed a contract with Henry Holt and Company. The publisher wanted the text in about a year, James replied that he could hardly do it in less than two years, then he took nearly twelve years to actually finish. But on May 18, 1890, he wrote to Alice "The job is done! All but some paging and half a dozen little footnotes, the work is completed, and I see it as a unit" (Letters I:295). Two years later, James replied in the *Briefer Course*'s preface to critics who insisted that the order of *The Principles*' twenty eight chapters was "planless and unnatural." The order of those chapters, he wrote, was definitely not planless, "for I deliberately followed what seemed to me a good pedagogic order, in proceeding from the more concrete mental aspects with which we are best acquainted to the so-called elements which we naturally come to know later" (PBC:9; Writings I:3-4). The Turing Test asks us now to decide what really took place back in the last quarter of the nineteenth century.

After converting or translating the naïve-realist account into more accurate quintalist terms, the Turing Test asks no more than a decision as to whether James had some vague notion of what he wanted to accomplish and was able to constantly evaluate the 'words' coming from his pen in light of what he had earlier decided to accomplish and whether he could have known on May 18, 1890, that what he had willingly committed himself to almost twelve years earlier had— as a result of hours upon hours of thinking and 'writing'—actually been brought into existence. Either there was a consciously intelligent agent named "William James" whose experiences and decisions were as described, or there was not. James dealt with the basic issues behind the Turing-Test in Chapter V of *The Principles*, appropriately named "The Automaton Theory." Ultimately, he confessed, it was both common sense and a realization that the issues cannot be decided on 'positivist' principles that led him to insist that the theory that pure 'mechanical' principles could explain such phenomena as Shakespeare's plays or (we can add) Beethoven's scores was naïve.

In other words, it must be emphasized that the Turing Test, whether applied to 'words' teletyped from an 'anonymous' source or to the 'words' of James's *Principles* or to the entire ensemble of things and doings shorthanded by "cosmos," involves entire worldviews, so-called incommensurable philosophies, or rival unifying theories. Turing's presentation is rife with presuppositions which he either had not critically examined or had no desire to argue for. That sort of approach does not measure up to James's call for being either "impartially *naïf* or impartially critical" (PP I:137). It is far too unsophisticated for this third millennium.

Specifically. The best current view of physical bodies is that *there are no computers*, just as there are no brains or hands or pens or pieces of paper. Literally speaking, there are no 'James's Works,' 'Shakespeare's plays,' or 'Beethoven symphonies.' At most there may be swarming sub-atomic bodies whose motions are so complex that to describe them we need all the relevant 'laws' of physics and chemistry. Whoever believes <u>that</u> there is a conscious agent lurking among those swarming subatoms we collectively refer to as "a computer," and <u>that</u> that conscious agent has 'passing thoughts' which include complex memories of the past and complex thoughts about what is still to be written, is as free to assent to those thoughts as others are free to believe there are ghosts inhabiting human body-machines. In like manner, whoever believes <u>that</u> there is a sub-conscious agent lurking among the discrete subatoms collectively referred to as her or his "brain" and <u>that</u> that sub-conscious or un-conscious agent is 'sending up' into her or his conscious mind all of the complex, quasi-time-spanning thoughts—which include the contradictory thought-options <u>that</u> brain-agents exist and <u>that</u> brain-agents do not exist, etc.—is as free to believe that as others are to believe that society and language really exist and that we get thoughts from society's words rather than from our individual brains or higher minds.

To repeat, we deal here with decisions about entire belief-systems, not isolated claims. (A note. If a goal, presently existing in intention only, comes to fruition, these issues about sources and higher minds will be treated more fully in a third and final volume. It will conclude the Jamesian, quintalist system whose first parts are *William James on Common Sense* and this present volume.)

Honest Arbiters of What Is True. Among the common-sense convictions upon which these recastings of James's ideas are based is the conviction that all of us are born quite ignorant or lacking in knowledge. Among the things we learn and take for granted in our youthful years is the notion that some humans are far smarter or more knowledgeable than we and that we get much of our information from them. We 'instinctively' come to regard them as 'authorities' or 'experts.' If we grow up among people said to constitute a 'first-world' country, we are likely to change our ideas about which other persons deserve to be called authorities or experts. At first it is our parents, then we learn that they are not as smart as certain other experts, and so on. And, once we have undergone the kind of intellectual conversion discussed earlier in this chapter, whole roster-changes are likely to follow. Inevitably, though, if we continue learning the way we need to if we are to play our role in this new millennium, we will realize that—in James's words—each of us is a presiding arbiter or judge with respect to the truth of our own beliefs, even our own beliefs about who are the expert authorities on this and who are the expert authorities on that.

That, at least, is the hope. Not everyone does continue learning the way they need to. Not even when they have been told of their personal responsibility for trying to learn what is true lest, when they are regarded by the young as expert authorities, they unwittingly pass on error rather than truth. At what point does good-faith ignorance evolve into bad-faith? James, in his inspired great-law-of-habit paragraph, said that "the laws of the arbiter, of the *cogitandum*, of what we ought to think, are to the former [the laws of our actual thinking] as the laws of ethics are to those of history" (PP I:552-53). What *ought* we to believe? With that 'ought,' James joins Clifford in declaring that each of us—if we are ethical—ought to seek and assent to the truth.

Many 'presiding arbiters' do not. In some of his diatribes against those whom he accused of peddling nihilism, Nietzsche accused upholders of 'Christian' ethics of lying when they preached that, if there are no eternal values, then there are no temporal ones either. Nietzsche insisted, rightly, that such a claim is as absurd as saying there is no point to living today if we cannot also live tomorrow. If one of the laws of ethics is to not lie, then we may ask at what point absurdly erroneous thinking, stubbornly clung to, becomes lying.

Lying = Double Thinking. Nietzsche was not fond of Kant. He was particularly un-fond of Kant's thesis about the categorical imperative. Yet one of the things Kant insisted on was honesty. The opposite of honesty, as every child who has heard and understood the story of George Washington and the cherry tree knows, is lying. Whether lying is moral or immoral, it requires more intellectual effort—more swift thinking—than is required by simple honesty. In the same way that enkowntering 'werds' which are spelled in unfamiliar ways requires second thinking, lying to someone requires, first, that we hold in mind both what we believe is true but do not want that person to know and what we believe is false and do want the other to think and, then, that we knowingly choose to say words which we hope will make the other think what we think is false and to not say words which we fear would make the other learn what we think is true. On the contrary, when it does not occur to us to lie, we un-self-consciously utter the first words that come to us to express the thought being furnished by an unseen source when we are asked a question, at least if the thought is about something we can be expected to know.

Telling the truth or being honest, however, is not synonymous with knowing the truth. This interpreter of James's works is convinced James made mistakes and held on tightly to certain erroneous beliefs. But, has anyone ever accused James of lying in any of his lectures, articles, or books? Even if he did not have entirely consistent notions about the meaning of "true thought," and even if some of his notions of 'true thought' were false thoughts, all of the evidence points to the conclusion that James was honest and honestly wanted to find and express the truth. If, in any of his works, he used words to express error, it was unwittingly or nondeliberately.

It was mentioned above that introducing James's belief in a higher mind or minds would help to understand the main topic of this chapter, the full glory of a passing thought. The chief error of those who attribute 'reason' to beasts and 'intelligence' to computers is not so much their faulty ideas of beasts and computers but their lack of self-understanding. Able to think about such complexities as bestial behavior and electron racetracks, they are unable to grasp the complexity of the instant-by-instant ongoing thoughts whereby they think about those other complexities. How many fully appreciate what it takes to consciously and intelligently make a mistake or to deliberately deceive? Whoever has not understood the full depth of James's thought, from atoms and brains to thoughts and minds, will never grasp the full glory of a mature human's thought. Whoever has not grasped that, will never be able to play the 'Turing Test' game so important for understanding the meaning or purpose of the Kosmos.

Does the 'Higher Mind' Lie? If, however, all of our thoughts—including those we collectively refer to as our early, common-sense philosophy—are from a more-than-humanly-intelligent agent, and if that agent knows that part of our naïve-realist beliefs are false, then the moral law of trying always to tell the truth as we know it demands an honest admission that the deity or deities lie to us. This runs wholly against the tradition that God can neither deceive nor be deceived. When Descartes realized that many of his growing-up beliefs were false, he expended much thought and effort to explaining that those errors should not be attributed to God who is all-good but to his own hasty judgment, a lack of discretion concerning which ideas he should consent to. But when the thoughts proposed are not only false but not accompanied by any warning of their falsity, then—like Descartes—we have no resources for guarding against acquiescing in the deception. As well as revealing what is true, the god or gods deliberately deceive us. The god or gods literally lie.

James claimed that the 'Kosmos' is "an expression of intelligence rational in its inward nature," adding that the 'mentality' which is a feature of that intelligence is to be described as "the pursuance of future ends and the choice of means for their attainment" (PP I:8). Before we finally accept the hypothesis that the means include the deliberate presentation to us of false thoughts as well as true ones, we must ask what is the end or goal of such deception and whether lying can ever be moral. Or are those thinkers right who claim that the existence of so much evil in the world, part of which is a massive amount of ignorance and false beliefs, is more than enough evidence to prove there is no God?

Or are those thinkers too quick to call every deliberate deception "evil"? Are there, as 'literature experts' claim, various 'levels' in every 'text'? Are Aesop's fables lies? Only someone who takes Aesop to be claiming that a fox literally walked away from unattainable grapes muttering "They were probably sour anyway" or that a donkey literally put its hooves on the dinner table will be deceived. Are Jesus' parables deliberate deceptions? Taken literally, they are false, but what educated person takes them literally? Are geometers' pretenses, that dimensional lines of varying lengths all have the identically infinite number of dimensionless points or that curves are really tiny straight lines, wicked distortions of the truth? Who but the vast majority of students and probably not a few teachers take such patent fictions as literally true?

Should we side with Descartes who felt that the infinite goodness of God made it logically repulsive to believe that divine deception rather than human impatience is behind naïve-realist human thinking about the physical world? Or should we adopt a stance similar to Bacon's and conclude that God gave us the wherewithal needed to play a brilliantly conceived game of wits?

The King-David Gestalt-Shift. In the Book of Samuel, the story is told that God sent the prophet Nathan to confront King David with the horrible evil of the crimes he committed by his adultery with Bathsheba and the murder of Uriah, her husband. Because he had enough experience to anticipate that the king would become defensive if confronted directly, Nathan told the king that a certain rich man, rather than kill and eat one of his own many lambs, seized the only lamb of a poor traveler, killed it, and feasted on it. After listening to Nathan's tale of injustice, King David demanded to know the name of the rich man so that he could order him to be properly punished for his crime. Whereupon Nathan replied "You are the man!" (2 Sam 12:7)

If none of us who have progressed far enough in our learning career are exempt from having been confident for years that what we feel is a book, that what we see are words printed on the book's pages, that the thoughts we get while reading the book are thoughts coming from the book's words or from its author, then none of us is exempt from the obligation to reexamine all of our most confident convictions in order to learn whether, in Clifford's terms, we have been believing them upon insufficient evidence. It may be easy to believe it is only other people—the warring parties in Europe, Asia, Africa, South America, and Australia—who should reexamine the beliefs behind so much killing and destroying. But if we need to learn the truth, lest we form part of the 'society' which passes on to its young the stones of error in place of the bread of truth, then we must first learn the truth.

Were Nathan here and we could ask him, "Am I one of those who cling to pernicious errors because they refuse to see whether they have sufficient evidence for maintaining them?", what would he reply?

BIBLIOGRAPHY

Most of the James citations can be found in the following sources:

(Abbreviations)
CER (*Collected Essays and Reviews*)
ERE (*Essays in Radical Empiricism*)
HI (*Human Immortality*)
MEN (*Manuscript Essays and Notes*)
ML (*Manuscript Lectures*)
PBC (*Psychology: Briefer Course*)
PP (*Principles of Psychology*)
TT (*Talks to Teachers*)
WB (*Will to Believe*)

James, William, *Collected Essays and Reviews*. New York: Longmans, Green and Co., 1920.

James, William, *Essays in Radical Empiricism*. Cambridge: Harvard University Press, 1976.

James, William, *Human Immortality*. New York: Dover Publications, 1956.

James, William, *Letters of William James*, two volumes, ed. Henry James. New York: Atlantic   Monthly Press, 1920. (Abbreviated as *Letters I* and *Letters II*.)

James, William, *Manuscript Essays and Notes*. Cambridge: Harvard University Press, 1988. Grateful

acknowledgement is made to Harvard University Press for permission to cite several

passages from this volume.

James, William, *Manuscript Lectures*. Cambridge: Harvard University Press, 1988.

James, William, *Psychology: Briefer Course*. London: Collier-McMillan, 1962.

James, William, *The Principles of Psychology*, originally published in

1890. The text used for this book is the 1950 authorized Dover edition in two volumes, abbreviated as PP I and PP II.

James, William, *Talks to Teachers*. New York: Norton & Co., 1958.

James, William, *The Will to Believe*. New York: Dover Publications, 1956.

James, William, *Writings 1878-1899*. New York: The Library of America, 1992. It has the complete texts of *Psychology: Briefer Course*, *Will to Believe*, and *Talks to Teachers*, plus selected, important essays of James. The content in this collection is from the critical edition of James' works, published by Harvard University Press between 1975 and 1988. (Abbreviated as *Writings I*.)

James, William, *Writings 1902-1910*. New York: The Library of America, 1987. It has complete, pre-1975 editions of *The Varieties of Religious Experience*, *Pragmatism*, *A Pluralistic Universe*, *The Meaning of Truth*, and *Some Problems of Philosophy*, plus selected, important essays of James. (Abbreviated as *Writings II*.)

Other principal sources for information on James' thought are:

Barzun (Barzun, Jacques, *A Stroll With William James*. New York: Harper & Row, 1983.

Myers (Myers, Gerald E., *William James, His Life and Thought*. New Haven: Yale University Press, 1986.

Perry (Perry, Ralph Barton, *The Thought and Character of William James*, 2 vols. Boston: Little, 1935.

Other citation sources:

Allport, Gordon, "The Productive Paradoxes of William James," in *Psych. Rev.*, 50:97.

Barnes, W.H.F., "The Myth of Sense-Data," in *Perceiving, Sensing, and Knowing*, ed., R.J. Swartz.

Berkeley, G., *Of the Principles of Human Knowledge*. See E. Burtt, *The English Philosophers*.

Boring, E.G., *A History of Experimental Psychology*, 2nd ed. New York: Appleton-Century-Crofts, 1950.

Brown, D., *Human Universals*. New York: McGraw-Hill, 1991.

Burtt, E., *Metaphysical Foundations of Modern Science*. Garden City: Anchor, 1954.

Burtt, E., ed., *The English Philosophers from Bacon to Mill*. New York: Random, 1939.

Eddington, A., *The Nature of Modern Science*. Ann Arbor: University of Michigan, 1968,

Einstein, A., *Ideas and Opinions*. New York: Dell, 1954.

Frankl, V., *Man's Search for Meaning*. New York: Washington Square, 1959.

Fromm, E., *The Art of Loving*. London: Unwin, 1962.

Galileo, *The Assayer*, in *The Scientific Background to Modern Philosophy*, ed. M. Matthews.

Gibson, J., "Conclusions from a Century of Research on Sense Perception," in S. Koch and D. E.

Leary, ed., *A Century of Psychology as Science*.

Goodman, N., *Ways of Worldmaking*. Indianapolis: Hackett, 1978.

Gredt, J., *Elementa Philosophiae Aristotelico-Thomisticae*. Freiburg: Herder, 1932.

Hardin, C.L., *Color for Philosophers*. Indianapolis: Hackett, 1986.

Harrison, J., "Philosopher's Nightmare," in *Proceedings of the Aristotelian Society*, 1967.

Hirst, R.J., *Perception and the External World*. New York: Macmillan. 1965.

Hoffman, B., *The Strange Story of the Quantum*, 2nd ed. New York: Dover, 1959.

Horgan, *The End of Science*. Reading: Addison-Wesley, 1996.

Hume, D., *Enquiry Concerning Human Understanding*. See E. Burtt, *The English Philosophers*.

Koch, S. and Leary, D.E., ed., *A Century of Psychology as Science*.

Köhler, W., *Gestalt Psychology*. New York: Mentor, 1959.

Kuhn, T., *The Structure of Scientific Revolutions*, 2nd ed. Chicago: University of Chicago, 1970.

Locke, J., *Essay Concerning Human Understanding*. See E. Burtt, *The English Philosophers*.

Lonergan, B. *Insight*. New York: Philosophical Library, 1956.

Maritain, J., *Creative Intuition in Art and Poetry*. Cleveland: Meridian, 1953.

_____, *Degrees of Knowledge*, 4th ed. (Trans., G.Phelan) New York: Scribners, 1959.

Maslow, A., "Existential Psychology: What's In It for Us?", in *Existential Psychology*, ed. R. May.

Matthews, M., ed., *The Scientific Background to Modern Philosophy*. Indianapolis: Hackett,

May, R., ed., *Existential Psychology*. New York: Random House, 1961.

Menninger, K., *The Vital Balance*. New York: Viking, 1967.

Natanson, M., *The Journeying Self: A Study in Philosophy and Social Role*. Reading: Addison-Wesley,1970.

Novak, M., *Belief and Unbelief*. New York: New American Library, 1965.

Owens, J., *An Elementary Christian Metaphysics*. Milwaukee: Bruce, 1967.

Pais, A., 'Subtle is the Lord...' Oxford: Oxford University Press, 1982.

Pepper, St., *World Hypotheses*. Berkeley: University of California, 1942.

Perkins, M., *Sensing the World*. Indianapolis: Hackett, 1983.

Pinker, S., *How the Mind Works*. New York: Norton, 1997.

Plato, *Meno*, trans. B. Jowett.

_____, *Phaedo*. trans. B. Jowett.

_____, *Republic*. trans. B. Jowett.

_____, *Sophist*. trans. F. M. Cornford.

_____, *Theatetust*. trans. B. Jowett.

Price, H.H., *Perception*. London: Methuen, 1932.

Rorty, Richard, *Philosophy and the Mirror of Nature*. Princeton: Princeton U. Press, 1979.

Russell, B., *An Outline of Philosophy*. Cleveland: Meridian, 1927.

Ryle, G., *Concept of Mind*. Hammondsworth: Penguin, 1963.

St. Augustine, *Concerning the Teacher*, trans. G. Leckie. New York: Appleton-Century-Crofts, 1938.

_____, *Confessions*, trans. F. Sheed. New York: Sheed & Ward, 1943.

St. Thomas, *On Being and Essence*, trans. A. Maurer. Toronto: Pontifical Institute of

Medieval Studies, 1949.

Swartz, R.J., ed., *Perceiving, Sensing, and Knowing*. Garden City: Anchor, 1965.

Szasz, T., *The Myth of Mental Illness*, 2nd ed. New York: Harper & Row, 1974.

Watson, John, *Behaviorism*, 2nd ed. New York: Norton, 1970.

Whitehead, A.N., *Immortality*. In A.N.Whitehead, *The Interpretation of Science*. Indianapolis: Bobbs-

Merrill, 1961.

_____, *Science and the Modern World*. New York: Free Press, 1925.

Index